The Banality of Good and Evil

Moral Lessons from the Shoah and Jewish Tradition

David R. Blumenthal

Foreword by
James W. Fowler

GEORGETOWN UNIVERSITY PRESS / WASHINGTON, D.C.

to my students —

Rabbi said, "I learned much Torah from my teachers,
and more from my colleagues,
but I learned most from my students."
—*Talmud*, Makkot 10a

for Rodolphe Mérieux —

notre quatrième fils,
brutalement disparu dans sa vingt-quatrième année,
"Que notre Seigneur miséricordieux, l'abrite sous Ses ailes à jamais."

Georgetown University Press, Washington, D.C. 20007
© 1999 by Georgetown University Press. All rights reserved.
Printed in the United States of America.
10 9 8 7 6 5 4 3 2 1 1999
THIS VOLUME IS PRINTED ON ACID-FREE OFFSET BOOKPAPER.

Library of Congress Cataloging-in-Publication Data

Blumenthal, David R.
    The banality of good and evil : moral lessons from the Shoah and
Jewish tradition / David R. Blumenthal.
        p.   cm. — (Moral traditions & moral arguments)
    Includes bibliographical references and indexes.
    1. Good and evil (Judaism).   2. Holocaust, Jewish (1939–1945)—
Moral and ethical aspects.   3. Government, Resistance to—Religious
aspects—Judaism.   4. Helping behavior—Religious aspects—Judaism.
    5. Ethics, Jewish.   I. Title   II. Series.
BJ401.B58 1998
296.3'6—dc21
ISBN 0-87840-714-6 (cloth)
ISBN 0-87840-715-4 (paper)
                                                        98-43090

Contents

Foreword

You hold in your hands a singular book. Only David Blumenthal could have written it. The text is taken from his teaching hundreds of students in his Emory University course, "The Problem of Evil: A Social Psychological Approach." The author brings to this work his deep immersion in three thousand years of Jewish narrative, scriptures, philosophy, and commentary. At the same time, he correlates his study of Jewish theology and ethics with a penetrating and comprehensive account of the best social scientific inquiries into the twin mysteries of human goodness and human evil.

The overwhelming gash across human and twentieth-century history constituted by the shoah stands as the subtext of this work. In the corporate and personal behavior of its perpetrators, and in the complicity of complacent bystanders, we find the most extraordinary and sustained instances of human genocide and acts of evil. Blumenthal, following Hannah Arendt, points to the awful banality of the shoah's permeating evil in its routinization and legitimization of brutality.

In narratives that recall the behavior of rescuers and protectors of intended victims, the author brings us into close quarters with the equal mystery of human goodness. Avoiding the idealization that sets rescuers apart from the rest of us, Blumenthal pours over the careful studies of those who, at great risk, did all that they could "lest innocent lives be lost." In those acts of goodness, he finds a kind of ordinariness, a kind of habitual decency at work, that can be referred to as "the banality of goodness."

The passionate heart of *The Banality of Good and Evil* focuses on Blumenthal's shaping of educational approaches that intentionally seek to ground and equip children and youth for prosocial action through immersion in practice. He is not an idealist. The inculcation of values and principles through didactic approaches, he demonstrates, does not guarantee compassionate and courageous action. The equipment of adults with capacities to sense and respond to evil with courageous forms of unmasking and opposition depends on helping youth form an array of values, affections, skills, and abilities that can be modeled, taught, and learned. This book offers a comprehensive approach to moral education geared toward justice, compassion and, when necessary, vigorous forms of protest and opposition to authority when it abuses its power and responsibility. This is serious moral education in which the author honors the ethical humanism that derives from the Enlightenment, with its central affirmation of human rights. But it is clear that he wants religious communities to reclaim their places as moral educators who can develop men and women who are effective advocates for justice and human rights in contexts of economic, political, or religious oppression.

The middle section of this book sets forth a compelling model for such moral education. It provides a framework that civil societies as well as Christians, Muslims, and Jews can employ. The last third of the book illustrates how this framework can be used in Jewish education. In this section Blumenthal provides a remarkable series of studies in Jewish scripture and midrashim, making accessible to Jews and non-Jews the methods, spirit, and style of the intellectual, ethical, and living spiritual heritage of biblical and rabbinic Judaism.

This is a singular book. Enter it, and you will find yourself engaged with the mystery of human good and evil. In ways you would not have imagined, you will be equipped to see how we, and the young for whom we are responsible, can grow as teachers and agents of justice and goodness in an ethically struggling world.

—James W. Fowler

Author, *Stages of Faith*
Candler Professor and Director, The Center for Ethics
Emory University

Acknowledgements

To John Hines for permission to print his poem, "Clouds of Cousins"

To the Derekh Eretz Committee of the Educational Policy Committee of the Solomon Schechter Day School of Greater Boston 1994–1995 Board of Trustees for permission to reprint "The Ten Commandments of the Solomon Schechter Day School Community"

To Gene Sharp, author of *The Politics of Nonviolent Action,* and the Albert Einstein Institution for permission to reprint "198 Methods for Nonviolent Action"

To Intellectual Properties Management, Inc. of the King Estate for permission to reprint "Six Steps for Nonviolent Social Change" and "Six Principles of Nonviolence"

To The Epstein School, Solomon Schechter School of Atlanta, for permission to reprint the *"Na'aseh ve-Nishma'"* curriculum

To Facing Ourselves and History for permission to print excerpts from the Introduction to *Holocaust and Human Behavior*

1

Roadmap

I Knew a Jewish Nazi

I knew a Jewish nazi.[1] He was of European origin and a prominent leader of a Jewish community in the northeastern United States. He was not a member of the nazi party, nor was he particularly racist in his view of the world. That means he wasn't really a nazi, but he acted like many of the nazis I've read about.

He had terrible temper tantrums. He would scream. Rage, is the word. He would yell at the top of his lungs, hovering with his bulk over those at whom he was yelling. I came to know him later in life when he thundered and gesticulated, pointing his finger, banging his fist, and working his face into a visage of rage. His yelling knew no bounds. It was a fit whose purpose was to intimidate; he never used physical violence. He was a cultured, haut-bourgeois nazi.

In his rage, he would denigrate others: "That is just plain stupid!" "You don't know what you are talking about!" "How could you even think that that was right?!" "That is absolutely wrong!" "We don't do things like that!" It was important to make the other person feel small, stupid, ignorant, and unworthy. It was crucial to ridicule, to spew contempt at the other. It was vital to crush the will and independence of the other. He never praised, unless the praise was intended to motivate someone to do his will. The scenes were a ritual, a repeating pattern of rage and humiliation.

He always asserted his self-righteousness. "I-am-right-you-are-wrong" was one word. He did not say, "We are both right" or "We are both wrong," and never admitted, "I am wrong; I'm sorry." He certainly never said, "I hear you. I hear your pain." He never felt remorse or regret for that which he did. He never felt shame or guilt for the humiliation he inflicted on others. He never admitted things were beyond his control. Admitting weakness was beyond him. Weakness was a failure of mind and will. Acknowledging weakness was a sinful act. Rather, he would berate the other, blame the victim.

History was a malleable entity. Stories were told and retold so that he, or his point of view, always came out triumphant. Relatives and friends, business acquaintances and even strangers, were molded as interactions with them were recounted: His second ex-wife was a deceitful person. His help was always stealing. His cousin was after his money. Uncle so-and-so was a good for nothing. It was the big lie and he told it so often that his family, and sometimes friends and acquaintances, believed it, especially those who were younger and had no reason to question his version of the events. It was a *récit,* a litany, and at first others accepted it; only later were some able to question.

When history couldn't be molded, silence was the rule. What did happen to his father's brother? Why was so-and-so really dismissed from his job in the Jewish community? What did happen to the proposal to underwrite such-and-such a project? What did become of the funds in such-and-such an account? Why did his chosen successor not follow him in office? How did he feel knowing that his father had beaten his brother? These were questions that, if asked, would have produced a temper tantrum or, at best, evasive maneuvers. A voluble history that silenced history.

He demanded absolute loyalty. One had to agree with him, right or wrong. One had to admit he was right, regardless of the truth. One had to be loyal to him, independent of the cost to other relationships. Surrender of the will, obedient loyalty—that is what he demanded, and got, from most people. He always had an apt phrase ready to justify that loyalty: "Blood is thicker than water." "Our family sticks together." "The Jewish community is one." "We only have each other." "Brothers and sisters belong together." "The older generation knows what's best." "The older generation went through real events; your lives are so protected." "It's for your own good." He used these clichés to evoke loyalty to himself and his views, not really to strengthen the family or community.

To maintain his authority and control, he incited members of the family against one another. Even in games, he would set up one group of children as guards and charge another group to steal an object from the guards. He also set members of boards and committees working against one another. In later years, when his authority was severely questioned, he said, "I shall bring doom and destruction upon the family / community." And he did, setting child against parent, sibling against sibling, cousin against cousin, leader against leader, and follower against follower. He carefully cultivated the seeds of jealousy, bringing them to flower as fully developed interpersonal rivalry. He zealously left no one at peace, but vigorously and consistently pursued his agendum of contention and distrust. He destroyed relationships in the generation after him, all the time preaching family love and community unity.

He also whined. He played sick. They said of him at age ninety-two, "He's been dying since he was twenty-seven." At the slightest challenge to his authority, he would gasp, collapse into a chair, and reach for his pills. It worked, too. No one challenged him openly. He always thought of himself as the victim: of an authoritarian father who died when he was a teenager, of his fellow nazis who did not see his personal qualities but judged him by his race and drove him from their land, of his ex-wives who deceived him, of his family that placed enormous responsibilities on him and then did not show him the loyalty and gratitude he felt he deserved, and of members of the community who were constantly trying to take advantage of him or defame him. Only in business did he not complain: "Anyone who cheats me of my money deserves it."

He was very miserly with his money, doling it out in very small quantities. Occasionally, he would make what appeared to be a lavish gesture, but it was always a motivational gift, meant to reinforce his image as generous. It always had strings attached; one felt obliged to agree with him in the next family discussion or community dispute. Where there was ambiguity, he took credit for the generosity; close inspection often proved that others had actually paid the bills. There were even times when, as others told it, he would throw money on the desk or the floor and one had to pick it up to get it. In spite of his millions and communal prominence, he rarely gave to charity and then always meagerly and with restrictions.

He, and by extension those who knew him, were superior. Insofar as they were his, they were the elite—intellectually, socially, financially, and politically. After all, they (that is, he) had escaped early from nazi Europe. For him, being a "nazi" was a socioeconomic, not a racial, matter. "Nazis" were low class and low culture; those who were his were high class and high culture. They were also better than the average American Jew, who is also low culture even if economically better off. Those who were his were also above non-Jews, as long as the latter were not aristocracy. The haut-bourgeois status of those who were close to him, combined with generations of Jewish shrewdness, made them superior. Their taste in dress was better; so were their manners. Their knowledgeability of many areas was superior; so was their ability to survive. Everyone else was below them, in one way or another. They wouldn't exterminate others—that is for non-Jewish nazis—but the other was definitely inferior, wrong, in fact absolutely wrong.

He was always correcting people: on table manners, on politics, on morals, even in the usage of one's native tongue. And the tone was always absolutist, superiorist: "That is not done that way!" "We don't do that!" "You must get into the outside world!" "A man doesn't behave like that!" "Stand straight!" "Brush your hair!" "Lift your elbows!" "Don't laugh like that!" "If you do that again, I'll leave the table!" It didn't make a difference what the topic was. It made no difference how old one was or what position one occupied in the community. People over age fifty were corrected like children of five and, for serious matters, treated like rebellious teenagers of fifteen. Preservation of the elite required constant discipline.

His world was a world without supportive love. "You must be able to stand on your own!" "There is no such thing as being too tough on a child!" "It is not possible to be too demanding of someone else!" Networking, webs of support, understanding for failings (not just failures) were unknown. One was never hugged, or just held quietly and affectionately. No physical or verbal tenderness. No emotional comfort. No consoling presence. It was life in the marines; all survival, with survival being only for the fittest, which meant being prepared to be ruthless. No one is born ruthless; it has to be taught, cultivated. To love was to train someone to survive. It was not to support, to sustain, to nurture. To love was to interfere with one's full weight in the life of the other, to force each issue as early as possible, to give guidance which could not be refused. It was not careful and supportive consideration of options with benefits and costs, together with an affirmation of the other and a confirmation of her or his responsibility for his or her life. Even what looked supportive turned out to be manipulative, and it had the strings of later loyalty attached. Survival of the fittest, training of the elite, that was love.

And yet, this exceptionally authoritarian man was a leader in his community, a father-figure in his family, and an otherwise cultured middle-European Jew who lived, worked, and prospered in northeastern America. He was "normal" in most other ways. He ran a successful business. He raised a family. He read newspapers. He received guests. He was active in his community. He was, in short, a good man who paid his dues to life, did his duty, followed his conscience, and did what was expected of him.

Analytic Reprise

The literature on nazis talks about most of the qualities of my Jewish nazi. First, of the abusiveness—often physical, always emotional: the tirades, the intimidation, the screaming, the denigration of the other. And of the irrationality of such abuse, of its utter unpredictability. Always the abusiveness is clothed in morality, shrouded in loyalty. Always the abuse is presented as justified, as good for the recipient, as an act of love or duty by the abuser.

The literature talks, too, of the malleability of history, of the retelling of the past so as to create a worldview in which abuse can be justified.[2] It speaks, too, of the silence that is imposed upon truth where truth threatens the *récit* of accepted history. And of the whining, of the perpetrator seeing himself as the victim.[3] And of *Götterdämmerung,* of the need to impose a final solution on others as reality collapses, of the glory of a suicide which brings destruction and desolation.

The literature speaks, too, of the perfectionism of nazi culture. In a world of self-righteousness, there are no mistakes. In the realm of seamless strength, there are no errors. To put it another way, in a world of survivalist elitism, the only mistake is not being tough enough to survive.[4] In the realm of absolute loyalty, the only mistake is insufficient loyalty. In the kingdom of authority, the only sin is incomplete obedience.

Most important, the literature also talks about the banality of evil, about the ease with which normal people are drawn into doing unbelievable evil. As Hannah Arendt pointed out, Eichmann was not a madman. It was, rather, his good conscience that led him to be the diligent executor of the final solution.[5] As one child of a lower-level nazi relates:[6]

> My father killed, yes, that's true. Maybe he has hundreds of inmates on his conscience. He conducted experiments on people, he failed to help sick prisoners, and he did nothing to bring down the death rate at the camp. But keep in mind: whatever he did, he did out of deeply held convictions, not out of a lust for murder. He wasn't a pervert but a political animal who accidentally found himself on the wrong side.

The concept of "the banality of evil" is a very powerful analytic tool. Used originally by Hannah Arendt, the term has been construed to mean three things: (1) evil which is normal, prosaic, or matter-of-fact; (2) evil which is rationalized as good because it is obedient or because it serves a larger purpose; and (3) evil which is trite, hackneyed, or stale. The last implies that evil is not immoral or grossly wrong. Arendt never meant to imply that nazi evil was trite and hence not immoral. Rather, Arendt meant to say that nazi evil was "banal" both in being matter-of-fact and in being so because it was rationalized as good. I follow Arendt in this usage. In this sense, even abusiveness can be "banal," that is, normal, prosaic, matter-of-fact, and rationalized as a greater good. Indeed, as Alice Miller has pointed out, Hitler was a role model for abusiveness precisely because his actions were very close to the everyday reality of middle-European family life.[7]

My Jewish nazi was not a nazi in the racist sense. Nor was he guilty of participating in the dehumanization and extermination of Jews or others. He was not an SS officer, not even a concentration camp guard. Nor was he swept along in the enthusiasm of national socialist dogma or caught up in the charisma of Hitler. As a Jew, he was not, nor would he have been permitted to be, a part of those. However, he was part and parcel of the authoritarian milieu which was the soil of nazism. He was very much steeped in the abusive culture which constituted the air which nazism breathed. As such, he was a nazi—a Jewish nazi to be sure—but culturally as much a nazi as some of the men who served their fatherland and their führer[8] in the same authoritarian, obedient, and ultimately abusive spirit. His abusiveness is normal, psychologically natural. His evil is an integral part of his culture "which consist of beliefs, meanings, values, valuations, symbols, myths, and perspectives that are shared largely without awareness."[9] As such, it is seen by him as good. His evil is not demonic; it is banal, even though it is evil.

Nazis are not the only ones who can have their good judgment blinded by the banality of evil. All people can be caught up in it. Any person can slip into making very bad judgments in the name of some greater good. The interrelationship between evil and banality is explained, in part, by study of the obedience effect; that is, of people's deep need to be part of a hierarchy and of their natural penchant to do what they are told, especially if they are relieved of their responsibility by legitimate authority figures.[10] Everyone exists in a set of social hierarchies, and most people are above some and below others. Those below normally, and without thinking, follow those above—that is the nature of social trust—even when those above are wrong or ambiguous. Those below are being "good" when they follow those above; they are living a life of law and order, for what is law and order if not being respectful of social authority? The interrelationship between evil and banality is also explained, in part, by the study of child-rearing and personality-formation. Everyone is raised as a child. Some are raised in an environment that breeds fear, obedience, and violence. Such persons tend to relive their past in their own abusive lives, doing evil acts out of personal and cultural conditioning.

How does one assess guilt for such deep personal and cultural patterns? On the one hand, one must use the language of moral discourse and unqualifiedly condemn evil done in the name of banality—especially if it is an act of abuse—for exactly what it is: evil. There is no justification for scenes of rage and degradation of the other. There is no excuse for the distortion of history, for the demand for absolute loyalty, and for the deceit of clichés. There is no defense for acts intended to bring physical or emotional ruin on others. There is absolutely no justification for physical and sexual abuse, or for genocide. Furthermore, there is no excuse for those who clothe evil in rationalization of any kind. Nazis, and others, who do these things are wrong. They are guilty of misdeeds. They are guilty of not resisting the familial and cultural patterns that educated and molded them. Such perpetrators must be brought to justice by humanity and by God.

On the other hand, we must also use the language of honest intelletual analytic discourse[11] and admit that evil can be banal and that resistance to banal evil is difficult as, indeed, resistance would have been very difficult for my Jewish nazi. Some people come from a family psychology that obliges them to be abusive and a social psychology that compels them to obey. They do not know any better. In fact, they believe that what they do is correct, psychologically and socially. They believe that what they do is good, not evil. It is part of their tradition, part of the web of their being. Such phenomena cry out to be studied. Such patterns demand that their roots be exposed.

Pointing to the banality of evil does not make humans, nazis or others, less culpable morally. Humans are responsible for the evil they do, regardless of why they do it. They are accountable before humanity and God. Pointing to the roots of the banality of evil, however, does pose a new set of questions: How is evil generated, and how would one shatter the pattern of evil? How is willing obedience generated, and how would one break the cycle of authority and obedience? What sort of cultural teachings are necessary to create a reasonably disobedient society? What type of patterns are necessary to prevent family violence and abuse? If our goal is to prevent a resurgence of nazism, and if preaching about good and evil is not enough, what are our educational responsibilities—as teachers, parents, peers, clergy, political leaders, indeed as human beings? The goal of this book is to examine these questions and to propose some answers.

Counterpoint

On a field in the small French village of Le Chambon sur Lignon, a representative of the nazi regime concludes his speech about the glories of the third reich [12] with the traditional, "Heil Hitler." Silence is the response of the large group of people assembled; they are religious resistors. Finally, a lone voice shouts out, "Vive Jésu Christ!" [13]

In Haarlem (Holland), in a small watch shop, a family receives a Jewish baby to hide. Others have turned it away but the father of Corrie ten Boom says, "You say we could lose our lives for this child. I would consider that the greatest honor that could come to my family." [14]

In a farmhouse in Poland, a family takes in Jews, even though they know that the penalty for doing so is immediate death to the whole family and burning down the farm.

In the midst of the massacre in My Lai, Chief Warrant Officer Hugh Thompson sees the killing from his helicopter, knows it is wrong, and instinctively takes action. He lands his helicopter, places himself and his men between Lieutenant Calley (who outranks Thompson) and his Vietnamese victims, and orders his men to train their weapons on their fellow Americans and to open fire if Calley's men open fire on the Vietnamese. [15]

In a racially mixed school with tensions running high, a white student intervenes to protect a handicapped teenager from a black student who is attacking him. The white student breaks the hold of the black student with force and is ready to take the consequences for what might become a general racial fight in the school.

A bystander pulls a driver from a burning car. . . . A person jumps into a river to save a complete stranger. . . . A church votes to join the sanctuary movement to shelter refugees from South America even though it is illegal. . . . American blacks face southern sheriffs with their dogs and armed policemen. . . . A bystander comes to the aid of a mugging victim. . . . A young woman refuses to go home with her drunk date. When he insists, a male friend steps in and helps her.

Diana, Princess of Wales, dies. Billions of people see the funeral of the "people's princess." Tons of flowers are set out in her honor. Billions of dollars flow spontaneously to the charity set up in her memory. Everyone strives to acknowledge her kindness toward the oppressed and underprivileged. . . . Mother Teresa dies and the world honors her caring for "the poorest of the poor." Untouchables everywhere weep for her kindness; the rest of us weep with them. . . .

These moments—and there are many more like them, all over the world, in all kinds of situations—form the mystery of goodness. They tell us of the other side of the coin of human moral behavior. They recount acts of courage, of resistance, and of altruism; acts of caring, kindness, and human love. What motivates a simple Polish woman to hide Jews in her barn at extreme danger to her family and herself? What moves a Dutch teenager to kill a Dutch nazi in cold blood, without rancor and hate, because that policeman represents danger to people in hiding?[16] What propels a person to jump into a river to save a drowning person who is a complete stranger? What motivates people to form groups to resist terror and the encroachment upon the lives and civil rights of others? This is the mystery of goodness, and it is deeply a part of the picture of good and evil, for as there is evil, so there is good.

"Rescuers" is the appropriate title for bystanders who decide to take an active role in protecting victims. In interviews, they always deny that they have done anything special. They always refuse the epithets "heroic" and "extremely courageous." Part of the mystery of goodness, then, is its banality; that is, the normalcy and rationalized character of it. Doing good is natural, prosaic for those who practice it. Doing good is good because it serves a larger purpose, because it is obedience to some greater command. Indeed, one must speak of the "banality of goodness," just as one must speak of the banality of evil precisely because goodness, like evil, is natural to those who practice it.

How does one assess merit for such goodness? Some rescuers are professionals; others are motivated by financial gain; while yet others act spontaneously, out of some deep inner goodness or caring motive. Again, we must use the language of moral discourse and unqualifiedly declare goodness to be good, regardless of motivation while, at the same time, we must use the language of intellectual analytic discourse and study closely the factors that facilitate the doing of good.

Pointing to the banality of goodness does not diminish it in any way. An act is good when it is caring, when it protects the life and rights of others, no matter who does it, or where, or why. However, pointing to the banality of goodness does pose a new set of questions: What motivates altruists to do what they do? What conditions in life facilitate caring behavior? How does obedience fit into the doing of good? How would one teach this mystery of goodness? Indeed, can it be taught at all? Preaching and our usual methods of education don't seem to be effective, or else we would be living in a better society. What, then, ought religious and educational institutions to be doing to encourage prosocial behavior? The goal of this book is to examine these questions, too, and to propose some answers.

Getting from There to Here

As we approach the end of the century and try to bring some perspective to its most traumatic event, the shoah,[17] the task before us seems overwhelming. Can one really "bring some perspective" to such an event? Is the very attempt to do so a banalization of the lives of those who died, or survived?[18] As a theologian, two questions cry out for answers. First, where was God? How can we, as religious people, reconcile our belief in the continuous presence of God in the life of the Jewish people with the presence of God in the shoah? I have ventured an answer in *Facing the Abusing God: A Theology of Protest*.[19]

The second question is, where was humanity? Here, the issue is not the cruelty and sadism of the shoah for, although these were certainly present, cruelty and sadism were not peculiar to the shoah. Nor is the question one of numbers, for there have been other mass murders and even genocides in which large numbers of people have been killed.[20] The issue in the shoah is also not one of state policy, though that certainly sets off the shoah from previous forms of genocide.[21] The real horror of the shoah lies in the compliance of the masses with the final solution. The key question about humanity, then, is: Why did so many tens of millions of people go along with the shoah? How did the nazi regime persuade the overwhelming masses of Europe to remain bystanders? to accept passively, if not actively, the extermination of the Jews? Terror was certainly a factor, but it is not a sufficient answer.

An equally puzzling question is posed by those who rescued Jews: Why did they rescue? How did the rescuers manage to resist the persuasion of the nazi regime such that they defied it? If obedience characterized the masses, what describes the resistors and rescuers?

The answer to the question, where was humanity, lies first in careful historical study of the period of the shoah. Extremely useful data, however, can also be found in the field of social psychology. A series of social psychological experiments in compliance, known loosely as "the obedience experiments," were conducted and the results have been widely discussed. A series of experiments in prosocial action, known loosely as "the altruism experiments," were also conducted and their results are rather widely known too. Unfortunately, within the discipline of social psychology, experimental work in obedience and in altruism is not usually done together. Nor is analysis of these complementary phenomena usually undertaken as a whole.[22] Similarly, within the discipline of history, systematic social psychological questions are not often asked. To answer the question, where was humanity, however, one must study the obedience experiments and the altruism experiments, as well as the historical literature on perpetrators and rescuers during the shoah.[23] Such research generates a unified field theory of antisocial and prosocial human behavior and helps us address the issue of the nature of human responsibility.

As morally serious persons, it is incumbent upon us to look at the data from antisocial studies and ask: What have we learned in the fifty years since the end of the shoah about human moral behavior? What lessons, if any, can we draw for humanity from this event as we enter the next century? Especially theologians and religious educators must confront the fact that an overwhelming majority of the perpetrators and bystanders were religious. They were believers, energetic adherents of their churches and active participants in the various praxes of piety.[24] How did church leaders—priests, pastors, theologians, and others—allow themselves and their institutions to be drawn into evil? Why did some religious leaders resist, often taking their followers with them? What was it that religious institutions were teaching that enabled the shoah to happen? Western religion and culture has been discussing the problem of good and evil and preaching ethical behavior for three thousand years. We are not amateurs. Yet we failed miserably, and there is every reason to believe that we will fail again. Why? What **ought** we to be discussing and teaching?

As morally serious persons, it also is incumbent upon us to look at the data from prosocial studies and ask: What have we learned about human goodness? What do we know about the basic impulses to do good? And, how could we cultivate those impulses? In the century that discovered Auschwitz in the actions and motivations of humankind, what is goodness and how would one shape human society so as to surface goodness and not evil? Especially theologians and religious educators must confront the difficult question: Why hasn't organized religion succeeded in inculcating goodness in humanity? Judging from the history of this century, and indeed the history of organized religion before this century, we have failed to teach goodness, we have failed to so instruct those under our tutelage such that they will, in overwhelming numbers, act in a prosocial manner toward their fellow human beings. What have we done wrong, and what **ought** we to be doing to do it right?

If there are answers to the question of human compliance and resistance in social psychology and history, then it is the responsibility of educators in general and theologians and religious educators in particular to bring these insights back into the church, the synagogue, the mosque, the school, and the university, and to modify what one teaches and how one teaches it so as to increase resistance to evil and to encourage the doing of good.

The problem, where was humanity, then, implies two tasks: first, a descriptive-analytic task rooted in history and social psychology and, then, a normative-prescriptive task rooted in moral thought and theology intended to better humankind's ability to teach resistance to evil and to cultivate the doing of good. The goal of part 1 of this book is to do the descriptive-analytic work. In the first chapter of this part (chapter 2), the relevant studies in the fields of social and personal psychology as well as history will be surveyed and then a field theory for the factors which facilitate the doing of good and the doing of evil will be presented. In the second, third, and fourth chapters of this part (chapters 3, 4, and 5), a multilevel analysis rooted in social and personal psychology as well as in history will be elaborated, describing the centrality of hierarchy and role, teaching and praxis, and childhood discipline and personality development.

The goal of part 2 is to do the normative-prescriptive work. In the first chapter of this part (chapter 6), the problem will be summarized and restated and a theological perspective will be articulated. In the second chapter (chapter 7), eleven affections and twelve value-concepts of the prosocial life will be presented. The complex linkages between the affections, teachings, value-concepts, and the praxis and socialization patterns of the prosocial life will also be shown. In the third chapter (chapter 8), four specific recommendations for inculcating prosocial attitudes and behaviors, with detailed suggestions, will be made. The latter will be summarized as the "Ten Commandments for Resistant and Caring Living."

The goal of part 3 will be to apply the insights of the first two parts to Jewish ethical teaching. The aftermatter will contain various appendixes which I hope will be useful for readers and teachers of prosocial values and ethics in all situations.

After the shoah, as Langer and Shapiro have argued,[25] nothing should be written without caesura, without the disruptive in-breaking in the fullest terms possible of that event. I have tried to honor this by concluding many of the chapters with texts that shatter our most careful analysis; hence, the sections entitled, "Counter-text." The reader, thus, will encounter ideas and counter-ideas, expository analysis and irruption in the same chapter. Sometimes, however, a "Co-text" seemed more appropriate, and I have done that too.

On Matters of Personal Privilege

No book is written in a vacuum. This means that every author has the responsibility to identify himself or herself to her or his readers. I have done that in previous works and readers have often commented that they have found it helpful to be able to locate me in the space of academic, religious, and Jewish discourse. I telescope that autobiographical effort here:[26] I am a Jew, a rabbi, and the son of a rabbi, with a family and serious community commitments. As such, my involvement with the shoah is central to my identity, though it is not the whole thereof. I am a professor, well-trained in academic discourse, intellectually curious about other disciplines, and an experienced teacher and writer. I am also a religious person with a strong appreciation for the spiritual dimension of life and with a dedication, which grows out of that spirituality and whatever life has to teach me, to writing theology. My theology is personalist, rooted in psychology, and it always flows from Jewish sources and situations, though it takes into account the multifaceted nature of my setting and my interests. It also always takes up the challenge of speaking, at once, to God and to the people. In addition, I am male, middle-aged, heterosexual, married, and a father of three sons. I try to be inclusive and multicultural in my thinking, action, teaching, and writing, though I make an effort not to represent the views of others.

One cannot write about any subject without reflecting one's values and commitments. This is especially true of the shoah because the material is too searing and we, even if we are too young to have been touched personally, recoil in horror from what we learn. This, however, is healthy, for our involvement and our defensiveness are a sign of our humanness. The debate about "objectivity," known in professional circles as the issue of history and the historians,[27] is present in the materials used here. The range of attitudes, as I read them, includes: Blackburn's passionate anti-nazi rhetoric, Mayer's bewilderment and anger at the data he uncovered, Weinreich's suppressed horror, Browning's fine historical sense combined with his feeling of inadequacy when he comes to explanation, Müller's, S. Katz's, and Koonz's steady amassing of facts without a sufficiently broad analytic framework (the 'how' without the 'why'), F. Katz's very limited analysis, Klee's total lack of analysis, and Cocks's apologetic rhetoric. Many of these authors also attempt a prescription, a normative stance on what one should do to avoid another shoah: Adorno, Cohen, Bar On, and Miller want to apply psychotherapeutic principles that work with individuals to large masses; Mayer wants democratization of the grassroots political process; Sichrovsky wants young Germans to reject their parents; F. Katz preaches early resistance, while it is still possible; Davidowicz wants a Jewish consciousness alert to antisemitism, as well as anti-antisemitism; and Staub and Oliner have prescriptions for building a prosocial, altruistic society. My own preference is for solid, fact-oriented historical analysis that reaches beyond the facts for some larger social and psychological explanation. In addition, I favor a morally critical, prophetic stance toward the material; better to be outraged than to be "objective."

It is my practice to capitalize only nouns referring to God, together with nouns usually capitalized in English. This is a theological-grammatical commitment to the sovereignty of God. Thus, I spell "messiah," "temple," etc.[28] To infuse literature with ethics, I especially do not capitalize "nazi," "führer," "fatherland," "third reich," "national socialist," "final solution," etc., except in quotations. I am indebted to Hana Goldman who, as a plucky ten-year-old, defied her teachers by refusing to capitalize "nazi," thereby setting an example for all of us.

The task of transliterating Hebrew is enormously complex. I have used a commonsense method, indicating the Hebrew *het* with the sign "*ḥ*" and the Hebrew *khaf* with the sign "*kh*" (both pronounced like the "ch" in German "Loch").

For many years I used the word "holocaust" to designate the destruction of European Jewry during the Second World War. I have since been persuaded that "holocaust" should not be used for two reasons: First, it bears the additional meaning of 'a whole burnt offering,' which is certainly not the theological overtone to be sounded in this context. And second, the destruction of European Jewry happened to Jews and, hence, it is they who should have the sad honor of naming this event with a Hebrew term. The word "shoah" has been used for a long time in Hebrew to denote the catastrophe to Jewry during World War II and has even been adopted by many non-Jews as the proper designation. I now adopt this usage and acknowledge my debt to Professor Jean Halpérin of Geneva and Fribourg for the insight. However, since this word, too, refers to catastrophe and not to God, I have consistently not capitalized it.

It is my custom to use inclusive language, except when referring to God Who, for me, is experienced as male, though I respect and honor others who perceive and relate to God in other ways.[29] I also prefer to do my own translation of classical biblical and rabbinic texts even when they are cited in articles and books to which I refer. In these translations, I use inclusive language because I believe it to be in the sense of the text, though classic Jewish texts never use inclusive language because biblical and rabbinic Hebrew neither allow for, nor deem it ethically necessary, to use inclusive forms. In citing current articles, however, I have, except where indicated, left gendered language.

To make reading this book easier, several methods of text-referencing are used: A series of citations from the same author are noted by parentheses in the text. Full citations of works are repeated at the first occurrence in each chapter so that the reader need not search for the full reference. "Ibid." is usually avoided. Endnotes, not footnotes, are used to keep references and supplementary comments out of the way of the reader. In addition, chapters often contain headings and subheadings. For emphasis, I use italics in quotations and bold typeface in my own text.

This book is dedicated to the many students who have enriched my life. Their luminous intelligence and their radiant love have warmed my heart and stimulated my mind. Their willingness to engage material strange to them, ranging from medieval Jewish mysticism to enormously complex commentaries to the text of the Bible to the ideas and processes of the course on which this book is based, has never ceased to amaze me. The life-loving energy and the beauty and power of these youths have left me breathless. Truly, they have been my *haverim* and *haverot,* my friends and companions, over the years, generously giving of themselves to me and graciously receiving what I have offered them. It has been my privilege to bless some of these wonderful young people before they graduate. Some have written books, others have raised wonderful families, and still others have gone on to distinguished careers in every corner of the planet.

I want to single out in particular those students who have done social service as part of their work with me. One organized a major national demonstration on behalf of the homeless and brought the first forum on this subject to our campus. Another spent a summer caring for young men in gangs in a midwestern city. Yet another worked for peace in Ireland, a job so dangerous that his roommate was shot and killed. One worked in human rights on the West Bank. Another did research and drafted material for the Georgia law allowing the homeless to vote. Yet another worked finding employment for the thousands of refugees and illegals in Atlanta. One ran a halfway house for teenage drug addicts. Another administered tuberculosis medicine in the crack houses in Atlanta. And yet another worked endlessly with autistic children. The courage, insight, and dedication of these young people, in school and afterwards, have left me stunned, and embarrassed at my own inaction. Indeed, it is partly their example that has motivated this book.

Letters, visits, and e-mail keep all these wonderful people in touch with me. I cannot thank all of you for the joy and inspiration you have given me over the years.

This book is also dedicated to the memory of Rodolphe Mérieux who was, to my wife and myself, as a fourth son especially during the three years he studied at Emory University. Rodolphe, whose family we have known for decades, was a young handsome European prince. At any time of the day or night, he was proper, correct, and gracious to all, always ready with an act of support and solidarity. Rodolphe was compassionate and sensitive to the suffering of others. The night the Gulf War broke out, he stayed with us as we watched and worried about our son who was in Jerusalem. When friends needed help, he noticed it and made the necessary arrangements. He was also a lover of peace in a world which could be aggressive and uncaring. He urged friends and family to maintain contact, often acting as a young diplomat in training. Rodolphe Mérieux was killed in the midst of his youth by the explosion on TWA 800 in July 1996. His death is a great loss for his family, for us as his second family and, indeed, to all his friends. May his memory be a blessing to all those who knew him.

It is, finally, my custom to invite dialogue with readers of my books. I can be reached at my website: http://www.emory.edu/UDR/BLUMENTHAL (it is capital sensitive); through my e-mail address: reldrb@emory.edu; and by regular mail at: Department of Religion, Emory University, Atlanta, GA, 30322.

May 24, 1998
28 Iyyar 5758 / Yom Yerushalayim
the 31st anniversary of the liberation of Jerusalem

Counter-text

- The Lord was displeased with what David had done. So the Lord sent Nathan [the prophet] to David, and he came to him and said, "There were two men in the same city, one rich and one poor. The rich man had very large flocks and herds but the poor man had only one little ewe lamb that he had bought. He tended it, and it grew up together with him and his children. It used to share his morsel of bread, drink from his cup, and nestle in his bosom; it was like a daughter to him. One day, a traveler came to the rich man but he was loathe to take anything from his own flocks or herds to prepare a meal for the guest who had come to him. So he took the poor man's lamb and prepared it for the man who had come to him." David, then, flew into a rage against the man and said to Nathan, "As the Lord lives, the man who did this deserves to die! He shall pay for the lamb four times over because he did such a thing and showed no mercy." Then, Nathan said to David, "You are the man!" (II Sam. 12:1–8).

COMMENT: In the midst of a war, David, walking one evening on the roof of his palace, sees Bathsheba. He has her summoned and has relations with her, despite the fact that she is already married to Uriah, the Hittite. Bathsheba becomes pregnant and David, in an attempt to cover her pregnancy, summons Uriah home and orders him to sleep with his wife. Uriah, however, as a good soldier, does not wish to render himself impure by sexual relations while in the midst of battle and he returns to his post without having had relations with his wife. David, then, orders Uriah to be put in the forefront of the battle and arranges for him to be killed. At this juncture, the prophet Nathan comes to the king and confronts him on the subject of his adultery with Bathsheba and his complicity in the murder of Uriah. This is one of the most famous of acts of prophetic challenge to authority and is depicted powerfully by Rembrandt and other great artists. It is a calling to moral accountability and, as such, it is a paradigm for the ideals of justice and compassion expected even in the highest places.[30]

PART 1

The Descriptive-Analytic Task

> But I remember now
> I am in this earthly world, where, to do harm
> Is often laudable; to do good, sometime
> Accounted dangerous folly.
>
> —Lady MacDuff in William Shakespeare's
> *Macbeth,* Act IV, Scene II

2

The Field

The Studies

What enabled an ordinary, average human being to bind together the legs of a woman in childbirth, inflicting unbearable pain on the woman and the not-yet-born child and eventually killing them both? And, what enabled an ordinary, average human being to lie, to steal, and to cover up, often for long periods of time and at considerable danger to her or his family, the existence of hidden Jews in the home? These two questions—and they are representative of groups of people—are central to the understanding of the shoah and, indeed, of human nature. Answering them would seem to be crucial to the human hope for a better world. The context of social violence by individuals and social entities in which we live and the shadow cast by the shoah have created what I call "anticipatory guilt" among serious moral persons. We do not want to be responsible for more genocide, for more avoidable social violence. On the contrary, we want guidance for ourselves and for those who hold key roles in society on how to create a more prosocial and less antisocial environment—for the good of humanity and the future of the human race.

There are two intellectual disciplines that contain data for answering these questions: social psychology and history. In the area of social psychology, work has been done on obedience and social conformity as well as on prosocial action and altruism. In the area of history, work has been done on perpetrators, bystanders, and rescuers. A survey of this work seems prudent as a beginning point for this study.

In the beginning, no one was willing to believe. The world-famous photographer for *Life* magazine, Margaret Bourke-White, wrote: "I hardly knew what I had taken until I saw prints of my own photographs."[1] Yet the facts were there: The concentration camps had existed, the annihilation of European Jewry had almost been accomplished, and the "nazi beast" had somehow coopted not only sadists to whom it gave a field of action but also the vast majority of Europeans: Germans, Poles, Ukrainians, Austrians, even the majority of the French and the Dutch. The shoah or the holocaust, as the extermination of European Jewry came to be called,[2] had happened. But how? How had so many people

19

become willing accomplices to mass murder? This question, together with its haunting companions—Could it happen again? Could it happen elsewhere?— produced a flurry of studies, analyses, and experiments in the years 1950 – 1980. Some, like Adorno (1950)[3] and Allport (1954),[4] rooted their work in social psychology: in questionnaires and statistical analysis. Others, like Asch (1951),[5] Zimbardo (1971),[6] and Milgram (1974),[7] based their work in experimental psychology: in peer pressure, role playing, and obedience. Still others, like Arendt (1963),[8] Des Pres (1976),[9] Fein (1979),[10] and Davidowicz (1975),[11] grounded their work in history and drew social-psychological conclusions from that evidence. Mayer (1955)[12] even went to interview Germans in Germany. Yet others, like Bettelheim (1952, 1979),[13] Cohen (1953),[14] and Fromm (1965),[15] rooted their analysis in personal psychology, moving from the individual to the group.

But the problem of how the shoah happened did not go away; in fact, it got bigger. The 1980s and early 1990s saw a series of detailed historical studies on nazi educators,[16] psychologists,[17] women,[18] lawyers,[19] doctors,[20] theologians and academics,[21] big business,[22] SS officers,[23] ordinary soldiers,[24] and children of nazis.[25] Often these historians reached for an explantion of the larger phenomenon; most of the time, they remained puzzled by the facts and let history speak for itself. Psychological studies continued to appear such as: Dimsdale (1980),[26] Katz (1993),[27] and Staub (1989, 1991),[28] as well as Miller (1983)[29] who developed a new psychological-cultural explanation for nazi culture. In addition, a whole bibliography developed on the topic of genocide and masskilling,[30] and an excellent study on the My Lai massacre and its aftermath[31] appeared. A whole field that might be called "antisocial studies" located in the disciplines of social psychology, therapeutic psychology, and history has developed.

The year 1986 was crucial because two books appeared that tried to encompass the topic of aggression and altruism. Zahn-Waxler[32] compiled the papers of a multidisciplinary conference that had been held in 1982 which represented the fields of sociobiology, developmental psychology, socialization studies, psychotherapy, emotion studies, ethology (the study of violence), psychobiology, and personality studies. While many of the issues which still divide the field are present in this volume, Zahn-Waxler honestly analyzed the limits of work done and noted that "understanding the etiologies and interconnections of altruism and aggression has remained elusive" (xi). Olweus[33] also assembled a series of essays, some rooted in specific studies and others more theoretical, which ranged over many disciplines. Whether by intention or not, Olweus did not even try to draw any conclusions from this profusion of studies. It was too early for such a comprehensive analysis. So, aggression-obedience studies went one way while altruism-prosocial studies went another.[34]

Between 1989 and 1992, three reviews of the newer trends in altruistic studies appeared. Eisenberg[35] gathered some of the best theorists: Staub, one of the most persistent thinkers in this area, set forth basic definitions for most of the operative terms. Hoffman presented his types of empathy and distress. Deutsch wrote about prosocial values and the business world. Batson, one of the most systematic thinkers, set forth his critique of the basic assumptions in altruistic studies. Kaplan dealt with the history of gender distortions in the field. Piliavin[36] summed up work in the field under the following headings: the definition of altruism, the altruistic personality, the empathy-altruism hypothesis, the development of altruism, altruism in animals, and altruism in the public domain. And contributors to a volume edited by the Oliners[37] were able to point to forty-four different kinds of helping actions, three classes of motives, and the surfacing of mid- and late-life prosocial attitudes and actions. New historical evidence of altruistic behavior during the Armenian genocide, in nazi Holland, among the Bahais, and in the communist world were cited. Finally, two chapters on how to create more caring societies, one of which became the title of the Oliners' later book,[38] were included.

Several new data fields have been added to the area of prosocial studies. First, and from the point of view of this study most important, is the data from the shoah. The Oliners' study of rescuers[39] remains the most thorough social-scientific study, followed by Fogelman[40] whose bibliography is the most complete. The works of Tec[41] and the catalogue of Block and Drucker[42] add first-hand testimony, as do the many films on rescue.[43] Des Pres's observations on caring activities, especially gift-giving, in the death camps are also valid evidence here.[44] Evidence, most of it episodic, is also available from reports and studies of: the sanctuary movement,[45] conscientious objection,[46] racism,[47] the mothers of the Plaza de Mayo,[48] and American civil rights workers.[49] Attention has also been given in the legal and sociological communities to civil disobedience and the law.[50] Finally, as analysis has grown and as the need of society for guidance from social scientists on better ways to manage our communal lives has grown, some social scientists have turned to prescription, to setting forth things that we must do as individuals and as a society if we are to live in a more caring environment. Here, the later work of the Oliners[51] is crucial but so are the suggestions of Staub,[52] the projection of Kelman and Hamilton,[53] the insights of Kohn,[54] the social-activist proposals of Sharp and of Holmes,[55] and the activities of the Giraffe Project.[56] A whole field that might be called "prosocial studies" located in the disciplines of social psychology, therapeutic psychology, and history has developed.

Some Philosophical, Moral-Legal, and Methodological Problems

Any attempt to reach general conclusions about human behavior must encounter serious philosophical, moral-legal, and methodological problems. This study surely falls into that category.

Two Philosophical Problems

The first philosophical problem resides in the breaching of the specificity of a given historical situation. To generalize from the shoah to other areas of human behavior is to violate the sanctity of historical givenness. Resolution of this problem lies in realizing that, while human moral behavior during the nazi period was conditioned by many factors and combinations of factors that were unique to that time and place, the actors then were human and they were responding to human conditions and motivations which were not unique to that time and place. It is these general tendencies in human moral behavior, not just the details of a specific moment, which are of concern here. Hence, the data of this study ranges over many historical moments, with special focus on the shoah because of its centrality in twentieth-century history and its function as a paradigm of human behavior in our times.[57]

The second philosophical problem resides in the definition of good and evil. There is a long tradition of trying to define good and evil in western society. One stream goes back to the ancient Greeks and its interpreters; another goes back to the Bible and its interpreters. These are very rich traditions and, rather than attempting to sum up that whole tradition or to epitomize it, I propose, based on the commonsense understanding of the historical, social-psychological, experimental-psychological, and personal-psychological data cited throughout, the following functional definition of evil and good: **Evil is doing acts which inflict violence, physical or emotional, upon another; or which tolerate violent acts done to another.** And: **Good is doing acts which care for another and oneself, physically and emotionally; or which cultivate caring acts done to another and oneself.** These definitions have their limitations: Sometimes violence is good. The definitions of "evil" and "good" are not formal but rooted in some basic sense of what a harmful or caring act is—for ourselves and for others.[58] The definitions are also decidedly occido-centric. Still, they do reflect the moral consensus that underlies all the evidence I have seen. They also have the advantage of being commonsensical and not tied to any given western stream of thought. Most important, they are action-oriented, not abstract.[59]

The basic question for this study, therefore, will not be philosophical-theological; it will not seek definitional categories. Rather, the basic question will be inductive-analytic; it will search for concepts that describe the forces at work.[60] The questions, then, will be: **What conditions facilitate the doing of evil? What factors in the human environment facilitate the committing of violence, physical or emotional, against another; or the tolerating of violent acts against another?** And: **What conditions facilitate the doing of good? What factors in the human environment facilitate the doing of caring acts, physical and emotional, to another and to the self; or facilitate**

cultivation of caring acts done to another or the self? These questions require a descriptive answer while the questions 'what is evil' and 'what is good' require a philosophic or theological answer. The descriptive enterprise will, in my opinion, put a new perspective on the analytic table and, perhaps eventually, will bring us closer to a realistic, normative (prescriptive) stance which our times so badly need.

The Moral-Legal Problem

The moral-legal problem resides in seeing description and analysis as justification. Description and analysis, however, are not that; they are explanation. Study helps us understand human behavior. Analysis helps us grasp what has happened. Study and analysis, however, do not resolve the question of responsibility. They do not absolve anyone of any guilt or confer social approval on anyone. Justification, on the other hand, derives from moral judgment and law. It is grounded in moral reasoning and legal principle. Its purpose is to condemn evil and reward good.

The moral-legal problem of justification is soluble along the lines I noted above: Pointing to the banality of evil does not make humans, nazis or others, less culpable morally. Humans are responsible for the evil they do, regardless of why they do it. They are accountable before humanity and God. And: Pointing to the banality of goodness does not diminish it in any way. An act is good when it is caring, when it protects the life and rights of others, no matter who does it, or where, or why. **Whatever study reveals, humanity must maintain well-considered moral standards, and humanity must enforce those standards in law. Evil is evil and it must be treated as such, and good is good and it must be treated as such.**

Some Methodological Problems

The first methodological problem consists of several general pitfalls: The range of disciplines needed to accomplish this study—social psychology, experimental psychology, history, theology, and personal psychology—and the scope of people involved—sadistic perpetrators, ordinary perpetrators, bystanders, victims, survivors, and rescuers—is simply too vast for one person to encompass. The bibliography for such an inquiry is too large and most of the key studies have a secondary literature of critique and defense which requires analysis of its own. There is also the need to integrate, or at least relate, the psychological findings with the historical data from the shoah and other historical moments. Picking and analyzing key studies is always risky and, being a theologian and not a psychologist or historian, I am sure to miss a few important studies and to be wrong about the importance of others.

The second methodological problem centers around the complexity of the field of antisocial and prosocial behavior. Three configurations of problems can be noted in the areas of method, range, and motivation.

(1) Three methodologies have developed for studying antisocial and prosocial behavior and attitudes, each of which has its strengths and weaknesses. The first method involves studying "exemplars," people who have done prosocial or antisocial acts. The subjects are identified, questioned about their motives, given self-evaluations through psychometric testing, and then the results are correlated.[61] The advantage to this method is that one is dealing with live, real subjects; this generates data that is seen by some as "ecologically valid."[62] The disadvantage is that the subjects are not always articulate and, even when they are, they do not always fully understand their own actions and motives.[63] The second method is the "case method." It involves observing social interactions in real situations, or designing social-psychological experiments in as-close-to-real situations as can be achieved, measuring the results observed, and then correlating those results with psychometric measurements.[64] The advantage to this method is that it deals with close-to-real situations which also include variables that can be manipulated experimentally; this method, too, is considered by some as "ecologically valid." The disadvantage is that such case studies are often contrived and, at the same time, not fully controlled. The third method is the "laboratory experiment." It involves highly restricted laboratory situations in which carefully designed experiments can be carried out.[65] The advantage to this method is that well-constructed hypotheses can be thoroughly and systematically tested; this is considered by some to be "science" in the strict sense of the word. The disadvantage is that the results are disconnected from social reality and are considered by others as "ecologically invalid." All three methodologies have been pursued and all are accompanied by theorizing.[66]

(2) The range of activities that qualify as prosocial or altruistic is enormous. It includes: rescuing another under great stress, rescuing another when there is no special stress, donating blood, volunteering for a charitable organization, visiting the sick, helping the poor, caring for the elderly, civil disobedience, political activity such as demonstrating, giving gifts, participating in self-help groups, sharing food or toys, caring for pets, giving money, making interest-free loans, sheltering the homeless, conscientious objection, and participation in the peace movement, in the sanctuary movement, in the civil rights movement, etc.[67]

Similarly, the range of activities that qualifiy as antisocial or aggressive is enormous. It includes: knowing about antisocial behavior but not protesting it, performing ancillary administrative tasks that result in antisocial activity, rounding up victims, transporting them, guarding victims, killing them indirectly, killing victims directly, torturing them, torturing them for no ulterior reason, etc.

(3) The motivation for prosocial or altruistic behavior is also very complex. Some people act prosocially because that is their profession (doctors, therapists); others receive payment for specific acts (rescuers who took money to save Jews). Some do it for the fame, or the challenge, or the fun; others do it for no reason they can identify but just because it is the decent, or human, thing to do. Sometimes the rewards are as subtle as self-esteem, which itself can be positive (fulfilling norms and following principles) or negative (avoiding internal or external censure); sometimes there appear to be no rewards at all. Sometimes such persons act out of obedience to a moral authority; sometimes out of a stubborn independence of mind. For some, it is a matter of principle; for others, a matter of empathy. And then, there is aggressive action which establishes a dominance hierarchy which itself stabilizes groups in a positive way, especially in times of stress, thus turning an act of aggression into a potentially prosocial act.

Similarly, the motivation for antisocial or aggressive behavior is very complex. Some people act antisocially believing they are doing good; others are sadists. Some act consciously and deliberately; others on impulse. Some conform to superior orders; others follow peer patterns. Some experience a welling up of feelings from the depth of their being; others seem to be involved only superficially. The rewards for antisocial behavior can range from praise from superiors to subtle feelings of having accomplished one's duty or having finished one's task.

Not much work has been done on resolving the problem of motivation for antisocial and prosocial behavior. The clearest way out of this morass of conflicting theories of motivation for the realm of prosocial action, it seems to me, has been outlined by Staub who begins by identifying "prosocial orientation" as a primary moral value orientation of human beings:[68]

> . . . *prosocial orientation* . . . three interrelated domains: (1) a positive view or positive evaluation of human beings; (2) concern about and valuing of other people's welfare; and (3) a feeling of personal responsibility for others' welfare.

Then, Staub differentiates "prosocial" from "altruistic" behaviors according to motive:[69]

> *Prosocial* behavior is behavior intended to benefit other people. However, the reason for benefiting them may be to gain reciprocal benefits, or approval—that is, some kind of self-gain. *Altruism* is behavior intended to

help other people for no other purpose but to improve their welfare, to benefit them.

Finally, Staub elaborates on the difference between values, goals, and motives, and then notes that these can be arranged into hierarchies and that reduction of conflict among them is a primary activity of human existence.[70]

> In this conception personal goals and values are similar constructs. Both refer to what is desirable, preferred. It is worthwhile to distinguish them by their content, by the types of outcomes they refer to. *Values* are desired outcomes that relate to the welfare of human beings. They guide human relationships in light of considerations of human welfare. . . . Thus, values are always moral or morally relevant, that is, they have clear moral implications. *Goals* are more self-related, they refer to desired outcomes that have no direct relationship to others' well-being. . . . use the generic term *motive* to refer to goals and values together. . . .
>
> An important characteristic of goals and values is that they can be arranged in a hierarchy, according to their importance. This is probably true not only of individual, but also of group goals and values. Goals and values function in a unified manner, so that they are best characterized by a single hierarchy. . . . *motive equilibration*. This refers to a process itself motivational, that works toward the reduction of conflict among motives. A special case of motive equilibration is moral equilibration.

A typology of antisocial and prosocial motivations needs to be added to Staub's definitions in the quest for the parameters for an analysis. Smolenska and Reykowski distinguish three classes of motivation:[71] "*Allocentric motives* originate when attention is focused on the persecuted person or persons and his or her situation. . . . *Normocentric motives* originate from the activation of a norm of helping. . . . *Axiological motives* originate from the actualization of moral principles such as 'justice', 'sanctity of human life', and so on." The Oliners, who list empathic, normocentric, and principled types of rescue,[72] base their typology on this work.

Using these basic parameters has three advantages. First, it is possible to be very inclusive in listing activities that count as prosocial. Second, it is possible to affirm that humankind does, indeed, have a truly allocentric orientation — that is, that human beings can, and do, act solely for the good of the other and without any egocentric motivation[73] — without having to limit positive evaluation of such prosocial behaviors only to allocentric acts.[74] And third, it is possible to note that it makes no practical difference if people do good deeds out of selfish motives, for professional reasons, because such actions are normative in their circles, or on ideological grounds.

A similar set of definitions, typologies, and parameters can be constructed for the area of antisocial studies.

The problems inherent in a descriptive-analytic study of antisocial and prosocial behavior are legion. Perhaps I have entered the realm where even angels fear to tread. However, in spite of all these difficulties, one must look for some answers. One must amass and analyze the data, in the hope that some conclusions can be reached that will inform us about the nature of evil and good, of human moral action. The context of social violence and the shadow of the shoah in which we live force upon us the search for definitions of antisocial behavior and evil and prosocial behavior and goodness. Our responsibility to prevent social violence obligates us to search for the motives and environments that will encourage good and discourage evil. Our anticipatory guilt compels us to try to make sense of this complicated field of human behavior. One must gather data and analyze, for without that, we are helpless. Motivated by anticipatory guilt, I shall, as an intelligent and concerned reader, do my best to resolve these methodological problems by displaying and analyzing the data as responsibly as I can.

Toward a Field Theory of That Which Facilitates Both Good and Evil

As has been shown, there are many studies on antisocial and prosocial behavior among both social psychologists and historians. However, while some scholars have speculated on the implications of the study of that which facilitates evil for the study of that which facilitates good,[75] to the best of my knowledge no systematic study exists which attempts a unified field theory for these two areas of human behavior. Since I have juxtaposed these two areas, I feel I must attempt such a field theory, bearing in mind that my qualifications for this are those of an intelligent reader of social psychology. It seems to me that there are six dimensions shared by the phenomena which facilitate good and those which facilitate evil. It is important to think about them as a whole, in a preliminary way, before we proceed to the details of the descriptive-analytic and prescriptive-normative tasks.

Human Character

It is unpopular to say so, but I think that some people are just born with aggressive, punitive characters and others are just born with caring, solicitous characters. This is part of humanity's collective genetic make-up. To be sure, nurture counts more than nature but, all things being equal, people are different and some are kind while others are nasty.

Furthermore, every person contains a measure of aggressive nastiness and a measure of caring kindness. Everyone has a lust for power and a capacity for violence, just as everyone has an impulse to be altruistic and a capacity for empathy.[76]

Both these observations seem self-evident but, when considering the factors which facilitate the doing of both good and evil, it is helpful to restate even the obvious—that some people are good by character and some are evil by character.

Personal Psychological History

Two related developmental patterns in childhood strongly influence the inclination of the adult to do good or evil. First, **the way discipline is administered in childhood** is a significant factor in forming the adult's penchant for doing good or evil. If discipline of the child is excessive, if it is erratic, if it is irrational, or if it is a combination of any or all of these, the adult is more likely to be aggressive and punitive toward others in his or her attitudes and behavior. There are three reasons for this: The rage at being unjustly punished is suppressed and surfaces in later abusing behavior. The impulse to protest and challenge authority is driven out by sheer force, inducing unquestioning obedience which is then internalized as a pattern of behavior and as a moral value. And, the model of authority for such a child is authoritarian and severe; the child identifies with the model and the adult acts according to this authoritarian model as those attitudes and behavior patterns are internalized.

Conversely, if discipline of the child is proportionate, if it is rather consistent, if it is reasoned, or if it is a combination of any or all of these, the adult is more likely to be inclusive and caring toward others in her or his attitudes and behavior. There are three reasons for this: The sense of competence in handling threatening situations carries over to adult life. The ability of the child to protest to authority empowers the adult to believe that all authority ought to be reasonable and, if it is not, authority can be challenged. And, the model of authority is one which permits challenge and responds to reason; the child internalizes this model through identification and the adult acts in the same way, accepting challenge and responding to reason.

Second, **the way empowerment and self-esteem are handled in childhood** is also a significant factor in forming the adult's inclination toward doing evil or good. A child who is deprived of the power to make age-appropriate decisions will have neither the skills nor the self-esteem necessary to defy social authority or to carry through on personal commitments that challenge social norms. A child whose self-esteem is verbally or physically battered will be an adult whose first reaction will be conformity and obedience regardless of the moral significance of the compliance demanded. Such adults have an exclusive worldview and, hence, lack empathy for victims. Such adults can be easily manipulated by legitimate authority as it rationalizes the doing of evil.

Conversely, a child who regularly makes age-appropriate decisions will have both the skills and the self-esteem necessary to evaluate the demands of authority and to act on personal commitments that challenge social norms. A child whose self-esteem is supported and sustained will be an adult whose first reaction will be evaluative and conscious of the moral significance in the situation at hand. Adults who come from a milieu that nurtures their self-esteem have an inclusive worldview and, hence, experience empathy for victims. Such adults respond empathically, normatively, or out of principle. Such adults cannot be easily manipulated by the rationalizations of legitimate authority.

All childhoods require discipline and all deal with empowerment and self-esteem. Personal psychological history is common to both the doing of good and evil. The way discipline, empowerment, and self-esteem are treated in childhood is a significant factor in forming the adult's penchant for doing these acts.

Socialization

All adults are socialized, as children and also later as adults, to "affections" and "value-concepts,"[77] that is, to moral and social values. People acquire a "moral orientation." Two aspects of socialization determine a person's inclination to do evil or good: content and process.

The content of socialization has a significant influence on a person's penchant for doing good or evil. If one is socialized to the value-concepts of abiding morality, inclusiveness, bonding and caring, and critical consciousness and protest, one is more likely to do good. If one is socialized to the affections of intelligent moral judgment, extensivity, empathy, and righteous anger, one is more likely to have prosocial attitudes and patterns of behavior. The converse is also true. If one is socialized to the value-concepts of hierarchy, authority, exclusiveness, and obedience, one is more likely to do evil. If one is socialized to the affections of allophobia (fear of the other), punitive judgment, duty and discipline, and survival of the self at all costs, one is more likely to have antisocial attitudes and patterns of behavior.

Similarly, it makes a difference whether one is socialized to the skills of empathy, perspective-taking, and challenging authority or to those of emotional toughness, unquestioning compliance, and self-surrender. It also makes a difference whether one is socialized to use the language of caring, bonding, and networking or the language of judgment, authority, and continuous criticism. Finally, it makes a difference whether one is socialized to splitting, repressing, and projecting anger or to seeking superordinate goals, bridging communication gaps, and conflict management and resolution. In a phrase: **Content counts.**

The processes of socialization, however, are the same for good and evil. (1) Modeling: All children and adults identify with legitimate authority figures and internalize their patterns of behavior and attitudes. Every culture creates heroes and antiheroes whose deeds are communicated in all sorts of media and who, by their role, shape one's expectation of oneself. (2) Formal instruction: All children and adults receive instruction in values and actions from the police, preachers, political figures, parents, the media, and teachers of all kinds. This flow of admonition to do this or that is much more pervasive than one would think. (3) Peer influence: All persons are sensitive to what others think of them and modify their attitudes and behaviors accordingly, whether those persons be friends, family, coworkers, or strangers. Everyone has some sort of network which provides emotional and material support for one's attitudes and actions. (4) The ecology of language, the linguistic environment within which one lives: Everyone has stereotypes, particularly of those persons and groups we know least, and our linguistic milieu shapes our perceptions, attitudes, and behaviors towards such persons. (5) Authority and hierarchy, the place of roles, norms, and rules, and the centrality of praxis: All these socialization processes are common to both the doing of good and evil; the last, however, deserve separate comment.

Authority and Hierarchy

All social situations comprise several hierarchies of authority. The workplace, the school, the playspace, the domains of religion, sports, and culture—all comprise explicit and implicit hierarchies of authority. There are always superiors and inferiors, hierarchically speaking, with the former exercising more and less direct authority, or influence, over the latter. Insertion into a multiplicity of these hierarchies is unavoidable; it is part of living together with other human beings. Hence, obedience to authority is also unavoidable; it is a natural part of being human.

Authority is always embodied in some social institution. It may be the family, the church, the school, the workplace, the sports team, the marketplace, the army, or the social group. These social institutions may be formal or informal, but hierarchy is never disembodied; it is always concrete.[78]

Hierarchies cultivate values in ways that are both manifold and subtle. Legitimate authorities sanction, validate, and rationalize actions and attitudes. They instruct us, formally and informally, what to value and how to act. Because hierarchical authority is pervasive, the values it teaches are pervasive—for better and for worse, for good and for evil.

To be sure, content counts. There are authorities that sanction evil and those that validate good, and there are hierarchies that facilitate the doing of good and those that facilitate the doing of evil. But, from a social-psychological point of view, all hierarchical authority functions the same way.

Roles, Norms, and Rules

Role develops from the processes of socialization mentioned above—modeling, formal and informal instruction, internalization of attitudes and behaviors, peer influence, the ecology of language, and insertion into an authoritative hierarchy—as well as from praxis itself (see below). Role enables people to know their place in the social hierarchy and to act appropriately.

Role enables one to set clear expectations and, then, to act in accordance with those expectations. Role functions through the setting of norms and the generation of rules of behavior from those norms. Because of role, people are basically "normocentric," that is, they act in accordance with their norms and accompanying rules.

Role also enables people to set an image of "self" and to mold oneself into that image. Role functions by projecting a sense of who one is, as well as of who one can be. The former keeps us located in human society; the latter allows us to see beyond our present situation to a different self. In a word, role enables us to become, as well as to be.

Again, content counts. There are exclusive, punitive norms with applicable rules and there are inclusive, caring norms with applicable rules. There is a "rescuer self" and a "perpetrator self." And, there is a "culture of cruelty" and a "culture of care." But roles, norms, and rules as such, with all the mechanisms by which they function, are common both to the doing of good and the doing of evil.

Praxis

Doing is the best form of learning. Action is the best form of self-formation. Praxis enables people to learn the skills required for finding and maintaining one's place in society. Praxis also creates community for, in acting, one belongs to others who act the same way. In doing, one shares the embodiment of common values. In addition, praxis allows human beings to follow their deepest impulses; it permits them to "act out" their innermost needs and values.

Doing has its own momentum. Action propels us. Praxis functions incrementally. A first, small step allows us to take a second, bigger step and, eventually, to walk quickly and surely on the way of action; perhaps, even to run on the path of doing. Practice also makes perfect. It empowers us to do more and to do it better. Praxis can even lead to routinization, to taking for granted an act that, a short time earlier, one would have considered unthinkable.

Again, content counts. Murder is a learned skill, just as is rescue. The capacity for selfless care of others is acquired, just as is the capacity for mass-killing. Getting away with murder is incremental, perhaps routinized, just as is healing the sick. But praxis is central.

The Art of Moral Living

The theory of the field of that which facilitates both good and evil includes: human character; one's personal pyschological history, particularly how discipline, empowerment, and self-esteem are handled; and the many modes of socialization: modeling, identification, formal and informal instruction, the ecology of language, and particularly one's socialization to authority and hierarchy, to roles, norms, and rules, and to praxis. These six dimensions seem common to the acquisition of attitudes and behaviors that are both evil and good. To study this area is to analyze the factors which facilitate good and evil precisely by using these rubrics. It is to design social-psychological experiments of all kinds and in all environments, and historical studies in all cultures and periods, which will enable us to analyze both the doing of good and the doing of evil; one side of the equation is no longer sufficient. Perpetrators and rescuers, subjects in obedience and altruistic experiments, must be studied together if we are to have a grasp of the full depth and range of human behavior.

The art of living in society is in identifying the hierarchies within which one lives and, then, evaluating them. The craft of living in society is in identifying the authorities who exercise influence over one and, then, ranking them. The teaching of the state may conflict with the teaching of God. The moral instruction of parents may stand in stark contrast with that of one's peer group. The ethical demands of the workplace may be very different from those of the church or synagogue. In fact, it should be the case that the mandates of the family, the church, the school, the workplace, the sports team, the marketplace, the army, and the social group are in conflict. To live intelligently is to recognize the authorities and hierarchies within which one lives and to negotiate their conflicting demands. To live morally is to invoke one authority against the others in order to achieve moral clarity and ethical propriety.

Similarly, the art of ethical living is in identifying the roles, norms, and rules according to which one lives and, then, evaluating them. The craft of the moral life is in identifying one's various roles and, then, favoring one over the others. It is in knowing and then choosing one's "self," insofar as that is possible. One's role as parent may conflict with one's role as citizen. The norms and rules of the workplace may differ strongly from the norms and rules of the synagogue or church. The expectations of peer behavior may contrast starkly with the expectations of family behavior. In fact, it should be the case that one's roles conflict, that the norms and rules that guide one through life are in dissonance with one another. To live intelligently is to recognize the roles, norms, and rules within which one lives and to negotiate their conflicting demands. To live morally is to invoke the moral content of one role or norm over and against others in order to achieve principled clarity and ethical propriety.

Finally, the art of living a moral life is in becoming aware of one's praxis. The craft of ethical living is in becoming knowledgeable about that which one does. To live intelligently is to know one's practices and, then, to prefer some behaviors over others. To live morally is to be intentional about one's praxis, resisting behaviors which are evil and persisting in behaviors which are good.

Content does count; I cannot repeat it enough. Scientists, historians, clergy, teachers, politicians, parents—indeed, everyone—must identify the value-concepts, affections, and praxes inherent in their lives, and must look for the literary and social-psychological resources in their moral traditions that will support the cultivation of a prosocial orientation. But **process also counts,** and scientists, historians, clergy, teachers, politicians, parents—indeed, everyone—must learn to identify the social processes in which one lives, to recognize the varied and subtle socialization forces at work in their past and present, and must learn how to manipulate those forces, or at least themselves within those forces, so as to avoid antisocial, violent ways and to act in prosocial, caring ways. It is to a more detailed analysis of these social processes that we now turn.

Counter-text[79]

10 But now, You desert and shame us.
You do not go out with our armies.
11 You put us to flight from our enemies.
Those who hate us tear us to pieces at will.
12 You hand us over like sheep to be devoured.
You cast us among the nations.
13 You sell Your people for nothing.
You do not make a profit on their sale price.
14 You make us an object of shame for our neighbors,
a thing of scorn and derision for those around us.
15 You make an example of us to the nations,
an object of head-shaking among the peoples.

(Winter, 1944):
"You desert and shame us"—as they cut our beards and mass-rape
our women.
"You do not go out with our armies"—with our resistance.

"You put us to flight from our enemies"—in mass exodus and
        transports.
"Those who hate us tear us to pieces at will"—using our skins for lamp-
        shades and our flesh for soap.
"You hand us over like sheep to be devoured"—in the gas chambers,
        crematoria, and gang burning-pits.
"You cast us among the nations"—as stateless and displaced persons.
"You sell Your people for nothing"—we are worth less than slaves, less
        than animals.
"You do not make a profit on their sale price"—our value is precisely
        calculated for work, starvation, and death.
"You make us an object of shame for our neighbors"—so that no one
        touches us, in the camps and even after liberation.
"A thing of scorn and derision for those around us"—they toss scraps of
        bread into the trains of our starving people; they make us defecate
        in our clothing.
"You make an example of us to the nations"—of degradation and de-
        humanization, a sign par excellence and a symbol of Jew-hatred.
"An object of head-shaking among the peoples"—in disbelief that
        something like this is happening to anyone, much less to us,
        Your chosen people.

To use this psalm and midrash liturgically on Yom Hashoah (Day of Re-
membrance) or at any other time, one person should read the psalm through,
out loud, with the rage in which the latter part of the psalm is written. That person should then repeat these verses, in a lower tone drifting into an undertone.
Another person or persons should, then, begin reading the midrash as an overtone. When the reading of the midrash is finished, one may conclude with the
final verse of the psalm, again read in the appropriate tone of protest.

3

Hierarchy and Role

Insertion into a Hierarchy Which Does, or Which Tolerates, Evil

Insertion into a hierarchy which does, or which tolerates, evil facilitates the doing of evil. The overwhelming evidence for this comes from social psychology, but the evidence from history is equally compelling.

The Milgram Experiments

Milgram's [1] famous experiments required subjects to administer what they believed were painful and / or lethal electric shocks to innocent people simply on the basis of the assertion of the authority of the experimenter. Quite contrary to expectations, 50 to 65% of the subjects followed instructions into the lethal range of shocks (35, 60–61). The percentage reached 85% in Germany (171) and among young people (173). No difference was registered for women (62–63). With unrelenting clarity, Milgram notes that these results are not a function of class, religious affiliation, gender, location, educational background, ideology, and general culture (62–63, 170). Nor are they a result of character or psychopathology (187). The results derive solely from the assertion of hierarchy-authority in the form of the experimenter.

Milgram concludes that hierarchy and authority are inherent in any society (152); that this hierarchy and authority are internalized and serve as the basis for obedience to legitimate authority (141); and that conscience, which regulates impulsive aggressive action, is diminished at the point of entering a hierarchical structure (132) such that the person enters an "agentic state" in contrast to the usual "autonomous state" (132–34). In the agentic state, morality becomes obedience to authority; that is, that which is good is obedience to the authority (145–46); the superego is shifted from independent evaluation of the morality of action to the judgment of how well one has functioned in the hierarchical-authoritative setting (146). The move to the agentic state, then, minimizes the damage to the ego and self-image, though a certain amount of strain is observable during the transition from, and in the ongoing tension between, the agentic and the autonomous states (154–57).

The Brown-Eyed / Blue-Eyed Children Experiments

The same results in a not-strictly experimental setting were obtained in Riceville, Iowa,[2] where a teacher, Mrs. Jane Elliot, in an attempt to teach her third-grade class about the nature of discrimination, set the blue-eyed children against the brown-eyed children. The bigotry shown by the class, which affected the learning curves of the students, was surfaced solely by the authority of the teacher, which is all the more remarkable since she reversed the hierarchy of blue-eyed and brown-eyed children on the second day simply by saying that she had been wrong on the previous day. The teacher's authority extended so far that the parents did not object to the bigotry shown in class. Later work by Mrs. Elliot showed that this "experiment" works in prisons and elsewhere; that is, among adults, because they too accept, and act upon, the authority of someone legitimately placed in the social hierarchy.[3]

My Lai and Its Aftermath

In a long and deep study of the trial of Lieutenant Calley for his part in the massacre at My Lai during the Vietnam War and of the aftermath of the trial, Kelman and Hamilton[4] explored the question of legitimate authority with great thoroughness. After devoting a chapter to the events of 16 March 1968, the authors spend a chapter discussing the problem of "legal crimes," putting it very succinctly: "When subordinates receive orders from duly constituted authorities operating in an apparent legal framework, they may well assume that the orders themselves are legal" (47, quoting Arendt). Kelman and Hamilton, then, devote chapters 3–6 to the problem of legitimate authority. They point to the "habit of obedience" (57) and to the fact that legitimate authority requires, it does not persuade; it, thus, has an obligatory character which is linked to the roles of the hierarchy (89–91). They also point to the temporary surrender of the right to choose which allows the influence of authority to be felt, thereby creating obedience (91).

To maintain its legitimacy, an authority must focus individuals on rule-, role-, and value-oriented decisions;[5] not on decisions based on personal, subjective preference. It must also be able to claim legitimate access to power, remain within the cultural norms, abide by the implicit rules for the use of power, and be generally accountable. If this is done, then even if there is doubt, most persons will insert themselves into the hierarchy and obey legitimate authority (122–25).

Surveying reactions to the events at My Lai and later to the trial of Lieutenant Calley, Kelman and Hamilton develop other typologies which generate the corroborative result that if the authority is legitimate and if the subordinates and superiors stay within their assigned roles, then if a legal crime is committed, most people feel that there should be no punishment because role-within-legitimate-authority takes precedence over independent moral judgment of the act itself (206), though there is some variation depending upon one's place in the hierarchy (207–8).

The SS

Historians studying the shoah have reached much the same conclusion. Hannah Arendt,[6] observing the trial of Eichmann, pointed out that he was not a fanatic or a monster. On the contrary, he was terrifyingly normal; he felt he did no wrong; and he would not have felt the slightest remorse had the nazis won and had he been able to carry out the final solution (146, 276, 288).[7] For Eichmann, the "führer's wish" and word were law and, when that law contradicted orders from superiors—as when Himmler ordered him to stop the deportation of the Jews to extermination camps—it was the law that he needed to, and did, follow; not the orders (137–46). It was, therefore, precisely his conscience that motivated Eichmann (146–47); his conscience was the law (293). Eichmann was so obedient that the Israeli judges got more information from him than either set of lawyers, precisely because they were high in the authority hierarchy (223). From this, Arendt reasoned that anyone could have filled Eichmann's place in the hierarchy (278) and that evil was banal[8] precisely because insertion into a social hierarchy made it normal.

More than thirty years after the war, Klee and his colleagues interviewed former SS officers.[9] Again, the thesis of insertion into hierarchy appears very strong: "'I am however convinced that very many men of lower rank under the then authoritarian regime and under such strict and tough commanders as Stahldecker never even entertained the thought of giving expression to their inner conflict, fearing privately that a refusal to take part in a shooting would have had very serious consequences. In my experience, amongst the lower ranks there was not so much an objective necessity to obey orders, more of a subjective one . . .'" (85, quoting). And again: "'We had been drilled in such a way that we viewed all orders issued by the head of state as lawful and correct. We police went by the phrase, "Whatever serves the state is right, whatever harms the state is wrong." I would also like to say that it never even entered my head that these orders could be wrong. Although I am aware that it is the duty of the police to protect the innocent I was however at that time convinced that the Jewish people were not innocent but guilty. . . . I followed these orders because they came from the highest leaders of the state and not because I was in any way afraid'" (220–21, quoting).[10]

Ordinary Germans

With the invasion of Russia, the crack troops of the German army and the SS divisions moved out of Poland to form the fighting units and the Einsatzgruppen. However, there were still almost three million Jews left in Poland who, according to the final solution, needed to be exterminated. Who was minding the store? Who would carry out this "project"? In a stunning book, Christopher Browning[11] follows the history of Police Battalion 101, a group of men who weren't fit for the fighting units, whose job it became to carry out the final solution in Poland. Sometimes, this meant shooting everyone, person by person; at other times, it included shooting the sick, the weak, the elderly, and the infants while forcibly deporting the rest. The transformation of this remarkably undistinguished group of men, only 25 to 30% of whom were members of the nazi party (48), into mass murderers is one of the most horrifying stories of the shoah.

Browning carefully reconstructs the actions of Police Battalion 101, taking into account all the appropriate problems of dealing with such historical sources, and concludes that 80 to 90% of the men continued to kill Jews while only 10 to 20% of the men refused, asked to be excused, or simply evaded the killing tasks (74, 160). Of those who continued to kill, a small percentage became hardened killers who enjoyed their work and volunteered for killing missions; the greatest number "did everything that was asked of them and never risked confronting authority."[12] Browning also points out that the work of this group of men who, by November 1942 had executed sixty-five hundred Jews and deported forty-two thousand more (121), was not an episode but an ongoing, relentless task that required sustained attention (132). It was, thus, not a battle frenzy as in My Lai but "atrocity by policy" (160–61). Furthermore, this was not depersonalized action but hands-on killing with high salience to the victims (162). Nor were these men specially selected, nor was the majority self-selected (165–69). There was no special coercion[13] and no "putative duress" (170–71). Revulsion, when it occurred, was physical; not ethical (74).

In an attempt to wonder why and how, Browning admits the effect of brutalization and numbing, of the context of racial war, of psychological splitting, and of ideology. However, he maintains that these factors were contributory, subsidiary (161, 163, 182, 184). The main mechanism that enabled these ordinary men to become "grass roots" killers was insertion into the hierarchy of army command. Their officers only needed to invoke the authority of their hierarchy to obtain obedience, even though it was sometimes accompanied by anger and upset (69, 74, 151, 171–75). Peer pressure—not to be "weak" but to be "tough" (150, 183)—reinforced authority; it did not create it (175).

In another study of ordinary Germans done in the 1950s, Milton Mayer[14] went to a small village in Germany and, hiding his Jewish identity, interviewed the local people about life under nazism. The motif of insertion into a hierarchy which does, or tolerates, evil was very strong: "When 'big men,' Hindenburgs, Neuraths, Schachts, and even Hohenzollerns, accepted Nazism, little men had good and sufficient reason to accept it. *'Wenn die 'Ja' sagen,'* said Herr Simon, the bill-collector, *'dann sagen wir auch 'Ja.'* What was good enough for *them* was certainly good enough for us. . . .' My friends were little men—like the Führer himself" (44–45). And again: "This immense hierarchism, based upon blind servility in which the man on the third rung would never dare to imagine that the man on the second would order him to do something wrong, since, after all, the man on the second had to answer to the man on the first, nourished the buck-passing instinct to fantastic proportions. . . . The only objection to the scheme is that men who always do as they are told do not know what to do when they're not. Without the thoughtful habit of decision, they decide . . . thoughtlessly. If they are forbidden to beat Jews, they learn how not to want to, something a free man who wants to beat Jews never learns . . ." (162–63). And again: "'The new National Socialist faith believed in God but not in the divinity of Christ. That's the simplest way to put it. . . . We little people didn't know whether or not to believe it. 'Is it right, or isn't it?' we asked ourselves. . . . One believed one way, one another. It wasn't ever decided. Perhaps, if the war had been won, it would have been decided finally.' 'By whom?' 'By the men on top. But they didn't seem to have decided yet themselves. A man didn't know what to think'" (232–33).

The German Judiciary

In a very thorough study of the nazi legal system, Ingo Müller[15] reaches a similar conclusion. Long before nazism, judges and law professors were purged of liberals and turned into a civil bureaucracy appointed by, and loyal to, the state (6–9). This created a very conservative judiciary and, since there are no jury trials, a very conservative legal system which gave preferential treatment to the radical right (13, 21). Volkist philosophy made it clear that every judge must "place the vital interest of the nation unconditionally above what is formally law" (52).

Gleichschaltung, or "coordination," included declarations such as the one by a state association of jurists which "placed itself jubilantly and dutifully under the leadership . . ."; an obligatory oath to Hitler, together with the compulsory use of the nazi salute; and the "coordination" of the encyclopedias of law by Carl Schmitt (a still-recognized figure in jurisprudence) to include antisemitism as well as the new theory of law (36–45). It also allowed the lawyers, the professors, and the judges to have such a "unanimity of aim" that defense attorneys would speak against their clients (64). As Müller puts it: "A judge's 'true nature and racial identity' ought to 'make him a part of the community which creates the law. . . .' A judge should therefore approach a case with 'healthy prejudice' and 'make value judgments which correspond to the National Socialist legal order and the will of the political leadership . . .'" (71–73, citing legal authorities from that time). This worked so well that judges began enforcing the ban on interracial marriage before it was promulgated (91).

In addition, the idea of "enemies of the state," that is, of defining disloyalty to the führer and the party as a crime, became common. As Müller puts it: "'. . . loyalty is the highest duty of the *Volk* and therefore a moral duty in National Socialist and German thinking. . . . According to these principles a violation of the duty of loyalty necessarily leads to the loss of honor. It is the task of the National Socialist state to require just expiation from the disloyal, who by their disloyalty have renounced their membership in the community'" (77, citing an official directive). This "enemies of the state" principle was easily linked with the racial laws. It was the basis for a policy to deprive such "enemies" of their civil rights (116) and to annihilate them (142–47). It was easily extended to include crimes of omission (134), "unfounded suspicion" of disloyalty (138), and even "psychological support" for resistance activities (160), including unintentional remarks made in private (147). It was also used to justify a series of appeals of sentences, each of which was intended to make the sentence more severe (129–34 on "pleas of nullity," 159, 181–82, 188–90). Of course, there were no appeals by victims (166). Finally, it led to the seizure, and often to the handing over by the court to the Gestapo of persons who had already been acquitted for further "treatment," the latter not being subject to the court system at all (174–82). This, in turn, led to the blurring of the distinction between the lawful and the illegal (75); between petty crimes, misdemeanors, and felonies; and between attempting and committing a crime (164–65). It led, too, to a policy of "the apprehension of every last asocial element" (133), to "decisions based less on law than on eliminating lawbreakers" (147).

Müller speculates that nazi justice evolved as it did because these men were genuinely conservative and had been cultivated to be so by the legal system. The conservative and racist ideologies of the state were, thus, not foreign to them. He points out, too, that, with the elimination of the Jews and Social Democrats early on, there simply was no other voice heard in Germany. Finally, he points to the friend-foe ideology of the law expounded by such an authority as Schmitt (296–97). However, it seems abundantly clear from Müller's evidence that insertion into a hierarchy which does, or which tolerates, evil was the primary factor that facilitated the doing of evil in nazi legal circles. Nazi jurists, especially in their capacity as civil servants, were part of such a hierarchy. Obedience was "normal," banal—especially since everything was rationalized and explained to them as being for the greater good, thereby reinforcing the legitimacy of the authority. It was "natural," therefore, to defer to superiors in their theories and in their actions.

Insertion into a Hierarchy Which Does, or Which Tolerates, Good

As insertion into a hierarchy works to facilitate evil, so it works to facilitate the doing of good. Here, too, evidence from social psychology, as well as from history, is probative.

The Princeton Experiment

In a well-known experiment, Darley and Batson[16] took a group of sixty-seven Princeton Theological Seminary students and administered to them a series of personality and religiosity psychometric tests. They then gave the students the parable of the Good Samaritan (Luke 10: 29–37) to read and assigned half of them to deliver a homily on the parable and half of them to prepare a brief talk on alternate ministry. The testing and reading were done in one building and the homily or talk was done in another. Each group was then divided into three subgroups: one was "high-hurry," that is, they were told to hurry to the second location to complete the assignment; one was "intermediate-hurry," that is, they were told to go directly to the second location; and one was "low-hurry," that is, they were told they had ample time to get to the second location. A suffering victim, who was actually a confederate in the experiment, was placed on the way to the second location.

The purpose of the experiment was to see how many theology students, who had just read the parable of the Good Samaritan and were preparing either to give a short homily on the subject or to talk about ministry, would stop to aid this experimental victim—as the Good Samaritan had stopped to aid a victim by the wayside—and to determine what kind of help they would offer. Sixty percent (60%), that is, more than half, did not stop to offer help to the victim on the wayside. Of the 40% who did stop, 10% were in the "high-hurry" group, 45% in the "intermediate-hurry" group, and 63% in the "low-hurry" group. The conclusions were quite clear:

> A person not in a hurry may stop and offer help to a person in distress. A person in a hurry is likely to keep going. Ironically, he is likely to keep going even if he is hurrying to speak on the parable of the Good Samaritan, thus inadvertently confirming the point of the parable. (Indeed, on several occasions, a seminary student going to give his talk on the parable of the Good Samaritan literally stepped over the victim as he hurried on his way!) . . . It is hard to think of a context in which norms concerning helping those in distress are more salient than for a person thinking about the Good Samaritan, and yet it did not significantly increase helping behavior (107, parentheses original).

Darley and Batson, then, speculated on the cause of this phenomenon:

> Why were the seminarians in a hurry? Because the experimenter, *whom the subject was helping,* was depending on him to get to a particular place quickly. In other words, he was in conflict between stopping to help the victim and continuing on his way to help the experimenter. . . . Conflict, rather than callousness, can explain their failure to stop (108, emphasis original).

This experiment confirms, in an ideologically dramatic setting, the insights of the previous section on obedience; to wit, that insertion into a hierarchy of authority is more important than ethical teaching or vocational aspirations in determining a person's willingness to do something ethically wrong.

The Helping Distressed Persons Experiments

In an equally dramatic series of experiments, Staub[17] took groups of various ages, assigned them an irrelevant task, and then gave them one of three sets of instructions: one group was given permission to leave the task room if necessary; one group was given no instructions on leaving the task room; and one group was prohibited from leaving the room. Then, from an adjacent room, cries of distress were simulated. The purpose of the experiment was to test resistance to authority in a situation evoking helping behavior as a response to the distress stimulus. When done with children, the experiment showed: "The frequency of help was similar in the *no information* and *prohibition* groups. Almost all subjects in the *permission* condition actively helped" (313, emphasis original). When conducted with adults, the experiment showed: ". . . while no information and permission resulted in almost identical, high-frequency helping behavior, prohibition substantially reduced active attempts to help" (314).

This experiment, too, confirms the insights of the previous section on obedience; to wit, that insertion into a hierarchy of authority is very important in determining a person's willingness to act—except that the inescapable result of this experiment is that **authority can permit ethically correct behavior; that is, that authority can function, as authority, to justify and permit prosocial behavior.** This result should not come as a surprise, but the implications for this are enormous as further analysis will show.

In a study of the influence of television on prosocial and antisocial behavior, Eron and Huesmann[18] showed that "[E]xposure to prosocial content [programs such as *Mr. Rogers, Lassie,* and *Father Knows Best*] led to increased prosocial behavior, whereas exposure to aggressive content led to increased aggressive behavior. . . . Those boys who watch violent television and identify with aggressive television characters are predictably more aggressive two years later regardless of their initial level of aggressiveness" (293, 304). Here, again, an authority—in this case, the cultural authority of television[19]—acts as an authority to sanction *both* prosocial and aggressive behavior.

Revisiting the Obedience Experiments

A closer look at Milgram's obedience experiments also reveals the power of authority and obedience to sanction prosocial behavior. One of the subjects was a professor of Old Testament. The subject discontinued the experiment after reaching 150 volts saying, "If he [the learner / victim] doesn't want to continue, I'm taking orders from him." In the post-experiment discussion, the professor said, "If one had as one's ultimate authority God, then it trivializes human authority" (47–49). Authority and obedience to that authority—in this case, the victim and then God—sanctioned prosocial action. In yet another set of experiments, two experimenters were brought into the action, one who advocated continuing the experiment and one who advocated discontinuing it (105–7). In this case of split authority, "[N]ot a single subject 'took advantage' of the instructions to go on; in no instance did individual aggressive motives latch on to the authoritative sanction provided by the malevolent authority. Rather, action was stopped dead in its tracks" (107). Milgram maintained that this was because of a "contamination" of the hierarchical system, noting that some subjects tried to ascertain which experimenter was the higher authority (107). The possibility also exists that, in some cases, the presence of two authorities, one sanctioning antisocial action and the other sanctioning prosocial action, allowed or permitted the subjects to follow the impulse to do good precisely because they had a choice of which authority to follow.

Rescuers Invoke Authority

The evidence from the historians confirms this view. Baron[20] notes that Dutch Calvinists rescued Jews: because they believed the Jewish people were the people of God and, hence, Christians were obligated to rescue them; because they had a ministry to the persecuted; or because they were predestined to rescue (318–19). Sauvage[21] cites the same testimony from Hugenot France and Fogelman[22] quotes one Christian as asking, "What would Jesus do?" (177) and another as saying, "I have to save these people, as many as I can. If I am disobeying orders, I'd rather die with God and against men than with men and against God" (201). She also observes: "Indeed, this conviction among religious rescuers—that they were accountable to a higher and more fearsome authority—was the most salient aspect of their rescuer self. It overcame antisemitism, transcended fear, and impelled them to action" (176–77). Kurek-Lesik[23] cites the following:

"I come from nationalist circles, often charged with anti-Semitism. Why did I save Jewish children? Because they were children, because they were people. I would save any man [sic] in danger of death, and a child—every child—is particularly dear to me. This is what my Catholic religion *orders* me to do. . . ." A persecuted Jew somehow stopped being a Jew and became simply a man, woman, or child in need of help. The Polish nuns were motivated by a Christian *duty* towards others and by their fidelity to the ideal that they were pledged to do so in a special way by their vows. . . . This is why saving Jews and Jewish children should first of all be seen in the broader context of monastic service to humanity (330–32, emphasis added).

Sometimes, the authority invoked was not religion but national resistance. Thus, Baron notes that 42% of the Dutch rescuers were also in the resistance and, hence, saving Jews was sanctioned by the political authority of the resistance even if one had no particular religious or social feeling for Jews (312–13).

The evidence, then, is quite consistent: People who do prosocial acts often invoke a higher authority to sanction their actions. The implications of this for building a better society are substantial.[24]

Peer Support as an Appeal to Authority

Peer support is another form of authority and it, too, sanctions prosocial action. In one part of the Milgram experiments, subjects had peers, who were actually confederates in the experiment, who objected to continuing the experiment (116–21). The results were noteworthy: "In this group setting, thirty-six of the forty subjects defy the experimenter (while the corresponding number in the absence of group pressure is fourteen). The effects of peer rebellion are very impressive in undercutting the experimenter's authority" (118). The peer "provides social confirmation for the subject's suspicion that it is wrong to punish a man against his will, even in the context of a psychological experiment. . . . dispersion of responsibility . . . every failure of authority to exact compliance with its commands weakens the perceived power of the authority" (120–21).[25]

Staub[26] observed the same phenomenon. First, he cited well-known experiments by Latané and Darley showing that increase in the number of passive bystanders leads to decreased bystander action (296). Then, on a variant of the adjacent-room distress experiments, Staub had confederates generate "positive verbal definition" of the situation ("That sounds bad. Maybe we should do something."); "negative verbal definition" ("That sounds like a tape recording. Maybe they are trying to test us."); "indirect help definition" ("I'll go try to find the experimenter."); "prohibition definition" ("I'll go try to find the experimenter. Don't go in there. I don't think we're supposed to."); and "maximum positive influence definition" ("I'll go try to find the experimenter. You go in and see what happened."). The results were very clear: "The behavior of the confederate greatly affected the frequency of active help. . . . *Maximum positive influence* produced the greatest helping behavior—all subjects helped" (318, emphasis original).[27]

Data from the historians support this thesis too. The Oliners[28] write about the importance of networks which, however, under conditions of terror must perforce be kept small and discrete (102–8). And Fogelman notes the "channel factors," a term drawn from Kurt Lewin, which were necessary prerequisites of rescue. They include the availability of a hiding place and a network to supply identity cards, ration cards, escape route, warning in case of impending raid, etc. (60–61). Furthermore, the Oliners point out that only one-third of the rescuers began helping Jews on their own initiative; the rest—fully two-thirds—of the rescuers undertook rescue activity only after being asked by a potential victim, a parent or other relative, a religious functionary or representative of the resistance, a teacher, or an acquaintance or a friend (312–17).

The evidence is clear: **Legitimate social authority—hierarchical or peer authority—facilitates both antisocial and prosocial behavior.** Staub sums it up well: ". . . most people seem to need social support to behave according to prosocial [and antisocial] ideals" (336).[29]

Role and Rule in Determining Antisocial Action and Responsibility

An emphasis on role and rule in determining action and responsibility is another factor that facilitates the doing of evil. This, to be sure, overlaps with the previous factor of insertion into a hierarchy which does, or tolerates, evil; but it seems of sufficient importance to merit attention on its own.

The Stanford Experiment and My Lai

The clearest evidence of the significance of the factor of role comes from the Zimbardo experiments which have been widely discussed in the literature.[30] The Stanford prison experiment was not so much an exploration of obedience as a study of the ease with which people adapt to their assigned roles. Students responding to an advertisement were tested and found to be nonpsychotic. They were, then, randomly assigned to act as prisoners or guards, with the faculty acting as prison administrators. The guards quickly adapted to their role, imposing arbitrary rules on the prisoners to degrade them and developing means to control any resistance. The prisoners quickly adapted to their role, allowing the guards to break their group solidarity and losing track of the fact that this was only a university experiment from which they could exit at any time. Visiting parents adapted to their role, behaving as visitors to a prison and feeling unable to "help" their children. Most astoundingly, the faculty adapted fully to its role as prison administrators, trying to prevent a rumored "breakout" and treating prisoners who broke down as shirkers who were trying to talk their way out of prison. The identification with the roles and rules of the experiment was so complete that the experiment, which was to have lasted fourteen days, was terminated on the sixth day.

The work of Kelman and Hamilton also supports the centrality of role and rule in facilitating the doing of evil. One of the most important results of their study of the trial of Lieutenant Calley and its aftermath is the double typology that they develop to account for the workings of the hierarchy-authority. First, there are the three "dynamics of authority" which account for why people obey: Compliance, that is, the need to attain reward or avoid punishment, motivates some. Identification with the authority, rooted in parental authority and transferred to professional role expectations, motivates others. And internalization of authority, that is, adopting behavior congruent with values and worldview, motivates yet others. These three dynamics of authority permit integration of the individual into society; violating them leads to guilt, shame, regret, etc. (104–15). Second, there is the typology of "rule- , role- , and value-oriented persons" which accounts for the different reasons why people obey. Rule-oriented persons obey because it is their duty to abide by the rules set forth by a legitimate authority; such persons need to know the exact rule and subrule for any given situation. Role-oriented persons obey because they accept their place in the social hierarchy and participate in the role assigned to them; such persons need to have a clear idea of where they stand and what is expected of them as persons standing in that place. Value-oriented persons obey because they accept the worldview of the hierarchy, including its values; such persons need to have reasoned convictions about why a certain action must be done in that society (119–22). Combining these two typologies, rule-oriented people obey by compliance, role-oriented people obey by identification with their role, and value-oriented people obey by internalizing the values of their social hierarchy. Also, as noted earlier, role-within-legitimate-authority takes precedence over independent moral judgment (206).

Teaching as Experimenting

It may be of some interest to add some narrative, episodic evidence in support of the claim for the centrality of role and rule in determining human action. In teaching this material at Emory University, I try to sensitize the students to the centrality of hierarchical authority and rule observance / role fulfillment. I spend much time discussing these matters in relation to our work in the classroom. Three recurrent issues seem worth mentioning. First: The course is divided into three parts: obedience studies, altruistic studies, and religious-philosophical considerations. At the end of the obedience section, I give an hour exam which is divided into three parts. The first part tests the students on the material. The second is composed of three questions: "Why did you take this exam?" "What could you have done to get out of it?" "Should I have given it?" And the third part asks that, for five points, the students write their names legibly seven times. Almost uniformly, students invoke their role as students as the reason why they took the test and my role as professor as the reason why I should have given it. As a result, they see no reason why they should seek exemption from it and, therefore, have no idea how to go about such a task. Only four out of thirty-two, 12½% (the same percent range that Browning found), refused to write their names (and received extra credit for that); the others obediently went along invoking, in subsequent discussion, rule and / or role (some invoked the points to be gained, that is, self-interest, but most noted during later discussion that that, too, is role-determined). Only one student, 3%, sought (and received) exemption from the final examination.[31]

Second: After considering the Milgram and Stanford experiments, we do a mind experiment in which the exits from campus streets are blocked and all cars which enter the campus are forced to keep moving in a circle. We discuss at length the means necessary to keep the persons driving the cars moving—students dressed in police uniforms, clear orders to keep moving without explaining why, etc.—and the penalties to be applied to anyone who stops—being yelled at by the authorities, having the car towed, etc. Students adapt quickly to the role of experimenter-policeperson and show some ingenuity in refining the "experiment." It is quite a shock when I, or a student, notes the role fulfillment and points out that the real "winners" in this experiment are those who stop driving in a circle early. We, then, discuss how one would resist in such an experiment.

Third: I did one session with totally nondirective teaching; this meant that my teaching assistant and I said nothing for the full class. After ten minutes of initial awkwardness, one student adopted my role and began a class discussion on the assigned reading. This lasted thirty minutes, during which students continued to play their role, even continuing to raise their hands. The single comment about the process of the class was suppressed. After this, the issue of what was happening (process) came up again; this part lasted another thirty minutes. One student walked out; the rest debated whether to appoint an authority to direct the discussion or asked of one another what they should do. There was great frustration and even some mild personal attacks which were not put down by the group. Toward the end, three more people walked out. The class was terminated five minutes early. At no point in this time period did anyone seize control of the class and direct the discussion to the material assigned, nor did anyone force the question of my silence on me. Discussion of what had happened in the following class revealed that, indeed, the students had felt an anomie during the class and anger towards the instructors and towards fellow students; that they had felt an authority vacuum in a place where they had expected authority to be asserted; and that they felt lost when the assigned roles of teacher and student had collapsed—so much so that some said they had "not gotten what they had paid for during the previous class."[32]

Hitler's Professors

Historians studying the shoah have reached the same conclusion. Weinreich,[33] in what I think is the first systematic study of a profession under nazi rule, dealt with nazi academics and research institutes. He deals thoroughly with nazi racial, legal, and political scholarship and describes in great detail the workings and "studies" of Walter Frank's institute, Goebbels's institute, the institute on German church life, Hans Frank's institute, Rosenberg's institute, and so on. The sheer number of academics involved is impressive and, as Weinreich points out, this may have been politicized scholarship, but it was not sham scholarship; it was research performed by scholars of high standing (7–9, 240). Furthermore, scholarship provided the intellectual grounding of nazi action; academic conferences were attended by high party and military personnel (7–9, 47–48, 239). Scholarship became policy (112), after *Gleichschaltung* (coordination), of course (67).

Weinreich devotes a great deal of space to academic scholarship and the Jewish problem. It was scholarship that fostered the idea of ghettoization (95) and it was scholarship that "proved" that the Nuremberg laws and ghettoization would not be sufficient to solve the Jewish problem (107). It was scholarship which discussed, and then rejected, *Eindeutschung* (Germanization) and *Umvolkerung* (refolking) of non-aryan elements (172–77). There was a *wissenschaftliche Abteilung* (scientific division) of the extermination camps (197). Even in 1944, there were scholary pamphlets and conferences on antisemitic themes being prepared (216, 219–34). And it was academic scholarship that provided the grounding for nazi racial "science" (chap. 5) and racial "law" (chap. 6).

In trying to account for this, Weinreich notes that scholars wanted to be part of the social hierarchy (37–38). Scholars knew they needed to be consciously political to accomplish that: "'The German historians are aware of their duty to provide the historical tools for the central problem of the present war and the forthcoming rearrangement of Europe and to envision and interpret the development of the past from the point of view of the present. By this publication they wish to profess the political character of their science'" (84–85, quoting). Weinreich, then, points to the long, distinguished German academic tradition which was appealed to in achieving "'close and loyal collaboration'" (102, quoting). Such academics needed to do their job well; hence, the following question: "'Please inform me whether your inquiry of October 31 is to be understood as a directive in the sense that all Jews in the Ostland are to be liquidated? Is this to take place without regard for age and sex and economic considerations . . .'" (149, quoting). It was, thus, a fulfilling of role and a following of rule that motivated the cooptation of German academics into nazi culture.

The SS

Sabini and Silver[34] contrast the Milgram and Zimbardo experiments, emphasizing the conclusions from the latter as follows: The former shows that, if one does not intend evil, one does not feel responsible; hence, if authority can succeed in shifting the intent to obedience, subjects will not even feel responsible (339–41). The latter shows that if brutalization can be made standard procedure, it will become legitimate; hence, only socialization to role is necessary to make brutalization morally acceptable. This means that, ". . . the similar brutality of the female guards [in concentration camps] suggests, at the same time, the superfluousness of this selection [of guards for brutality]; it suggests that the conditions of the camp were sufficient to socialize the guards into the brutality in a relatively brief period without prior selection" (354).

The centrality of role and rule is also confirmed by an account of a former nazi in Sichrovsky:[35] "A petty bureaucrat of high position, a man who'd started on the bottom and worked his way up to the very top, but who nonetheless remained a petty bureaucrat at heart. Decent, respectable, incorruptible . . . To him job performance was a physical concept—a given amount of work within a given amount of time. Merely doing his job was not enough. He took pride in the way he did his job, in not being a mere machine. Actively doing rather than just functioning, a hum switch in a circuit. The amount of work to be done within a given time period was the law by which he lived. . . . It was a system that functioned because of his transformation into what was expected of him before an order was even given. He had the gift of anticipating the needs of those about to take power and to prepare for them. . . . It's not that he wanted evil, but he was afraid to do good if it involved even the slightest resistance to authority. I think he simply didn't recognize the difference between good and evil. . . . He never broke any laws. On the contrary, he was the personification of probity. Whoever his superior, whatever the system, he was a model citizen" (49–56).

Klee, too, found that role played an important part in doing evil. Role was so central that one SS officer could write in his diary: "'On 17 July 1941 nothing much happened. I messed around with the Jews some more—and that's my work'" (99, total entry for the day). And another could make the following entry: "'In the afternoon another Sonderaktion, the 14th I have participated in up to now. In the evening cosy evening company in the Führerheim as guests of Hauptsturmführer Wirths. There was Bulgarian red wine and Croatian plum brandy'" (267, quoting). Both men were reporting fulfilling their job roles.

Others

The early study of Mayer also underscores the centrality of role and rule in facilitating the doing of evil: "Teachers teach what they are told to teach or quit, and to quit a public post meant, in the early years of the Third Reich, unemployment; later on, . . . it meant concentration camp" (79–80). Even after the end of the war, Mayer notes: "Always credulous and submissive, the Germans had just had twelve years' intensive training in total credulity and total submissiveness; the Occupiers found them marvelously docile, even unresentful, Germans to the manner born" (302).

Steiner,[36] himself a concentration camp survivor who worked on the death commandos, gives two reasons why rule observance and role identification work so forcefully. First, the role models and rule expectations usually neatly fit the personal needs and cultural expectations of the individual. Thus, national socialism was based on traditional values, traditional heroes, and a traditional scapegoat; the individual needed only to properly place himself or herself in this system. Second, in role identification, bonding, not truth or morality, becomes the cement of identity, and a strong leader provides a positive reinforcement and a focus for one's loyalty. Role identification, then, becomes a form of "affiliation as identity repair." Thus, membership in German organizations, especially the SS, allowed one to shed one's old identity and acquire a legitimate, new one (416–23). The "authoritarian sleeper" personality in Germany found institutional support in nazism for roles of violence, as well as "an ultrasignificant other" who demanded obedience (431–35). This allows a merging of role and person: "Depending on the degree of his identification with the 'cause,' the influence of his leaders, and the nature of his role, there would be a merger of role and person" (435).[37]

The importance of role in the doing of evil is also strongly supported by the work of Ervin Staub[38] who epitomizes his work by saying, "I believe, however, that the basic sources of genocide are cultural characteristics, difficult life conditions, and the needs and motives that arise from them" (32). He then lists the cultural preconditions for the shoah (chap. 8) and, after examining other cases of mass-killing and genocide, lists the following general cultural conditions for genocide: a weak cultural self-concept leading to nationalism, devaluation of subgroups, an authoritarian orientation to society in parenting and politics, a monolithic culture, and a strong ideology (233–36).[39] Most importantly,

Staub argues for the integration of the personality through role identification: "Originally this [violence] may have been justified as part of the war against subversion, but once violence becomes normal practice additional, totally self-serving motives for it can come into play, including greed, sex, or sadism. . . . ideological and identity-related motives became integrated with other personal motives (e.g., power, stimulus seeking, sadism). People function better when their different motives join and support each other, especially if they have to overcome personal inhibitions or social prohibitions" (225–56).

Role and Rule in Determining Prosocial Action and Responsibility

Normocentrism among the Rescuers

One of the most fascinating results of the study of rescuers by the Oliners is the development of the threefold typology of motivation: [40]

> Rescuers who were characteristically *empathically* oriented responded to an external event that aroused or heightened their empathy. Rescuers who were characteristically *normocentrically* oriented responded to an external event which they interpreted as a normative demand of a highly valued social group. Rescuers who characteristically behaved according to their own overarching *principles,* in the main autonomously derived, were moved to respond by an external event which they interpreted as violating these principles (188, emphasis original).

Analyzing the normocentric orientation, the Oliners found:

> Unlike an empathic reaction, a normocentric reaction is not rooted in a direct connection with the victim, but rather in a feeling of obligation to a social reference group with whom the actor identifies and whose explicit and implicit rules he [or she] feels obliged to obey. The social group, rather than the victim him- or herself, motivates the behavior. The actor perceives the social group as imposing norms for behavior, and for these rescuers, inaction was considered a violation of the group's code of proper conduct. . . . For their first helping act, the *majority* of rescuers (52 percent) responded to a normocentric expectation (199, emphasis added).[41]

This means that over half of the rescuers did what they did, not out of sympathy [42] and not out of principle, but because they felt that some social authority expected it of them, as it expected such action of everyone in the social group. As noted above, the authority can be hierarchical or peer authority, and it can be religious or political, etc., but it is the expectation of the group which counts: "People with strongly internalized norms can demonstrate considerable autonomy within the parameters allowed by the group or even strain the boundaries of permissible group behaviors. Nonetheless, they are not entirely independent of their groups, for they will stop short of acting in any way that would jeopardize their group membership" (208).

Smolenska, who participated in the Oliners' research,[43] also notes that normocentric motives included those of helpfulness, solidarity, etc.; that these motives were religious or secular in origin; and that such norms were rooted in a reference group (family, church, political organization), in an internalized commitment to the norms of the group, or in a self-concept that identified the norms of the group with the self (218). Kurek-Lesik, in the quotation cited above on the behavior of Polish nuns, maintains that 62% of the women's religious communities in Poland participated in rescue (329)[44]—not out of sympathy with Jews but out of normocentric motives: it was, indeed is, the role of a nun to give shelter to the oppressed. Baron, working with Dutch rescuers, concludes: "Since positive attitudes towards Jews represented a pre-war consensus in Dutch public opinion, the rescuers of Jews stemmed more from the mainstream of Dutch society than from its margins. Their aid to the Jews represented a *normative altruism* in keeping with typical Dutch values . . . deep roots in the soil of Dutch history" (322–33, emphasis added). Sauvage, too, in his film reportage on Le Chambon sur Lignon underlines the normocentric nature of the actions of those rescuers.

Eron and Heusmann reach a similar conclusion based on their study of the influence of television on prosocial and aggressive behavior in children: ". . . by consistently observing either aggressive or prosocial behavior, the youngster comes to believe these are expected, appropriate ways of behaving, and that most people solve problems that way. Norms for appropriate behavior are established. . . ."[45]

The evidence is clear: **Most people respond normocentrically, that is, they grasp the demands of hierarchical and peer authority on them and assume the role of loyal follower of those norms / authorities.** To act prosocially, one need only follow—follow the prosocial norms of one's reference group(s).

The "Rescuer Self": Role Internalization among the Rescuers

Norms alone only set standards. To be effective, norms must be internalized, identified with the ego, or self. Fogelman,[46] in one of her most important contributions, set forth the concept of the "rescuer self":

A rescuer's life was intricate and terrifying. A careless word, a forgotten detail, or one wrong move could lead to death. . . . A core confidence, a strong sense of self, and a supportive situation had allowed bystanders to undertake the rescue. But once the decision to help had been reached and the rescue had begun, a different self—a *rescuer self*—emerged, to do what had to be done and to keep rescuers from becoming overwhelmed by new responsibilities and pressures. A "transformation" had taken place. It was not simply their behavior that changed. Successful rescuers became, in effect, different people (68, emphasis original).

Citing Lifton, Fogelman notes that rescuers became "de-centered" by the events around them and then, in the effort to reestablish equilibrium, they had to "create new selves," to "re-center" themselves (68–69).

This new self, in the case of the rescuers, was built on strong moral foundations. It allowed them to do what was necessary—including plotting, stealing, lying, taking risks, enduring hardships, putting loved ones in jeopardy, and living in fear—all in the service of setting the world (and their place within it) on solid ground (68–69, parentheses original).

The "rescuer self" enabled rescuers to deal with feelings of guilt, rage, fear, terror, and sadness; to cope with the enormous problems of everyday life: feeding their charges while not buying so much as to arouse suspicion, disposing of their bodily wastes, washing them and their clothes without letting laundry give them away, keeping the hidden ones busy, dealing with their illnesses and their instabilities, fears, and anxieties; managing their own families: children, spouses, friends, etc., who also had fears and needs; and leading a "normal" life to the outside world. Rescuers, then, had two roles but only one self:

From day to day the rescuer self played the part of innocent bystander concerned solely with getting by in these difficult times. It minded its own business and kept out of people's way. . . . Rescuers had to be ready on a moment's notice to shift smoothly from one role to another. . . . They lived their roles day and night. Their roles had to contain a kernel of truth, part of their real experience, or else. . . . Rescuers were able to play various roles and take required actions because, at the deepest level of their beings, it was who they were and what they believed that really mattered. . . . consistent with their moral beliefs, identities, feelings, and attitudes (76–80).

The two roles could be played precisely because the self identified with only one, internalized only one role.[47]

Blood Donors and Exemplars

The evidence from the social sciences supports the internalization of norms and the development of the role of the prosocial activist. Piliavin, in her study of blood donors,[48] notes that internalization is fuller if no external rewards are present—in this case, that blood donation was more of a role / identity issue among donors who were not paid than for those who were paid. She concludes: "The actions of the self, however, can come to be more and more controlled by the 'me,' through the development of commitments to certain images of the self. . . . the gradual development of commitment to a self-identity of 'regular blood donor' and its effects . . ." (253).

Colby and Damon,[49] in their study of exemplars, develop the concept of "goal transformation" to explain how people, many of whom were in mid-life and hence already had commitments, suddenly were transformed into exemplars of prosocial activity. One of the exemplars is quoted as saying:

> "It changed my goals. It didn't change my values. . . . I don't think my values have changed from early on in life. I think I've always tried to do the best I could under the circumstances with whatever the job was. That's just a very simple sort of thing, that you do the best you can, in school, or whatever. I've grown, I've learned more and more about what's important. . . . Now the goals have changed as the opportunities have changed. . . . And so I try to seize that moment, that opportunity, and maximize the potential of that opportunity. So that changed my priorities. It gave me new goals. I didn't have a goal five years ago of . . . So it's the opportunity that created the new goal" (252).

On the basis of their study, Colby and Damon conclude:

> They were not setting their moral interests in opposition to their personal ones. Nor were they setting their own interests against those of others. The exemplars were starting from the assumption that their own interests were synonymous with their moral goals. Their real dilemma was in deciding how to parcel out their limited time and energy to all the others whom they felt called upon to serve. . . . Rather than denying the self, they *define it with a moral center.* They seamlessly integrate their commitments with their personal concerns, so that the fulfillment of the one implies the fulfillment of the other. . . . None saw their moral choices as an exercise in self-sacrifice. To the contrary, they *see their moral goals as a means of attaining their personal ones, and vica versa* (299–300, emphasis added).

Similarly, in writing about the workers in the civil rights movement who are also prosocial exemplars, Beardslee comments:[50]

> All the workers reported a sense of joy and accomplishment in taking action, in not being passive. . . . Taking action, being an organizer, was for

them the visible expression of a new consciousness. They were aware of themselves as actors and aware of a new sense of self-worth and valued in their own actions. Mr. L. put it this way: "Being involved tended to free you. . . . gave a new sense of pride, it was a new sense of identity, really" (39).

People who are prosocially active develop a "prosocial self," often by transforming goals and values they already possess, and this "prosocial self" enables them to internalize the role of the helping person, thus facilitating the doing of prosocial acts.

Summary

In seeking an answer to the question of what facilitates good and evil, social hierarchy occupies a very important place. All persons are brought up in social hierarchies of family, school, peer group, workplace, and state. These hierarchies inculcate obedience to authority as a behavioral norm and as a moral value. People, therefore, have a strong tendency to invoke authority to justify their acts—for good and for evil. Further, these social hierarchies, behavioral norms, and moral values become strongly embodied in rules of human behavior and in roles assigned within the various hierarchies. Adherence to role becomes constitutive of personal identity. People, therefore, have a strong tendency to identify the rules and roles set for them and to follow those rules and to fill those roles. In so doing, they become who they are—for better and for worse.

Counter-text[51]

- Judges must also be experts in worldly matters so that they do not rule erroneously. For if they are not expert in such matters, then even if they are expert in Torah law, the result will not be "a completely and truly correct" judgment. . . . Therefore, the judge must be an expert in both fields. . . . wise in matters of Torah . . . and astute with regard to worldly affairs.[52]
- Rabbi Shmuel bar Naḥmani said in the name of Rabbi Yoḥanan: Every judge who issues a judgment which is thoroughly true, causes the presence of God to dwell in Israel. . . . and every judge who does not issue a judgment which is thoroughly true, causes the presence of God to depart from Israel.[53]
- "One law shall apply to you. The citizen and the stranger shall be alike. I am the Lord your God" (Lev. 24:22)—a law which is equal for all of you.[54]

COMMENT: Judges, as the arbiters of the human legal system, bear enormous responsibility. In this, the human judge shares with God the responsibility for the moral order of the universe. As Falk puts it: [55] "All the mitsvot [commandments] of the Torah are given in the framework of the covenant which God made on Mt. Sinai with the Jewish people. Since God chose this way, it means that God recognizes the legal and moral capacity of humanity and its natural autonomy too. Religion is not put upon humanity by a decree from on high; rather it is presented to humanity as the outcome of a dialogue and the result of an agreement. . . . The covenant is also the source for mutual responsibility. . . . Furthermore, the covenant serves as the basis for historical continuity for it includes all the generations."

- It is permissible to work one's non-Jewish slave excessively. However, even though the law is so, it is *middat ḥasidut* (the standard of the pious) and the way of the wise that a person should be merciful and pursue justice and not increase the yoke of one's slave and oppress him or her. Rather, one should give them to eat and to drink of every food and beverage—the early sages would give their slaves of every dish of which they ate—and one gives food first to the animals and slaves before one eats oneself. . . . Similarly, one may not abuse a slave with the hand or with words. . . . one may not yell or be angry at them overmuch but one should speak with them gently and listen to their complaints. . . .[56]

COMMENT: In the context of the shoah, the rabbinic treatment of non-Jewish slaves is remarkable. The nazi attitude is clearly caught by B. Ferencz in the title of his book, *Less Than Slaves* (Cambridge, MA, Harvard University Press: 1979).[57]

- Rabbi Ishmael the son of Rabbi Yose was walking on the road and met a man who was transporting a package of kindling wood and who had set it down to rest. "Help me reshoulder it," he said. Rabbi Ishmael replied, "How much is it?" "A half a *zuz,*" said the man. Rabbi Ishmael gave him a half a *zuz.* . . . Was not Rabbi Ishmael an old man and therefore it was not in accordance with his venerable state [that is, he was not obligated at all because of this age to help despite the Torah injuction to aid someone who has set down a burden to reshoulder it]? Rabbi Ishmael the son of Rabbi Yose acted *lifnim mi-shurat ha-din* (within the line of the law).[58]

COMMENT: Everyone is obligated by biblical law to help another person reshoulder a heavy load that that person has put down (Ex. 23:5). The elderly, a priest, and some others, however, are exempt from this because it might be unseemly for them to do such heavy manual work. Rabbi Ishmael the son of

Rabbi Yose, who was elderly, met a person who had put down a heavy burden and bought the load from him so as not to have to help him reshoulder it. He did not have to do this; he could just have walked on and ignored the burdened person. However, desirous of fulfilling the commandment to help one who has put down a heavy burden and yet physically unable to do so, Rabbi Ishmael bought the burden from the other person, thus making it his own and no longer that of the over-burdened person. In so doing, Rabbi Ishmael acted *lifnim mi-shurat hadin* (within the line of the law), embodying the value-concept of "caring."[59]

4

Teaching and Praxis

"You've got to be taught to hate and fear. You've got to be taught from year to year. It's got to be drummed in your dear little ear. You've got to be carefully taught." With these words, the central character of Rogers and Hammerstein's *South Pacific* explains that antisocial attitudes are not inborn; they must be taught. Prosocial attitudes, too, are not inborn; they, too, must be taught. Process counts, but so does content.

Teaching That Leads to Evil

Staub[1] differentiates culture and ideology as follows: "It is useful to distinguish between the *existing culture,* which consists of beliefs, meanings, values, valuations, symbols, myths, and perspectives that are shared largely without awareness, and *ideology,* which I define as primarily a consciously held set of beliefs and values [concerning an ideal social organization and way of life]." Legitimate social authority, as Staub observes, takes an existing culture and channels, focuses, and expands it through ideology; that is, social authority molds culture through specific teachings about the ideal society. The clearest evidence for this comes from historians, particularly from those who have studied the shoah in its cultural context, for it is in historical study, seen from the social-scientific perspective, that one sees most clearly the influence of ideology on culture.

The interrelationship between ideology and culture in nazi Germany can be seen in three fundamental areas: in racial thinking, in its positive as well as its negative aspect, including antisemitism; in authoritarian teaching in the home, in the public arena, and in its extreme forms; and in Darwinian survivalism as a way of defining the meaning of life.

Racial Thinking

Racial thinking was a cultural concept in pre-nazi Germany that was raised to an ideological commitment by nazism. Racial "science" became one of the mainstays of nazi ideology in medicine, law, and politics.[2] Everyone was given racial education in school[3] and in the army.[4] Racial thinking taught the inherent, natural superiority of the aryan race and, hence, its victory over other races which, by definition and accumulated biological and historical "evidence," were inferior. Racial thinking worked by preaching and practicing racial purity, that is, by urging aryans to remain pure and undefiled by inferior races, and by culturally compelling the isolation and devaluation of inferior races. This led to a whole series of praxes: racial laws which were vigorously observed and enforced which made it a crime to have sexual, and then social and cultural, relations with inferior races;[5] breeding policies which encouraged aryan Germans to breed, even out of wedlock though that contradicted the teaching of German motherhood;[6] a bureaucracy which generated and evaluated family trees for racial purity and mental health, and included eugenics and euthanasia programs;[7] and discrimination against, persecution of, and eventually liquidation of inferior races.

Two major contradictions existed in racial thinking, aside from very bad science. The first is that racial superiority was a function of genetics and will.[8] Logically, one would think that genetics could not be modified by will and that will could not affect genetics; yet both became a part of standard nazi racial ideology. The second is that racial superiority was a function of genetics but that it could be controlled by the state. Indeed, there were substantial scientific and political discussions about aryanization of non-aryans and "folking" of non-Germans[9] though, again, it would seem illogical that the state could make biological determinations.

Belonging to the superior race was wonderful. It created a *Volksgemeinschaft,* a folk-community, which was united by a deep sense of racial kinship, folk symbols, youth and adult group activities, an accent on health and strength, a panoply of heroes and rituals, and character traits that were carefully cultivated in school, in the workplace, in the home, and in the public sphere, such as hard work, diligence, obedience, punctuality, thrift, honor, loyalty, womanly steadfastness, comradeship, duty, order, joy, and peace.[10] Racial thinking also broke down rigid class thinking: "'I remember Wedekind,' said the teacher. 'I didn't know him before I joined the Party, and I don't know him now. Why? Because he was my inferior. A baker is nothing, a teacher is something; in the [nazi] Labor Front we belonged to something together, we had something in common. We could know each other in those days.'"[11] It created a sense of eliteness: "After a detailed study, Tom Segev concluded that 'joining the SS was to become part of an elite, an aristocracy, a religious order, a secret society, a gang, an army and a family all at the same time. . . . At times the SS was something of a mentality, a way of life.' An SS veteran who served as a concentration camp commander described the comradeship this way: '. . . Comradeship is everything. It gave us the mental and physical strength to do what others were too weak to do.'"[12] Sichrovsky, quoting the child of an SS officer, put it as follows: "The Nazis looked great!...it must have been exciting then." [13] There was, indeed, a sense of purpose, an esprit de corps,[14] generated by living in a racially coherent community. The film, *Triumph of the Will,* catches this so well. Blackburn calls it a "mystical community." [15] This was the bright side of racial thinking and, while we today also know its dark side, the bright side was certainly attractive to Germans, then and now and, if we are to be honest, it has its attractions for each of us.

The dark side of racial thinking was its exclusiveness and what it led to. Everyone who was not aryan was excluded: Slavs,[16] Blacks and Asians,[17] even women in a certain sense.[18] However, it is especially the Jews who were excluded in racial thinking, for antisemitism was another cultural concept in pre-nazi Germany which was raised to an ideological commitment by nazism—so much so that Davidowicz, followed by S. Katz and others, has argued that anti-semitism was the core and center of nazism.[19] The long, and continuing, history of Jew-hatred[20] has been well-documented and need not be rehearsed here.[21] It is enough to note, first, that there was no compromise on this subject: Unlike Gypsies, some of whom were aryanized or permitted to slip through extermination; unlike homosexuals, Jehovah's Witnesses, criminals, and others who could be "reeducated"; Jews—all of them—were destined for extermination.[22] Second, one must let the realization sink into one's consciousness that, to the best of their ability, the nazi authorities did in fact exterminate the Jews.[23] And third, had Germany been victorious, or less territorially greedy, those Jews who survived the initial killers would also have been exterminated.[24]

Racial thinking in general, and Jew-hatred in particular, brought to the surface the phenomenon of scapegoating. This human behavior was, and is, not peculiar to nazi society and ideology, but it was brought to a fine art by nazi propagandists. It also was (as it always is) a quick and easy solution to many complex, and perhaps insoluble, problems. It is, therefore, a very effective psychological and social tool. Staub has noted: "When there is no aggressor or the aggressor is too powerful or the source of responsibility cannot be identified or the responsibility is one's own (or one's group's), identifying a scapegoat will have 'beneficial' side effects. A cause is found, and life problems become comprehensible. Known danger is preferable to a vague anxiety about an unspecified threat. Finding a scapegoat makes people believe their problems can be predicted and controlled; and it eliminates one's own responsibility, thereby diminishing guilt and enhancing self-esteem" (48).

Authoritarian Teaching

Authoritarian teaching in the home, in the public arena, and in its extreme forms was another cultural concept in pre-nazi Germany which was raised to an ideological commitment by nazism. In one of the most remarkable essays on German culture, Alice Miller,[25] citing manuals for raising children, pointed out the authoritarian, indeed the emotionally and physically abusive, nature of child-rearing philosophy and praxis before and during the nazi period. She called this "poisonous pedagogy." Two selections will illustrate:

> "Such disobedience amounts to a declaration of war against you. Your son is trying to usurp your authority, and you are justified in answering force with force in order to insure his respect, without which you will be unable to train him. The blows you administer should not be merely playful ones but should convince him that you are his master. Therefore, you must not desist until he does what he previously refused out of wickedness to do. If you do not pay heed to this, you will have engaged him in a battle that will cause his wicked heart to swell with triumph and him to make the firm resolve to continue disregarding your blows so that he need not submit to his parents' domination. If, however, he has seen that he is vanquished the first time and has been obliged to humble himself before you, this will rob him of his courage to rebel anew. . . ." For parents' motives are the same today as they were then: in beating their children, they are struggling to regain the power they once lost to their own parents. . . . Although parents *always* mistreat their children for psychological reasons; that is, because of their own needs, there is a basic assumption in our society that this treatment is good for children. . . . Beatings, which are only one form of mistreatment, are *always* degrading, because the child not only is unable to defend him- or herself but is also supposed to show gratitude and respect to the parents in return (citing and responding, 15–17, emphasis original).

> "Only humiliation can be of help here. . . . Someone who is unduly proud of his accomplishments should be assigned tasks far beyond his abilities and should not be dissuaded if he attempts to take on more than he can handle; halfhearted measures and superficiality should not be tolerated in these attempts. . . . Hold up to a talented lad the examples of living or historical figures who possess far more splendid talent than his. . . ." The conscious use of humiliation (whose function is to satisfy the *parents'* needs) destroys the child's self-confidence, making him or her insecure and inhibited; nevertheless, this approach is considered beneficial (citing and responding, 21–22, emphasis original).

Miller's evidence occupies eighty pages and includes a list of methods used to raise children in an authoritarian way (59) and quotations from Eichmann, Höss, Himmler, and Hitler (67–70).

Authoritarian child-rearing continued after the nazi period. Sichrovsky cites two examples: "Punishment was administered ritually. I had to stand against the wall with raised arms. Then he would hit me across the rear end five times with a thin bamboo stick. My mother would stand next to him and watch, after which she'd take me into her arms and console me. Father would leave the room. Afterward I had to go to his room and apologize. After all, I had hurt the poor man's feelings" (43). And: "Once one of them was supposed to memorize a poem, and every time he stumbled Father let him have it. I can still hear the screams. Mother took me [a girl] by the hand and led me out of the room. 'Father's going to kill Erich. We better leave,' she said to me. Things really got bad later on when we lived in our own house, with no next-door neighbors and no danger of being overheard. After that there was no stopping him" (95).

Authoritarian teaching for the public arena is embodied in the following quotation from Hitler:[26] "My pedagogy is harsh. Weakness must be chipped away. The youth that will grow up in my fortress will frighten the world. I want a brutal, authoritarian, fearless, cruel youth. Youth must be all of this. It must be able to bear pain. It must not have anything weak and gentle. The light of the free, marvelous beast of prey must once again shine from their eyes. I want my youth to be strong and beautiful."

On the authoritarian view of the state in German thinking, Mayer notes:

> The German people have never, as single individuals, had to assume the responsibility of sovereignty over their government. The self-governing American regards his government as his mere agent, an animated tool in his hands. If it doesn't suit his purposes, he discards it and tries a new one. He, the constituent, constitutes the State; his ministers minister to him (152). . . . Twice in our time, at Weimar and at Bonn, Germany's victorious enemies have tried to turn Germany upside down and install government (as my Nazi friends see it) without rule. Hitler turned Germany (as they see it) right side up. He was an independent Sovereign, popularly supported, in part for no other reason than that he was an independent Sovereign. *This* was government (155). . . . He [the German] was habitually deficient in the *sense of political power* that the American possesses. . . . He saw the State in such majesty and magnificence, and himself in such insignificance, that he could not relate himself to the actual operation of the State (157, emphasis original).[27]

Indeed, the entire *Führerprinzip,* the leadership principle, which envisions the head of state as the authority for the folk, parallel to the father as the authority for the family, derives from this authoritarian teaching. As Mayer has commented: "All ten of my friends gladly confess this crime of having been Germans in Germany. . . . 'But,' I said, 'is this the *Herrenrasse,* the superior race?' 'Morally and mentally, yes,' he said. 'We are industrious and orderly, too. But we are unfortunate in this one respect: we cannot rule ourselves; *wir brauchen eine starke Hand,* we require an iron hand.' 'Why?' 'I don't know. That's the way we Germans are'" (164–65).

The authoritarian view of law is amply documented by Müller: The new ideology was given form through the legal process, specifically through the various decrees, regulatory rules, trials, etc. (48), as well as by the longing of the jurists for an authoritarian system (45). Even after the nazi period, jurists were so convinced of their having been "good" that they were bewildered by the mistrust the Allies had in their system (201) and maintained that they had only been enforcing the law (220); that they did not share the base motives of the nazi regime but were only obeying orders (247); that they had not knowingly broken the law (274); that fanaticism had led to blindness to injustice, which exonerated them (277); and that the conviction of one jurist would have led to the conviction of all, therefore none were guilty.[28] All this is rooted in an authoritarian view of the law and its relationship to society, especially to its practitioners. *Zucht und Ordnung,* discipline and order, were the order of the day (Mayer, 283–85).

Authoritarian teaching reached its acme in the preaching of, and justification of, brutality. Sabini and Silver point out that as long as brutality is a function of the individual, it is regarded as depravity. However, when it becomes standard procedure, it acquires legitimacy and, in acquiring legitimacy, it becomes socialized, institutionalized, and then it becomes policy.[29] The institutionalization of brutality within authoritarian teaching has produced two readings of the concentration camp guards. Staub has maintained that:

> In late 1933 Dachau, where many such murders occurred, was reorganized into a highly efficient facility in which systematic, policy-based brutality was institutionalized, although capricious individual brutality was discouraged. . . . Many of the SS who set up the [later] camps and then remained as personnel were veterans of the euthanasia program and thought of themselves as having special skills or expertise. They could focus their attention on the use of their professional skills. . . . The "ideal" SS man was not personally brutal and did not enjoy the suffering of victims. He could even treat individual Jews well while serving the machinery of their murder. . . . Not all SS men became "perfect." Even in a total organization like the SS, some traveled unique paths. Despite self-selection some had initially greater capacity for empathy for Jews, whereas others had deep-seated hostility or found pleasure in harming people (135–38).

F. Katz,[30] on the other hand, has maintained that:

> The Culture of Cruelty at Auschwitz. *The mission of Auschwitz was the systematic extermination of innocent people. To accomplish this mission*

there were official, formal procedures for carrying out massacres. Yet in addition to these official, formal procedures there emerged other forms of massacre. These were produced by the Auschwitz personnel who, using their own autonomy, informally developed a distinctive culture of cruelty that augmented the officially prescribed patterns of cruelty. In this culture of cruelty behavior evolved where new forms of cruelty were invented, refined, and repeatedly reenacted; where evil was deliberately courted, with full knowledge that it was evil; where a guard's personal reputation, one's status as an Auschwitz guard, was based on innovative contributions to cruelty.

It seems to me that both views are correct. There was indeed a form of authoritarian teaching that encompassed brutality at its extreme and that this brutality had two forms: an institutionalized form and an individual, "creative" form which was itself institutionally sanctioned. The latter represents the most extreme form of authoritarian teaching.[31]

Darwinian Survivalism

Darwinian survivalism was another cultural concept that was prevalent in pre-nazi Germany but was raised to an ideological commitment by nazism. Blackburn, who consulted thirty-six history textbooks and many collections of nazi speeches, notes that one must count Darwin among the intellectual precursors of nazism. Darwin's theories were popularized into the teaching that life is a struggle for existence, a fight to survive and, indeed, only the fittest survive. This, in turn, led to the need for *Lebensraum,* room for life to survive, and to the consequent right to seize such space from others (22, 50), as well as to the besieged and betrayed mentality: "We won *both* wars, and *both* times we were betrayed."[32] Most important, survivalism taught that war was the normal condition of humankind (22–23), the dimension of deeper meaning in life: "War was ideal for bestowing meaning in a society torn loose from its moorings" (127). Evolution, thus, came to mean the selection of oneself for survival with war as the ultimate selection agency (35, 49): "The rule of 'tooth and claw' thus served a beneficial function because it prevented 'universal decay and ensured further achievement . . .' determined the outcome of the 'cosmic struggle for survival and greatness. . . .' 'Even today it is not by the principles of humanity that man lives or is able to preserve himself above the animal world, but solely by means of the most brutal struggle'" (67–68, quoting Hitler).[33]

The teaching of survivalism led to two strange, though logical, results. First, the Jews were grudgingly admired because they had survived (68–69). And second, defeat in war implied loss of survival (72–73). Defeat was "more than a lost battle, a lost war. It was a 'shame, disgrace, humiliation'—and at the same time 'deserved'" (78). Hence *Götterdämmerung,* suicide in the face of defeat, was a logical conclusion to this popular Darwinism (72–73).

Because of the prevalence of the survivalist and war motifs, education had as its purpose the building of strong character; that is, the building of character that would survive. The teacher was not a "knowledge monger" but a soldier on the cultural-political front. Soldiering was the epitome and model of character building and, hence, of education. Furthermore, education was violent: "Character comes about only through force and counterforce" (93–96). To teach this, textbooks were rewritten, especially in the area of history, to reflect this survivalism and its eschatological tone (35–39, 51–56) with special emphasis on "blood witnesses," that is, those who were martyrs for the survival of the folk (43–45). Religion, too, was recast in this survivalist-eschatological tone (chap. 4). Race- , class- , spiritual- , ethnic- , and anti-liberal-education were all molded to fit into the pattern of Darwinian survivalism in the following "principles": Blood-mixing reverses the evolutionary process (144). Organic spiritual evolution is interrupted by the Asian spirit forced on the German people in Christianity (155). Democracy and liberal freedom are counter survivalist (171–74). In sum: "The Nazis considered education an exercise for development of human will . . . the school's function was to equip Germans to prevail in this struggle for existence" (178). Furthermore: "The contention within the National Socialist Philosophy between the physical and the metaphysical . . . arose from a common source: fear of a reversal of the evolutionary process . . . Hitler feared that without ceaseless vigilance, Germany would be plunged into oblivion . . ." (179–80, italics omitted).

Rationalization of evil by higher authorities is the process by which authority takes an existing culture and molds it through ideology. Rationalization of evil facilitates the doing of evil. In the case of Germany, racial thinking, authoritarian teaching, and Darwinian survivalism were present in German culture before nazism. Nazi authorities took these ideas and focused and expanded them through specific teaching into ideological commitment, thus rationalizing and facilitating the doing of evil.

All teachings, when elevated to ideology, enable legitimate authority to rationalize the doing of evil. As Milgram notes: "Ideological justification is vital in obtaining *willing* obedience, for it permits the person to see his behavior as serving a desirable end" (142, emphasis original). At the end of his published study, Milgram also presents a scenario for militarizing a personality (181–86). There, he writes: "The end of the war comes not through the disobedience of individual soldiers, but by the alteration in governmental policy; soldiers lay down their arms when they are ordered to do so" (183). Kelman and Hamilton also talk about "ideological zeal" and "transcendent mission" as components in obedience (49, 29). They go to great lengths to point out that legitimate authority, in order to maintain its legitimacy, must always remain within the normative framework of the culture (122–24). Thus, legitimate authority must use ideology, teaching, symbols, and justification as part of its strategy to evoke obedience, especially with role- and value-oriented persons (132). Conversely, authority must be judged illegitimate before disobedience can be called forth; one way that delegitimization of an authority occurs is through the development of a new ideology (56–57, 135).[34]

Teaching That Leads to Good

Prosocial attitudes also must be "carefully taught." No one is born with a prosocial orientation. What teachings, then, facilitate the doing of prosocial deeds? What ideas and concepts sustain altruistic motivation? Put differently, what is the teaching of goodness? What is the ideology of caring? The social-scientific and historical evidence suggest five such teachings.

Personal Competence

Personal competence—also called self-esteem, internal locus of control, and certainty—is one of the teachings at the core of prosocial action. Midlarsky,[35] in studying late-life development of altruistic behaviors, reports that, in a staged emergency, fewer older adults will attempt to help but, if they have received some training, older adults are more likely to try to succeed than is the case with younger subjects. She attributes this to a heightened sense of actual and perceived competence, as well as a willingness to help others (264). Midlarsky, then, points out that such helping behavior increases self-esteem and social integration, so much so that one may talk about "helper therapy" as a way of increasing competence and well-being among older adults (268). Similarly, Piliavin and Charng[36] note that, ". . . people high in self-esteem, high in competence, high in internal locus of control, low in need for approval, and high in moral development appear to be more likely to engage in prosocial behaviors" (31). Staub,[37] however, points out that too much self-esteem (overcompetence) can lead to a loss of sense of connectedness; hence, he proposes that competence and self-esteem need to be moderate in order to facilitate prosocial behavior.

As self-esteem and internal locus of control are part of the teaching of competence, so are several related personality configurations. Colby and Damon[38] report that the exemplars they studied had little dogmatism and disclaimed any special degree of courage. Rather, they were motivated by persistent truth-seeking, had a core commitment to honesty, possessed a sense of certainty about the moral rightness of what they were doing, remained open to new situations and ideas, and were able to focus their energies on the tasks at hand (76–82).

In particular, the ability to manage fear and doubt is part of the sense of personal competence. As Colby and Damon note:

> They were not wholly insensate when it came to feelings of fear. But they were able to manage such feelings so the fear did not emerge in consciousness as a formidable emotion to be reckoned with. . . . Their success lay in not allowing those intimations to become full-blown emotional forces capable of determining moral action. . . . that the roots of moral courage are not so much to be found in wrestling with fear as in preventing it, which can be done in a variety of ways, all of which stem from a fundamentally moral perspective on life (87–88).

The evidence from the historians supports the observations of the social scientists. The Oliners[39] found that rescuers had a strong belief that they could influence the events around them: "In fact, more than others, rescuers felt they could control events and shape their own destinies and were more willing to risk failure. . . . A sense of internal control did allow more rescuers to recognize a choice where others perceived only compliance and to believe they could succeed where others foresaw only failure" (177–78).

Fogelman[40] agrees with the Oliners and Midlarsky: ". . . competency . . . Rescuers were no fools; nor were they suicidal. . . . They needed to have faith in their capacity to assess situations and find solutions, not just in their ability to outsmart the Nazis. There was seldom time for measured thought. There was only time for a quick assessment of self and situation" (59; see also 237). In writing about children of rescuers, she comments: "Their work enhanced their self-esteem and gave them a feeling of competency and importance. In many families, children were included in family councils and given a voice in rescuing decisions" (224). Similarly, the Oliners agree with Staub that self-esteem among rescuers was important but that moderate self-esteem contributed to competence more than high self-esteem (178). Finally, Fogelman cites three stories of rescuers who conquered fear (chap. 7) and concludes by quoting one rescuer: "'The best antidote to fear is action'" (141).

Commitment to Intelligent Moral Judgment

Commitment to intelligent moral judgment is another teaching at the core of prosocial behavior. A commitment to trying to think through and analyze problems as fully as possible, together with the use of moral categories of thought and judgment, is a central teaching of the prosocial life.[41]

To be sure, intelligent moral judgment presupposes cognitive and moral abilities. The capacity to abstract ideas and moral principles from reality, to label them, and to discuss them is a prerequisite to committing oneself to a life in which such abilities are used. A veritable library exists on the development of these cognitive and moral abilities.[42] Most of these theories seem unduly rigid, utilizing "invariant" stages of development in a hierarchy of intellectual and moral competencies.[43] A typology of factors which facilitate prosocial attitudes and behaviors in personality development would seem more reasonable. Piliavin and Charng seem to share this view: "A more fruitful approach might be to look at certain theoretically promising dimensions of personality and see whether they are related in sensible ways to altruistic action."[44] However, the evidence is unambiguous that intellectual and moral capacities do develop through childhood, the adolescent years, and into adulthood; and, further, that not all adults fully develop their intellectual and moral abilities.

Having said that much, it is clear that prosocial action requires intellectual effort and agility. Fogelman reports the following story:

> Desperate times called for both creative solutions and constant vigilance. The rescuer always had to be alert. . . . On one occasion, the Nazis burst in unexpectedly at the Kowalsky's residence. Jean Kowalsky, who lived with her mother, had practically no warning. Her charges had barely enough time to hide before the soldiers climbed the stairs to the attic. There in plain view was a table littered with cigarette butts and cards. Cigarette smoke still lingered in the air. At this dangerous moment, Kowalsky's nine-year-old nephew spoke up. He confessed that he and his friends had been secretly playing cards and smoking. He pleaded with the soldiers not to tell his mother, as she would beat him if she knew. The Germans promised to keep his secret and left (75–76).

A similar remark showing the need for quick-witted thinking is made by an exemplar in Colby and Damon: "'If you don't have courage, you have to fake it. . . . If you don't fake courage, you aren't going to do those things that you really want to do, you are going very quickly to develop the reasons why you can't do that which your heart and your head say you should do'" (161–62). Indeed, in each of the stories that they relate, Colby and Damon are careful to document the variety of tasks undertaken and the sheer intellectual ingenuity that accomplishing those tasks took. The Oliners, Fogelman, and others are also careful to list the sheer variety of tasks involved in rescue—including evaluating who, among the rescuers and the rescued, were trustworthy and who, among the persecutors, could be bribed and with what—and to show that rescue required great thought and much careful planning. All these cases of inventive intelligence display the commitment to thinking quickly and decisively under pressure, even under extreme threat.

It is also clear that moral sense and moral judgment are central to thinking and decision in prosocial action. Thus, Colby and Damon note:

There is nothing Hamlet-like about this group. . . . Their overwhelming response was that it had never been necessary for them to muster their bravery once they had determined the right course of action. Their feelings of moral necessity had given them their great sense of certainty, and this in turn had relieved them of their fears and doubts. Courage became irrelevant, an unexercised affective appendage (70–71).

And, again, in their conclusion, the centrality of moral judgment is highlighted:

For most people, of course, moral and self-interests become linked, but only up to a point. There remain prominent schisms between morality and self after childhood and, indeed, all through life. The resolution of the two at the end of childhood remains only partial . . . that morality and self grow closer together during the course of normal development, but they still remain relatively uncoordinated for most (but not all) individuals . . . a person's moral judgment does not determine the place that morality occupies in the person's life. To know this latter key quality we must know not only how the person views morality but also how the person understands the self in relation to his or her moral beliefs. . . . In the end, moral behavior depends on something beyond the moral beliefs in and of themselves. It depends on how and to what extent the moral concerns of individuals are important to their sense of themselves as people. . . . the extent of the unity between morality and the self (305–7).

The evidence from the historians supports the social-psychological thesis of the centrality of moral reasoning and judgment in rescue. The Oliners report:

For most rescuers, then, helping Jews was an expression of ethical principles that extended to all of humanity. . . . While other feelings—such as hatred of Nazis, religion, and patriotism, or even deference to an accepted authority whose values the rescuer shared—influenced them, most rescuers explain their actions as responses to a challenge to their fundamental ethical principles. This sense that ethical principles were at stake distinguished rescuers from their compatriots who participated in resistance activities only . . . (170).

They also note that rescuers scored "significantly higher" on the Social Responsibility Scale than others (173) and, in their three-fold typology of rescuers, one category is that of those with "principled motivation," which constituted 11% of the sample (188, 209–21).

Smolenska, too, in her typology of rescuers, lists those with "axiological motives."[45] She writes:

Axiological motives originate from the actualization of moral principles such as "justice," "sanctity of human life," and so on. When an individual notices that his or her basic values are impinged upon, he or she may feel aroused in their defense. . . . since they are based upon his or her moral convictions. Axiological motives sensitize people to discrepancies between their principles and reality (219).

Fogelman, too, notes the centrality of moral thinking in rescuers: "The reward for most rescuers was the personal satisfaction of doing the right thing and remaining faithful to their consciences" (60). In her five-fold typology of rescuers, moral rescuers is the first category. Fogelman comments: "Moral rescuers, however, were doing more than just reciprocating affection. Moral rescuers had a strong sense of who they were and what they were about. Their values were self-sustaining, not dependent on the approval of others. To them, what mattered most was behaving in a way that maintained their integrity. The bystanders who ultimately became rescuers knew that unless they took action, people would die" (162). And again: "The essential characteristic of moral individuals is that they do not remain passive when faced with conflicting choices. Their conscience can transcend an evil society because that conscience is independent and has its orgins in early childhood" (180). And yet again, quoting a rescuer: "'We find it more important for our children to have parents who have done what they felt they had to do—even if it costs their lives. It will be better for them—even if we don't make it. They will know we did what we felt we had to do. This is better than if we first think of our safety'" (178).[46]

Extensivity

Personal competence and a commitment to intelligent moral judgment, however, are not enough to account for prosocial orientation, for many people have a good sense of their own personal, intellectual, and moral abilities yet lack a full orientation toward goodness. Extensivity—also called inclusiveness, attachment, connectedness, openness, acceptance, and diversity—is another teaching that facilitates prosocial attitudes and behaviors.

In their original study of rescuers,[47] the Oliners essayed a composite portrait of the rescuers. They concluded that the "capacity for extensive relationships" was what characterized their subjects. This extensivity included: parental modeling of caring behavior; reasoned discipline for children; communicating of the value of helping others for moral rcasons and without respect to reward; encouraging the qualities of dependability, responsibility, and self-reliance; willingness to take risks; inclusiveness with respect to others who are different; openness to new experiences; and positive self-evaluation (249–51). In their second reflection of this topic,[48] the Oliners again presented extensivity as the overarching teaching which facilitates prosocial attitudes and action, and linked it more systematically with attachment and inclusiveness (370):

> [E]xtensivity means the tendency to assume commitments and responsibilities toward diverse groups of people. Extensivity includes two elements: the propensity to *attach* oneself to others in committed interpersonal relationships; and the propensity toward *inclusiveness* with respect to the diversity of individuals and groups to whom one will assume obligations. . . . Conceptualizing extensivity as a two-dimensional continuum allows us to better understand the responses of nonrescuers as well as rescuers. Several nonrescuers were highly attached people, who were quite capable of altruistic behaviors on behalf of their families, church groups, or nation but who nonetheless shut their doors in the face of supplicant Jews. Other nonrescuers were more detached generally . . . not so much a matter of excluding Jews as it was a general sense of remoteness from others. Highlighting this distinction also helps explain why inclusive people, such as those who are intent on saving humankind, may nonetheless inflict great cruelties on individuals. Because of their disconnection from real people . . . they may become inured to the suffering of those around them (370–74, emphasis original).

Fogelman, calling this teaching "acceptance," reaches a similar conclusion:

> I found that one quality above all others was emphasized time and time again: a familial acceptance of people who were different. This value was the centerpiece of the childhood of rescuers and became the core from which their rescuer self evolved. From the earliest ages, rescuers were taught by their parents that people are inextricably linked to one another. No one person or group was better than any other. The conviction that all people, no matter how marginal, are of equal value was conveyed to children of both religious and nonreligious households (259).

The evidence from the social sciences supports the thesis of extensivity, openness, and inclusiveness. Beardslee[49] reports: "The Civil Rights Movement in the South, in these people's perception, was not a movement of rigid ideology, either religious or political. Rather it focused on relationships with others, on black and white together, on human, social interaction" (41). Similarly, Colby and Damon note:

> This quality of staying alive to social influence and moral growth all throughout life is a special mark of the moral exemplars in our study. . . .

All new ideas must owe their shape to some interaction between external guidance and internal belief: the transformation is, in one precise word, a "co-construction". . . . a balanced relationship between stability and change. Such a relationship is made possible by the expansive (rather than the restrictive) nature of certain personal qualities. These qualities, such as open-mindedness . . . Morality is an interpersonal matter, even when it takes the form of a transcendent faith in a supernatural power. This is because it is inevitably implemented through the quality of a person's interactions with the social world (183, 184, 187, 196).

This openness to the diversity of the world requires an ability to build bridges from one's current perceptions and analytic constructions to new constructions. Colby and Damon call this "scaffolding" (171) and it, too, presupposes extensivity and openness. At the end of their study, they note: "The exemplars' expansive moral concerns, and their steadfast moral commitments, are extensions in scope, intensity, and breadth of normal moral experiences. . . . *What is extraordinary about moral exemplars is that they apply this habitual moral mode to the farthest reaches of their social vision*" (303, 308, emphasis original).[50]

Empathy

Empathy is the fourth teaching that facilitates prosocial attitudes and behaviors. Unfortunately, the discussion of empathy is clouded by unclear definitions of empathy, by attempts to link empathy directly to altruism, and by unclear definitions of altruism.[51] Hoffman[52] and Batson[53] present two views which bear summarizing.

Hoffman defines empathy "not as an exact match of another's feelings, but as an affective response more appropriate to another's situation than to one's own" (71). He then goes on to point out that "empathic distress" is an affective response to the distress of another, "a parallel response—a more or less exact replication of the victim's presumed feeling of distress" (71). Empathic distress remains an internal feeling. Finally, he identifies "sympathetic distress" as follows: "[T]hey may continue to respond in a purely empathic manner—feeling uncomfortable and highly distressed themselves—but they may also experience a feeling of compassion, or 'sympathetic distress' for the victim, along with a conscious desire to help, because they feel sorry for the victim, not just to relieve their own empathic distress" (71). Empathy can be combined with anger to produce "empathic anger" (73), with self-blame to produce "guilt" (74–77), and with righteous anger to produce "empathic injustice" (77–78). The categories here overlap but Hoffman's basic typology is clear: Empathy is a feeling for the other. If the other is distressed, one experiences empathic distress oneself and there is a pressure to relieve that distress in the self. However, one can also experience sympathetic distress, which is empathic distress plus the desire to help the other for the other's sake, not just to relieve one's own distress. Relieving empathic distress is an egoistic act, while relieving sympathetic distress in an altruistic act.[54]

Batson rejects Hoffman's distinction between empathic distress which produces egoistic motivation and sympathetic distress which produces altruistic motivation. Rather, he proposes a unified definition of empathy which evokes a truly altruistic—that is, allocentric—response:

> Empathy, at least as I am using the term, does not mean feeling the same emotions one might imagine the person in need is feeling, nor does it mean feeling the emotions one would if suffering the other's plight. Instead, it is a more other-oriented emotional response elicited by and congruent with the perceived welfare of someone else. . . . When perceiving someone in distress, empathy will be an unpleasant, aversive emotion. But it is suggested that empathy—unlike personal distress—does *not* evoke egoistic motivation to have this aversive arousal reduced; *instead* it evokes altruistic motivation directed toward the ultimate goal of reducing the other's need.
>
> The proposal that empathic emotion can evoke motivation directed toward the ultimate goal of reducing the other's need has been called the *empathy-altruism hypothesis.* According to this hypothesis, the magnitude of the altruistic motivation is assumed to be a direct function of the magnitude of the empathic emotion. Of course, reducing the other's need is likely also to bring social and self-rewards, avoidance of social and self-punishments, and reduction of the helper's own feelings of personal distress. But it is proposed that feeling empathy for the person in need evokes a motivation to help in which these benefits to self are *not* the *goal* of helping; they are simply *consequences* of helping (in Eisenberg, 220–21, emphasis added and cross-references omitted).

Batson, then, while recognizing the presence of egoistic motivations in an altruistic act, insists that empathy—the feeling for the other—evokes the altruistic, and not the egoistic, response. He devotes his book to proving, in my opinon successfully, this "empathy-altruism hypothesis."

The evidence from the historians supports the centrality of empathy in prosocial activism. The Oliners, in their three-fold category of rescuers, enumerate those who are "empathically oriented" (188–99). Of this group, they write:

> An empathic orientation is centered on the needs of another, on that individual's possible fate. It emerges out of a direct connection with the

distressed other. Compassion, sympathy, and pity are its characteristic expressions. The reactions may be emotional or cognitive; frequently they contain both (189).

Rescuers with empathic orientation constituted fully three-eighths (37%) of the sample (221).[55]

Fogelman, too, recognizes the centrality of empathy, especially in the first phase called "awareness" (42). She also points out that the nazis knew very well that empathy was their enemy: "Compassion for others rests on the recognition that the one asking for help differs little from the one offering it. By making empathy with Jews difficult, Nazi propaganda became an integral part of the Final Solution" (46).[56]

Righteous Anger

For some people, righteous anger—also called moral outrage, the principle of justice, or empathic anger—facilitates prosocial attitudes and actions. Not all people experience righteous anger. Research shows that some people are motivated by caring, sympathy, and empathy while others are motivated by principle, ideology, rights, justice, and the feeling which comes from observing that those principles have been violated.

The distinction between an ethic of caring and an ethic of rights, together with the corresponding affects, is present in Gilligan[57] and this differentiation has become increasingly accepted in the field. Montada[58] conducted two experiments which indicated this double-sided motivation. The first showed that "[t]he best predictor was not sympathy for the needy . . . but, rather, moral outrage about the unjustness of differences between the privileged (the social stratum the subjects themselves belonged to) and the disadvantaged . . ." (235). The second study showed that "considerations of justice and entitlements and personally experienced moral oughts and responsibilities . . . were largely irrelevant to the prediction of actual social commitment. They were predictive only of the intention to act prosocially. Actual prosocial behavior seemed to be motivated by love (sympathy) alone . . ." (249).

Similarly, Colby and Damon, following Carlson, distinguish "two kinds of altruists which she calls reformers and helpers. These two types exhibit distinctive personality styles and emotional reactions. The reformers are oriented to correcting social injustice. They tend to show a zest for combat and adventure and are much more likely to express anger or contempt. The helpers are motivated by a desire to alleviate suffering. They are more nurturant and tend to identify with the distress of the people they are helping. The helpers are less likely to exhibit anger than the reformers." The exemplars studied by Colby and Damon divide equally into these two groups (277).

The Oliners, too, recognize the distinction between "two kinds of moral principles—the principle of justice (the right of innocent people to be free from persecution) and the principle of care (the obligation to help the needy). Those motivated by the principle of justice tended to exhibit different emotional characteristics than did those who were motivated by the principle of care. They usually had more impersonal relationships with those they assisted and reserved strong emotions (anger and hate) for those who violated the principle of justice they held dear. Rescuers motivated primarily by care, on the other hand usually focused on the subjective states and reactions of the victims. Kindness toward the victim was the dominant theme, while hate and indignation toward the violators were more transitory" (209).

All this leads me to think that while, morally, each ethic has an equal place and while, practically, it does not matter which motivation is predominant—and it is not to be excluded that one person would have more than one type of motivation and / or that motivation within the same person would vary over time—motivation from empathy and motivation from righteous anger remain two separate teachings in the facilitation of prosocial attitudes and actions.

Racial, authoritarian, and survivalist thinking create a teaching of evil. They are the content of antisocial ideology. Personal competence, commitment to intelligent moral judgment, extensivity, empathy, and / or righteous anger create a teaching of good. They are the content of prosocial ideology.[59]

The Praxis of Evil

It is not enough to have a hierarchy which does, or tolerates, evil. Nor is it enough to have a social context which places the emphasis on rule and role. It is not sufficient to have a teaching of evil. Nor is the rationalization of evil through intense ideological indoctrination by legitimate authority sufficient to bring about the doing of evil. In the end, evil must be done; it must be acted out. Evil is composed of concrete acts, and someone must actually do them. Three factors facilitate the actual praxis of evil: First, most people are not asked actually to commit evil acts; they are only asked to be passive bystanders. Second, the doing of evil is incremental; lesser acts prepare the way for more grave acts. And third, "practice makes perfect"; routinization facilitates the doing of evil. Each will be dealt with separately.

The Passivity of Bystanders

The passivity of bystanders was carefully studied by Staub.[60] He noticed that, if there are many bystanders, responsibility is diffused among them and each one is less likely to take action (87). He also noted that if bystanders are told to be observers and not to be active, they will do just that and will suppress empathy for the victim (120, 124). Denial and rationalization also increase passivity; so does deindividuation of the victim (163–65). Finally, Staub observed that just as dogs who are given shocks which they cannot avoid will learn to stop trying to avoid the shocks and will become passive, so humans who face terror and intimidation will learn to stop resisting and become passive (164). This means that the doing of evil is facilitated by making it clear to people that they should not intervene, by providing them with reasons not to intervene, and by intimidating them into observer status. Kelman and Hamilton remark that absent any countervailing authority, obedience is almost always the simplest and most prudent course (76).

Historians of the shoah, too, have noticed the passivity of the bystanders in the praxis of evil. Mayer, writing in 1955, already noted that: "The German community—the rest of the seventy million Germans, apart from the million or so who operated the whole machinery of Nazism—had nothing to do except *not to interfere* (57). . . . They only need to watch out for themselves: 'You were sorry for the Jews . . . sorrier, later on, that they lost their jobs and their homes . . . sorrier still that they had to leave their homeland, that they had to be taken to concentration camps and enslaved and killed. But—*weren't you glad you weren't a Jew?* You were sorry, and more terrified, when it happened, as it did, to thousands, to hundreds of thousands, of non-Jews. But—weren't you glad that it hadn't happened to you, a non-Jew? It might not have been the loftiest type of gladness, but you hugged it to yourself and watched your step, more cautiously than ever'" (59, emphasis original). Staub also notes: "Once in power, the Nazis created order, stability, and material well-being. Germans who were not opponents or victims of the system lived increasingly comfortable, satisfied lives under the Nazis until the Second World War began. . . . government-created jobs and emotional experiences like sitting around campfires with other young people . . . 'the continuing loyalty of many Germans was a personal one, a willingness to believe, in the face of all the facts, that the man who had done so much for them in his first years could do no wrong and would somehow emerge, victorious and immaculate, to confound his enemies and detractors'" (116–17).

Müller points to the passivity of the jurists: They were not asked to do evil in any grand or cruel sense; they were only responsible for the "regular and uninterrupted administration of justice" (125); they were only political and social conservatives doing their jobs (296).[61]

The clearest case of a profession which adopted a stance of rigorous passivity, blatant bystandership, and studiously self-serving ethical silence is the case of the psychotherapists. Cocks[62] notes that there is no evidence that neurosis was especially prevalent in the third reich (24–25); hence, psychotherapists of all schools saw it as their purpose, not to do evil, but to use a variety of short-term therapies to reintegrate people into nazi society (9). Since the master race, by biology, could not contain genetic mental disorders, all mental stress was a function of lack of adjustment to the folk-community, and was correctible (12–3, 98–9, 103, 161, 179, 186). The task of psychotherapy was to maintain the health of the folk-community and contribute to the nazification of society (22). There was a philosophical harmony between psychotherapy and national socialism (84). "The psychotherapist in this *völkisch* view of things was not to be simply an analyst but an active agent of the community, performing the vital function of leadership" (79).

In terms of actual deeds, psychotherapists were not asked to murder Jews; they only had to remain passive and protect themselves. Thus, to accomplish their goals, professionals had to be trained, associations formed, institutes kept open, and professional standards maintained (189–91, 228). Psychotherapists were Jew-haters, but not extremely so (83).[63] As a result, Jews, for the most part, were not treated (21), Freud's works were burned publicly (90), references to Freud were eliminated (95), various technical terms were "renamed" (161, 227), and fifteen Jewish analysts died in the camps while the rest fled Germany never to be invited to return (91). Doctors were "constrained within the new ethics" (100) and self-censorship was the order of the day (17, 117). The only resistor, Rittmeister, was executed in what became known as "the unhappy affair of Rittmeister" (165–68). Göring, the head of the Göring Institute and relative of the nazi leader, did not use nazi rhetoric in his own scientific work and did tolerate "Jewish" ideas (119, 161, 227), and the Berlin Psychoanalytic Institute had, in the beginning, pictures of Freud and of Hitler (93). However, as Cocks notes: ". . . it is true that for most people it was easiest (and most advantageous) to continue along the path of least resistance, making the daily moral compromises which kept them safe, sane, and comfortable (20). . . . There are no heroes in this book; it is an unhappy fact that most, if not all, of the psychotherapists in the Third Reich were more concerned about their own, and their profession's, survival than they were about the fate of others. But to dismiss their work on this basis alone would be to ignore common human frailties as well as a significant degree of accomplishment during very difficult times" (21).[64] These were "Germans on the job" (62, 95, 162). Their praxis of evil was largely passive.

Incremental Praxis

The incremental nature of the praxis of evil has been clearly stated by Staub: "If there is harm to others, progressively the victims' well-being and even their lives will lose value in their eyes" (80). After studying work on Greek torturers, he observes: "The more they participate, the more difficult it is for them to distance themselves from the system's goals and deviate from its norms of conduct, not only overtly but internally" (82). Citing other experiments, Staub adds: "Even without any instruction to do so, teachers [in Milgram-type experiments] tend to increase the intensity of the shocks over time" (81). Finally, drawing on Kurt Lewin's concept of "goal gradient," Staub reasons: ". . . the closer you are to a goal, the stronger the motivation to reach it. Interruption of goal-directed behavior is a source of tension: the closer the goal, the greater the tension. . . . The further you have progressed toward a goal, the more difficult it is to give it up" (85).

Based on these observations, Staub concludes that one learns by doing and that the more one participates in evil, the harder it is to break away from the pattern of doing evil, behaviorally and mentally. This leads Staub to conclude that there is a "continuum of destruction" (17–18) which begins with minor acts and escalates, incrementally, to more and more serious ones (chap. 6, 9). This "continuum of destruction" also makes "equilibration," that is, moral rationalization, easier (147).

The incremental nature of the praxis of evil is also confirmed by the Zimbardo prison experiment.[65] The guards were initially ill-at-ease with their role but, as they identified more and more with their role, they tried more severe repressive measures. As those measures were tolerated by the prison authorities (the professors) and not resisted effectively by the prisoners (fellow students), the (student) guards increased the irrationality and severity of their actions. A true "continuum of destruction." The Milgram experiments,[66] too, confirm the incremental nature of the praxis of evil. The shocks began at a harmless level and proceeded to ever higher levels in clear increments; subjects were not asked to begin at the lethal levels but to progress toward them.

It seems to me, too, that while factors such as insertion into a hierarchy, role identification, rationalization, bystander passivity, deindividuation of the victims as well as the perpetrators, and lack of resistance facilitate the incremental praxis of evil, the ability of perpetrators to "get away with it," that is, to practice evil without punishment, allows perpetrators to conclude that they can loosen their inhibitions and pursue their roles and / or their evil impulses with impunity. "Getting away with it" allows a new increment in the praxis of evil.[67]

Historians of the shoah have also noted this incremental phenomenon. The nazi system accomplished *Gleichschaltung,* coordination, in incremental stages, slowly taking over the schools, the unions, the universities, medicine, law, business, psychiatry, the churches, the courts, and even women's organizations.[68] The assault on the Jews was also carefully organized along a continuum of destruction.[69] Browning's account of the transformation of Police Battalion 101 from the initial shock of the *Aktion* in Jóséfow (chap. 7) to the "Jew Hunt" of November 1942 (chap. 14), to the "Harvest Festival," the mopping-up *Aktion* in November 1943 (chap. 15), is a remarkable essay on the incremental praxis of evil.

The continuum of destruction is so fundamental to the praxis of evil, and particularly to the reality of the shoah, that it has engendered a very serious debate among historians, known as the fight between the "intentionalists" and the "functionalists."[70] The issue is whether the actual extermination of the Jews was a full-fledged part of nazism from the beginning or whether it developed within nazi ideology and especially within nazi praxis. On the one hand, Hitler was explicit about his designs for the Jews in his earliest writings and, as head of state, in 1939 he said: ". . . that if the rest of the world would be plunged into a general war by Jewry, then the whole of Jewry would have finished playing its role in Europe! They may still laugh today at that, exactly as they laughed at my prophecies. The coming months and years will prove that I also saw correctly here."[71] On the other hand, the actual mass-murder and then the systematic extermination of the Jews did not begin until 1941, though Jews were discriminated against, persecuted, imprisoned, and deported before that. This would imply that mass-murder and extermination were later developments. One of the better arguments for the functionalist theory is that it was the fact that the nazis pursued an incremental attack on the Jews and "got away with it." This, in turn, allowed them to escalate that attack until it reached extermination camp proportions; that is, until extermination as an idea and a praxis, together with its "culture of cruelty," was within the purview of what would be "normal" enough to be tolerated.

Routinization

Routinization is the third element that facilitates the praxis of evil. Routinization means two things: First, it means actual practice at doing what one does. "Practice makes perfect," as the popular saying has it. Second, it means being linked to a bureaucracy, being sanctioned by institutionalization. In both senses, routinization facilitates the doing of evil.

In the first sense, Milgram has shown that the training of soldiers consciously employs the "practice makes perfect" phenomenon to enable the doing of evil (181–83). The historians of the shoah have also pointed to this phenomenon. Thus, Browning has noted that actually killing Jews made subsequent killing easier (124, 127) and, in *Schindler's List*,[72] the "target practice" of Amon Goeth allowed him to do what he did with greater and greater freedom. To be sure, "practicing" evil is linked to obedience, to being able to "get away with it," and to many other phenomena already examined; but it is the actual doing that establishes the precedent.

The routinization of evil by bureaucracy is clearly pointed to by Kelman and Hamilton in reference to the My Lai massacre (17, 165), though they are very careful to distinguish between bureaucracies, professional organizations, and the military (309–14). Staub points it out for aggressive cultures in general (54, 122–23, 233). In the field of shoah studies, routinization by institutionalization was noted most forcefully by Arendt[73] and is clearly seen, for example, in the study of the jurists.[74] Usually, routinization is eased by euphemistic language.[75]

The Praxis of Good

In retrospect, it seems self-evident to note that prosocial behavior, too, is learned by doing and that prosocial attitudes are acquired and reinforced by action. Still, this observation merits restatement: All behaviors are learned by doing, including prosocial behaviors, and all attitudes are learned best by socialization that is followed by action, including prosocial behaviors. As Staub puts it: "Children who taught a younger child, wrote letters to hospitalized children, or made toys for poor hospitalized children became more helpful on later occasions than children who spent the same time in activities that were similar in nature but not helpful to others. . . . Morality is learned through moral action. Learning by doing is a basis for developing values, motives, the self concept, and behavioral tendencies. . . . If there are benefits to others, even imagined ones, they begin to find the activity worthwhile and its beneficiaries more deserving" (80).

Sometimes, prosocial praxis begins with a request. Thus, the Oliners[76] note that two-thirds of the rescuers in their sample agreed to rescue only after having been asked by a victim or a respected intermediary. Sometimes, prosocial praxis begins with a "triggering event" such as confrontation with poverty, racism, war, etc. (Colby and Damon, 296) or a "transforming encounter" with Jew-hatred or cruelty (Fogelman, 52–53). And sometimes, prosocial praxis is rooted in a cumulative series of encounters. Thus, the Oliners report that some rescuers first observed Jewish stars, then they saw signs excluding Jews, then they noted that Jews were disappearing, then they heard reports about brutality and summary executions, then they witnessed the brutalization of a Jew or Jews. In such cases, it was the cumulative effect that propelled them into rescue (117–21). Fogelman confirms this analysis (41, 54) and devotes a whole chapter to the process of "becoming aware" (chap. 3). Salience to the victim increases the motivation to prosocial action.

Once committed to prosocial action, activists, too, follow the rule of incremental action; that is, they expand their sphere of activity to include more people or other causes. Fogelman cites research on the "foot-in-the-door effect" that demonstrated that "when people are asked for a small favor and comply, they are more likely to agree later to a larger favor" (150).[77] This fits in well with her own research on rescuers:

Some rescuers figured that as long as they were going to be shot for hiding one Jew, they might as well hide more [in spite of the increased dangers of discovery]. Dutch rescuer Wilto Schortingnuis and his wife began by agreeing to a request from a friend that they hide a Jewish doctor and his wife. Soon, a Jewish nurse from a psychiatric hospital where Schortingnuis's wife worked asked if they would harbor her and her two brothers. "If we could have two," Wilto said, "we could have four or six" (80).

One of the most moving stories told by Fogelman is that of Stefania Podgórska Burzminska who, as a teenager of sixteen years, began by sheltering one boy and wound up saving thirteen men, women, and children (87–104). In addition to being a powerful witness to religious faith and simple courage, this story illustrates the incremental nature of prosocial commitment. Piliavin and Charng also note this incremental principle among volunteers (55–56). Furthermore, almost all the stories told by Colby and Damon illustrate the same principle: prosocial activity generates itself.

Research also shows that prosocial action in one area of life almost always reflects a more general commitment to an altruistic ethic. Fogelman cites research conducted with Vietnam protesters which "found that their antiwar acts were part of a longer series of concerned stances, not unique, one-time, one-cause involvements" and a study of civil rights workers that showed "a continuity in their moral values" (82). She concludes that this was consistent with her findings on rescuers and cites a case of a rescuer who also fed German soldiers (82). The Oliners cite a case of a rescuer who was sheltering Jews in one room and fleeing German soldiers in another (228). Both the Oliners (199, 245) and Fogelman (273, 292, 297) point out that rescuers continued to be involved in prosocial activities after the war, caring for the sick, the addicted, the poor, etc.[78] In one of the great ironies of the outcome of the shoah, the perpetrators do not feel guilt and generally live out their lives without remorse, while the rescuers continue to feel guilty about all those they did not help (the Oliners, 229; Fogelman, 289).

Finally, incremental action leads to full moral commitment. The prosocial activist whose action grows by increments, ends up firmly committing himself or herself to action. Colby and Damon write: "Among our exemplars, we saw no 'eking out' of moral acts through intricate, tortuous cognitive processing. Instead, we saw an unhesitating will to act, a disavowal of fear and doubt, and a simplicity of moral response. Risks were ignored and consequences went unweighed" (70). Similarly, the Oliners observe: "This internal sense of compulsion was characteristically so strong that most rescuers reported rarely reflecting before acting. Asked how long it took them to make their first helping decision, more than 70 percent indicated 'minutes.' Asked if they consulted with anyone prior to making the decision, 80 percent responded 'no one'" (169).

Staub,[79] drawing on social-psychological research, states the case for praxis generating praxis most clearly:

> Just as the ancient philosophers had proposed, moral behavior is learned through action, through engagement in moral conduct. . . . In fact, learning by doing is a hidden aspect of most socialization. . . . There is substantial evidence that prior participation in prosocial behavior increases adults' subsequent positive actions as well as children's.

Piliavin and Charng note the same phenomenon: "'With repeated performance of a voluntary act over time, the sense of personal, moral obligation assumed increasing importance as a motivator; a supportive and favourable context in general became much less vital'" (43, quoting).

Summary

Antisocial attitudes and behaviors must be taught; so must prosocial attitudes and behaviors. Racial and other forms of exclusivist instruction, authoritarian education for the family as well as for the public realm, and survivalist training constitute the teaching of evil. They are the core of antisocial education and they facilitate antisocial attitudes and behaviors. Personal competence, commitment to intelligent moral judgment, extensivity, and empathy and / or righteous anger are the five core ideas that constitute the teaching of goodness. They are the core of prosocial education and they facilitate prosocial attitudes and behaviors.

Teaching alone cannot bring about either evil or good. Both antisocial and prosocial attitudes must be translated into behaviors through praxis. Incremental praxis and routinization aid praxis of both good and evil, while the passivity demanded of the bystander facilitates the praxis of evil.

Counter-text [80]

- "God will seek out those who are persecuted" (Eccl. 3 : 15)—Rabbi Huna said in the name of Rabbi Joseph: ". . . [Where] you find a righteous person persecuting a righteous person—'God will seek out those who are persecuted.' Where a wicked person persecutes a righteous person—'God will seek out those who are persecuted.' Where a wicked person persecutes a wicked person—'God will seek out those who are persecuted.' Even where a righteous person persecutes a wicked person—'God will seek out those who are persecuted.' Whatever the case—'God will seek out those who are persecuted.'" Rabbi Judah ben Shimon said in the name of Rabbi Yose ben Nehorai, "The Holy One, blessed be He, demands satisfaction for the blood of the persecuted at the hands of the persecutors . . . Therefore God chose Abel . . . Noah . . . Abraham . . . Isaac . . . Jacob . . . Joseph . . . Moses . . . David . . . Saul . . . and Israel."[81]

COMMENT: This passage highlights the moral principle that God Godself will take up the cause of the persecuted and applies it to the three logically possible cases—righteous exploits righteous, wicked exploits righteous, wicked exploits wicked—and then extends it even to the case where it would seem least likely—righteous exploits wicked. The source, then, returning to the motif of the wicked persecuting the righteous, asserts that God systematically chose the persecuted. It lists these "chosen" biblical figures and concludes by noting that the Jewish people is the righteous one whose cause will surely be taken up by God Godself, as the verse teaches. It is instructive to note that the rabbis mentioned are part of the stream of nonviolent teaching which developed in Jewish Palestine between 250 and 400 C.E.[82]

- He who hired someone to make a trip and that person was killed [while on the trip] should properly do penance [during the ten days of repentance].[83]

COMMENT: The situation here is that someone has hired another to go somewhere and the employee died on the trip. Since the employer is paying the person hired, the latter is responsible for his or her own safety (as long as the trip was not a trap planned by the employer for the person hired). The problem here is that the employer is, in some moral if not legal way, still "responsible" for the death of the person hired. After all, had that person not been on the trip, he or she would not have died under those circumstances. The norm, therefore, is that the employer should do some form of penance to express his or her remorse for the killing of the person employed.

5

Childhood Discipline and Personality

The previous chapters presented evidence from social psychology, experimental psychology, and historical study dealing with patterns of behavior and long-term attitudes that are observable in society at large. This enabled us to identify several factors composed of complex social conditions, attitudes, and feelings which facilitate the doing of evil and of good. This chapter will look at patterns of personal behavior in order to try to explain, from the perspective of psychotherapeutic and developmental psychology and personality theory, why the social patterns observed in the previous chapters exist. Admittedly, any attempt to generalize from personal to cultural history, from therapeutic to social analysis, is subject to the criticism of over-generalization. Still, society is made up of individuals and, so, the method which moves from the individual to society generates an understanding of some of the roots of social phenomena as they grow out of individual experience.

Insights from the Model of the Abused Child

Listening to Hitler's speeches and watching him speak in films such as *Triumph of the Will,* one is impressed with his screaming. Everything he seemed to have said was screamed, especially in his public appearances. This ranting and raving was one of the main motifs of another twentieth century classic film, Charlie Chaplin's *The Great Dictator.* Intended as a spoof on Germans and nazi Germany, Chaplin depicts Hitler screaming nonsense syllables. The same phenomenon of continuous screaming was also noticed in the camps. Survivors report the yelling, the screamed commands, no matter what the task at hand. Here, too, a spoof developed in American films: American GIs are stopped by German soldiers, the Americans yell "Heil Hitler," the Germans snap to attention and give the nazi salute, the GIs then hit them and escape. To Americans the screaming was a puzzle, even comical; to Germans it was not.

Alice Miller,[1] in her profound study of German culture, looks into the personal-developmental history of Germans using the tools of both cultural history and therapeutic case-history. The case of Hitler's screaming serves as a paradigm for Miller's general theory of the origin of social evil: Authoritarian culture permits a father to abuse his children—verbally, emotionally, and physically—and this child abuse generates the phenomena of splitting and projection, as well as those of repression and identification. These phenomena, in turn, allow the adult abused child to do evil with one aspect of the self, to be "normal" with the other, and to sustain both "selves" in a tense but workable coexistence. This model requires further explanation.

The literature on child abuse is vast and increasing every day as we become more and more aware of these stories of terror and of the difficulties of treating such persons.[2] There are many forms of child abuse: cult-related abuse, which is really a form of torture; sexual-physical abuse, which is rape and other forms of forced entry into the body of the victim; physical abuse, which is beating and other forms of nonsexual aggression against the body of the victim; sexual abuse by seduction, which is emotionally if not physically violent; abuse by a parent or intimate adult, as opposed to abuse by a spouse or a stranger; emotional and psychological abuse, which can be verbal or behavioral; and physical neglect or emotional indifference. Then there are combinations of these forms of abuse. There is also one-time abuse: rape, kidnapping, and assault. And there is abuse by identification, that is, when one sees or hears any of these forms of abuse, one identifies with the victim and participates in the survivor's pain. There are also many approaches to, and protocols for, therapy.[3] The outlines of child abuse are clear enough to enable a few generalizations.

The Dynamics of Abuse

In the usual situation of child **sexual** abuse, a child—usually female, though not always—is approached by an adult. The adult is usually someone already known to the child: a parent,[4] an older sibling, an uncle, a teacher, a sports coach, or a clergyperson. The child is asked, threatened into, or forced to perform sexual acts that are appropriate for adults but not for children: fondling, masturbation, and / or genital- , oral- , or anal-sexual intercourse. Usually, the act is put under the seal of secrecy by promise, oath, or threat of harm to the child, to a sibling, to a pet, or to the other parent. The child—who can be anywhere from two years old to eighteen—never has the ability to refuse or stop the abuse for three main reasons: First, the child is by definition a child and the child knows that she or he is obligated to do what the older adult demands even if that request seems irrational, harmful, or wrong;[5] second, the child is usually in deep fear of the adult because of direct or indirect threat; and third, the child may not understand what is happening.

The long- and short-term effects of child sexual abuse are disastrous, for a sexually abused child must not only submit to physically and emotionally painful acts but is also deprived of the basic control of what happens to her or his body and inner being. Child sexual abuse—and such abuse can go on for years—invades the physical and psychic space of the child, depriving her or him of that inner human dignity that comes with a secure immediate surrounding. Child sexual abuse seriously distorts the meaning of such positive human experiences as love, caring, and trust, for if one cannot trust / love those in one's inner circle, one cannot trust / love anyone. Child sexual abuse also seriously distorts the human emotions of anger, rage, and indignation, for such emotions, which are naturally felt against the abuser, are strictly controlled and repressed, leaving a child and later an adult who cannot express normal, justified anger.

In the usual situation of **physical,** and not sexual, child abuse, the adult will find some act the child has done and use that act as a pretext for physical violence which can range from severe spanking, to beating, to bondage, to burning, to other methods of torture. Often, the adult will tell the child that this abuse "hurts me more than you," that it is "well-deserved punishment," or that it is "for your own good." This is never true. The child is never responsible for the abuse because the "punishment" is never proportional to the offending act. Utilizing the rationale of punishment, however, makes the child feel responsible and diverts attention from the true motives for the abuse.[6] Sometimes, no pretext is even sought and the adult will break into physical abuse without any apparent reason. As in sexual abuse, threats and secrecy are usual concommitants and, as in sexual abuse, physical abuse can go on for many years.

The long- and short-term effects of child physical abuse are also disastrous for many of the same reasons that the effects of sexual abuse are destructive. The child victim of physical abuse must not only submit to very painful acts but also has her or his private physical and emotional space forcibly invaded, destroying the ability to trust and distorting the meaning of love and of anger. Here, however, the teaching of "for your own good" makes this kind of abuse very complex because the child is expected not only to suffer but to love the abuser and to recognize the "good" in her or his own suffering.[7]

Not all child abuse is physically or sexually violent. **Emotional** abuse includes screaming at a child, intimidating a child, and improperly caressing a child. There is also behavior which includes expecting too much of a child,[8] improperly praising a child, and neglecting a child physically or emotionally through distance, coldness, and lack of responsiveness. The range, then, of abusive behavior is enormous.[9] Nor is abuse limited to children. Indeed, the symptoms and effects of abusive relationships between adults are similar to those for abused children; hence, the phenomena of battered wives, abuse of the elderly, denigration of the poor, and punitive persecution of political and racial enemies.

In all cases, child and adult abuse are supported by culture; they survive within a social and ideological framework. Thus, cultural teaching which supports the right of a man to have sex with his wife at any time permits, morally and legally, sexual violence within a marriage—marital rape—though disapproving of rape outside marriage (Fortune, 19, 29). A social framework which presupposes that a "loose" woman has less human dignity than a woman who has a "proper" relationship permits, morally and legally, sexual violence with such women—rape of prostitutes or of women who engage in extracommitment sex (ibid.). Cultural teaching that distinguishes between "natural" and "unnatural" sex acts permits violence within the category of "natural" acts (Fortune, 63–64). An ideological position that assumes that violence is an uncontrollable natural "instinct" justifies violence, or at least excuses it as an irresponsible moment; women who accept this teaching will see violence against themselves as unfortunate but necessarily a part of social nature.[10] A social framework that presupposes that "boys will be boys" creates a double standard of moral and sexual behavior for men and women (Bolton, 56–57). Culturally taught child-rearing expectations, which teach that the will of children must be broken or that performance in school and society determine one's value, shape the inner worth of every child in that culture (Miller, 3–62). Indeed, the entire patriarchal stance which understands women and children as the property of men—it is the men who have rights and the women and children who must submit—sanctions physical, sexual, and emotional violence against women and children.[11]

How does a child protect itself from physical, sexual, and emotional abuse? Indeed, how does anyone who is being abused protect herself or himself from abuse? In one sense, a person, especially a child, cannot protect himself or herself from such abuse. Physical strength, size, role, and age create a power differential which puts the abused person in a totally helpless position. However, there are psychological mechanisms which abused persons employ by which they cope; that is, through which they create a psychological distance which helps them protect themselves. Several such mechanisms deserve attention: splitting, repression, identification, idealization, projection, displacement, and scapegoating. All of these mechanisms are largely subconscious; that is, people use them without thinking and their effects are not consciously molded or even consciously desired.

Splitting

Splitting[12] is the process by which the abused person is able to develop two (or more) selves, one of which is abused while the other retains a certain human dignity. The following narrative shows this phenomenon clearly:

> At first he would just stand by the bed and touch me. Later he began to lay in the bed beside me. Although he began by being gentle, as time went on, his touch became rougher and rougher. He would leave me feeling sore

and bruised for days. It was as if he completely lost touch with the fact that I was a child. He was a bully who physically dominated everyone in our family. I saw and heard him beat up my mother so many times that I was in constant fear that he would kill her. I knew that I was no match for him, and I guess I believed that his sexual abuse was somehow better than the physical abuse my mother received. Total detachment became my way of dealing with what went on at night. I would roll into the wall when he came in, pretending to be asleep, trying to be part of the wall. I would cry hysterically in order to get so far into my own pain that I wouldn't notice what he was doing. With the pillow over my face, I taught myself to detach my mind from my body. I could actually see myself from the far upper corner of the room; I saw the little girl crying in bed and felt sorry for her.[13]

Splitting is also reported by rape victims, by children suffering physical abuse, and by concentration camp inmates. In very severe instances, the splitting can be so deep that there are many selves in one person. Furthermore, sometimes the selves are unaware of one another. This is known as "multiple personality disorder" and therapists are just realizing the deep inner connection between MPD and abuse. While splitting is common among abused persons, almost everyone "splits" his or her personality in moments of deep frustration, though we do not call the phenomenon "splitting" because the effect is not as intense as in abused persons.[14] In any case, splitting is actually healthy because it enables the abused person to preserve some inner humanity at the very moment when, objectively, her or his humanity is being invaded.

Repression, Identification, and Idealization

Repression is the process by which people push painful memories out of their minds, blanking out the incident as well as the bodily and emotional feelings that went along with the incident.[15] Frequently, these repressed bodily memories, impulses, and feelings surface in dreams, fantasies, compulsive behaviors, and fleeting thoughts. Everyone represses memories which are painful and humiliating; part of normal therapy is to recover these repressed memories and feelings. However, repression is particularly common in abused persons.

Repression is also reported by rape victims, by children suffering physical abuse, and by concentration camp inmates. In very severe instances, the repression can be so deep that "numbing" results; that is, a complete lack of feeling or an inability to have feelings at all.[16] Repression, too, is healthy because it enables the abused person to put out of his or her mind memories and incidents which are simply too painful to deal with.

Identification is the process by which a child observes the behavioral patterns and emotional attitudes of her or his parents, imitates them, and then internalizes those patterns and attitudes. The range of these behaviors and attitudes is great and includes, among many others: patterns of speech, hand motions, dress, eating habits, and attitudes toward work, money, leisure, sexuality, and gender role. Identification is also present with other authority figures: close family, older friends, teachers, clergy, political leaders, and cultural heroes.

For an abused child, identification complicates the picture tremendously for several reasons. First, by identification, the abused child internalizes the abusive patterns and attitudes of the abusing parent. The abuser, thus, becomes part of the abused. Indeed, if the identification is strong, the abused will see herself or himself as guilty while seeing the abuser as justified. Then, later in life, when the abused has power, he or she may become an abuser in spite of, or rather precisely because of, her or his background as an abused person. Second, the abused may identify so fully with the abuser that he or she has no clear sense of her or his own and separate identity. This is especially so if the abuse itself was severe enough to provoke severe repression. Third, the cognitive dissonance between the abuser as intimate authority and the abuser as abuser can be so strong that "idealization" takes place; that is, the abused reshapes the image of the abuser into a more emotionally acceptable form. The abused may seize upon the positive traits in the abuser, repress the evil behaviors and attitudes, and create an idealized vision of the abuser which the abused can then safely identify with and internalize. This accounts for the frequent positive images which abused persons have of their abusers.[17]

While identification is a very prominent process in understanding abused children, it is also present in rape victims, battered wives, and concentration camp victims. Thus, Cohen maintains that identification with the SS, and even with their antisemitism, was very common, especially among the *kapos*. Even Jewish self-hatred in the camps was not unknown.[18]

Idealization and identification were also prominent factors in German society. Miller points out that all the leading figures of the third reich had very severe upbringings with yelling, screaming, beating and, in general, "poisonous pedagogy." They were all brought up to know what was expected, to obey, and to be tough on themselves and on others (65–70).[19] Hitler fit in with this picture perfectly. First, he claimed, as an authoritarian father would, to know what was best for the German people; he, thus, became the wise father of the German people (70). Second, by his very screaming, Hitler established himself as father. The way he spoke, more than what he said, gave him his unquestioned authority (73). The screaming, which was puzzling, even comical, to Americans, was crucial to the identification process by which Hitler became the father of all Germans because so many individual Germans had screaming, authoritarian fathers.[20] Third, seizing upon the wisdom and the abusiveness of Hitler, the Germans formed an idealized image of him with which they strongly identified (75). On this basis, Göring said: "If the Catholic Christian is convinced that the Pope is infallible in all religious and ethical matters, so we National Socialists declare with the same ardent conviction that for us, too, the Führer is absolutely infallible in all political and other matters. . . . And only with the Führer standing behind him is one really powerful. . . . It is not I who live, but the Führer who lives in me" (cited in Miller, 71). Naturally, obedience was due to this idealized father: "Once feelings have been eliminated, the submissive person functions perfectly and reliably even if no one is going to check up on him. . . . It is not a loss of autonomy that occurs here, because this autonomy never existed, but . . . his whole value system is dominated by the principle of obedience. He has never gone beyond the stage of idealizing his parents . . . this idealization can easily be transferred to a Führer or to an ideology" (83).

Projection, Displacement, and Scapegoating

Projection is the process by which a person takes an aspect of himself or herself and integrates that into another person even though that characteristic may not be present in the other. This is particularly true in times of failure, stress, or anger. In times of failure, people tend to blame others, even inanimate objects ("blaming their tools"); that is, they take their own proper failure and project it onto others. In times of stress, people expect parental-type support and comfort from friends, spouses, and even employers; that is, they take their own legitimate need for unconditional support and comfort and project it onto others, even though that is not the role of those others. In moments of anger, too, it is very common for people to project; that is, to take anger that may be justified in one context and to express it in a context in which it has no place. When an aspect of oneself is projected onto someone lower in a given social hierarchy, the usual proper term is "displacement." Projection which results in the victimization of an innocent person or group is sometimes labeled "scapegoating."

For an abused child, projection often offers a way of expressing strongly repressed feelings and memories. When combined with splitting, projection also allows the split-off personality, the one that was set aside because it was abused, to be expressed (Miller, 91). This is Miller's thesis about splitting and projection as a main cause of the shoah, for, according to Miller, the Germans in general, and the nazis in particular, came from homes that were authoritarian and abusive. This led to splitting off the abused part of themselves and to strong repression of any form of expression of anger. This repressed and split identity was, then, projected onto the Jews in the form of scapegoating:

"We had the moral right, we had the duty to our own people, to kill this people that wanted to kill us. . . . By and large, however, we can say, that we have performed this most difficult task out of love for our people. And we have suffered no harm from it in our inner self, in our soul, in our character. . . ." In order to make the struggle against these humane impulses easier, the citizens of the Third Reich were offered an object to serve as the bearer of all these qualities that were abhorred because they had been forbidden and dangerous in their childhood—this object was the Jewish people . . . everything they had feared in themselves since childhood could be attributed to the Jews . . . (Miller, citing Himmler and responding, 79–80).

Germans had a sense of relief in reading *Mein Kampf* and learning that it was permissible to hate the Jews because this meant that all their sibling envy could be projected onto the Jews and that their despised and abused selves could be projected onto the Jews (Miller, 166, 187–88). Indeed, the good aspect of themselves—the innocent, fun-loving, natural child—needed to be repressed, abused, and exterminated. It, too, was projected onto the Jews:

[They] led a million children, whom they regarded as the bearers of the feared portions of their own psyche, into the gas chambers. One can even imagine that by shouting at them, beating them, or photographing them, they were finally able to release the hatred going back to early childhood. From the start, it had been the aim of their upbringing to stifle their childish, playful, and life-affirming side. The cruelty inflicted on them, the psychic murder of the child they once were, had to be passed on in the same way: each time they sent another Jewish child to the gas ovens, they were in essence murdering the child within themselves (Miller, 86–87).[21]

Cohen, working with a more classical Freudian model of personal psychology, but with the same cultural setting of nazism, maintains that the ego of the average German and especially that of the SS was crushed by the educational and socialization forces of nazi culture and child-rearing (235). He, too, points to obedience as central to the new personality and notes that in order to be an inner member of the SS, one had to kill someone. This was called the *Blutkitt,* the "blood cement" (236). This, in turn, led to the development of "the criminal superego" in Germans and especially in the SS: "The content of the average German's superego was different from ours" (242). When set in the cultural context of the authoritarian father, the youth movement, *Gleichschaltung,* and nazi racial teaching, a criminal superego was natural (261).[22] On the subject of Hitler, Cohen notes that "for almost all Germans . . . he [Hitler] became the father, in Freud's hypothesis on the primal horde even the primal father . . . as a father image he controlled the superego of his followers and particularly the SS, who were his 'elite sons'" (275).

The model of the abused child turned abusing parent[23] is, then, one model drawn from personal psychology which helps clarify the social patterns that facilitate the doing of evil. When supported by an authoritarian cultural teaching, social framework, and ideological orientation, this model has very serious consequences because an environment in which children and others are abused and in which that abuse is culturally sustained by society gives moral permission to those so inclined to be abusers. Such an environment allows people to project their pain and humiliation and their repressed rage and shame onto others, doing them harm, indeed violence. Such an environment can easily facilitate the doing of evil by cultivating the authoritarian personality as a social norm.

Insights from the Model of the Authoritarian Personality

The classical study on the authoritarian personality, known as the Adorno study,[24] was done in America by a large team of psychologists over a period of time stretching from 1943 to 1950. Its intent was to describe prejudice, to measure it, and "to explain it in order to help in its eradication" (ix). Questionnaires were used, revised, used again, and statistically correlated to develop three scales: the A scale which measured antisemitism, the E scale which measured ethnocentrism, and the F scale which measured fascism. To help analyze the results of the scales, in-depth interviews were held, various psychological tests were administered, and more interviews were held. Finally, an overall theory of why people turn authoritarian was developed. The study came under substantial criticism but its main insights seem relevant to the task here.

Xenophobia and Rigid Adherence to Conventional Values

The authoritarian personality can be characterized as systemically xenophobic: "[W]e are faced here not with a particular set of political convictions and a particular set of opinions about a specific ethnic group but with a *way of thinking* about groups and group relations generally" (51, emphasis original). "It is not the experience [with members of minority groups] as such that counts, but the way in which it is assimilated psychologically. . . . his [the authoritarian person's] approach to a new and strange person or culture is not one of curiosity, interest, and receptivity but rather one of doubt and rejection. The feeling of difference is transformed into a sense of threat and an attitude of hostility. The new group easily becomes an outgroup" (149). Put differently: "*Ethnocentrism is based on a pervasive and rigid ingroup-outgroup distinction; it involves stereotyped negative imagery and hostile attitudes regarding outgroups, stereotyped positive imagery and submissive attitudes regarding ingroups, and a hierarchical, authoritarian view of group interaction in which ingroups are rightly dominant, outgroups subordinate*" (150, emphasis original).

The authoritarian personality can also be characterized as possessed of conventional values which are adhered to rather rigidly: "The goals which such parents have in mind in rearing and training their children tend to be highly conventional. The status-anxiety so often found in families of prejudiced subjects is reflected in the adoption of a rigid and externalized set of values: what is socially accepted and what is helpful in climbing the social ladder is considered 'good,' and what deviates, what is different, and what is socially inferior is considered 'bad'. . . . The more urgent the 'social needs' of the parents, the more they are apt to view the child's behavior in terms of their own instead of the child's needs" (257). Indeed: "They [conventional values] might also have been called 'authoritarian values,' since they are based on the assumption of conformity to external authority rather than on inner moral responsibility. . . . The prototypic examples of this value system are the Emily Post book of etiquette, the military 'rules of behavior,' and certain custom-ridden cultures, literate and nonliterate. The main content of these values, at least for individuals with a strong middle-class identification, deals with conformity and loyalty to ingroup standards" (291). In the family situation, this means that "[f]aithful execution of prescribed roles and the exchange of duties and obligations is, in the families of the prejudiced, often given preference over the exchange of free-flowing affection" (257–58).

The Need to Submit

The authoritarian personality can be characterized as one which has a deep need to submit, to surrender its identity, to an authority. This thesis was made famous by Erich Fromm in his book, *Escape From Freedom*.[25] Staub[26] also pointed to this phenomenon: "The officers produced by this system were far from being simple-minded robots. Instead, they formed a corps of 'true believers' who were effective leaders because, in addition to conviction about their own superiority to other men, they felt a common racial bond with their troops and were imbued with a medieval sense of noblesse oblige toward them. Furthermore, since most of these officers had virtually surrendered their sense of personal identity to Hitler and the SS, they were rarely troubled by the personal doubts which can divert men from putting total energy into their work."

Mayer,[27] writing about the same time as Adorno but from his study of Germans who had lived through the nazi period, noted that the need to submit is so strong that responsibility is subsumed under it: "Goebbels' immediate subordinate testified at Nuremberg that he had heard of the gassing of Jews, and went to Goebbels with the report. Goebbels said it was false, 'enemy propaganda,' and that was the end of it. The Nuremberg tribunal accepted this man's testimony on this point and acquitted him. . . . Responsible men never shirk from responsibility, and so, when they must reject it, they deny it. They draw the curtain. They detach themselves altogether from the consideration of the evil they ought to, but cannot, contend with" (73–76).

Adorno, too, noted that: "M's [the interviewee's] respect for authority comes into conflict with his explicit value of independence. . . . if the authority is sufficiently powerful, it becomes possible to submit without losing altogether the sense of independence. If dependence and passivity are to be accepted, it must be in circumstances that are beyond his control. . . . [M] wants to belong to or be 'in with' the ruling group. It is not so much that he himself wants to dominate, but rather he wants to serve powerful interests and so *participate in their power* (52–54, emphasis original).

Indeed, in a world in which "[t]he will of the adult must be a fortress, inaccessible to duplicity or defiance and granting admittance only when obedience knocks at the gates" (cited in Miller, 42), the desire to surrender one's identity to the adult authority is very great. In a world in which legitimate authority—be it a parent, political or religious leader, or God—is understood to be omniscient and benevolent, the need to relinquish the burden of responsible, individual identity in favor of that authority is enormous. The authoritarian personality embodies and acts on this deep desire and need.

Psychological Totalitarianism

The authoritarian personality can also be characterized by psychological totalitarianism, by a deep need for *Gleichschaltung.* Adorno, writing about Americans, noted: "The extremely prejudiced person tends toward 'psychological totalitarianism,' something which seems to be almost a microcosmic image of the totalitarian state at which he aims. Nothing can be left untouched, as it were; everything must be made 'equal' to the ego-ideal of a rigidly conceived and hypostasized ingroup. The outgroup, the chosen foe, represents an eternal challenge. As long as anything different survives, the fascist character feels threatened, no matter how weak the other group may be. . . . This mechanism makes for the complete distortion between 'guilt' and punishment . . . the 'expropriation' of the superego by the anti-Semite's punitive moralism obtains its full significance. . . . extermination fantasies . . . The disproportion between guilt and punishment induces him, rather, to pursue his hatred beyond any limits and thus to prove to himself and to others that he *must* be right" (324–25, emphasis original). "It is as a defense against the possibility of being grouped with the outcast and underdog that he rigidly has to assert his identification with the privileged groups" (279). This need to be totally a part of a larger whole is so strong that ". . . the removal of prejudice from the potentially fascist person may well endanger his psychological balance" (275).

Mayer, too, contrasted the psychological totalitarianism of the German character with the psychological freedom of the American character:

> External pressure—real or imaginary, it doesn't matter which—produced the counterpressures of German rigidity and German outbreak, the ordered, explosive propensity of the pressure cooker . . . (252). His personality, under pressure, is just as excessively submissive as it is assertive. Its essence is excess. . . . The German breakout—call it liberation, call it aggression, call it what you will—is a kind of periodic paranoid panic. In between times . . . the next panic cooks silently, symptomlessly, in *Zucht und Ordnung* [discipline and order]. To blame Germany—still less the Germans—is to blame the thistle for its fruits . . . (283–85).
>
> . . . incapable of quiet without melancholy or frustrated fury; insatiably hungry for the heights or the depths, sober or roaring drunk; forever insisting that man is born to suffer—and then begrudging the suffering; unresponsive and over-reactive; stodgy and unstable; . . . exhausted, unable to remain fully awake unless they are angry or hilarious—these are . . . the ways and the woes of men under pressure. . . . Organization and specialization, system, subsystem, supersystem are the consequence, not the cause of the totalitarian spirit. National Socialism did not make men unfree; unfreedom made men National Socialists. Freedom is nothing but the habit of choice (276–77).
>
> What they needed was the town meeting, the cracker barrel—to see, to hear, and at last to join the war on the totalitarianism in their own hearts. . . . the thunderous cry of American authority; "Let 'im talk, let 'im *talk*. . . ." What the Germans needed, so sorely that without it no effort, no expenditure, no army would ever help them, was to learn how to talk and talk back (305–6).[28]

Sichrovsky, interviewing nazis thirty years later, pointed again and again to the denial of history, to the denial of personal guilt, to the lack of remorse (72, 87); and more important, to *récit* which many nazis, and their wives, had evolved (98). This denial, even thirty years later, has a deeply panicked tone, a profoundly desperate quality to it. As Adorno has suggested: "Thus a basically hierarchical, authoritarian, exploitative parent-child relationship is apt to carry over into a power-oriented, exploitatively dependent attitude toward one's sex partner and one's God and may well culminate in a political philosophy and social outlook which has no room for anything but a desperate clinging to what appears to be strong and a disdainful rejection of whatever is relegated to the bottom" (475). It is the very desperation of the denial that enabled, and continues to enable, authoritarian personalities to stay within the psychologically totalitarian world in which they have grown up and acted, without having to confront the past from the perspective of new wisdom.[29]

Abuse, Authoritarianism, and the Culture of Cruelty

The authoritarian personality, then, can be characterized as one which grew up in, and perpetuates, an atmosphere of harsh discipline: "Prejudiced subjects tend to report a relatively harsh and more threatening type of home discipline which was experienced as arbitrary by the child. Related to this is a tendency, apparent in families of prejudiced subjects, to base interrelationships on rather clearly defined roles of dominance and submission in contradistinction to equalitarian policies. In consequence, the images of parents seem to acquire for the child a forbidding or at least a distant quality. Family relationships are characterized by fearful subservience to the demands of the parents and by an early suppression of impulses not acceptable to them" (Adorno, 256–57).

> . . . punishment implies the need to curb some intrinsic wildness or evil intent. Routine gratuitous punishment implies that powerful persons have the right to exert their will arbitrarily. . . . Having had little influence over their parents' behavior, [such children] are more inclined to feel a sense of helplessness in influencing others generally. . . . Human relationships are construed in power terms, superordination and subordination viewed as the inherent social condition of humankind. The best one can do in the face of power is to succumb.[30]

The more abusive the environment, the more the child is subject to the whim of the abusive parent. Punishment becomes more and more erratic, unpredictable, and capricious as well as more and more invasive and violent. This is both physically harmful as well as psychologically destabilizing.[31] In its extreme form, "harsh" discipline can turn very ugly. As F. Katz has commented:[32]

> Evil can be, and sometimes has been, *developed into a culture of cruelty,* a distinctive culture in its own right. As such it is systematically organized to reward individuals for their acts of cruelty: for being creative at inventing cruelties and for establishing a personal reputation for their particular version of cruelty. Here cruelty can be a macabre art-form . . . here, too, cruelty can be a distinctive "economy," where one's credit rating depends on one's level of cruelty—the more cruel, the higher one's standing. By contrast, acts of kindness can lead to publicly declared bankruptcy, and in some situations the punishment for this bankruptcy is a death sentence (31, emphasis original). . . . we must admit that, *under some circumstances, individuals will deliberately choose to do evil.* For example, a culture of cru-

elty can be highly attractive. It can offer an individual the opportunity to live creatively, and creative living touches on a profound human yearning. At times individuals may discover that acting cruelly is a way, perhaps the only way, they can be creative. They are then likely to embrace a culture of cruelty when some facilitating conditions exist in their immediate context (127, emphasis original).

One can conclude, then, that early childhood discipline which is excessive and erratic—that is, abusive in its broad sense—helps to create the authoritarian personality, thereby facilitating the doing of evil. Excessive and erratic discipline does this by instilling an attitude of obedience, by bullying and frightening the child into submission. Excessive and erratic discipline also creates a deep anger in the abused self. This anger, indeed rage, must be suppressed because the child cannot retaliate against the parent; however, it is very likely to surface in later hostile acts which will be directed against a helpless, socially stigmatized other. Abusive childrearing cultivates the xenophobic, rigid, submissive, and totalitarian personality, creating thereby the possibility for the doing of evil.

The Prosocial Childhood and the Altruistic Personality

The key factor uniting rescuers of Jews during the shoah was not economic status, religious or political conviction, hatred of the nazis, or even a special relationship to Jews. Rather, it was, as the Oliners have shown, a commitment to caring for other human beings which was deeply rooted in childhood attitudes toward authority and punishment. A disciplinary milieu characterized by reason and proportion is central:

> . . . significantly fewer rescuers recalled any controls imposed on them by the most intimate persons in their early lives. . . . parents of rescuers depended significantly less on physical punishment and significantly more on reasoning. . . . Thus, it is in their reliance on reasoning, explanations, suggestions of ways to remedy the harm done, persuasion, and advice that parents of rescuers differed most from nonrescuers (*The Altruistic Personality,* 179–81).

Fogelman, too, notes that studies of anti-nazi German men show their homes to have been "more accepting and less rigid" while studies of rescuers show that they experienced "a loving and trusting relationship with an affectionate mother [and] had a communicative and nonauthoritarian father." These studies supported her own findings of parents of rescuers "who explained rules and used inductive reasoning."[33]

The Oliners account for this phenomenon as follows:

> Reasoning communicates a message of respect for and trust in children that allows them to feel a sense of personal efficacy and warmth toward others. It is based on a presumption of error rather than a presumption of evil intent. It implies that had children but known better or understood more, they would not have acted in an inappropriate way. It is a mark of esteem for the listener; an indication of faith in his or her ability to comprehend, develop and improve (*The Altruistic Personality,* 182).

The social scientific evidence also supports the conclusion that caring authority in childhood is crucial in the formation of prosocial attitudes.

> Parents whose disciplinary techniques are benevolent, particularly those who rely on reasoning, are more likely to have kind and generous children. . . . Induction focuses children's attention on the consequences of their behaviors for others, drawing attention to others' feelings, thoughts, and welfare . . . more inclined to develop empathy toward others.[34]
> A great deal of laboratory and socialization research shows that prosocial behavior is influenced by a combination of (1) parental warmth and nurturance, (2) *induction,* pointing out to children the consequences of their behavior on other people, and (3) firm control by parents, so that children actually behave in accordance with important values and rules. . . . The more parents and socializers in other settings, such as schools, particularly in the early school years, use such a pattern, the more we can expect prosocial orientation, empathic responsiveness, and behavioral tendencies for increased altruism and less aggression in children. . . . While reasonable parental control is important, it is also important that parents respond to the child's own reasoning and be willing to consider the child's point of view.[35]

Parental behavior, then, which is supportive and loving, and which adopts a reasoning but firm attitude toward early childhood discipline facilitates prosocial attitudes and behaviors in children.[36]

If abusive childrearing cultivates the authoritarian personality, then one should expect that prosocial childrearing would cultivate the altruistic personality. In a series of three books, the Oliners[37] wrestle with defining the altruistic—prosocial, would be a better term[38]—personality. In their first work, the study of rescuers, they propose a "composite portrait" which is rooted in "extensivity":[39]

> It begins in close family relationships in which parents model caring behavior and communicate caring values. Parental discipline tends toward

leniency; children frequently experience it as almost imperceptible. . . . Simultaneously, however, parents set high standards they expect their children to meet, particularly with regard to caring for others. They implicitly or explicitly communicate the obligation to help others in a spirit of generosity, without concern for external rewards or reciprocity. . . . children are encouraged to develop qualities associated with caring. Dependability, responsibility, and self-reliance are valued because they facilitate taking care of oneself as well as others. Failures are regarded as learning experiences. . . .

. . . they risk forming intimate relationships outside it [the family]. Persuaded that attachment rather than status is the source of basic life gratification, they choose friends on the basis of affection rather than social class, religion, or ethnicity. . . . They feel more comfortable dealing with people different from themselves. . . . More open to new experiences, they are more successful in meeting challenges. . . . they find no reason to exclude them [outsiders] in an emergency. . . . evaluate themselves positively (*The Altruistic Personality,* 249–51).

Returning to the theme of the altruistic personality in their second book, the Oliners elaborate the concept of "extensivity" as follows:

As we define it, *extensivity* means the tendency to assume commitments and responsibilities toward diverse groups of people. Extensivity includes two elements: the propensity to *attach* oneself to others in committed interpersonal relationships; and the propensity toward *inclusiveness* with respect to the diversity of individuals and groups to whom one will assume obligations (*Embracing,* 370, emphasis original).

They also propose eight social processes that promote prosocial behavior and may be important in developing the altruistic personality: bonding, empathizing which includes perspective-taking, caring norms, participating in altruistic behaviors, diversifying, networking, developing shared problem-solving strategies, and making global connections (*Embracing,* 379–86).

Finally, in their third work intended to encourage the pursuit of caring norms and behaviors, the Oliners elaborate on the above-mentioned social processes that promote prosocial attitudes and behavior, devoting a chapter to each process and making concrete suggestions for how to teach them and bring them into action.[40] Caring and reasoned childhood discipline, then, cultivates the prosocial personality which is characterized by extensivity, attachment, and inclusiveness. These, in turn, are expressed in prosocial expectations of authority and a commitment to caring for other human beings.

Modeling, Prosocial Discipline, and the Culture of Care

Modeling turns out to be especially important in forming the prosocial orientation. Piliavin and Charng summarize the literature on cases involving civil rights, school children, and blood donors, concluding: ". . . children display greater generosity when they are exposed to generous models than to selfish models."[41] Similarly, Hoffman notes: ". . . children socialized to be empathic are, later on in life, disposed to select principles and ideologies that support society's disadvantaged members. . . ."[42]

Fogelman, too, observes: "The overwhelming majority of rescuers I interviewed, 89 percent, had a parent or adult figure who acted as an altruistic role model. . . . nearly every person I talked to mentioned a person who influenced their helping behavior. . . . many rescuers were not just encouraged but were expected to help others. When a neighbor was ill or a school friend was in trouble, rescuers report that their parents took it as a matter of course that they would help. In many religious homes, children were part of the whole family's charity work" (263, 265).

Reading the evidence from prosocial childhood discipline, together with the evidence drawn from the modeling of prosocial behavior in the formation of the altruistic personality, the Oliners note:

> Parents have power over children; they are not only physically stronger but also have access to material resources they can bestow or withhold. Societal norms generally support their superior position. . . . When adults voluntarily abdicate the use of power in favor of explanation, they are modeling appropriate behavior toward the weak on the part of the powerful. Faced with powerless others, children so raised in turn have at their disposal an internal "script"—a store of recollections, dialogues, and activities ready to be activated. They need not depend on innovation or improvisation but rather simply retrieve what is already imprinted on their memories (*The Altruistic Personality*, 183).
>
> It [parental punishment] includes a heavy dose of reasoning—explanations of why behaviors are inappropriate, often with reference to their consequences for others. Physical punishment is rare: when used, it tends to be a singular event rather than routine. Gratuitous punishment—punishment that serves as a cathartic release of aggression for the parent or is unrelated to the child's behavior—almost never occurs (*The Altruistic Personality*, 249).

Finally, reaching beyond the individual altruistic personality, the Oliners hope for a whole culture of care rooted in prosocial processes:

No single process itself . . . can be sufficient for the task of creating this type of care. We view the processes we have identified as mutually reinforcing, each one strengthening the other and capitalizing on the particular strengths of each. We also view them as occurring concurrently—that is, not in a sequenced pattern . . . but rather synchronously . . . for all these processes should communicate the message that care is a valued goal (*Caring Society,* 206).

Summary

Authoritarian childrearing practices range from unnecessarily strict to outright abusive. The more authoritarian the childhood discipline, the more the child is likely to develop the coping mechanisms of splitting, repression, identification, idealization, projection, displacement, and scapegoating. These patterns, in turn, cultivate the authoritarian personality which is characterized by xenophobia, rigid adherence to conventional values, the need to submit, and psychological totalitarianism. Such persons are conditioned to obedient behavior to the demands of legitimate authority, even when those demands are immoral. If these demands are immoral enough, a culture of cruelty can be created and sustained by such authorities.

Prosocial childrearing practices are characterized by the administration of punishment that is proportionate to the offense, by reasoning and explanation, and by the child's right of appeal of the punishment. The more prosocial the childhood discipline, the more the child is likely to develop behaviors that are responsible, risk-taking, caring, open, and reciprocal. These patterns, in turn, cultivate the prosocial personality which is characterized by extensivity, inclusivity, attachment, empathy, and active caring. Such persons are trained toward resistance to the immoral demands of legitimate authority as well as to ongoing caring practice vis-à-vis other human beings. If these patterns are deep and broad enough, a culture of caring can be created and sustained.

It seems good common sense to want to create a society in which evil is discouraged and resisted and in which good is advocated and encouraged. To do that, we must address the prescriptive-normative task. Having completed the descriptive-analytic task, it is to the hope for a better society and how to bring that about that we now turn.

Counter-text [43]

- Resh Lakish said, "Sometimes the cancellation of the Torah is its [re-] founding as it says, 'the tablets which you broke' (Ex. 34:1). The Holy One, blessed be He, said to Moses, 'May your strength be straight [that is, your actions are proper] because you broke them.'" [44]

COMMENT: This midrash rests on a question derived from Exodus 34:1: How did God react when Moses dared to break the tablets with the Ten Commandments, especially since the first set of commandments were written by the very hand of God (Ex. 31:18; 32:16)? The answer is that God was more than pleased that Moses resisted the temptation to hallow objects and that he preferred moral behavior to sacrality.

> • It is the way of people to be drawn in their attitudes and actions after those acquaintances and to follow the custom of the people of one's place. Therefore, one should always associate with righteous people and dwell among sages—so that one learn from their ways. Further, one should distance oneself from the wicked who walk in darkness—so that one not learn from their ways. . . .[45]
> • It is a commandment upon every person to love every other person as much as one loves one's own body as it says, "You shall love your other as yourself" (Lev. 19:18). Therefore, one should speak the other's praise and be vigilant concerning the other's possessions, as one is vigilant concerning one's own possessions and one's own honor. And, one who exalts oneself at the shame of another has no share in the world-to-come.[46]
> • A teacher who taught but the students did not understand should not get angry with them and abuse them verbally. Rather, the teacher should go over the material yet again, even several times, until they understand the depth of the halakha. Similarly, a student should not say, "I have understood" when she or he has not understood. Rather, he or she should ask again, even several times. And, if the teacher gets angry and abuses the student verbally, she or he should say to the teacher, "Teacher, this is Torah and I must learn it, even if my capacity is inadequate."[47]

COMMENT: Maimonides takes a clear stance in these passages concerning the proper attitude of authority toward others, especially children, although he does teach that one who kills a child or student in the course of teaching him or her Torah, wisdom, or a craft from which the child can earn a living has exercised just force and is not liable for manslaughter.[48]

PART 2

The Prescriptive-Normative Task

The Lord spoke to Moses saying, "Go down" (Ex. 32:7)—What is
"Go down" [and not "go"]? Rabbi Elazar said: "The Holy One,
blessed be He, said to Moses, 'Moses, go down from your greatness.
Did I give you greatness for any reason other than Israel and, now
that Israel have sinned [with the golden calf], what need do I have of
you?' Immediately, Moses lost his strength and did not have the force
to speak. But, when God said, 'Leave Me alone and I will destroy
them' (Dt. 9:14), Moses said to himself, 'The matter depends upon
me' and he stood up, gathered his strength to pray and ask mercy.
The matter is like a king who got angry with his son and struck him
a mighty blow. The king's friend was sitting in front of him and was
afraid to say anything. The king said, 'Were it not for my friend who
is sitting here before me, I would kill you.' The friend then said, 'The
matter depends upon me' and he stood up and saved [the son]."

—*Talmud,* Berakhot 32a

6

Transition

Recapitulation

In Roadmap (chapter 1), I drew a sketch of a "Jewish nazi" and compiled a collage of rescuers and altruists, juxtaposing these two sets of figures so as to set forth the twofold task of this book: the identification of the psychological and historical factors which facilitate the doing of good and of evil, and the outlining of the values and norms necessary for a more prosocial environment.

In the chapters of part 1, The Descriptive-Analytic Task, I set about amassing and ordering the data from the disciplines of social, experimental, therapeutic, and developmental psychology, as well as from history, which would accomplish the first task.

In chapter 2, I listed the studies and presented several philosophical, moral-legal, and methodological problems and my proposed solutions to them. I, then, set forth a unified field theory of the factors that facilitate good and evil attitudes and behaviors: character; personal psychological history; socialization; authority and hierarchy; roles, norms, and rules; and actual praxis. In the following three chapters, I presented more detailed analysis of these factors.

In chapter 3, I drew on data from social psychology and history to illustrate the centrality of hierarchy and role in cultivating both antisocial and prosocial attitudes and behaviors. The data clearly shows that insertion into a hierarchy and socialization to roles, norms, and rules which do, or tolerate, evil facilitate the doing of evil. The converse was also shown to be true: Insertion into a hierarchy and socialization to roles, norms, and rules which do, or tolerate, good facilitate the doing of good.

In chapter 4, I turned from social process to content. I identified the teaching of evil as consisting of exclusivism, authoritarianism in the personal and public realm, and survivalism, and I described the teaching of good as consisting of a commitment to personal competence, intelligent moral judgment, extensivity, empathy, and righteous anger. These constitute the substance of antisocial and prosocial ideology. I also noted that content alone does not educate; praxis does, and I pointed to incremental praxis and routinization as factors that facilitate both the doing of good and evil.

In chapter 5, I turned from content to personal psychology. I identified insights to be drawn from the childrearing patterns of the abused child, including the dynamics of abuse and the various mechanisms developed by abused persons to cope with such trauma: splitting, repression, identification, idealization, projection, displacement, and scapegoating. I also examined the characteristics of the authoritarian personality, including xenophobia, rigid adherence to convention, the need to submit, and psychological totalitarianism. I also drew attention to the connection of this data with the broader social phenomena of antisocial behavior and the culture of cruelty. I, then, did the same for prosocial childrearing patterns, noting that proportionate, reasoned, and caring discipline tends to create an altruistic personality which, in turn, is characterized by extensivity, attachment, inclusiveness, willingness to take risks, self-competence, and empathy. I also connected this data with the broader social phenomena of prosocial behavior and the culture of care.

In the chapters of part 2, The Prescriptive-Normative Task, I will outline the values and norms necessary to cultivate a more prosocial environment. In chapter 7, I shall set forth the affections and value-concepts of the prosocial life and deal with the interrelatedness between prosocial affections, prosocial praxis, prosocial value-concepts, and various socialization processes. And in chapter 8, I shall make strong and detailed recommendations for how to inculcate prosocial attitudes and behaviors, recommending particular processes as well as specific content. First, however, a brief theological interlude.

God's Grief

Theology is the art of seeing the world from God's point of view. We humans, however, see the world from our point of view, especially since the Enlightenment. We establish our action as determinative. We set the parameters of our intellectual and moral knowledge. Our view is anthropocentric. In this view, it is humans who create God in their image. Theology, however, works with traditions and experiences which see God as the determining actor in nature and history, or at least as an active partner in these realms. Human awareness of God through personal experience becomes central in the theological perspective. We sense God in nature, in our personal lives, and in our life as a society and we acknowledge God's influencing presence. Human awareness of God through the voices of others embodied in traditional texts is also central to the theological perspective. We read these texts and they echo in our hearts. We listen to these other voices and they resonate in our minds and souls. This point of view is theocentric. Theologians try to give expression and coherence to it. In this view, humans are formed in the image of God.[1]

How does humankind's dealing with good and evil look from the theocentric perspective? How does the human record of doing evil and good look from God's point of view?

In the beginning, there was only God. And God was personhood personified—capable of joy, anger, love, appreciation of beauty, humor, frustration, contentedness, relief, and many other affections. But there was no being outside God's self with whom God could relate. So God created the universe, first the forces of nature and afterwards humanity, for the forces of nature do not have personhood while humanity has been given that special divine gift. Initially, God set humanity fully within nature, unaware and incapable of good and evil but, in this state, humanity was not fully person. So God offered humanity knowledge of good and evil, which made them wholly person.

When humankind turned to evil, "God regretted that He had made humanity in the universe and He was deeply sad in His heart. God said, 'I will obliterate humanity which I made from upon the face of the universe, humanity together with the animals, the creeping things, and the birds of the sky, for I regret that I made them.'"[2] When humanity was restored, God established a general covenant with them but chose one man to be a loyal servant. When that man's family grew large, God gave them a Torah with laws, instructions, warnings, and promises, intending that these should guide them toward good and away from evil. Again and again, God's people sinned and God punished them but still humanity did not avoid evil and do good. And God was deeply pained and knew grief:

> "Is Ephraim not a beloved child to me? Is he not a child with which one plays? Whenever I speak of him, I remember and will remember him forever. For that reason, my insides churn for him. I love and have compassion for him," said God.[3]

> God said to the angels, "Come, let us go together, you and I, and let us see My house and what the enemies have done to it. . . ." In that moment [when He saw the destroyed temple], the Holy One, blessed be He, cried and said, "Woe unto Me for My house. Where are you, My children? Where are you, My priests? Where are you, My lovers? What could I have done? I warned you and you did not repent."[4]

> Elijah said to Rabbi Yosi, "Did you hear anything when you went into that ruin?" He replied, "I heard the sound of a voice that moaned like a dove and said, 'Woe unto Me that I destroyed My house, burned My sanctuary, and exiled My children among the nations.'" Elijah said to him, "This is said each day in the [heavenly] liturgy."[5]

From God's point of view, then, God gave humanity commandments but we ignored them, or denied them, or reduced even the ethical commandments to ritual, making instruction into magic and guidance into superstition. From God's point of view, God gave us reason and the power to legislate for ourselves but we distorted that reason and abused that power, "fattening our hearts, stopping our ears, and averting our eyes lest we really see with our eyes, hear with our ears, and understand in our hearts."[6] From God's point of view, God gave us freedom and responsibility, especially after the Enlightenment, but we betrayed that responsibility and turned against that freedom, replacing liberty with tyranny and tolerance with bigotry. From God's point of view, God gave us all the technology we could possibly want but, even though we used it to create good, we also used it to do evil, creating concentration camps as well as antibiotics, and nuclear bombs as well as computers. To put it simply, from God's point of view, humanity has been repeatedly sinful. Even though God has been gracious and forgiven us, we have turned again and again to sin.

This is God's distress, God's anguish. This is God's sorrow, God's grief. One might say, this is God's despair.

> "I have brought up and exalted children but they have rebelled against Me. An ox knows its owner and an ass the trough of its master but Israel does not know, My people does not understand."[7]

> God said to Jeremiah, "Today, I am like a man who had an only son for whom he had made a wedding, but the son died under the wedding canopy."[8]

And so it is. Parents do their best for children (even if the children think the parents could have done more for them), and children go astray. Parents educate, and children reject the knowledge and the skills given them. Parents proffer moral advice, and children ignore or defy it. Parents hope and pray for children to be what they envision, and children go their own way. Sometimes this is in the best interests of the child but, from the parents' point of view, it is distress and anguish. And, if it is not in the best interests of the child and the child is genuinely tending toward evil, parents experience deep sorrow and great grief. Indeed, parents feel despair.[9]

Humanity's Response

From God's point of view, humanity's penchant for sin is humanity's problem.[10] God has already given humankind the ability to form moral judgments, the capacity to do good, and a revelation intended to guide us toward that good. If we have failed, it is we who have failed and we who must repent. God can only call us to *teshuva,* repentance.[11]

> Return, Israel, to the Lord, your God, even though you have been undone by your sins.[12]

I shall erase your rebellious sins as a mist and your inadvertent sins as a cloud; return unto Me, for I have redeemed you.[13]

Return ever-turning children, I shall heal your turnings-aside . . .[14]

There is nothing greater than repentance . . .[15]

Repentance is greater than prayer . . . than charity . . .[16]

Maimonides summarizes well the definition of *teshuva* and the ideal of repentance:

> What is *teshuva?* That the sinner should desist from his or her sin, should remove it from her or his thoughts, and should decide in his or her heart that she or he will not do it again, as it says . . . , such that the One Who knows secret things would testify on his or her behalf that she or he will not ever turn to this sin again, as it says. . . . And one must make verbal confession and say those things which one has decided in one's heart.[17]

> What would complete *teshuva* be? That a person have the occasion to sin in the same manner as he or she had previously sinned, that such a person be capable of committing that sin, and then that the person refrain and not commit that sin—because of [the power of] *teshuva,* and not out of fear or lack of ability.[18]

According to Maimonides, then, the essence of *teshuva* is refraining from committing the sin one has previously committed. As integral parts of the process of *teshuva,* Maimonides mentions removing the thought of that sin from one's mind, deciding deep in oneself not to do it again, and verbal confession, though there are also other recommended steps.[19]

To do *teshuva,* then, requires four steps: becoming aware of sin, confession, protest, and renewed love of God and covenant.

To know error, to be aware of sin (Heb., *hakarat ha-het'*), is the first step in *teshuva.* One of the purposes of this book is to identify the subtle sins of obedience and conformity which facilitate the doing of evil. Part of the process of *teshuva* is studying these social-psychological processes and making ourselves aware of these sins, though obedience and conformity themselves are not sinful since they can also produce prosocial attitudes and behaviors.

After awareness of sin comes confession (Heb., *vidui*). Confession is so important that Maimonides gives it the status of a biblical commandment.[20] Jewish authorities differ on whether one must make public confession of personal sins or not. Maimonides rules that, if the sins are interpersonal, they require specific public confession; however, if they are between humans and God, one is required to specify them in private prayer but, in public, one recites only the general confession contained in the liturgy.[21] The custom, however, is contrary to Maimonides. One does not make public personal confession even for inter-personal sins. Rather, one uses the liturgical confessions only, for interpersonal sins as well as for sins against God. The two classical liturgical texts are al-phabetical acrostics and, hence, symbolically include all possible sins.[22] When praying them privately, one thinks of one's private sins and, when praying them publicly, one thinks of the sins of the people.[23]

In this spirit, I offer the following twelve lines as a supplement to the *'Al Ḥet'* form of the confession of Yom Kippur:[24]

על חטא שחטאנו לפניך באדישות.
על חטא שחטאנו לפניך בדמוי כוללני.
על חטא שחטאנו לפניך בהאטם אזן בהשע עינים.
על חטא שחטאנו לפניך ביראת השלטון.
על חטא שחטאנו לפניך בנטיה אחרי רבים לרעות.
על חטא שחטאנו לפניך בסור מרע ועשה טוב.
על חטא שחטאנו לפניך בנטישת מעשים טובים.
על חטא שחטאנו לפניך בעמידה על דם רעינו.
על חטא שחטאנו לפניך בפחדנות בתחום המוסר.
על חטא שחטאנו לפניך בצייתנות.
על חטא שחטאנו לפניך ברחמנות מפליגה ובאכזריות יתרה.
על חטא שחטאנו לפניך בשתיקה מול פני הרע.

For the sin which we have sinned before you with indifference.
For the sin which we have sinned before You by stereotyping.
For the sin which we have sinned before You by closing our ears
    and shutting our eyes.
For the sin which we have sinned before You with inordinate fear
    of authority.
For the sin which we have sinned before You by following the majority
    when it was wrong.
For the sin which we have sinned before You by ignoring the command,
    "Avoid evil and do good."
For the sin which we have sinned before You by avoiding the doing
    of good.
For the sin which we have sinned before You by standing idly by
    the blood of our neighbors.
For the sin which we have sinned before You with moral cowardice.
For the sin which we have sinned before You with blind obedience.
For the sin which we have sinned before You by being too merciful
    or too tough.
For the sin which we have sinned before You with silence in the face
    of evil.

The third part of the process of *teshuva,* not mentioned explicitly by Maimonides but inherent in the biblical and rabbinic sources,[25] is the summoning of human courage to defy earthly, and even divine, authority when injustice has been done. Walter Brueggemann[26] has put it very clearly, arguing that God's relationship to the Jews, and indeed to the world, is bipolar. It is composed, on the one hand, of a contractual theology, which is based upon revealed demands of behavior with appropriate rewards and sanctions (40) and, on the other hand, of an embracing of the pain of the other, which forces a change in the calculus of the contract (398). Contractual theology generates order, rationality, and coherence; it establishes legitimate authority (39–42). Embracing the pain of the other generates "an assault on the throne of God . . . 'brinkmanship' with legitimated structure" (400, 404). This bipolarity describes the basic dialectic of God's relationship to humanity.

Within this bipolar relationship, God experiences a tension between God's response of anger and God's response of enduring loyalty:

> On the one hand, there is an *intensification of Yahweh's anger and impatience.* Israel grows more wayward and less inclined to obedience. . . . Yahweh grows more taut and harsh. . . .[27] In the heart of God, there is an enormous patience, a holding to promises, even in the face of disobedience . . . there emerges an unbearable incongruity [which] concerns a God committed to a structure of sanctions, and yet with a yearning for a relationship with this disobedient partner (397, emphasis original).

Humanity, too, experiences this tension but, precisely because God is ordering and contractual and at the same time pain-embracing and in loyal relationship with humankind, humanity even in its sinfulness is able to find

> the nerve and the faith to risk an assault on the throne of God with complaint . . . [which] pushes the relationship to the boundaries of unacceptability. . . . It requires deep faith, but not only deep—it requires faith of a new kind . . . that this God does not want to be an unchallenged structure, but one who can be frontally addressed . . . that this ultimately legitimated structure is indeed open to the embrace of pain, open both for Israel and for God. . . . Obedience turns out to be not blind docile *submissiveness.* . . . It is rather a bold *protest* against a legitimacy that has grown illegitimate because it does not seriously take into account the suffering reality of the partner. Where the reality of suffering is not dealt with, legitimate structure is made illegitimate when the voice of pain assumes enough authority to be heard (400–1, emphasis original).

Resistance and protest, too, then, are part of the process of *teshuva.*[28]

Finally Maimonides, in considering the ultimate step in the process of *te-shuva,* proposes that true repentance must grow out of one's love for God.

> A person should not say, "I will observe the commandments of the Torah and occupy myself with its wisdom so that I will receive all the blessings written in it, or so that I will merit life in the world-to-come; and I will re-frain from the sins about which the Torah warns so that I be saved from the curses written in the Torah, or so that I do not get cut off from life in the world-to-come." It is not proper to worship God in this way, for one who does so, worships God out of fear. . . . [but] when one loves God with a love that is worthy, one immediately does all the commandments out of love.
> What is love that is worthy? That one should love God with a great, excessive, very powerful love such that one's soul is bound up in the love of God and one, therefore, meditates on God always . . . as we have been commanded, "with all your heart and with all your soul" (Dt. 6:5) and as Solomon said as a metaphor, "for I am sick with love" (Song 2:5); [in-deed] all of the Song of Songs is a metaphor for this matter.[29]

And so it is. We, who claim religion as the basis for our commitment to avoiding evil and doing good, must do so, not because behaving in this way will bring about a better world, or because it is rationally best for human society, or because it realizes the greatest of our human potential—though, if that is the best motivation one can offer, it is more than sufficient because it is the deed that counts. Rather, those of us who claim the presence of God as a motivation for avoiding evil and doing good should do so out of sensitivity to God's grief, out of understanding of God's pain, out of sympathy and compassion for God. This is the deepest love for God. Empathy, sympathy, compassion, and love cannot be a one-way process; they must be reciprocal. Reciprocal loving must be in the center of our religious consciousness, not on the periphery.

Furthermore, we who are religious should avoid antisocial attitudes and ac-tions and cultivate prosocial attitudes and actions as part of the dynamics of the covenant that binds us to God. God's presence among us is the center of who we are, as we are the center of God's universe. Refraining from evil and doing good must be an expression and embodiment of the love of that covenant; otherwise, we are secularists with religious traditions. Covenantal living em-bodies and sustains the religious consciousness of the d/Divine. Covenantal living brings us into relation with God and gives us the right to claim spiritu-ality as a basic dimension of our lives, and indeed to claim it as a constitutive part of all human existence.

If humanity does *teshuva*—that is, if we out of self-interest, or out of a compassionate desire to ease God's grief, or out of a commitment to covenan-tal living, respond in conscience and in concrete action to our own sinful tendencies to follow authority to evil, to be indifferent and passive, and to avoid resistant and caring living—then God, Godself, will respond and help us on the path of *teshuva:*

"Return to Me and I will return to You," says the Lord of hosts.[30]

When Cain went [into exile], he met Adam who said to him, "What has happened as regards the judgment passed upon you?" Cain replied, "I repented, and I am pardoned." When Adam heard that, he smote his forehead and said, "Is the power of *teshuva* so great as that? I did not know it was so."[31]

Anyone who comes to be purified will be helped [by Heaven].[32]

This is God's responsibility in the matter of discouraging evil and encouraging good—to call humanity to repentance and, if we respond, to support and help us in that effort.

A concluding prayer:[33]

ויהי רצון . . . חבר רע.

דבקנו ביצר הטוב ובמעשים טובים.
חזקנו לעשות משפט. לעמוד בפני שלטון הרשע.
ולנהוג בצדק ובהגינות עם בני אנוש.
פתח עינינו לראות ולבנו לחוש את מכאוב הזולת.
נצור לשוננו מרע ושפתנו מדבר מרמה
ושים בפינו דברי אמת, יושר, וחסידות.
עזרנו ללמוד. ללמד, ולשמש דוגמא אישית
לגמילות חסדים ולמעשי צדקה.
אמצנו להביא שלום בין אדם לחברו
ולעשות לתקון העולם.

ותננו היום . . . חסדים טובים.

May it be Your will, our God and God of our ancestors, to establish us constantly in Your Torah and to cause us cling to Your commandments. Do not bring us into unintentional sin, nor into trangression or purposeful sin, nor into temptation or into shame. Do not let the evil impulse have control over us. Keep us far from evil people and from evil friends.

Cause us cling to the good impulse and to the doing of good deeds. Strengthen us to do justice, to resist evil authority, and to act in just and attentive ways towards others. Open our eyes and our hearts to the pain of the other. Guard our tongues from evil and our lips from speaking deceit, and put into our mouths the language of truth, responsibility, and caring. Help us to study and to teach, to model and to do good deeds and works of charity. Give us courage to bring peace between people and to work toward the restoration of the world.

May we find favor, grace, and mercy, this day and every day, in Your eyes and in the eyes of all those who behold us and may You grant us abundantly of Your good gracious deeds. Blessed are You, Lord, Who grants abundantly of God's good gracious deeds.

Co-text[34]

Clouds of Cousins

One large dark cloud . . .
The children expectantly awaited another warm shower.
Dark, no thunder, one cloud . . .
   Rose in the west,
   Drifted ominously,
   Churned black swirl,
   Dry as tasteless chalk,
   Mid-day night,
Rolled over them as the Warsaw ghetto burned.

American boy.
They mocked him for weeping.
Hide the Jew in you, boy!
The cloud's the dust of the Jew boys.
Crybaby!
Cry, baby.
Cry.
The dust's your cousins.

COMMENT: Historians, recording the big events of wars, overlook little pocket scenes that affect us deeply. In the summer of 1943, a densely dark black cloud blew up before children who saw in it the prospect of a summer shower. They gleefully dressed in bathing suits and awaited its slow coming, expecting a romp in the warm rain it promised. That cloud passed drily over a disappointed brood of kids, silently darkening their afternoon. Probably coal dust from some Pennsylvania mine explosion. . . . Who knows now the source of that ominous portent?

7

The Affections and Value-Concepts
of the Prosocial Life

Perhaps it is the shadow of the shoah or of the atomic bomb.[1] Perhaps it is the growth of communication which enables us to see more and more quickly. Perhaps it is the ever-increasing bureaucratization of human life or the rise of political and religious fundamentalism in all cultures. Whatever the cause, researchers in the area of altruistic studies have felt called upon to do more than just describe and analyze. They have felt summoned to articulate a mission which would prescribe norms that cultivate prosocial behavior. I, for one, think that that is a perfectly acceptable goal for scientists and historians, as well as theologians and educators, and I am glad that these colleagues have brought their expertise to bear on the subject of prosocial human motivation and behavior. Each of the key writers on this subject—the Oliners[2], Staub[3], and Kelman and Hamilton[4]—has important insights on this subject and deserves to be read separately, particularly Pearl and Samuel Oliner's *Toward a Caring Society: Ideas Into Action* which is the most recent and fullest explication of what needs to be done in order to make our world a better place. I shall attempt here a reworking of these insights, dividing my comments into the affections and value-concepts which inform the prosocial life and then dealing with the complicated relationship between teachings, value-concepts, affections, socialization, and praxis.

"Affections"

Modern thought distinguishes between "emotions" or "feelings" which are transient (even if intense) and "affections" or "dispositions" which are ongoing emotional attitudes, sustained desires, long-term feeling-concepts. Feelings come and go; affections, however, are feelings which we are supposed to feel, emotions which we are expected to cultivate. Affections are feelings which are oughts. As Don Saliers notes:[5]

Being angry and feeling angry are different in many cases, just as being thankful and feeling thankful may be. . . . What we are in our intentions and actions, is more adequately revealed by referring to the dispositions which constitute a 'sense' of the heart than by referring to what we feel or what ideas we have at the time. To say that a person has a deep sense of gratitude is to remark upon his or her character. . . . The evidence of such gratitude will be found in his or her actions, perceptions, and feelings. Such a deep sense is what we shall call . . . an affection. It is not a feeling as such since it cannot be an episodic event 'inside' the person. Neither can it be a mood . . . [it] is a disposition. Such emotions, when found in the context of teachings about God, are religious affections in this 'dispositional' sense, rather than complex sensations, feelings, or moods (15–17).

In this perspective, "to choose a certain moral or religious view of the world and to adopt a way of life congruent with it *is* to take up a particular set of passions and emotions . . . the function of literature and poetry, and much of Scripture as well, is to arouse, sustain, and articulate deep emotions, not by 'causing' certain subjective feelings, but by offering evaluative images and descriptions of reality . . . metaphors, images, symbols . . . stories, concepts, and practices . . ." (12, 18, 19, emphasis original).[6]

Eleven Affections of the Prosocial Life

There are many affections of the prosocial life. I shall list only eleven.

Commitment to intelligent moral judgment is the sustained dedication to working towards informed moral decision making. It embodies the feeling that one ought to strive to judge truly and morally. It also requires careful thinking, a moral sense, and active and ongoing practice. Having such a commitment is also one of the teachings of goodness.[7]

Intellectual perseverance is the sustained effort to think through situations and positions critically. It is sticking to a topic until one has encompassed as much of the data as possible, and given it order. It embodies the feeling that one must create order out of chaos. While not unique to the prosocial life, intellectual perseverance is necessary for the prosocial life.

Moral strength is the persistent desire to have and to use moral power. It is the need to exercise, in an ongoing and growing way and together with others, one's moral judgment. It also is the sustained urge to help others exercise their moral judgment in a continuing and maturing way. To have moral strength is rooted in feeling strong and confident in one's moral judgments.

Righteous anger is the ongoing feeling that elementary justice has not been done. It is one's sustained response to injustice. It is one's continuing desire to see fairness prevail in human relations. Righteous anger is the affection that sustains one's sense of justice. It is also one of the teachings of goodness.[8]

Moral courage is the persistent feeling that one can challenge, even defy, authority because one feels one is right. It is the enduring feeling that one can face adversity. Courage is not the lack of fear; it is, rather, a perspective which sees fear as one piece in a larger moral picture.

Love is the sustained desire to help another human being. It is the long-term need to support another with as much ongoing energy as one can give. Love involves knowing the other's needs, figuring out how to meet them, and then doing acts of love. Love has many other meanings[9] and, as a concept, it could also be a teaching of goodness.

Compassion is the continuing feeling-with other persons. It is an ongoing commitment to feel their feelings, to understand them, and to judge them mercifully. Compassion is one's sustained effort to reach out to others, to put oneself in their place, and to help and care for them. Compassion is closely related to empathy and sympathy.

Respect is the sustained effort not to degrade, harm, or otherwise deprecate someone or something else. It keeps one from destroying that which is different or other. Respect is the ongoing "Thou shalt not" of human existence. Sometimes, it is accompanied by a feeling of awe; at other times, it is felt only as an abstract warning or prohibition.

Honor is the sustained effort to hold the other dear. It is the ongoing effort to act in reverence and care toward persons and objects. Honor is the ongoing "Thou shalt" of human existence. Sometimes, it is accompanied by a feeling of love; at other times, it is felt only as deference.

Devotion is the persistent willingess to be present to another. It is a continuing effort to meet the other's needs, to be of service, to help someone else. It involves ongoing acts of care and embodies the feeling that such acts are natural and good. It is close to the affection of love.

Friendship is the continuing effort to seek companionship from another and, at the same time, to be a companion to another. It is an ongoing sharing of presence and being. It involves sharing burdens as well as joys, tasks as well as moments. Friendship is the social affection.

"Value-Concepts"

"Value-concepts," a locution devised by M. Kadushin,[10] are terms which embody both ideas as well as values. Value-concepts contain conceptual, as well as normative, content. They are a fusion of our moral experience and of our need to abstract and think about that experience. They are a function of the deep interrelationship between cognition and moral judgment, as well as of the need to communicate moral values in some articulated form. "The component 'concepts' tells that the values referred to are communicable ideas, that is, ideas that may be shared by the group as a whole; whilst the component 'value' tells that these ideas are nevertheless also, in a degree, personal and subjective, and that they are ideas held warmly" (4). As such, value-concepts inform our thinking and our action in all situations, especially those involving intelligent moral judgment.[11]

Thus, "justice" is a value-concept of the prosocial life. Rooted in our personal psychological and social history, justice is an idea which we can formulate, analyze, debate, and communicate. But it is also a value that has a normative thrust in our personal and collective lives. It is an "ought," an ideal which we strive to embody. Similarly, "caring" is a value-concept of the prosocial life. It, too, is rooted in our personal and social history but has a moral thrust of its own. It is an idea we can discuss but it is also a value which we strive to embody.

In any given culture, the value-concepts must be in the language of that culture (chap. 3). Hence, in writing about the value-concepts of the prosocial life, I use English terms while later, in writing about the value-concepts of the Jewish ethical tradition, I shall use Hebrew terms.

All value-concepts imply all others. They overlap with one another such that a Venn diagram of overlapping circles is a good representation of the dynamic relationship of value-concepts one to another (chap. 2). Sometimes, one can identify an "emphatic trend," that is, a group of value-concepts that seem to have a common thrust or underlying motif (297–98, 321–24). Also, some value-concepts seem to be subsets of others (chap. 3). My own intellectual instinct is to take value-concepts that are more closely related and to call those "ancillary value-concepts" while leaving those which are more indirectly related as "related value-concepts." However, these distinctions really make no difference because the system of value-concepts is not a hierarchical system; rather, it is an organic, webbed system (chap. 2). I have, therefore, adopted the term "associated value-concept" to cover all value-concepts related to one another. The overlapping and interweaving is the strength of the idea of value-concepts.

The webbed nature of value-concepts is nicely illustrated by the debate over the "ethic of justice" vs. "the ethic of care." While these two value-concepts may characterize different gender groups, they are simply not separable ethically or morally. Justice and caring are two circles in a Venn diagram. They are two nonhierarchical values, which are also concepts. Justice and caring are organically webbed to one another, so much so that it is hard to know, morally or intellectually, whether any given act was one of justice or caring. They are so interrelated, even interdependent, that it is difficult to discern how much justice and how much caring comprise any given moral act. Perhaps justice and caring constitute "emphatic trends" in the world of moral thought and action; that is, perhaps they represent agglomerations of value-concepts that manifest differing moral thrusts. But they are surely overlapping value-concepts.

The plurality of value-concepts embodied in any given situation allows the practitioners of those value-concepts freedom legitimately to choose which value-concepts their action does, or will, embody. The very multiplicity of value-concepts provides for the human freedom to choose one, or more, over others (chap. 4). Thus, certain personalities will choose "justice" and act accordingly, while others will choose "caring" and also act accordingly. The realm of morality, thus, becomes flexible enough to encompass moral practitioners of all types and tendencies. It also generates a plurality of opinions, which can be discussed, concerning moral action.

A value-concept need not be present verbally in order to be active as a concept and as a value that informs a text or situation (chap. 1). Thus, an act of "caring" may be an act of deep "justice," even though the term "justice" is not part of the discussion of the situation; and vice versa.

Finally, because all value-concepts overlap and intersect, it is misleading to choose a limited number to illustrate the prosocial life, or even to gather value-concepts into groups. Nonetheless, I have chosen and clustered the following twelve value-concepts which seem to me to be more central, or more illustrative, than others. Still, the reader needs to know that there are many, many more value-concepts that inform our moral, intellectual, and affectional life. A little reflection will make that quite clear.[12]

Twelve Value-Concepts of the Prosocial Life

There are many value-concepts of the prosocial life. I shall list only twelve.

Morality is a basic value-concept that informs the prosocial life. Batson,[13] in a sparkling history of the altruism debate (chapters 1–4), notes that Western tradition, in its philosophical and psychological expressions, clearly assumes that altruistic action is really a form of egoism; that is, that all altruistic activity is really intended to gratify some egoistic need—for approval, for heightened self-esteem, to avoid guilt, etc. Morality, in Western tradition, then, is the brokering of various self-interests; all altruistic behavior is motivated by enlightened self-interest. In thinkers as varied as Aristotle, Hobbes, Nietzsche, Freud, Kant, and Darwin, there is no truly allocentric motivation for morality; that is, there is no motivational state in which the need of the other is truly the center. Batson devotes the rest of his book to designing and carrying out experiments intended to refute that widely-held hypothesis, demonstrating that truly altruistic, that is, allocentric, motivation does indeed exist.[14] Using overlapping circles, Batson then concludes that some prosocial activity is motivated by egoism, some by altruism, and some by both; the debate is only over how much prosocial activity is motivated by which factors (206–8). The existence of morality—that is, of prosocial attitudes and behaviors—which is rooted in egoistic, allocentric, or mixed motivations should be self-evident, for morality is one of the basic value-concepts of the prosocial life: We, humans, are capable of intelligent moral judgment, and we are capable of genuine allocentric motivation. We, humans, have the capacity for moral reasoning and for prosocial action of all types, including genuinely altruistic action. The affection closest to the value-concept of morality is commitment to intelligent moral judgment, the sustained dedication to work towards informed virtuous discernment and action.

Justice is also a basic value-concept of the prosocial life. Perhaps, it forms an emphatic trend; that is, a general thrust in moral thought and action. Justice is the basic human demand for moral reciprocity, for order and fairness in human interactions. It is rooted, on the one hand, in considered moral principle and, on the other, in an intuitive sense of what is, or would be, fair. Justice is not always egocentric; usually it is based on an imagined mutuality. Hillel's interpretation of the Golden Rule, "That which is hateful to you, do not do unto others," [15] is a good beginning toward understanding of the value-concept of justice. The affection closest to the value-concept of justice is righteous anger, the sustained anger that demands justice. [16]

Caring is another basic value-concept of the prosocial life. Perhaps it, too, forms an emphatic trend; that is, a general thrust in moral thought and action. Caring is the basic human ability to reach out and help another. It is rooted in active awareness of the needs of the other and in a deep human desire to aid a fellow human being. Caring is our ability to nurture the other to be that which it is within the other to be. It is assuming responsibility, stewardship, for our fellow human being. Caring is usually allocentric, but it can also be the result of egocentric motives, especially the subtle motives of self-reward. Perhaps the Golden Rule, "Love your fellow human being as yourself," [17] best catches the multidimensional motivation for caring. From the point of view of moral action in the world, motivation makes no difference; caring is still a basic value-concept of the prosocial life. The affection closest to the value-concept of caring is love, the sustained desire to support and nurture the other.

Inclusiveness [18] is another value-concept of the prosocial life. As a value and as a concept, it includes a positive valuation of human life, a sense of our shared humanity in its very particularity, and a respect for human being-in-the-world. Inclusiveness, as a thought and as a moral aspiration, encompasses an openness to the diversity of human existence in all its shapes and forms, a receptivity to the sheer difference of the other. Inclusiveness means learning about the culture of the other—language, body expressions, art, music, literature, and religion—and respecting the dignity of human expression everywhere, honoring the difference of the other in one's speech and behavior. The affections closest to inclusiveness are respect and honor, that is the sustained effort, at least, not to deprecate the being of the other and, at best, to hold the other dear in one's own eyes. Humans are capable of inclusiveness, though it is more easily preached than practiced.

Extensivity[19] is another value-concept of the prosocial life. It includes a positive evaluation of all life, indeed of the entire biosphere. Extensivity requires a global view of human life, an ecological perspective on human action.[20] In this perspective, every human action needs to be weighed morally in the scales of extensivity and **globalism.** Extensivity and globalism require avoiding pollution of one's political and social, as well as one's natural, environments. Indeed, these value-concepts require a proactive program for creating a human context that is wholly prosocial. Again, respect and honor are the affections closest to extensivity and globalism.

Bonding[21] is another value-concept of the prosocial life. Bonding is not just a social and psychological process; it is a value we strive to embody, as it is also a concept we can analyze and discuss. Bonding, as a value-concept, is one's ability to become deeply attached to another human being—through touch, play, conversation, ritual, and sharing of joys, tensions, satisfactions, and griefs. Bonding is intimate; it is contact, connectedness with a fellow human being. Bonding means bonding with others and not only with those who are like us. We begin with our families but we reach outward. Bonding enables us to see ourselves in relation to the other. It is the mirror of our being-in-the-world. The affection closest to the value-concept of bonding is devotion, the sustained desire to be in the presence of the other.

Attachment,[22] by contrast, is social. It, too, is not just a process but is the value-concept which embodies our need for social contact with one another. Attachment is our ability to maintain networks of people. Sometimes we are attached to a person or group for a particular goal or purpose; sometimes we are attached to a person or group just for friendship and fellowship. Sometimes attachment is rooted in kinship; sometimes it is chosen. Almost always attachment can lead to bonding.[23] The affection closest to the value-concept of attachment is friendship, the sustained effort to build and maintain contacts with others.

Empathy[24] is another value-concept of the prosocial life. Empathy, too, is not just a psychological process. It is, rather, a value we strive to embody and a concept we can analyze and discuss. Empathy, as a value-concept, is our ability to see the other as she sees herself or as he sees himself. Empathy, as a value-concept, is rooted in our own suffering and in our own joy. For it is from within ourselves that we reach out to feel-with the other. To empathize with another means to draw on the range of our own experience, to clarify in our own inner self the feeling of the other and, then, to identify with the pain, or with the joy, of the other. As a value-concept, empathy moves us to be the other, for a short period of time. Empathy is also a teaching of goodness.[25] The affection closest to the value-concept of empathy is compassion, the sustained openness to the feelings and states of others.

Critical consciousness[26] is yet another value-concept of the prosocial life. Critical consciousness, as a concept and as a value, is our ability to think, and to think against the grain of prevalent social consciousness. It is the embodiment of the value that urges us to differentiate truth from falsehood, fact from fantasy. Critical consciousness forces us to measure and weigh the data we receive, no matter what degree of self-evidence and authority lies behind the thought or behavior. It is our ability to apply ourselves intentionally to the study and evaluation of ideas, values, and social processes. Critical consciousness is also our ability to think long and hard about a subject, to consider a proposal from many sides, and to reach reasoned and reasonable conclusions. It is our ability to take multiple perspectives and to evaluate them in an orderly way. Critical consciousness is our ability to reason morally. The affection closest to the value-concept of critical consciousness is intellectual perseverance, the sustained effort to think through, and to think through critically, the situations we are in and the positions we take.

Empowerment[27] is also a value-concept of the prosocial life. Empowerment is not only a psychological process; it is a desideratum of human moral existence. Empowerment is the accumulating of correct judgments such that one develops confidence in one's ability to make further, and more difficult, moral judgments. In this sense, empowerment is self-empowerment—as a value and as an idea, not only as a process. Empowerment is also the value-concept that motivates us to help others make responsible moral decisions such that they develop confidence in their ability to exercise their own moral judgment. The affection closest to the value-concept of empowerment is moral strength, the sustained desire to have, use, and share moral power.

Protest,[28] or resistance, is another value-concept of the prosocial life. Protest is our ability to express and communicate our critical evaluation of the other. It is our way of saying that injustice has occurred, that elemental fairness has been violated. Protest, or resistance, is our ability to challenge, sometimes to defy, authority on moral grounds. It is the ground from which we question human, and even divine, authority. Protest, or resistance, is our insistence that morality is universal and binding upon all. It is the assertion of universal justice and caring. The affection closest to the value-concept of protest is moral courage, the sustained desire to see fairness done even if one must challenge authority to accomplish that.

Weaving the Web: Value-Concepts, Affections, and Teachings

The list of eleven affections and twelve value-concepts given here does not begin to exhaust the number of value-concepts and affections. There still remain: sympathy, forgiveness, and concern as affections; and equity, intimacy, integrity, virtue, righteousness, humaneness, meaning, and goodness as value-concepts. There is no such thing as too many prosocial value-concepts and affections, especially since hierarchy is not the issue. Then there are the five teachings of goodness: personal competence, commitment to intelligent moral judgment, extensivity, empathy, and righteous anger.[29]

The affections and value-concepts of the prosocial life do not stand alone. Rather, they are interwoven with one another. Thus, among the value-concepts, morality, justice, and caring are close to one another. They are so closely woven together that they cannot really be separated. Similarly, bonding, attachment, and empathy are very close; perhaps too close to be separated. Further, bonding leads to caring for, most often, we care for those with whom we have bonded. In this sense, bonding is accepting the other while caring is sustaining the other in her or his very being. Sometimes, however, we are caring first and that leads to bonding. Actually, any act of bonding is also an act of caring; and vice versa. Similarly, critical thinking which remains in the realm of thought, that is, which is only a concept and not a value, is socially and hence morally useless, while protest, which is not informed by thought, is only rebelliousness. Critical thought, however, which accepts the call to moral action, becomes protest, and protest, which accepts the discipline of moral reasoning, is critical thought in action. Thus, too, among the affections, moral courage and moral strength overlap, as do commitment to intelligent moral judgment and intellectual perserverance, as well as devotion and friendship, and devotion and love. In fact, considered reflection will show that all these affections and value-concepts are related to one another, bound into a bond that cannot be easily undone.

Value-concepts are concepts that have cognitive content and a normative thrust; that is, they are ideas that are oughts. Affections are feelings that have intellectual substance and a normative thrust; that is, they are emotions that are oughts. And teachings are thought-feelings that are, by definition, oughts. While I have listed teachings above and tried to distinguish value-concepts from affections in these pages, the overlap among these categories may be greater than the distinctions. Thus, caring (a value-concept) and love (an affection) are really very close. So are empathy (a teaching and value-concept) and sympathy (an affection),[30] and extensivity (a teaching) and inclusivity (a value-concept). Thus, too, commitment to intelligent moral living falls into two categories (a teaching and an affection) as does empathy (a teaching and a value-concept). In addition, there is the overlap internal to each category mentioned in the preceding paragraphs.

It seems to me that each of these three categories has its own purpose. Thus, in my opinion, value-concepts are more consciously intellectual and more intentionally moral than affections. Further, the realm of value-concepts is, in my view, more organized than the realm of affections, though one must bear in mind that its structure is that of a web not a hierarchy. Finally, it seems to me that the idea of value-concepts accounts better for the transition from feelings to affections to values. I, thus, justify the use of value-concepts as separate from affections. It seems to me, further, that both value-concepts and affections get formalized into teachings, that is, into a message that is consciously conveyed from one person to another in formal and informal settings. Thus, I justify the use of teachings as separate from value-concepts and affections, though I admit that there is a great deal of intellectual and pedagogical overlap. Because these categorizations are so complex, I understand that others will think otherwise, classifying and organizing these terms differently. In the end, it is prosocial action that counts and, in that perspective, it makes no moral difference whether we are dealing with ideas warmly held, or feelings firmly sustained, or teachings deeply rooted and embodied in moral acts.

Weaving the Web: Moral Structures and Patterns of Behavior

The patterns of behavior examined in part 1 and the affections, value-concepts, and teachings examined here also overlap and interrelate. The teachings, value-concepts, and affections of the prosocial life are generated by the praxis of, and socialization for, prosocial attitudes and behaviors; and vice versa: The teachings, value-concepts, and affections of the prosocial orientation inform, and are the axiological force behind, the praxis and socialization patterns observed earlier. Life is not linear; rather, life is a complex irregular weaving of a fabric. It is a kaleidescope of overlapping and ever-changing shapes and colors.

There are two ways of dealing with the complex interrelatedness of life. The first is to acknowledge that life is, indeed, an evolving web. In this case, one does not "begin" at a specific point and "proceed in an orderly manner" toward some "fully articulated goal." Rather, one tacks back and forth through life, just as one must tack to sail a boat into the wind.[31] Following this way, one becomes conscious of being in an intricate living process and one slowly assumes responsibility for parts of that process. On one tack, one identifies teachings, affections, and value-concepts, reflects on them, and relates them to observed attitudes and behaviors. On the other tack, one identifies processes of socialization, types of roles, rules, and norms, modes of authority, patterns of behavior, reflects on them, and examines their relationship to teachings, affections, and value-concepts. Slowly, one reaches an understanding of what is going on and one evolves a plan of action. Slowly, one changes a pattern here and an attitude there. Eventually, the changes evolve into new moral commitments.

The second way to deal with the evolving-web nature of life is not to reflect on it at all but simply to respond to the needs of the moment. Some transforming event may evoke a strong commitment or someone may ask for help, and one is moved to respond. The first response is action and that action evolves, by increments, into a deeper commitment and broader range of activity. Following this way, life becomes a series of sudden shifts in course in the middle of the sea. Praxis rules; reflection, if it comes at all, comes later.

It makes no difference how goodness comes about, for goodness is good unto itself. However, through the study of those factors which facilitate goodness and the identification and examination of the value-concepts, teachings, and affections of the prosocial life, a small piece of the mystery of goodness is unveiled and the knowledge which is gained by looking at the working of goodness helps us better analyze, teach, and practice goodness.

Co-text [32]

- Concerning flesh and blood, if one does wrong to one's fellow, it does not leave the heart forever. Not so the Holy One, blessed be He. The Israelites were in Egypt and the Egyptians enslaved them with brick and mortar. Yet after all the evils that they did to the Jews, the Holy One, blessed be He, had mercy on them and said, "'You shall not abominate the Egyptian for you were a stranger in their land' (Dt. 23:8). Rather, pursue peace as it says, 'Seek peace and pursue it'" (Ps. 34:15).[33]

COMMENT: The commandment "you shall not abominate" is said of Egyptians and of Edomites in Deuteronomy 23:8. It is said of them because, though one cast children into the Nile and the other made war on the Israelites, they did not try to undermine the structure of their religious teaching. Therefore, they are not to be abominated. Here, God sets the example of loving one's enemies as an act which embodies the value-concept *hesed*.[34]

8

Do This

Pre-text[1]

Rabbi Judah ben Simon said in the name of Rabbi Yoḥanan: Moses heard three things from the Almighty and was strongly taken aback.[2]

• When God said to him "They shall make for Me a sanctuary" (Ex. 25:8), Moses said before the Holy One, blessed be He, 'Master of the universe! "Behold the heavens and the heavens above the heavens cannot contain You" (I Kings 8:27) and yet You say, "They shall make Me a sanctuary'"?! The Holy One, blessed be He, replied, 'Moses, it is not as you think. Rather, "[the sanctuary] shall be twenty boards [wide] on the northern side, twenty boards [wide] on the southern side, eight on the west" [etc. as detailed in Ex.] and I shall come down and contract My Presence among you below, as it says, "And I shall meet you there"' (Ex. 25:22).

• When God said "You shall be careful to present to Me at the proper time My offering, My food, as a fire-sacrifice, as a pleasing odor to Me" (Nu. 28:2), Moses said before the Holy One, blessed be He, 'Master of the universe! If I were to gather together all the animals of the world, would there be sufficient to offer up to You even one offering?! Or, would all the trees in the world be enough for one sacrifice?! For it says, "The Lebanon does not have enough fuel nor are the animals sufficient for an offering" (Is. 40:16)?! The Holy One, blessed be He, replied, 'Moses, it is not as you think. Rather, "You shall say to them, 'This is the fire-offering which you shall bring . . .'"' (Nu. 28:3).

• When God said "Each person shall give a ransom for his or her soul" (Ex. 30:12), Moses said to the Holy One, blessed be He, 'Master of the universe! Can a person give a ransom for her or his soul as it says . . . "Ah! A person can never pay ransom for his or her soul, no matter how precious the ransom is"' (Ps. 49:8)?! The Holy One, blessed be He, replied, 'Moses, it is not as you think. Rather, "This is what they shall give"' (Ex. 30:13). [Rabbi Meir said, "The Holy One, blessed be He, took something like a coin of fire from under the throne of glory and showed it to Moses saying, 'Something like this shall they give.'"][3]

COMMENT: In each of these three cases, human beings are asked to do something that, on the surface, seems impossible to accomplish: to build a sanctuary to contain God's presence, to make an adequate offering to God, and to pay ransom for one's soul and person. Yet, in each case, the text teaches us that, while the task may seem impossible, there is definitely something we human beings can do. This is the theme of this chapter.

Religion and the Secular Humanist Tradition

Social scientists often control for "religion" in their work, administering one of the well-known scales of religiosity to establish this factor. They also often control for political views or attitudes of prejudice. However, there are not many who control for general prosocial belief and behavior. This is a serious error, for there is an entire humanist secular tradition that begins with the Enlightenment, is embodied in American, French, and United Nations declarations of human rights, and which has spawned political revolutions in the United States, France, Germany, and elsewhere. This secular political human rights tradition, which is now understood to include economic, social, cultural, and health rights, as well as political and civil rights,[4] has created and spread the democratic process throughout the Western world and even into other cultures. It is this tradition that motivates prosocial beliefs and actions in many persons; hence, the need to control for it in social-psychological and historical studies.

One can call this general prosocial orientation "the human rights tradition," or "the Enlightenment tradition," or "the humanist tradition," or, in short form, "humanism," "secularism," or "modernity."[5] The existence of this tradition, no matter what its label, is very widespread. Indeed, it is so much a part of the fabric of Western culture that we are often not even aware of it, unless we go to a part of the world where this tradition is not taken for granted and see how other cultures handle such issues as the democratic vote, the separation of church and state, and women's rights—all issues strongly shaped and deeply informed by the secular humanist tradition.

The humanist or secular tradition has its own moral teachings, value-concepts, affections, stories, social structures, symbols, rituals, even its own spirituality—just like the more familiar religious traditions. Sometimes, however, the moral and social values of the secular tradition conflict with that of traditional religion; this is to be expected. In addition, some of the people who most publicly claim the name "secularist" or "humanist" are atheists.[6] This, unfortunately, has led neofundamentalist thinkers to label the very existence of the humanist secular tradition as bad and, as a result, the words "humanist" and "secular" have acquired a negative valence in many circles. However, this need not be so. Religious, as well as secular, thinkers have claimed the humanist tradition, Martin Buber's *Biblical Humanism* being a fine example, though there are many others. Traditional religion has nothing to fear from humanism, secular or religious. Indeed, to live in the contemporary world is, to my mind, to be heir to both secular humanism and traditional religion. The art of modern moral and spiritual living is cooking these varying, and often differing, traditions into one elegant and nourishing dish.

I propose, therefore, to recognize, indeed to honor, secular humanism together with traditional religion. The value-concepts and teachings of the prosocial life, elaborated above, are drawn from the secular humanist tradition. A parallel set, drawn from Judaism, is to be found in part 3. A similar set drawn from Christianity or other traditional religions could be constructed. I very strongly urge colleagues from other religions to do just that and to let the similarities and differences between secular humanism and traditional religion, as well as among traditional religions, surface. In this chapter, I shall offer specific suggestions for inculcating prosocial attitudes and behaviors and I shall do so from within the secular humanist tradition. In this way, the value-concepts and prosocial suggestions that I advocate here can be used by businesspersons, clergy, educators, community leaders, and others, regardless of religious affiliation, while those I make in part 3 can be used by Jewish leaders and can constitute a model for other religious traditions.

Failure Creates a Problem

In an earlier chapter, I presented the Princeton experiment [7] in which sixty-seven Princeton Theological Seminary students were asked to study the parable of the Good Samaritan (Luke 10: 29–37) and then requested to proceed to another facility where they were to be filmed giving a sermon on the parable or on alternate ministry. Between the two buildings, the experimenters placed a "victim," the goal being to find out how many of these theology students, who had just finished studying the parable of the Good Samaritan, would stop to aid the victim and what kind of help they would give. As noted, only 40% stopped to help, a rate above the usual helping rate of 12 to 25% but not high enough for those who take the parable, and similar prosocial religious teaching, seriously. The conclusion relevant here is that religious prosocial teaching helps a little but not enough.

The evidence from other sources is even more discouraging for those in both secular and religious moral education. The social-psychological evidence indicates that religious affiliation and praxis is not a determining factor in antisocial, or in prosocial, behavior. Thus, religion did not help or hinder subjects, in any systematic way, in the Milgram,[8] Staub,[9] Colby,[10] or other social-psychological studies. In yet another study, Batson and Ventis [11] noted, after studying closely three people from very different but actively religious backgrounds, that it was not the religious teaching but the context of social roles, norms, and reference groups that provided the best predictors of religious identity (31–48). Further, asking about people's attitudes and then checking their actual behaviors, Batson and Ventis concluded that seeing oneself as prosocially motivated and actually performing prosocial actions were not the same: "The more religious may *see* themselves as more helpful and caring; they may even be seen this way by others. But when it came to action, there is no evidence that they are" (289, emphasis original).

The historical evidence, too, indicates that religious affiliation and praxis is not a determining factor in antisocial, or in prosocial, behavior. Thus, religion was not a determining factor among the rescuers for, while some rescuers rescued out of specifically religious motivation, most did not.[12] Nor was it a salient factor in the organized resistance to the nazis, though some activists were certainly moved to resistance by their religious convictions.[13] Religion also was not a significant factor, in any systematic way, among the soldiers of the German police battalions.[14] In addition, it must always be born in mind that the shoah took place in the midst of Christian Europe; that is, that Christian religious teaching did not stop, or even hinder seriously, the realization of the discrimination against, persecution of, and eventual extermination of the Jews of Europe. No one knows for sure, but I have speculated publicly that, had the Pope ordered that any Catholic who participates in the killing of Jews be excommunicated, perhaps 30% of European Jewry might have been saved because Eastern Europe, the site of most of the mass killing, was devoutly religious and such an exercise of papal authority, even if followed half-heartedly by local church authorities, would have been taken very seriously. Finally, it must also be born in mind, *mutatis mutandis,* that the Jewish resistance in the ghettoes and in the forests was also not significantly composed of people with religious training.[15] Religion was simply not a determinative factor during the shoah, except for the very few—not for the rescuers or the resistance; not for the perpetrators, active or passive; and not for the resisting victims—although the religion of the Jewish victims was always their death warrant.

The case is not better in the least for the secular humanist tradition, as Richard Rubenstein has shown in *The Cunning of History*[16] as well as in several other books. The secular state, which was supposed to protect all citizens regardless of race, religion, ethnic origin, and economic status, responded during the shoah by declaring Jews stateless and, hence, without the protection of the secular state. No human or civil rights obtained for Jews, and for some others, during the shoah. Indeed, under all of the totalitarian regimes set up in the tradition of the Enlightenment, the prosocial tradition bearing the values of modernity collapsed; hence, the state-approved, or state-tolerated, persecution of Jews, gypsies, homosexuals, and others under fascism, communism, and certain types of socialism. The "people's republics" embody the failure of the secular humanist tradition.[17]

Much to the consternation of adherents and advocates of both religious and secular moral traditions, then, the fact is that the role of religious and of secular moral teaching in prosocial and in antisocial behavior is episodic. Some people, indeed most, use these traditions to justify antisocial behavior while others, a minority, use them to justify prosocial behavior. To put it differently: There is no overall consistent pattern of prosocial influence in secular or religious moral teaching. **Religious as well as secular moral teaching accounts for very little of humankind's ability to resist evil and do good.**

Several theorists have tried to rectify this situation. Avi Sagi, in an insightful article,[18] has pointed out that there are two models of authority in rabbinic Judaism, each of which implies a different basis for obedience. The first is the "epistemic model" in which authority is a function of knowledge, not of any charismatic quality or social position (2–10). Precisely because it is a function of knowledge, epistemic authority is always dependent upon the truth of the knowledge claimed and the consensus which recognizes that truth. Einstein's authority, for example, was a function of his knowledge, not of his charisma or social status, and could be challenged by anyone with the erudition to dispute it. Similarly, in classic rabbinic tradition, the rabbi or rabbinic judge derives his[19] authority from his knowledge, and his authority can be challenged by anyone with the erudition to show another view to be correct. The most senior of sages can be overridden if proven to be wrong, or if he changes his own mind. When the student surpasses the teacher, the student becomes the authority, though such supersession must be exercised with utmost deference and respect.

The second model is the "deontic model" in which authority is a function of the individual person, not of that person's knowledge (11–21). Such authority is derived from the community which invests that person with authority. In this model, once authority is given, obedience is unconditional, it being assumed that the spirit of God and the halakhic process keep that authority within proper rabbinic bounds. The root metaphor for this model is the absolute nature of judicial discipline in rabbinic Judaism[20] and, more importantly, the absoluteness of the covenantal relationship once assent to it was given (11–18).[21]

Both the epistemic and the deontic models are available in halakhic Judaism, each generating its own type of elite (21–23). Sagi's elegant analysis can be generalized to non-Jewish models of authority and leadership. However, it still does not answer the question: **How** does one cultivate an elite that will model prosocial behavior as well as a following that will actually do prosocial acts? Neither knowledge nor charisma guarantees the doing of good.

In an attempt to incorporate the insights of the social scientists, particularly Batson, into Christian theology, Rigby and O'Grady have looked at the question of agape, altruism, and eros.[22] The options for defining these terms are clearly set out: First, agape is altruistic love and eros is self-love, the former being the only true Christian love;[23] second, agape implies eros, both being forms of Christian love; [24] and third, agape is love of one's enemy or sacrificial love, altruism is love of the other, and eros is self-love, with the realization that "here [in agape] altruism finds its true meaning in undreamed of possibilities of being and loving." [25]

This effort to engage "the possibility of empirically grounded altruistic motivations" based on the work of Batson creates a theological construct for Christians. Perhaps it, too, can be generalized to non-Christian authority and leadership. However, it, too, does not answer the basic question: **How** does one cultivate prosocial attitudes and actions? How does one translate the construct into reality? Theology, in itself, as Batson and others have shown repeatedly and as common sense and history teach, does not yield ethical action and it is action, and not construct, that is important.

Sharon Welch [26] has articulated a theology which moves towards prosocial action. She begins by identifying clearly the "ethic of control" and the "theology which valorizes absolute power" through an "erotics of domination" (23 – 47, 111 – 13). She, then, contrasts this with the "ethic of risk," the "heritage of resistance," and the "epistemology of solidarity which posits the value of all traditions" (20 – 22, 75 – 80, 137 – 42). Most important, Welch makes some concrete proposals: to tell the stories of resistance, that is, to preserve the "dangerous memories" and to use them to empower one to prosocial action; to acknowledge the political and cultural matrix of (even religious) thought and, on the basis of that avowal, to proceed to a critique of particular institutions; to acknowledge and celebrate interdependence; to cultivate a "complex, fluid, concrete love . . . [which] enables us to maintain rage and vision in the face of the disclosure of more forms of oppression"; to acknowledge the plurality of images and experiences of the divine; and to network relationships which embody an attentiveness to life (75 – 76, 154 – 79).

Intellectual construct and practical suggestion combine in Welch's work. Still, in comparison to the specific measures taken in altruistically-oriented businesses, schools, and other institutions, [27] one could have wished for more process-oriented suggestions: **How** does one acknowledge and celebrate interdependence (especially in a religion that preaches individual salvation)? **How** does one cultivate a love which remains open to rage in the face of oppression? **How** does one affirm religious or secular authority and cultivate intelligent disobedience at the same time? [28]

Finally, studying ethics, moral theology, and the intersection of law and ethics, together with work in comparative ethics, is a major goal in intellectual academic circles. Books are written, conferences are held, dialogue is engaged in on these subjects. There is a whole field of moral education with a professional organization, conferences, and publications. Sometimes even ethical grand rounds are held in hospitals. Still, one must ask with the Talmud, *mai nafka minah,* "What results from all this? What difference does it make?" The study of ethics and moral theology does not make us better people. Analyzing the teaching of morality and dialogue in comparative ethics do not, in and of themselves, inculcate prosocial values or lead to prosocial behavior. Remember Hitler's professors, and clergy, and educators, and lawyers—all serious persons and professionals who, despite their personal, spiritual, and professional concern with the doing of good, ended up doing evil.[29] What, then, is needed? What do we need to do, as morally responsible people and leaders, to encourage prosocial attitudes and behaviors?

Four Very Strong Recommendations for Encouraging Prosocial Attitudes and Behaviors

Resistant and caring behaviors come from a background of proportionate and reasoned discipline, combined with modeling, practice, and the teaching of caring attitudes and behaviors. The following four recommendations, with specific proposals where appropriate, then, should be incorporated in any program, religious or secular, intended to encourage the doing of good and discourage the doing of evil.[30]

Admit Failure

As noted, the results of social-psychological and historical research indicate that secular and religious moral education is not a factor, in any systematic way, in people's choice of good and evil. Bluntly put: Religious and secular moral education has failed to discourage antisocial behavior and to encourage prosocial behavior. This, however, does not seem to have penetrated fully into the minds of secular and religious educators. To put it most simply: If religious and secular moral education works, why do we not see more prosocial action in human society?

Give Formal Instruction

Formal instruction, while not sufficient, is necessary. Content does count, even if it is not determinative. A plan of instruction intended to educate and inculcate prosocial values must include the following five areas.

(1) **Teach prosocial value-concepts.** There are a large number of prosocial value-concepts.[31] Discuss the terms: inclusiveness, extensivity, globalism, goodness, kindness, justice, fairness, law, integrity, virtue, uprightness, rectitude, equity, impartiality, righteousness, ethics, caring, morality, protest, resistance, bonding, humaneness, and humanity. And the complements: exclusiveness, isolationism, ethnic superiority, injustice, oppression, prejudice, un-

fairness, uncritical compliance, inhumaneness, and inhumanity. In a religious setting, discuss specifically religious prosocial value-concepts.[32]

(2) **Use the language of justice and caring.** The way we phrase what we want to say forms who we are and who we become. Discuss the words: pity, compassion, concern, affection, love, care, cherish, nourish, protect, understanding, empathy, kindness, mercy, sympathy, attachment, devotion, heart, feeling, respect, awareness, recognition, intimacy, attention, warmth, and consideration. And the complements: pain, sorrow, grief, worry, anxiety, distress, suffering, trouble, sensitiveness, stress, intimidate, persecute, threaten, and terror. Be sure to use these words in conversation on all topics and issues.

(3) **Identify and actively teach prosocial texts and traditions.** For the secular tradition, this would include stories and poetry from the American and French Revolutions, the period of slavery, the civil rights movement, and the antiwar protest; exemplars from industry and education;[33] and stories of ordinary citizens who have accomplished prosocial tasks.[34] For the biblical tradition, this would include the stories of Shifra and Pu'ah, the midwives who resisted Pharoah's genocidal decrees; Raḥab, the prostitute, who resisted the Jericho secret police to hide the spies; Nathan, the prophet, who confronted King David forcefully on his adultery with Bathsheba and the murder of her husband; Saul's officers who refused to kill the priests of Nob who had sheltered David; Abraham who argued with God about the justice of destroying the cities of Sodom and Gemorra; Moses who consistently defended the people of Israel against God's unjust threats; and the author of Psalm 44 who protested vehemently against God's desertion of God's people in time of war.[35]

(4) **Teach the nature of social processes.** The whole thrust of this book has been to show that social process is the determinative factor in the avoiding of evil and the doing of good. Secular and religious educators must, therefore, provide formal instruction about the social processes within which we live and make moral decisions. Discuss the terms: authority, obedience, disobedience, resistance, protest, heteronomy and autonomy, norms, rules, values, normocentric, agentic shift, salience, permission, ingroup-outgroup, conflict management and resolution, win-win, socialization, identification, modeling, peer support, and incremental learning. Discuss the nature of hierarchies and the effect of excessive vs. caring discipline. Read the books by Milgram, Kelman and Hamilton, the Oliners, Browning, and so on. Show the films and discuss them.[36] An understanding, no matter how tentative, of these processes is an important first step.

(5) **Teach critical thinking.** Thinking against the social grain is crucial. People must be consciously taught to ask: How does one identify a lie? What is propaganda? Who is manipulating whom? Whose power is at stake here? Do I agree with the truths being expounded here; and if not, why? What do I

think, independent of what I feel? The instinct for truth and good common sense needs to be reinforced and developed.

Teach Prosocial Skills

Intellectual knowledge is not enough; one must learn how to do things. Therefore, religious and secular authorities must teach concrete prosocial skills. I recommend teaching the following seven prosocial skills:

(1) **Perspective-taking and empathy**—This enables one to understand how the other feels, to appreciate the affective dimension of the other's situation. Ask: "What do you think he or she feels?" "What does she or he feel even if she or he cannot express it?" "How angry, happy, ashamed, proud . . . is he or she?" "What would you feel in that person's place?" "What is empathy? What is sympathy?" Everyone is capable of perspective-taking and everyone will need to be the object of perspective-taking by others in the course of life. Being able to empathize is an important prosocial skill.

(2) **Identifying and coding one's own feelings**—Our feelings are basic to who we are; they are the ground for much of our being and the agency for much of our action. We need to know our own feelings. Ask: "What did you feel when you saw . . . ?" "Can you recall feeling ashamed, guilty, joyous, powerful, hurt, nurturing, modest, immodest, content?" "What is the difference between anger and rage?" "Have you ever felt either?" "What was it like?" "How do you feel when someone threatens you, challenges you publicly, or praises you in front of others?" Almost everyone has experienced every one of these emotional states at one time or another. Being able to recognize and label them is an important prosocial skill.

(3) **Identifying authorities, hierarchies, norms, roles, and social processes**—As noted, everyone exists within a series of social hierarchies. Ask: "What is the social hierarchy in this particular situation?" "To whom are you subordinate?" "To whom are you superior?" "Is there more than one authority at work here? more than one set of subordinates?" "Upon what is the legitimacy of the authority in this situation based?" "What would you have to do to break the rule, the norm?" "What would you have to do to challenge the authority?" "Are you, as an authority, acting in a responsible way, within the limits of your legitimacy? And, if not, how do you as an authority challenge your own authority and reshape it?" Knowing one's place in various hierarchies and, hence, imagining how one might challenge these hierarchies is a major prosocial skill—and it can be learned.[37]

(4) **Externalizing repressed prosocial impulses**—Doing good, as Batson has shown and as rabbinic tradition teaches, is a basic part of being human. All people want to do good to others, even if the motivation for that is, sometimes, egoistic. Yet, many people hesitate to do good. Ask: "What does your impulse

to do good tell you to do?" "What act of caring have you done today?" "What can you do that would be really kind?" "Whom do you know who is a really good person?" "What does she or he do?" "How do you know he or she is good?" Realizing that one does know good when one sees it, recognizing good impulses in oneself, and realizing that the impediments to doing good are not as formidable as they seem is an important prosocial skill.

(5) **Conflict management skills**—Conflict does not need to be "overcome" or "eliminated." Quite the contrary, conflict is a natural part of life. It does, however, need to be managed so that human relationships do not deteriorate into resentment, hatred, and violence. Teach the skills of mediation. Instruct people in the art of finding superordinate goals. Ask: "What is at stake behind the surface issues for each party?" "What are the common goals of these people?" "Why should these persons cooperate with one another? And if they cannot live in harmony, what intermediate relationship could they have?"

(6) **Networking**—No person is an island, as the poet says. Everyone needs support, even those who do good. A network provides moral, as well as tactical, support. Because doing good is contagious, a network also supports increased prosocial action. A broad network also distributes the impulse to do good over a larger number of areas of one's life. Teach how to build and broaden a network. It is not enough for prosocial action to be a "school (or, church or, professional) activity"; it must become part of the larger lives of the participants. Teach how to make all participants stakeholders in the activity and how to use participatory democracy to involve everyone—the disadvantaged, the willing, the reluctant, even the opposition. Also, show how to involve legitimate authority figures because authority does count; it is only a matter of which side it will count on.

(7) **Protesting**—At some point, social protest may be necessary in order to effect a prosocial goal. There is a long history of this in the West in this century. Teach the skills of coalition-building.[38] Teach the techniques of nonviolent protest: persuasion, social noncooperation, economic noncooperation in the form of the boycott and the strike, and political noncooperation, especially with state authorities. Teach how to organize the various types of demonstration: sit-ins, stand-ins, ride-ins, pray-ins, and hunger strikes, as well as the skills of direct action, negotiation, and reconciliation.[39] Familiarize people with how to find the resources for further training in these areas.[40]

Pay Attention to Context and Process

Religious and secular authorities must recognize that it is not only **what** one teaches but **how** it is taught that makes the difference. It is not only the **content** of the teaching but the social-psychological **context** in which it is taught that makes the real difference between successful and unsuccessful

moral education. In order to accomplish this goal, I make the following additional five practical recommendations for how to teach prosocial values:

(1) **Establish a means by which authority can be challenged.** All social
structures need discipline to give them form. To be as certain as one can that
discipline is proportionate and reasoned, set up a mechanism of criticism and
appeal within the disciplinary process, and be sure that that mechanism functions fairly. In a school, business, hospital, government, synagogue, church, or
volunteer organization, even in a family, I recommend the following, bearing
in mind that these mechanisms must be used honestly and in good will, not as
ploys to pacify underlings or as shields for superiors:

(a) Set up an **ombudsperson** or an **ombudscommittee** who will hear appeals of disciplinary action taken by the central hierarchy.
(b) Set up a **whistle-blowing mechanism** which will enable criticism of
the hierarchy.
(c) Set up a **care team** which will evaluate, not the efficiency with which
the task of the organization is being carried out, but the caring quality of the relationships between members of the organization, particularly those relationships that are hierarchical.

(2) **Act. Do. Implement prosocial action.** It is relatively easy to plan and
to build programs. It is much harder to make sure that the action one intends to
motivate actually takes place. One needs to have some mechanism for checking
the efficacy of what one does, even (perhaps, especially) in education for prosocial action. In a school, business, hospital, government, synagogue, church,
or volunteer organization, even in a family, I recommend the following:

(a) Undertake a **specific project:** visiting the sick, lobbying for a cause,
being part of a watch organization, caring for the homeless, and so on.
Do not let prosocial commitment remain vague.
(b) See to it that there is **personal contact with the disadvantaged person.** Salience to the victim is critical to prosocial activity. Do not let
prosocial commitment be only financial or administrative.
(c) Create a **feedback mechanism** in the form of a journal or report in
which one records what one has actually done. In addition, one should
record feelings and thoughts for later sharing and discussion.

(3) **Model prosocial attitudes and behaviors.** People have a very fine instinct for hypocrisy. This comes from an equally fine ability to observe what
others do and hear what they say, and then compare the two. It is, therefore,
very important to practice what one preaches, that is, to do prosocial acts, for in
the doing is the teaching. In a school, business, hospital, government, syna-

gogue, church, or volunteer organization, even in a family, I recommend the following:

(a) **Model prosocial behaviors yourself.** It is easy if one is in charge of organizing or implementing a program in altruistic behavior to forget to actually do altruistic acts. No matter where one is in the organization, a deed of kindness counts.

(b) **Hire staff** who have a record of prosocial action. The criterion of prosocial action is not usually used in hiring professors, teachers, engineers, doctors, business executives, government employees, or hospital staff. It is used more often, but not systematically enough, in hiring clergy, social workers, and in engaging volunteers. Make prosocial action a part of the resumé that candidates must submit to apply for a job and, if it is not a part thereof, ask.[41]

(c) **Evaluate and promote** using prosocial activity as one of the criteria. Prosocial action is not usually used in evaluating and promoting professors, teachers, engineers, doctors, business executives, government employees, or hospital staff. It is used more often, but not systematically enough, in evaluating and promoting clergy, social workers, and in engaging volunteers. Rewards do not always work;[42] however, process establishes norms. By making it known that prosocial action is approved and used in professional assessment, prosocial action acquires the sanction of the hierarchy and becomes a norm.

(d) Acknowledge **heroes and heroines.** Set up a publicity mechanism which will highlight the activity of those who do perform prosocial acts. Recognition, too, sets norms and standards, as well as reinforces the impulse to do good.

(4) **Develop syllabi and curricula in prosocial action.** There are texts and methods which inculcate prosocial value-concepts and actions. Identify the questions. Prepare the materials. Find the teachers. Teach the texts. There is no other way.[43]

(a) Find the **texts** in Judaism, Christianity, and other world religions, as well as in the secular tradition and in American and European civilization. Find the material in the media, on the internet, anywhere it is available.

(b) Be sure to use the **applied learning methods:** study-buddies (small units that prepare and work together), field observation of prosocial organizations, and project-oriented tasks.

(c) Provide a **full-time person** to encourage and supervise the program in prosocial education and action.

(5) **Be intentional about what you are doing.** It is so easy to let matters slide, to drift into complacency. These recommendations demand a great deal of effort. Indeed, doing good requires much energy, thought, questioning, and care. Still, consciousness is what renders us human. Intentionality is what makes us a part of humanity. Especially in doing good, we must be conscious, intentional.

The Ten Commandments for Resistant and Caring Living

As a question on the final examination of the course which I give on this material, I ask students to write the "Ten Commandments for Resistant and Caring Living." The following represents a digest of their suggestions and mine, and is yet another reworking of the material we have been considering:[44]

1) **Identify the authority that is demanding your obedience as well as the authority that is demanding your resistance.** Recognize the hierarchy of authorities in which you exist. Analyzing the social-psychological processes, knowing these processes consciously, will help you choose.

2) **Establish salience with the victim(s).** Learn about them by seeing their suffering, by making person-to-person contact with them, and by identifying your feelings and theirs.

3) **Identify the values in the situation using the language of care, attachment, and inclusiveness.** Analyze the situation from the justice and the caring perspectives. Lean toward the caring perspective and accept universal human worth as the norm.

4) **Invoke a higher authority.** If you are in doubt, consult your higher authority, whatever it is—conscience, God, tradition, or inner self. Use it consciously as the justification for doing good.

5) **Act! Remember that inaction is a form of action.** Identify the means of empowerment and use them. Take risks. The proof is in the doing, not in the words or intentions.

6) **Follow your good instincts; do not worry about being inconsistent.** Think less and act more. It's okay to be good.

7) **Use your own social-psychological authority for the good.** Ask others to help. Everyone has some authority; so do you. Invoke it. Use it.

8) **Act incrementally. Practice.** Don't be afraid to get more involved, to do more. Also, routinize caring acts. Make them second nature to you. Model caring behavior for those around you—children, parents, friends, followers, bystanders, even strangers.

9) **Network with others.** Identify your community of consensus for the val-

ues of good and evil. Find others like you. Seek collateral support for those values. Pool resources and share tasks with your community.

10) **Explore your own personal history.** If you must think about yourself, identify your own narrative. Examine your own childhood discipline patterns as well as the behavior of those who were models in your life. Know more about your psychological reflexes and your personal belief system so as to identify your ultimate authority/ies and loyalty/ies.

Co-text[45]

- Alexander of Macedonia asked the sages of southern [Judea] . . . "What should a person do to be beloved by one's fellow humans?" They said to him, "One should hate politics and power."[46] He said to them, "My [advice] is better than yours: One should love politics and power and one should do good [with them] for other human beings."[47]

COMMENT: This is a profound comment on the relationship between politics and ethics. Very interestingly, it is Alexander the Great, and not the rabbis, who seems to have the better advice.

- "You shall love the Lord, your God, with all your heart, with all your soul, and with all your might" (Dt. 6:5). "With all your heart"—with both your impulses, with *yetser tov* and with *yetser ha-ra'*.[48]
- May it be Your will, Lord my God, that you lay me down to sleep in peace. Cast my lot in with Your Torah. Make me accustomed to do mitsvot and do not make me accustomed to commit sins. Bring me not into a state of unintended or intended sin, nor into temptation or shame. Let *yetser tov* (inclination to do good) have dominion over me and do not let *yetser ha-ra'* (inclination to do evil) have dominion over me. Save me from . . .[49]

COMMENT: The word "heart" (Heb., *levavekha*) could be spelled *libkha,* that is, with one letter *bet.* The doubling of the letter *bet* is the occasion for this midrash which depicts humanity as having "two" hearts, one which is our inclination to do good and one which is our inclination to do evil. The midrash is followed by a rabbinic prayer. This psychology of the double heart is basic to rabbinic psychology.[50]

PART 3

The Voice of Jewish Tradition

Do not hate your fellow in your heart. You shall surely reprove
(Heb., *hokheah tokhiah*) your acquaintance, and do not bear sin on
his or her account. Do not take revenge or bear a grudge against
your people, but love your other as yourself; I am the Lord
(Lev. 19:17–18).
Whoever can remonstrate with the members of his or her household
and does not, will be caught [in the sin] of the members of her or his
household; with the people of his or her city, will be caught [in the
sin] of the people of her or his city; with the whole world, will be
caught [in the sin] of the whole world . . .
"God will come in judgment with the elders of His people and with
its [chief] leaders" (Is. 3:14).—Though the leaders sinned, what
was the sin of the elders? Rather, say of the elders that they did not
remonstrate with the [chief] leaders.

—*Talmud,* Shabbat 54b–55a; *Zohar* 3:42b

9

The Tradition and the Problem

The Tradition and the Social Sciences

Judaism has assumed the task of making human beings into good people for almost 4000 years and it has an enormously rich repository of legal, narrative, and hortatory literature on the subject which scholars of every age have used and expanded.[1] This literature, drawn from the biblical and rabbinic traditions, includes sources dealing with resistance, caring, and various types of religiously sanctioned violence. These varied and sometimes contradictory traditions deserve a rigorous legal and theological analysis. This is not the place for that. Rather, I will attempt here a compilation of certain of the Jewish sources relevant to the normative goals set forth in part 2. It seems prudent to begin by listing some of the texts, though many will be dealt with more fully later on.

The tradition of resistance to human and divine authority on matters of justice has biblical roots in the following stories, though there are many more:

- Abraham arguing with God over the destruction of Sodom (Gen. 18)
- Tamar insisting on her right to have a child (Gen. 38)
- The rescue of Jewish male infants by the midwives Shifra and Pu'a (Ex. 1:15–22)
- The hiding of the spies by the prostitute Raḥab (Josh. 2)
- Nathan confronting David over his arranging the murder of Bathsheba's husband (II Sam. 12:1–25)
- Ritspa protecting the corpses of Saul and his sons contrary to King David's orders (II Sam. 21)
- Amos confronting the priest Amazia on the emptiness of the cult (Amos 7)[2]
- Elijah's confrontation with the Ahab and the prophets of the Baal (I Kings 18)
- Vashti refusing to appear before the king (Esther 1)
- Esther's defiance of court etiquette and power (Esther 4:11 and 7:1–10).[3]

The rabbinic sources for the tradition of defiance of authority include:

- The justification of Abner's death because he did not protest (or protested, but not vigorously enough) the killing of the priests in Nob (*Talmud,* Sanhedrin 20a with Rashi)
- The accusation that Job (the protestor against God *par excellence*) was really a sinner in that he protested only his personal danger and not that of the people (*Talmud,* Sanhedrin 106a)[4]
- Moses seizing God's garments and dissolving God's oath as a protest against the impending punishment of the Jews (*Talmud,* Shabbat 54b)
- The ethical teaching that whoever does not reprove others will eventually suffer at their hand (*Talmud,* Berakhot 32a).

Finally, the most important rabbinic contribution to the tradition of resistance to authority comes in the substantial halakhic discussions on the topics of the obligation to obey and the obligation to disobey, the duty to rescue and its limits, and the proper and improper uses of violence. In addition, rabbinic literature contains the recounting of heroic acts of resistance to persecution, some of which ended in martyrdom, during the periods of the Romans, the Crusaders, medieval Spain, and the nazis.[5]

The long and rich biblical and rabbinic traditions on caring behavior also have biblical roots:

- Miriam taking care of her brother Moses (Ex. 2:1–10)
- The devotion of Ruth to Naomi (Book of Ruth)
- The love of David and Jonathan (I Sam. 18–20)
- Various verses from Proverbs about being caring even towards one's enemies (Prov. 24:29 and 25:21–22).

The rabbinic sources include:

- The midrash about God feeling pain when the blood of the wicked is shed (*Talmud*, Sanhedrin 39b)
- The midrash of Jacob using mitsvot and good deeds, not his sword and bow (*Bereshit Rabba* 97:6 commenting on Gen. 48:22)
- The tradition that, in his confrontation with Esau, Jacob feared as much that he might kill someone else as that he might be killed himself (*Bereshit Rabba* 76:2)
- The ethical teaching that one should be among the insulted and not among those who insult (*Talmud*, Shabbat 88b).

Indeed, the definition of a *hasid* (a pious person), the development of *middat hasidut* (the standard of piety which is beyond the law), and the elaboration of the value-concept of *gemilut ḥasadim* (the doing of good deeds) is part of the rabbinic tradition on caring behaviors.

The tradition that demands, or at least sanctions, aggressive activity toward the other also has biblical roots:

- The flood (Gen. 7:21–23)
- The command to wipe out Amalek and the confrontation between Samuel and Saul on this subject (Ex. 17:14–15, Dt. 9:1–5, Dt. 25:17 19 with I Sam. 15)
- The order to destroy the six nations resident in Canaan and Joshua's attempt to do this (Dt. 20:16–18 with Josh. 6:20–21, 8:20–29, 10:28–43, 11:10–15)[6]
- The destruction of the peoples of Midian and Bashan (Nu. 31 with Dt. 3:3–7)
- David's Philistine wars (I Sam. 27:8–12)
- The absolute obedience commanded by social authorities such as the court system and parents (Dt. 17:11 and Dt. 21:18–21)
- The many cries and demands for bloody revenge (e.g., Pss. 44, 109, 136)
- The various "texts of terror" and "painful passages" against women and even against Israel.[7]

Rabbinic teaching, on the one hand, mitigated many of these "tough" laws and incidents in the Tanakh. Examples include the development of qualifications for administering capital punishment which, in practice, abolished it and the substitution of flogging for the anxiety of a "trial by heaven."[8] On the other hand, rabbinic thought continued some of these very firm lines. The rule which did not allow a *mamzer* (the child of an adulterous or incestuous union) to marry into the Jewish community is the example most often cited. The ethical teaching that one may, indeed must, hate one's neighbor if he or she persists in her or his sin until the other changes his or her ways, although one may never hate in one's heart, is another example.[9]

The texts, then, are plentiful, as one would expect in a tradition so old and experienced. In addition, they include various, indeed contradicting, teachings on resistance, caring, and religiously-sanctioned violence. The problem here is quite direct: What does this collection of conflicting texts and traditions have to do with anything that can be learned from the social sciences about cultivating good and discouraging evil? What do these texts about religious commandments have to do with "The Four Very Strong Recommendations for Encouraging Prosocial Attitudes and Behaviors" and "The Ten Commandments for Resistant and Caring Living"?[10] To put it another way: Given the plurality of texts in Jewish tradition, how does one choose those texts upon which one will act? Given the command not to follow a majority which is in error and the equally obligatory command to conform to instructions from duly instantiated authorities,[11] how does one decide what to do—especially in light of the evidence cited earlier that these decisions are the sum of a complex of factors which are not specifically "religious," "intellectual," "ethical," or "theological"?

This question becomes particularly sharp when one looks at the historical evidence. Organized Jewish religion has not always been on the good, or caring, side of social conflict. The biblical priests backed the monarchy even in its corruption, as the prophets testify. The organized Jewish community, in both its religious and its Zionist embodiments, did not behave impeccably during the shoah.[12] Even in contemporary social issues, the rabbinate is not among those leading the fight for caring behavior. The Israeli peace movement, for example, has not been led, or even well-populated, by people who identify as "religious."[13] Jewish religion has not succeeded in several thousand years in making the world a better place, except in very limited circles of pietists. Jewish ethical preaching has not worked to make ordinary Jews significantly more caring people. What, then, would be effective? The questions of part 3, then, will be: **How ought Jewish tradition be taught so that people will become more caring, as individuals and as groups? What are the resources within Judaism which facilitate the doing of good and the discouraging of evil? What can Jewish religion and ethics learn from the social-scientific study of obedience and altruism to help it articulate, teach, and practice the doing of good?**

There are no studies which deal with this matter. Much has been written from the philosophical and the halakhic points of view,[14] but nothing, to my knowledge, from the point of view of social psychology and history. The task of part 3, then, will be to present some major classical texts and principles, and then attempt to relate these to the insights gained in the previous parts, with the avowed purpose of generating a praxis, a theology, and texts which will facilitate the doing of good and the condemning of evil.

Four chapters in this part will present the voice of Jewish tradition on prosocial attitudes and behaviors. Chapter 10 will display four key value-concepts in the halakha dealing with these issues: *tselem* (image), *brit* (covenant), *tsedek* (justice), and *hasidut / hesed* (caring), together with associated value-concepts. Chapter 11 will collect biblical and rabbinic stories of resistance and goodness, including those which condone resistance to God. Chapter 12 will assemble biblical and rabbinic teachings of resistance and goodness, including the rabbinic psychology of *yetser tov* (good impulse) and *yetser ha-ra'* (evil impulse) as well as the norms governing *kiddush ha-Shem* (martyrdom). Chapter 13 will deal with four case studies: military disobedience, judicial dissent, the obligation to rescue, and rabbinic views on violence and nonviolence. After this presentation of the Jewish voice, Chapter 14 will attempt a synthesis of the Jewish sources with the insights from the social sciences gleaned in parts 1 and 2 of this book.

Reading Rabbinic Texts

Reading rabbinic texts is not like reading other genres of literature. Rabbinic texts are not narrative, as are the biblical books of Genesis or Kings; nor are they expository, orderly essays on a topic. Rabbinic texts are not philosophical, in a systematic way; nor are they poetic or visionary compositions. For the most part, they are not legal, in the sense of an organized code of laws; nor are they belle-lettres or fiction, though they are certainly highly imaginative. Rabbinic texts are not exegetical or commentative, in that they expound the direct meaning of texts; nor are they homiletical, in the sense of well-developed sermons. They are not scientific tracts; nor are they grammatical or philological analyses. Rabbinic texts are not theology, in any comprehensive way; nor are they extended polemical essays. They are not mystical treatises, though the presence of God is always felt under the surface; nor are they, in any sense, academic works.

Most of the rabbinic texts we shall encounter are midrash, a unique and highly problematic genre.[15] The word *midrash* means three things: a process, a particular literary unit, and an anthology of midrashim (*midrash,* singular; *midrashim,* plural). As a process, midrash is a way of studying a text closely and discovering the gaps, the unsaid dimensions, of the text; or it is studying two or more texts closely and discovering the variants and contradictions in them. Often midrash is a juxtaposition of two or more texts with a view toward interpreting those texts together, intertextually. The result of these types of close study is a revealing of holes in the textual fabric and a reweaving of the texts into a new whole. A "third text" is most often the result of the midrashic process. Such deconstruction and reconstruction is, usually, quickly accomplished in a few lines, forming a particular unit, called "a midrash"; the units are, then, sometimes edited into an anthology, also called "a midrash," forming yet another, greater, whole.

There is only one way to learn how to read midrash—by doing it. Hence, study is the way into rabbinic literature and, thence, into the world of rabbinic values and teaching. In the chapters that follow, I will present rabbinic midrashim. Because of the unfamiliar character of this literature, I will take the time to explain how to read such selections, as well as to explicate the value-concepts which inform them. The biblical and rabbinic texts will be indicated by the use of a bullet and the explication will be indicated by the notation, COMMENT:. There are many, many more midrashim which I could use; I have scattered some of them at the end of earlier chapters. Readers are welcome to contact me if they do not understand the texts I present, or if they have trouble understanding the additional texts I have included in other places in this book.

As noted above,[16] I prefer to do my own translation of classical biblical and rabbinic texts even when they are cited in other articles and books. In these translations, I use inclusive language for humans because I believe it to be the sense of the text, though classic Jewish sources never use inclusive language because biblical and rabbinic Hebrew neither allow for, nor deem it necessary, to use inclusive forms. I also usually use inclusive language when writing about God. However, it is my custom to use gendered language when citing texts which refer to God because, for me, God is experienced as male, though I respect and honor others who perceive and relate to God in other ways.[17] In citing current articles, I have, except where indicated, left gendered language.

The further we get from the shoah, the easier it is to forget. I have, therefore, returned to the custom of introducing counter-texts at the end of each chapter.

Counter-text[18]

It was Pesach. Every man, woman and child were [sic] taken into the ghetto. We had about a dozen SS guards. A lot of people don't understand how a dozen or two dozen SS men can guard 1,000 or 1,500 in the ghetto. The way they did it was to open fire, kill a few people and then say, "The first one to move, I'll blow your head off." Do you think you would move? You think you would be a hero? You're right, no one would move. You might plot something, that you want to get him; but, you ain't going to move. That's exactly what happened to us. They came in with machine guns and hand grenades. They didn't just stroke us on the back and say, "Nice boy, nice boy. Now take it easy." Bull! He took a whip and whipped you real good and took a brick and split your head open just to show the other people what he's going to do in case you open your mouth. Those SS men were bent on killing you and torturing you, and there was nothing you could do.

We had no shelters and it was very cold. The typical day in our area in the winter was ten to fifteen degrees below zero with snow up to your chest. We cleared out the ovens where the bricks were made and we crammed four or five families in there; maybe forty to fifty people. We didn't care how filthy it was; at least it was covering us from the snow and ice.

They did not give us any food or water; absolutely nothing. They had us throw bricks to each other to catch and throw to the next person. By the time we loaded up the end of the camp, they started the process to get the bricks back all over again. By the end of the day there was no skin left on our hands. The ghetto was really nothing but a temporary station on the road to death. They were so devious. They promised us that they would relocate us to a decent place of work and living quarters away from the local "Jew-hating anti-Semites."

10

Some Jewish Prosocial Value-Concepts

In contemporary English, the word "norm" has two meanings. One is descriptive and refers to patterns that are widely present; hence, "normal." The other refers to guidelines for behavior, desiderata of action; hence, "normative." The former constitutes the "is"; the latter comprises the "ought." In what follows, I shall use "norm / normative" in the sense of guideline or desideratum and, sometimes, will use "moral norms" to indicate that.

Halakha is the all-encompassing mode of Jewish self-articulation in rabbinic tradition. It is the system of rules, practices, and norms which expresses and shapes rabbinic Jewish identity. Coming from the Hebrew root "to go," halakha is the Jewish "way."

There are two senses to the word halakha. In its technical sense, halakha is law, that is, a system of rules for resolving conflicts among people using a tradition and a duly instantiated authority which has powers of enforcement. In its larger sense, however, halakha is a set of attitudinal and behavioral norms, embodied in stories, exegesis, and moral exhortation. All laws are informed by norms and such norms are clearly part of the halakha. However, some of the moral norms of the halakha, often contained in literature known as "aggada," are not legally binding and, hence, are not part of halakha in its technical sense but are very much a part of halakha in its larger sense. Functionally, halakha-as-norm influences and shapes halakha-as-law, and vice-versa. Halakha, in its fullest meaning, is a combination of law and moral norm. Morality and law are not separate in rabbinic Judaism; they are under one rubric called halakha. Together they articulate Jewish identity and God's will for humankind.[1]

Halakha, in both its senses, is informed by, and undergirded with, value-concepts. "Value-concepts"[2] are terms which embody both ideas and values; they contain conceptual, as well as normative, content. Value-concepts are a fusion of our moral experience and our need to abstract and think about that experience. They are a function of the deep interrelationship between cognition and moral judgment, as well as of the need to communicate moral values. "The component 'concepts' tells that the values referred to are communicable ideas, that is, ideas that may be shared by the group as a whole; whilst the component 'value' tells that these ideas are nevertheless also, in a degree, personal and subjective, and that they are ideas held warmly."[3] As such, value-concepts inform our thinking and our action in all situations, especially those involving intelligent moral judgment. There are four central value-concepts which inform halakha, the Jewish "way," in matters of prosocial attitudes and behaviors.[4]

Tselem (Image)

Tselem[5] means "image" and, more specifically, it is shorthand for the image of God in which humanity is created.[6] It is the value-concept which underlies the theological doctrine of *imitatio Dei,* that one should imitate God's ways, that one should try to be God-like. In rabbinic culture, this value-concept underlies many teachings:

> • "This is my God and I shall beautify Him . . ." (Ex. 15:2). How can a person "beautify" God? . . . Abba Shaul says: Be like Him. As He is merciful and gracious, so shall you be merciful and gracious.[7]

COMMENT: This midrash starts with a verse, raises a question, and then proposes several answers, only one of which is given here. This is one of the major literary forms for midrash: the "verse-problem-solution" form. Here, the verse is taken from the triumphant song of Moses after the crossing of the Red Sea. The problem is clear: How can the verse mean what it says, that one can actually "beautify," or for that matter "praise" or "extol," God? God is transcendent, beyond human beautification and praise. The answer of Abba Shaul is that we beautify God by imitating God, that we praise God by acting in ways that God acts. Abba Shaul teaches that we fulfill the demand of the verse to beautify God by acting in the image of God in which humanity was created.

> • Rabbi Akiva says: Whoever spills blood [that is, kills someone], it is as if he or she had annihilated the likeness (Heb., *demut*), as it says, "He who spills the blood of a person, by a person shall his blood be shed, for He made humanity in the image of God" (Gen. 9:6).[8]

COMMENT: This midrash starts with a moral and legal norm and then cites a verse as a prooftext.[9] This literary form is also one of the major literary forms for midrash: the "principle-prooftext" form. Here, Rabbi Akiva establishes that killing (purposeful, as well as accidental) is not only a crime punishable by the law but a violation of the moral order of the universe. He formulates this by saying that whoever kills another human being diminishes the likeness and image of God in the universe, alluding to Gen. 1:26–27, "Let us make humanity in our image, according to our likeness." As a prooftext, however, he cites the biblical text which links the killing of humans to the image (Gen. 9:6).[10]

• Rabbi Elazar ben Azaria says: Whoever does not attempt to be fruitful and multiply, it is as if he had spilled blood and annihilated the likeness, as it says: "He who spills the blood of a person, by a person shall his blood be shed for He made humanity in the image of God. Be fruitful and multiply . . ." (Gen. 9:6–7).[11]

COMMENT: This midrash follows the principle-prooftext form and uses the same verse cited above. Here, Rabbi Elazar draws the conclusion that whoever refuses to reproduce has in effect "killed" the unborn. He does this by reading Genesis 9:6 in the context of the next verse which deals with the divine command to reproduce. It is the juxtaposition of the injunction against killing, with its reference to image, to the command to reproduce that leads him to his conclusion.

• Rabbi Ḥiyya son of Rabbi Medafti taught: "The people stood over Moses from morning to night [as he judged them]" (Ex. 18:13)? Is it possible that Moses sat and judged all day long? What would happen to his study of Torah?! Rather, this teaches that every judge who issues a judgment which is thoroughly true, even only once, Scripture considers him as if he had become a partner to the Holy One, blessed be He, in the work of creation, for here it says "from morning to evening" and there it says (Gen. 1:5, etc.) "and there was evening and there was morning."[12]

COMMENT: A verse-problem-solution form. Here, the verse from Exodus about Moses judging the people all day is cited. The problem is that Moses could not possibly judge the people all day because then he would not be able to study Torah, a problem common to all rabbinic judges. The solution is to cite another verse, from Genesis 1:5, which shows that God, too, worked all day in creating the world. Using the common phrase "morning-day," even though they are reversed, Rabbi Ḥiyya draws a moral conclusion that any rabbinic judge, including Moses, acts in the image of God when he reaches a thoroughly true judicial decision, which would, to be sure, imply study. Such a judge becomes like God, a partner in bringing moral order to the universe.

• Rabbi Shmuel bar Naḥmani said in the name of Rabbi Yoḥanan: Every judge who issues a judgment which is thoroughly true, causes the presence of God to dwell in Israel . . . and every judge who does not issue a judgment which is thoroughly true, causes the presence of God to depart from Israel.[13]

COMMENT: This is an expansion of the above; it is rooted in a midrash on other verses (not quoted).

In each of the sources cited above, the value-concept of *tselem* (image) is present. It informs and generates value and conceptuality for the exegesis of the passages in question, for the legal principles enunciated, and for the moral norms that educate society and inform the law. *Tselem* is, however, not the only value-concept present. The following are easy to discern: *rahamim* (mercy) in the first source; *midah keneged midah* (measure for measure) in the second and third texts; *peru urevu* (be fruitful and multiply) in the third; and *din* (law) and *Shekhina* (God's felt presence) in the fourth and fifth.[14]

Brit (Covenant)

Brit is another key value-concept underlying halakha. The word means "covenant" and, with that term, the rabbinic tradition teaches that God, having created the world and humanity, entered into an agreement with God's creation. In this agreement, God reveals God's will and gives humans their (free) will. The will of each is sovereign and cannot be violated by the other. Still, in determining what God's will is, humanity and God are in dialogue, each able to make demands, to ask for clarification, to remonstrate, even to protest. God, in rabbinic theology, submits God's revealed will (the Torah) to the judgment of humanity, within certain limitations, and humanity submits its will to God, within certain limitations. As Falk has noted:[15]

> From the outset, there are two foundations which give the Torah authority, one divine and one human. On one side, the command of God is the classic expression of a heteronomous legal norm but, on the other side, the covenant at Sinai is described as a voluntary autonomous engagement. . . . "We will do and we will obey. . . ." "The Holy One, blessed be He, held Mt. Sinai over them as a dome and said to them, 'If you accept the Torah, fine; if not, here shall be your grave. . . .'"[16] On one side stand "the righteous acts of God" as a summary of the acts of God according to the covenant and, on the other side stand "the righteous acts of Israel" according to the very same covenant. . . . "Accepting the yoke of the kingdom of God . . ." In one sense, there is a "yoke" here, indicating the heteronomous nature of the mitsvot but, together with it, there is an "accepting" which is the principle of human will. . . . Autonomy, therefore, is not the opposite of heteronomy; it is its completion.

In the words of the midrash:

> • On that day Rabbi Eliezer answered all possible questions but the sages did not accept his answers. He said to them, "If the law is according to me, let this carob tree prove it." The carob tree, then, was uprooted and re-

planted one hundred measures away. Some say 400 measures. They said to him, "One cannot bring proof from a carob tree."

He replied to them, "If the law is according to me, let this stream of water prove it." The stream of water, then, was moved and flowed behind them. They said to him, "One cannot bring proof from a stream of water."

He replied to them, "If the law is according to me, let the walls of this study hall prove it." The walls of the study hall, then, leaned and were about to fall. Rabbi Joshua rebuked the walls saying, "If scholar-students[17] (*talmidei ḥakhamim*) are arguing with one another on a matter of law, what is your place here?" So, the walls did not fall because of the dignity of Rabbi Joshua and they did not straighten up because of the dignity of Rabbi Eliezer. They remained leaning.

Rabbi Eliezer spoke to the sages yet again, "If the law is according to me, let heaven prove it." A voice, then, came out of heaven and said, "Why are you arguing with Rabbi Eliezer for the law is according to him in all matters?" Then, Rabbi Joshua stood up and said, "'It is not in heaven' (Dt. 30:12). What does it mean to say that the Torah is not in heaven? Rabbi Jeremiah taught that [it means] that the Torah has already been given on Mt. Sinai. We, therefore, do not take note of the voice from heaven for You have already written in the Torah on Sinai, 'one must turn with the majority to vote'" (Ex. 23:2).

Rabbi Nathan found Elijah and said to him, "What was the Holy One, blessed be He, doing at that time?" He said to him, "He smiled and said, 'My children have had the better of Me. My children have had the better of Me.'"[18]

COMMENT: This is yet another literary form, the "narrative" form. The point in this widely-cited text is that miracles, even a voice from heaven, are rejected in determining the law. The value-concept of *brit* clearly gives the law into the hands of the sages. There is, here, an associated value-concept[19] called *Talmud Torah* (the study of Torah); it works hand-in-hand with *brit*.

• "It is time to act for God, for they have violated your Torah" (Ps. 119:126). [Concerning this] they said, "Better to uproot the Torah than that the Torah should be forgotten in Israel."[20]

COMMENT: A verse-problem-solution form, though the problem is not explicitly stated. The question from the verse is, How can one act for God and yet violate the Torah? The answer is that the sages do indeed have such judicial authority, within *brit*, for use in extreme circumstances. This fulfills the meaning of the verse. Falk, citing this passage, notes that these are "values *contra legem*, against the letter of the law" which are, nonetheless, part of the law.[21]

The covenantal nature of obligation in Jewish thought and practice does not, however, exclude the possibility of legitimate difference of opinion. In fact, there are whole areas of the law that are specifically left open for the discretion of the rabbinic judge and of the individual.[22] Even in serious matters, pluralism within *brit* was acknowledged as logically, textually, and socially necessary. This idea is embodied in the phrase *'elu ve-'elu divrei 'elohim hayyim* (these and those are the words of the living God).

> • Shmuel said, "For three years the school of Shammai and the school of Hillel sat and disagreed. These said, 'The halakha is according to us' and those said, 'The halakha is according to us.' Then, a heavenly voice came forth and said, 'These and those are the words of the living God. . . .'"[23]

COMMENT: A narrative form. The point is that even the most distinguished and revered schools (Hillel and Shammai preceded Shmuel by two hundred years and their schools were very old and held in high honor) disagreed, but always within *brit*.

> • "Masters of gatherings" (Eccl. 12:11)—These are the student-sages[24] who sit in groups and occupy themselves with Torah. Some declare impure while others declare pure, some forbid while others permit, some render unfit while others render fit. Lest someone should say, "How, then, can I learn Torah," Scripture says, "They were given from one shepherd" (same verse)—one God gave them, one Sustainer said them, [they come] from the mouth of the Lord of all creation, blessed be He, as it says, "God spoke all these words" (Ex. 20:1). You, too, therefore, make your ear a funnel and acquire a heart that knows to listen to the words of those who declare impure and to those who declare pure, to those who forbid and to those who permit, and to those who render unfit and to those who render fit.[25]

COMMENT: The disjunction between the two clauses of the verse from Ecclesiastes, together with the omnipresent problem of legitimate disagreement among legitimate authorities, gave rise to the principle and value-concept of *'elu ve-'elu divrei 'elohim hayyim* (these and those are the words of the living God) even though it is not present textually.

> • Even if one's words are directed against faith and religion, do not tell a person not to speak and suppress his or her words. Otherwise there will be no clarification in religious matters. On the contrary, one should tell a person to express whatever she or he wants . . . and he or she should never claim that she or he would have said more, had he or she been given the opportunity. . . . Thus, my opinion is contrary to what some people think.

They think that when it is forbidden to speak against religion, religion is strengthened; but it is not so. The elimination of the opinions of those who are opposed to religion undermines religion and weakens it.[26]

The issue is well summarized by Y. M. Epstein:[27]

Every dispute among the *Tannaim,* the *Amoraim,* the *Geonim* and the *Poskim* in pursuit of true understanding constitutes the word of the living God and each has a place in the *halakhah.* That is indeed the glory of our holy and immaculate *Torah.* The whole *Torah* is called a song and it is the glory of the song that its different sounds are various but harmonious.

Many rabbinic texts on *brit* contain another associated value-concept called *mitsva.* This value-concept expresses, first, the sense that what one is asked to do is actually a command from God. It is not an act based in natural or moral reason. Nor is it an act based on culture and custom. Certainly, it is not an act rooted in human impulse and feeling. Rather, a *mistva* is a mandate from God, a commandment. The value-concept of *mitsva* in this sense is most easily seen in those commandments that seem to have no inner logical sense:[28]

- He said to them, "By your lives! The dead do not render [other things] impure nor does the red heifer or the water render [them] pure. Rather, the Holy One, blessed be He, has said, 'I have issued an edict and made a decree, and you are not permitted to transgress my edict, as it says, "This is the edict of the Torah"'" (Nu. 19:1).[29]

COMMENT: In biblical and rabbinic law, a dead body is ritually impure. Anything that comes in contact with it also becomes impure. This impurity, however, may be removed by sacrificing a red heifer, preparing it properly, and sprinkling the impure person or object with a mixture of ashes from the heifer and water (Nu. 19). Here, the authority in the text has been asked about this nonrational procedure. He gave an answer which did not satisfy his students and, in the ensuing discussion, he expanded his answer, teaching that God's *brit* includes those demands made of us that seem completely counterintuitive. Such demands are still *mitsva,* that is, part of *brit.*

- The clothes of everyone who deals with the red heifer are rendered impure but the [ashes of] the red heifer render impure clothes pure. Rather, the Holy One, blessed be He, has said, "I have issued an edict and made a decree, and you are not permitted to transgress my edict."[30]

COMMENT: This strange phenomenon—that the person who prepares the purifying ashes of the red heifer, together with his clothes, is rendered impure by the very act of preparing the means of purification—is scriptural (Nu. 19). Here, the text leaves the issue of counterintuitivity implied and goes directly to the answer, again stressing that the counterintuitive is included within *mitsva* and *brit*.

Mitsva, in the sense of commandedness, however, is not limited to "non-rational" mitsvot.

> • Rabbi Elazar ben Azaria said, "From whence do we know that a person should never say, 'I don't [even] want to wear garments made of wool and linen [which are forbidden],' 'I don't [even] want to eat the meat of a pig [which is forbidden],' 'I don't [even] want to have forbidden sexual intercourse'? Rather, one should say, 'I [really] want to do [such things], but what can I do? My Father in heaven has decreed [them forbidden] for me!' Therefore, the Torah says, 'I have set you apart from the nations to be Mine' (Lev. 20:26)—from which [one learns that] one must separate oneself from sin and accept the yoke of heaven."[31]

COMMENT: A principle-prooftext form, though the principle is phrased as a question. Here, the situations implied are familiar to everyone: On the one hand, one can be tempted to boast of one's piety and to brag that one is never tempted by certain sins; this is surely not modest and could encourage over-confidence about one's piety. On the other hand, one can wish devoutly to sin and be genuinely tempted, or at least fully embarrassed that one is tempted; this is surely dangerous, for one might give in to such temptation. The authority in the text, therefore, interprets the verse about God having set us aside to be God's people to teach a general moral norm—that one must be ready to separate oneself from sin, not on the basis of virtue but on the basis of obedience to God's will for separateness for God's creatures. Note the presence of the value-concepts of *malkhut shamayim* (the kingdom of heaven) and *het'* (sin), together with *mitsva* and *brit*.

> • A person should never intend to do anything except by the decree of God, as it says, "Many are the thoughts in the heart of a person but the advice of the Lord is that which lasts" (Prov. 19:21).[32]

COMMENT: A principle-prooftext form. Note that this is a moral norm, not a specific legal standard of behavior. Nonetheless, it can be invoked as a value-concept at any time.

The second sense of *mitsva* is that what one is asked to do is something one ought to do even if it is not obligatory.

> • It is the nature of sheep to [be domesticated and] graze, but antelopes dwell in the desert and it is not their nature to enter places of human dwell-

ing. This antelope, however, has entered and dwelled with us. Shall we not be grateful to it that it left the great open desert, the place where antelopes and wild rams graze, and left them to come to us? For this, we must be grateful. So the Holy One, blessed be He, said, "I must be grateful to the convert for he or she has left her or his family and parental house and has come to dwell with Me. Therefore, I command (Heb., *metsave*) you, 'You shall love the convert' (Dt. 10:19) and 'You shall not oppress the convert'" (Ex. 22:20). Therefore, too, it is written, "The Lord watches over converts" (Ps. 146:9).[33]

COMMENT: The word *ger,* which in biblical Hebrew means "stranger," very often has the meaning in rabbinic Hebrew of "convert." Here, the text begins with a metaphor (an implied *mashal*) drawn from nature, proceeds to a moral norm stated as the speech of God, and concludes with the verses which support (or, read in reverse, are the source of) the norm. Two of the verses are legal and one is a moral maxim; note that the genres are mixed to establish the norm. In this case, the value-concept of *mitsva* is very close to the value-concept of *middat ḥasidut* (the standard of the pious). In this sense, *mitsva* is used in popular contemporary Jewish discourse as in "it's a *mitsva* to do such-and-such," e.g., to visit the sick, to telephone a parent, to help someone in need, etc.

In each of the sources cited above, the value-concept of *brit* (covenant) is present. It informs and generates the value and conceptuality for the exegesis of the verses in question, for the legal principles enunciated, and for the moral norms which educate society and inform the law. *Brit,* however, is not the only value-concept present. The following are also active: *talmud Torah* (study of Torah), *'elu ve-'elu divrei 'elohim ḥayyim* (these and those are the words of the living God), *mitsva* (commandedness, oughtness), *malkhut shamayim* (the kingdom of God), and *middat ḥasidut* (the standard of the pious). There are others, too.

Tsedek (Justice)

Tsedek (justice) is another key value-concept underlying halakha. Falk has put it very well:[34] "Just as the religious mystic relies on direct experience and on intuition in order to receive illumination, so does the philospher yield to his feeling of truth, and the lawyer fulfills his task by following his passion for justice and order. . . . A need for *immediate* perception of justice seems, indeed, to be required. . . . If the idea of *justice* is to rule in the divine as well as in the human sphere, divine law must be understood as a system of layers, the lower layer being controlled by a higher one representing justice." The texts embodying this sense for justice are legion.

In the words of Scripture itself:

• Do not give a hand to a wicked person to be a false witness. Do not be after the majority to do evil. Do not respond to a dispute by tending toward the majority to cause others to tend [that way]. Do not give honor to the poor in his or her dispute. . . . Do not distort judgment in the dispute of the poor. Stay away from false words. Do not kill the innocent and the righteous for I will not justify the wicked (Ex. 23:1–7).
• Do not do evil with the law. Do not forgive the poor. Do not give honor to important people. Judge your friend in justice (Lev. 19:15).

In the words of the midrash:

• "Do not put a stumbling block before the blind" (*lifne 'iver lo titen mikhshol*) (Lev. 19:24). To one who is blind in any matter do not give advice that is not fitting. Do not say, "Sell me your field for a donkey" for you are going around him when taking it from him.[35]

COMMENT: A verse-problem-solution form with the problem not stated explicitly. The implied question here is, Can the verse be limited to the specific case stated in Scripture? Obviously not, for there are many "blind" people. Hence, the moral norm and legal rule that one may not mislead anyone who is unfamiliar with the subject matter at hand. One may not even mislead someone intellectually. So strong is this norm that the phrase *lifne 'iver lo titen mikhshol* (Do not put a stumbling block before the blind) became a major justice principle, a value-concept that is a phrase, and is often invoked.

• He [God] first says that you should obey His laws and precepts that He commanded you, and immediately afterward He says that even in regard to matters as to which He did not command you, you should be scrupulous to do what is right and good in His eyes (*ve-'asita ha-tov veha-yashar be-'einei Hashem*) [Dt. 6:17–18; see also Dt. 12:28] because He loves goodness and equity. This is a matter of great consequence. Inasmuch as it is impossible for the Torah to mention explicitly all the ways in which people relate to their neighbors and fellows and to cover all the types of business transactions and all the things necessary for the proper ordering of society and government, it mentioned a great many such things . . . and then stated generally that in all things one should do what is right and good. . . . A person who acts according to the technical and formal sense of the Torah's laws, that is, who carefully follows only the explicit rules but not those implicit from the general spirit of the text, is a "scoundrel within the bounds of the Torah" (*naval bi-reshut ha-Torah*). Therefore, the Torah's method is to particularize and generalize; for after stating the specifics of the law . . . it states in general terms "Do what is right and good," in order to establish an affirmative commandment to behave with uprightness and fairness. . . .[36]

COMMENT: The prominent medieval biblical commentator, Naḥmanides, addresses here the tension between the long list of specific laws in the tradition and the sheer variety of life that must perforce bring up new situations. In his commentary to Deuteronomy 6:17–18, Naḥmanides invokes the biblical phrase ve-'asita ha-tov veha-yashar be-'einei Hashem (You shall do what is right and good in His eyes) to establish the general principle and moral norm that one is also obligated by law to behave with uprightness and fairness, even when the law or the situation is vague. This phrase itself became a major justice principle, a value-concept that is a phrase, and is often invoked. Elon cites another medieval commentator who proposes that we must be righteous and straight because God is "righteous and straight" (Dt. 32:4).[37] Note the overlapping of the value-concepts tselem and tsedek in this version.

Using these and other verses, the rabbis derived an etiquette for courts meant to ensure just consideration for everyone:

• It is a positive commandment for a judge to judge justly as it says, "Judge your friend in justice" (Lev. 19:15). What is just court procedure? It is the equal treatment of the parties in all matters. One may not speak his full mind while the other is told, "Keep it short." The judge may not be pleasant with one, speaking softly to one, while being unpleasant with the other, speaking harshly to that person.

If there are two parties, one dressed expensively and the other poorly, the judge must say to the wealthier one, "Either clothe the other as you dress before you come into court, or you dress as he or she dresses." This is so that they be equal; then, they may come before the court.

One may not sit while the other stands, rather, both should stand. If the court wishes, it may seat them both but one may not sit higher than the other but next to one another.[38]

In an interesting contemporary rereading of "Do not give honor to the poor in his or her dispute" (Ex. 23:3) and "Do not forgive the poor" (Lev. 19:15), Israeli Supreme Court Justice Cohn formulates his own norm:[39]

I fully confess, however, that I shall neither rest nor remain silent in trying to find for the poor, the oppressed and the miserable some legal right, and I shall not believe those who tell me that my efforts will be in vain. If counsel for the respondent expects an explicit verse to warn me also of that, here it is: "How long will ye judge unjustly and respect the person of the wicked? Judge the poor and the fatherless, do justice to the afflicted and the destitute, rescue the poor and needy, deliver them out of the hands of the wicked" (Ps. 82:2–4).

All these laws and moral norms are intended to ensure that justice be done. They embody and shape the value-concept of *tsedek*. They are part of halakha-as-law and halakha-as-norm. With and without formal sanction, they exert a formidable moral weight. Note, too, that a value-concept is sometimes expressed as a law; sometimes as a catchword, phrase, or verse that becomes a principle; and sometimes as a general norm or teaching. This, too, is part of the strength of value-concepts. While *tsedek* is the central value-concept here, others are also active: *patur mi-dinei adam ve-ḥayav be-dinei shamayim* (one is exempt from human law but liable by divine law),[40] *latse't yedei shamayim* (fulfillment of duty in the sight of heaven),[41] *'ein ruaḥ ḥakhamim noḥa hemenu* (the sages are displeased with him or her),[42] and *tom lev* (purity of heart).[43] There are, of course, many more.

Ḥasidut / Ḥesed (Caring)

Ḥasidut / ḥesed (adjective *hasid*) is another key value-concept of halakha. The word has a complicated history. In biblical Hebrew, *ḥesed* means "covenantal love"; we ask God to act out of God's love which is rooted in the fundamental loyalty of the covenant.[44] In the Middle Ages, it means "grace," "unmerited love."[45] In usual rabbinic Hebrew, however, the root signifies "piety," "super-erogatory action," and sometimes "special mercy." In the context of this book, it is best to translate it as "caring," which is quite close to the rabbinic usage. The texts are legion.

• Just as the Holy One, blessed be He, is caring (Heb., *ḥasid*) as it says, "and He is caring in all His deeds" (Ps. 145:17) for He acts within the line of the law, so shall you be caring.[46]

COMMENT: This text could also have been cited above under the value-concept *tselem*. It is a good example of the same text embodying more than one value-concept, for it surely belongs in both categories, *tselem* and *ḥasidut*. (On acting "within the line of the law," see below.)

• The *hasidim rishonim* (former pious ones) used to put their thorns and glass fragments [that is, destructive garbage] in the ground three hand-breadths deep so that it would not interfere with the plow.[47]

COMMENT: A very early teaching on caring for the environment as a value though, in rabbinic culture, this teaching is set in a theology of "you shall not [wantonly] destroy" (Dt. 20:19–20)[48] and within the value-concept of *middat ḥasidut* (the standard of the pious).

- He says to others, "Come and save for yourselves" [and they may]. But, if they are clever, they settle accounts with him after Shabbat. . . . "Settle accounts"?! What are they doing? They have taken from ownerless property! Rav Ḥisda said, "This is *middat ḥasidut* (the standard of the pious)."[49]

COMMENT: A person can allow others to salvage objects from a burning house because those who do this are taking *hefker* (ownerless property); that is, since the owner knows his goods will burn anyway, it is as if he had declared them ownerless. Anyone taking such an object may keep it. If, however, one returns such an object to the owner after Shabbat, it is, according to one authority, an example of supererogatory behavior, of *middat ḥasidut* (the standard of the pious).[50]

- "A householder who was traveling and [was needy and] had to take of the poor-taxes may take and, when he or she returns [and has money], she or he must pay," so says Rabbi Eliezer. Rav Ḥisda said, "This is a case of *middat ḥasidut* (the standard of the pious)." Rava argued: "The text continues and says, 'he or she shall pay' and you argue that this is *middat ḥasidut*?! Furthermore, Rabbi Eliezer says . . . The reason is that if he or she were poor [she or he does not pay] but, if he or she is [really] wealthy, she or he must pay."[51]

COMMENT: A wealthy person who is on a trip and runs out of money and, hence, is poor may take of the tithes for the poor and other special poor-taxes to feed oneself. Rav Ḥisda maintains that, since the person was poor at the time she or he took from these funds, he or she is not obligated to repay and, if she or he repaid what had been taken upon reaching home, this is *middat ḥasidut* (the standard of the pious). The talmudic discussion goes on to refine the position: that only if the householder was poor even at home is such an act *middat ḥasidut,* a supererogatory act; but, if the person is wealthy at home, he or she is actually obligated to pay.

- Great is the dignity of the creatures (Heb., *kevod ha-beriyot*) for it takes precedence over [even] a negative commandment of the Torah.[52]

COMMENT: The commandments which are stated directly in the Torah, positive and negative, stand highest in the hierarchy of rabbinic law and practice. There are, however, exceptions. The most famous is the rule that saving a human life takes precedence over observance of the Sabbath or even Yom

Kippur. Thus, one **must** ride on Shabbat to take a person to the hospital if hospitalization is the only way to save that person's life. Thus, too, a person **must** eat on Yom Kippur if her or his life is in danger should he or she not eat. The quotation cited here teaches the general rule that the dignity of the elderly and the sages also takes precedence over certain positive commandments and even over certain of the more-strictly observed negative commandments. Thus, an elderly or distinguished person need not lift heavy burdens, etc. The phrase, *kevod ha-beriyot,* became a general caring principle and it is invoked in varying contexts. It is an associated value-concept to *tsedek, hasidut,* and *tselem.* This overlapping and interweaving of value-concepts is part of the strength of rabbinic Judaism.

> • Rav Nahman said in the name of Rabba bar Avuha, "'You shall love your other as yourself' (Lev. 19:18)—choose for him or her a beautiful death." [53]

COMMENT: In the ancient world, the methods of capital punishment were extremely cruel. Since the Bible requires capital punishment under certain conditions, the rabbis decided that one should choose the quickest and least painful ("beautiful") death for a condemned person. This rule embodies the *hesed* principle. I do not know whether the American provision prohibiting "cruel and unusual punishment" is connected to this exegesis of this famous biblical passage.

One of the ways that the value-concept *hasidut* / *hesed* expresses itself is in a phrase that itself became a value-concept and teaching, *lifnim mi-shurat ha-din,* variously translated as "within the line of the law" or "on the inside of the line of the law." It means "acting more generously than the law requires" [54] and embodies the value-concept of *hasidut* / *hesed.* [55]

> • If one shows a coin to a moneychanger [to determine the quality of the coin and the moneychanger rules that it is good] but it turns out to be bad, one authority says that a professional moneychanger is obligated to pay and an amateur is not, while another authority says that both the professional and the amateur moneychanger are obligated to pay. . . . Rabbi Hiyya [who was himself a moneychanger paid because] he acted *lifnim mi-shurat ha-din,* within the line of the law, as Rabbi Joseph had taught [exegeting Ex. 18:20]: "You shall show them"—the source of their livelihood; "the way"—deeds of lovingkindness; "they must walk"—the visitation of the sick; "in"—the burial of the dead; "and the work"—the *din;* "which they must do"—that which is *lifnim mi-shurat ha-din.* [56]

COMMENT: The issue is professional responsibility: Are moneychangers responsible, indeed liable, for opinions they render? One authority rules that liability is a function of knowledgeability; the other rules that ignorance is no excuse. Rabbi Ḥiyya seems to hold the opinion that all moneychangers are liable in case of error and they must make good when they are wrong. Experts, however, are exempt from this so as to ease the business of moneychanging. In his own case Rabbi Ḥiyya, who was an expert, nonetheless made good on an error acting *lifnim mi-shurat ha-din* on the basis of Rabbi Joseph's exegesis of Exodus 18:20. The exegesis, in classic midrashic style, takes one verse, splits it into its component phrases, and then uses each phrase to add on a new teaching. Here, the various phrases are signaled by quotation marks and the teachings drawn from them by midrash follow the dash.[57]

- *Lifnim mi-shurat ha-din*—This the case of the father of Shmuel who found donkeys in the desert and returned them after twelve months.[58]

COMMENT: Everyone is obligated by biblical law to care for a lost animal which has been found until the owner can reclaim it (Ex. 23:4). However, no one is obligated to bear the maintenance costs for a lost animal for more than twelve months. The father of Shmuel, however, continued to maintain a lost animal after twelve months, thus acting *lifnim mi-shurat ha-din* (within the line of the law).[59]

- It was taught: Rabbi Ishmael ben Elisha said: "I once entered into the innermost part [of the temple] to offer incense and saw Akatriel Yah, the lord of hosts, who was seated upon a high and exalted throne. He said to me, 'Ishmael, my son, bless me.' I replied, 'May it be Your will that your mercy suppress Your anger. May your mercy prevail over Your other attributes so that you may deal with Your children according to the attribute of mercy. May you enter *lifnim mi-shurat ha-din* on their behalf.' He, then, nodded to me with his head."[60]

COMMENT: This strange narrative reports an event that once happened to Rabbi Ishmael son of Elisha who was himself a rabbi and a priest. Rabbi Ishmael entered the innermost part of the temple and had a vision of Akatriel Yah, lord of hosts. Some scholars, basing themselves on Rabbi Ishmael's prayer that God have mercy on Israel, a prayer addressed properly only to God, think that Rabbi Ishmael saw a manifestation of God. Other scholars, identifying the figure with others with similar names, think that he saw a vision of an angel. To capture the ambivalence of the text, I have alternated capital letters for pronouns referring to the figure.[61] In any case, this text is an example of how even God must act *lifnim mi-shurat ha-din*.[62]

In sum: *lifnim mi-shurat ha-din* is a case "where that [the act performed] would produce a result more beneficial to the other party . . . produces a more equitable result [than the law alone]."⁶³ Interestingly, the phrase of *lifnim mi-shurat ha-din* became so rooted in halakha that, although such an obligation is not enforceable, it was given the force of positive law in the Middle Ages: "[W]e too enforce the perfomance of an obligation that is greater than what the law strictly requires if it is within the individual's capacity, i.e., if he is wealthy. . . . It is the practice of all Jewish communities to compel a rich man to pay where it is fair and fitting to do so, even though he is exempt from any positive liability."⁶⁴

Gemilut ḥasadim (the doing of good deeds) is also an associated value-concept to *ḥasidut / ḥesed*. It always has concrete acts of *ḥesed* at its core. The following passages speak for themselves as they define acts of *gemilut ḥasadim*.

• Rabbi Ḥama bar Ḥanina taught: "You shall follow the Lord your God" (Dt. 13:5). Is it possible for a person to "follow the Lord"? Does it not say, "For the Lord your God is a consuming fire" (Dt. 4:24)? Rather, follow the good qualities of the Holy One, blessed be He. Just as He clothes the naked, as it says, "The Lord God made clothes of leather for Adam and his wife and He put them on them" (Gen. 21), so should you clothe the naked. Just as He visits the sick, as it says, "The Lord appeared to him [Abraham, right after his circumcision] in Elonei Mamrei" (Gen. 18:1), so should you visit the sick. Just as He comforts the mourners, as it says, "After the death of Abraham, God blessed Isaac his son" (Gen. 25:11), so should you comfort the mourners. Just as He buries the dead, as it says, "And He buried him [Moses] in the valley" (Dt. 34:6), so should you bury the dead.⁶⁵

COMMENT: This text lists: clothing the naked, visiting the sick, comforting the mourners, and burying the dead. The presence of the verses which show how God Godself does these acts makes the midrash very powerful. Note, too, that this text also embodies the value-concept of *tselem*.

• These are the things which have no limit [in their observance]:⁶⁶ leaving the corner of one's field for the poor, bringing the first fruits, pilgrimage on the holidays, *gemilut ḥasadim* (doing good deeds), and study of Torah. These are the things which bear fruits in this world but whose main reward is reserved for the world-to-come: honoring one's parents, *gemilut ḥasadim* (doing good deeds), and bringing peace between others, but study of the Torah is the greatest of all.⁶⁷

COMMENT: The deeds associated with *gemilut ḥasadim* help define the category, as well as expand the meaning of *ḥasidut / ḥesed*. Note that "honoring one's parents," "bringing peace between others," and even Torah study fall within this value-concept.

• In three ways, doing good deeds (*gemilut ḥasadim*) is greater than charity (*tsedeka*). Charity applies only to a person's financial resources, but doing good deeds applies to a person's resources and to his or her body. Charity can be given only to the poor, but doing good deeds can be done for the poor and for the rich. Charity can be given only to the living, but doing good deeds can be done for the living and for the dead.[68]

COMMENT: The commentators expand this text. To do good deeds "with one's resources" includes lending money and allowing someone to borrow utensils and cattle. To do good deeds "with one's body" means to eulogize the dead, to cause the bride and groom to rejoice, to accompany a visitor on the way, to visit the sick, and to comfort the mourner. To do good deeds "for the dead" includes burying the dead personally and not through hired persons, and doing this even if the deceased is not a relative.[69] *Gemilut ḥasadim* also includes speaking caringly to the poor, giving good advice, and praying for the sick and for those who are oppressed.[70]

• The world rests on three principles: Torah, worship, and the doing of good deeds.[71]

COMMENT: "Torah," here, means the study of Torah, as well as its practice. "Worship" meant, first, the sacrificial order and, later, liturgical prayer. "Doing of good deeds" is that which has been illustrated by all the examples cited above, as well as analogous actions.

Finally, in writing about the tradition of nonviolence in rabbinic Judaism, Kimelman has noted:[72] "We have seen that alongside the normative legal tradition there existed, in this period, a concomitant current which may be considered the standard of the *ḥasid*. The *ḥasid* was not one who stood on his legal rights, but always sought a solution which would find favor in the eyes of God. He was a self-sufferer who avoided the remotest possibility of doing harm. He sought good and shunned evil. Quick to forgive, he was pacific in human relationships, basing his life on what he had learned. Valuing life above possessions, he never arrogated anything to himself. Above all, he sought to prevent injury and acted lovingly to his fellowman."

In each of the sources cited above, the value-concept *ḥasidut / ḥesed* (caring) is present. It informs and generates the value and conceptuality for the exegesis of the verses, for the legal principles, and for the moral norms which lie behind those verses and principles. *Ḥasidut / ḥesed,* however, is not the only value-concept present. The following are also active: *tselem* (image), *middat ḥasidut* (the standard of the pious), *kevod ha-beriyot* (the dignity of the creatures), *lifnim mi-shurat ha-din* (within the line of the law), and *gemilut ḥasadim* (the doing of good deeds). There are others, too, such as *shalom* (peace) which, in the form of the phrase, *mipnei darkhei shalom* (for the sake of peace), became a major principle in halakha.[73]

*   *   *   *   *

These four key value-concepts—*tselem* (image), *brit* (covenant), *tsedek* (justice), and *hasidut / hesed* (caring)—together with their respective phrases, verses, principles, and associated value-concepts, are central to halakha, both in its technical legal sense and its larger normative sense. They express and embody the ideas and the values, the rules and the norms, of halakha. They also give it its enormous flexibility. As Kadushin has noted,[74] the plurality of value-concepts functioning in any given situation allows the practitioners of halakha freedom to legitimately choose one (or more) over others. Thus, certain personalities will tend toward *tsedek* and will choose to emphasize and interpret the halakha that way. Other personalities will tend toward *hasidut / hesed* and will choose to emphasize and interpret the halakha that way. Halakha, thus, becomes flexible enough to encompass practitioners and decisors of all types and tendencies. In the process, it also generates a plurality of opinions which balances the binding rabbinic consensus on most issues.

Counter-text [75]

Finally, the Russians came closer to liberating the camps; the German army was being defeated. Obviously, the Germans were very, very careful to make sure no evidence was left of their beastiality. They started evacuating the camp. When they marched us from Buna to Gleiwitz, by the time we got there only eight thousand people from between forty and sixty thousand humans remained alive. Anybody that slowed down was automatically shot. I remember one incident very clearly. One of the boys from near our town came over to me and he says, "Yankele, you know my family? Will you tell them, if you make it, that I really tried? I've given it everything, I can not go on anymore." So I just went down on my hands and knees and put him on my back. He started shuffling his feet in the deep snow and we just continued on. We kept on going. Anyone that slowed down, quite frankly, was automatically shot. They were then thrown onto the truck, until the trucks were filled up; then they dug ditches and they poured gasoline over the bodies and they burned them. All evidence of their beastiality was destroyed. . . .

They shoved and crammed a bunch of us into coal carrying railroad cars, without a top, to be taken to the interior of Germany. It was bitter cold. It was about December when they started taking us in. The temperature over there gets somewhere around ten below zero. This was an everyday occurrence. The weather itself was not the worst thing. I experienced the worst pain in the world. Real hunger pains, as painful as it is, or big cuts and bruises and broken bones, as painful as they are, are absolutely no comparison to thirst pain. Thirst pain is so bad and so terrible that there is no way that anybody will ever be able to describe it. I have seen people actually bite their skins open hoping to get a little blood on their lips. I have seen when it started snowing a little bit, people trying to jump up to catch a snowflake. I have seen people tear their guts out, with their own fingers, because they could not take the pain any longer. In that car, I even saw it when there was ice formed on the corner and somebody asked to be picked up so he could bite the ice, or lick the ice, only to have his lips frozen to it. When he came down, there was [sic] no lips. By the time we arrived in Buchenwald, which was probably eight days later, there was [sic] only eight, out of a hundred or more, of us to get off alive.

11

Stories of Resistance and Goodness

Prosocial action must be modeled and Jewish tradition has many stories of resistance to unjust authority as well as of spontaneous goodness. These stories, read and told from generation to generation, become models for prosocial attitudes and behaviors. In and of themselves, the stories are not enough, for prosocial orientation requires also living models, "text-persons" as Heschel used to call them, and it requires practice, a network of support, and so on. But stories set a tone for a culture; they form a model for society.

In Jewish tradition, the stories divided themselves into those which illustrate resistance and those which embody spontaneous kindness. The former can be divided into those which show resistance to human authority, public and personal, and those which demonstrate resistance to divine authority.

Resistance to Human Authority

There are many biblical stories of resistance to human authority, some of which were expanded upon by rabbinic tradition. Only a few examples can be given. Among the stories that show resistance to public authority (the king, the priest), four deserve mention:

> • And she [Rahab, the prostitute] took the two men [the spies sent by Joshua to Jericho] and hid them saying, "Yes, they came to me though I did not know where they were from and, when the gates were about to close, the men left and I do not know where they went. Pursue them quickly and you will catch them" (Josh. 2:4–5).

COMMENT: The setting is the conquest of Canaan by Joshua. He has sent spies to the city of Jericho and the king of Jericho is anxious to capture them. The spies find refuge in the home of Rahab, who is a prostitute whose home is in the very thick walls of the city. Rahab hides the spies and, when the guards of the king come to search for them, she lies and then sends the guards off on a wild-goose chase. Meanwhile, she lets the spies down a rope through her window and they escape. When Joshua comes and marches around Jericho blowing the rams horns, "the walls come tumbling down," the city is conquered and Rahab is saved. To appreciate Rahab's position, imagine the SS banging on her door in the Ukraine in 1943.

> • David took them [all the male descendants of Saul except Mefiboshet, the son of Jonathan] and gave them to the Gibeonites who impaled them on the mountain. . . . But Ritspa bat Aya took a sack and spread it out on the rock, from the beginning of the harvest until water fell from the heavens upon it, and she did not let the birds of the sky rest on them [the corpses] by day nor the beasts prey upon them by night. When David was told what Ritspa bat Aya, the concubine of Saul, had done . . . he gathered the bones of Saul and Jonathan . . . and the bones of those who had been impaled and buried them . . . and God turned to the land after this (II Sam. 21:1–14).[1]

COMMENT: The setting is the consolidation of David's rule as king. He has been chosen as king of the southern tribes but the family of the previous king, Saul, controls the northern tribes. The Gibeonites have a score to settle with the house of Saul and David agrees. In the midst of King David's political calculations, the concubine of Saul, a social nobody, defies everyone and asserts the moral rectitude of protecting the corpses of the royal family—a very courageous act for anyone, especially a concubine. This is, eventually, recognized by King David.

> • This is what the Lord showed me: He was standing on a wall [which had been] checked with a plumb line and He was holding a plumb line. The Lord asked me, "What do you see, Amos?" "A plumb line," I replied. The Lord declared: "I am going to apply a plumb line to My people, Israel; I will pardon them no more. The shrines of Isaac will be laid waste, the sanctuaries of Israel reduced to ruins, and I will turn upon the house of Jeroboam with the sword." Amaziah, the priest at Beth El, then sent word to Jeroboam, the King of Israel, saying, "Amos is conspiring against you within the house of Israel. The land cannot endure the things he is saying. . . ." Amazia then said to Amos, "Go, flee to the land of Judah, seer! Eat bread and prophesy there. And don't ever prophesy at Beth El again, for it is a king's sanctuary and a royal palace." And Amos answered Amaziah, "I am not a prophet, nor a son of a prophet, but a tender of animals and a trimmer of trees. It is the Lord Who . . ." (Amos 7:7–17).[2]

COMMENT: A plumb line is a string with a weight attached to it that, when suspended from the top of a wall, will show whether the wall is straight or not. Using this image, Amos, in God's Name, proclaims the kingdom of Jeroboam crooked and, hence, subject to God's judgment. Amos does this in a speech in the royal sanctuary of Beth El. Here, it is not the king who is defied but the king's royal priest. Imagine such a defiant speech in the cathedral of nazi Berlin.

> • The king of Egypt said to the Hebrew midwives—the name of one was Shifra and the name of the other was Pu'a—"When you birth the Hebrew women, look at the birthing stool. If the child is a boy, kill it but, if it is a girl, let it live." However, the midwives feared God and did not do as the king had commanded them and they let the boys live (Ex. 1:15–22).[3]

COMMENT: The setting is the persecution of the Jews in ancient Egypt after they had been made slaves. The king of Egypt embarks on a state policy of genocide, killing all the newborn males. Two women resist his command and let the boys live. This story, the first recorded instance of nonviolent civil disobedience,[4] is only a few lines long and is easily lost in the larger dramatic story of the Exodus. But stories of resistance are always local, small pieces of the larger picture of oppression and injustice. To get a feel for it, imagine the nazis issuing such an order in 1943 in Poland and imagine the situation and the courage of the midwives. Remember, too, that this was not a one-time activity but a form of resistance that continued for several years.[5]

> • "And they let the boys live" (Ex. 1:22)—It is taught: Not only did they [the midwives] not kill them but they also would provide them with bread, water, and food. [Rashi: This means that they would help to keep them alive, hiding them in their houses and bringing them up.][6]

COMMENT: The rabbis recognized the moment of resistance of Shifra and Pu'a and, reading the text closely, they asked: Why does the text say "and they let the boys live"? It was enough to say that the midwives did not do as the king had asked and kill the boys! If they didn't kill them, the boys would, naturally, live! The rabbis respond by reading the verb "let them live" more actively and, in so doing, they add meaning to the sentence: The midwives not only did not kill the male children, they also "let them live" by sustaining them—an insight expanded even further by the medieval commentator, Rashi. Rescuers during the shoah, too, sustained their charges, sometimes for long periods; they did not just refrain from killing them or turning them over to the authorities. We have before us, here, a biblical text telling of events which took place about 1200 B.C.E. in ancient Egypt, that was edited about 1000 B.C.E. in ancient Israel, that was commented upon in about 150 C.E. in a talmudic text written under Roman persecution, expanded upon around 1096 C.E. by a commentator who lived in France during the Crusades, and read by ourselves at the end of the twentieth century in the light of horror and resistance in our own times—a venerable tradition indeed.

There are other biblical stories of resistance to public authority: Moses' murder of the Egyptian taskmaster who was abusing Jewish slaves (Ex. 2:12), Pinḥas's killing of the Israelite man and the non-Israelite woman who had profaned the camp (Nu. 25:7–8),[7] Elijah's confrontation with Ahab (I Kings 18), the refusal of Saul's officers to kill the priests of Nob,[8] the resistance of Shema'ia to King Reḥoboam (I Kings 12:21–24), the running critique of the king by Jeremiah which eventually landed him in the stocks (Jer. 20:1–6), Vashti's refusal to come before King Aḥasuerus (Esther 1:10 –2:1),[9] and Daniel's defiance of the king on eating kosher food (Dan. 1), on not worshiping the idol which resulted in Daniel's being thrown into the fiery furnace (Dan. 3), and on not praying to the king which ended with his being thrown in the lion's den (Dan. 6). Among the later sources, one can count: the rebellion of the Jews against the Syrian-Greeks under the Maccabees in 176–74 B.C.E., the revolts against the Romans in 68–73 C.E. and under Bar Kokhba in 132–53 C.E., and a mass demonstration by Jews before Petronius to protest regulations imposed by the Emperor Claudius, sometimes referred to as the first mass nonviolent act of civil disobedience on record.[10]

There are also stories that show resistance to personal, in contrast with social, authority. Among those, three deserve mention:

- About three months later, Judah was told, "Your daughter-in-law, Tamar, has been a harlot; in fact, she is pregnant by harlotry." "Bring her out and let her be burned," said Judah. As she was being brought out, she sent this message to her father-in-law, "I am pregnant by the man to whom these belong." And she added, "Examine these: whose seal and staff are these?" Judah recognized them and said, "She is more right than I . . ." (Gen. 38).

COMMENT: The setting is the patriarchal narrative of Genesis, in the midst of the story of Joseph and his brothers. Tamar had been married to Judah's son, Er, but he died. Judah's second son, Onan, had come to her in levirate relationship, had refused to give her his seed, and had also died. Judah's third son, Shela, was destined for Tamar but Judah refused to give him to her for fear that he, too, would die. Tamar, asserting her right to bear a child, disguised herself as a prostitute and had relations with Judah. When he found out that she was pregnant, not knowing that he was the father, he ordered her execution. Tamar challenged Judah and confronted him with the pledges he had left the "prostitute." To Judah's credit, he admitted she had justice on her side. From this relationship, King David eventually descended (Ruth 4:18–22). This is resistance to personal authority in a family setting.

- Moses said to Aaron, "'. . . You shall surely eat it as I have commanded' (Lev. 10:18)—in mourning you shall eat it." Aaron replied, "'If things like this have happened to me and I eat a sin offering today, can this be pleasing in the eyes of God?' (Lev. 10:19). . . . Just as the tithe, which is a lesser form of holy offering, cannot be eaten in a state of mourning as it says . . . , so, *a fortiori* the sin sacrifice, which is a greater form of holy offering, [should not be eaten in a state of mourning]." Immediately, "Moses listened and it was good in his eyes" (Lev. 10:20), for Moses was not ashamed to say, "I did not hear [that reasoning]" but said, "I heard [that reasoning] and had forgotten it."[11]

COMMENT: Right after the dedication of the sanctuary in the desert, Nadav and Avihu, two of the sons of Aaron the high priest, did something wrong and they were killed while in the sanctuary itself (Lev. 10). Moses orders Aaron to continue with the ceremonies of the day and to eat, together with his two remaining sons, the sin offering, even though Aaron and the two remaining sons were in mourning (actually, in pre-mourning). Aaron, however, reasoned differently, arguing *a fortiori* from the case of tithes which, according a specific verse, cannot be eaten in a state of mourning. When confronted with Aaron's challenge on a matter of Torah teaching, Moses admitted he was wrong and agreed with Aaron's ruling; that is, Moses listened to this challenge to his personal authority and then agreed that Aaron was right.

• The Lord opened the mouth of the ass and it said to Balaam, "What have I done to you? Why have you struck me three times?" Balaam replied to the ass, "You were making fun of me. If I had a sword in my hand, I would kill you." So the ass replied to Balaam, "Am I not your ass upon whom you have ridden from earliest times until now? Have you lost your mind?" And he said, "No." . . . Then the angel of the Lord said, ". . . Now, I should kill you and let her live" (Nu. 23:28–34).[12]

COMMENT: It is hard to know which is the ass in this story. But that is exactly the point: Even an animal can protest human authority when that person is just plain wrong. In this case, the ass' protest reflects truth and was justified. To his credit, Balaam admits his error at the end.

There are, to be sure, many other stories of defiance of social or personal authority, including those drawn from the shoah.[13]

In considering these stories of resistance, it is important to note, first, that each embodies the value-concepts of *tsedek* (justice) and *hesed* (caring), among others, and each is embodied within *brit* (covenant). Stories, too, embody, even as they teach, value-concepts. Second, in three of the stories cited (that of David, Judah, and Moses), the authority figure, when challenged, admits the justice of the claim and reverses himself. This openness to challenge by authority is itself reasonable and caring, and sets a model of reasonable and caring authority.[14]

Stories of Goodness

In addition to stories of resistance to social and personal authority, there are many, many stories which model prosocial attitudes and behavior. Three popular hasidic stories will have to suffice:

> • Every morning, at midnight, the community would rise to recite the penitential prayers. They would dress warmly, trudge their way through the snow to the synagogue, and cry out mightily to God. Yet, the rebbe [the spiritual leader] was not present. One of the opponents of the rebbe derided this behavior and, when he asked one of the followers where the rebbe was during prayers, he was told, "He has gone to heaven but he will return." Finally, the opponent decided to find out for himself what it was that kept the rebbe from these holy services. The opponent hid under the rebbe's bed while the latter was at evening services and remained there until the midnight hour came. At that moment, the rebbe rose, dressed as a peasant, and left the house, with the opponent following discretely. The rebbe went to a remote cottage in the forest and entered. When the opponent drew near, he saw the rebbe conversing with a non-Jewish peasant woman who was an invalid. The rebbe then left, cut wood for her, returned, lit the fire for her, prepared strong tea for her, spoke a while longer, and left. Abashed, the opponent followed the rebbe back to the village. When the followers asked where the rebbe had gone, he replied, "He has gone higher than heaven."[15]

COMMENT: This story is told by hasidim anxious to dispel the skepticism of their opponents who did not believe in the spiritual power of the rebbes and certainly not in claims that a rebbe ascended to heaven and returned. However, its strength lies in the simple act of *ḥesed* (caring) peformed by the spiritual leader, for someone who does not even know who he is. It is an act of caring which is a blessing. In contrast with the followers who cry loudly in the synagogue and with the skepticism of the opponent, it serves as a model for caring attitudes and behaviors.

> • One day the rebbe's wife came into his study dressed in her finest. When he asked where she was going dressed so well, she replied that she was taking the servant girl to court because the latter had broken things and was insolent. A few moments later, the rebbe caught up with his wife and the servant girl on the street. "Why are you here? I do not need your help,"

said the wife. The rebbe replied, "I know you do not need my help. But, she may."[16]

COMMENT: This somewhat sexist story captures well the class conflict of the situation, and that is the point. The rebbe's wife represents social power and the law, while the rebbe represents *hesed,* the caring dimension of life.

- The rebbe was on his way to pay a call upon a distinguished rebbe in a nearby city. As was the custom, one of his followers was driving the car. As the vehicle approached the toll-booth, the driver took out the exact change and turned into the lane with the automatic toll-collecting machine. Seeing this, the rebbe quickly admonished him, "Turn to the other lane, the one with the toll-collector. Given a choice between a machine and a person, one must always choose the person."[17]

COMMENT: This is a very contemporary story of *hesed* embodied in the action of a spiritual leader.

Resisting God

There are sources in which people defy even God, the ultimate Authority. Challenging God has two dimensions. The first is a calling of God to God's ultimate justice. If God has acted unjustly, *brit* (covenant) provides that humanity can call God to account. If God has not acted in accordance with God's own standard of *tsedek* (justice), the sources show that humankind can call God back to that higher, ultimate standard. This type of challenge is rooted in a deep love of God and of the covenant God has made with humankind for the just administration of creation. By the same reasoning, God calls humans to account on justice issues.

The second type of challenge to God is an intercessory calling of God to God's *rahamim* (mercy and love) on behalf of individuals, the Jewish people, or all humanity. If God has not acted mercifully, *brit* (covenant) provides that humanity can call God to account. If God has not acted in accordance with God's own *middat hasidut* (standard of mercy and love), the sources show that humankind can call God back to that higher, ultimate standard. This type of challenge is also rooted in a deep love of God and of the covenant God has made with humankind for the merciful and loving administration of creation. By the same reasoning, God calls humans to a standard of caring.

All these sources appeal to God's "higher" or "better" nature.[18] Stories of the first type embody the value-concept of *tsedek* (justice) while those of the latter type embody the value-concept of *hasidut* (caring), always within *brit* (covenant). To be sure, each case is a mixture of both justice and caring.[19]

• Abraham came forward and said, "Will You sweep away the innocent along with the guilty? What if there should be fifty innocent people within the city? Will You then wipe out the place and not forgive it for the sake of the innocent fifty who are in it?! Far be it from You to do such a thing, to bring death upon the innocent as well as the guilty, so that innocent and guilty fare alike! Far be it from You! Shall not the Judge of all the universe do justice?!" (Gen. 18:23–25).

COMMENT: The setting is God's announced intention to destroy the wicked cities of Sodom and Gemorra. When Abraham hears that God is about to do this, he did not rejoice in the downfall of the wicked but immediately began to argue with God, speaking these words, the most famous protest lines in all literature.

• Though you crushed us into a desolate place and covered us with deep darkness, did we forget the Name of our God or spread our hands in prayer to a strange deity?! Truly, for Your sake we are killed all day long, we are considered sheep to be butchered. Wake up! Why do You sleep, Lord? Arise! Do not abandon forever! . . . (Ps. 44: 20–24).[20]
• Look from heaven and see that we have become a derision and curse among the nations. We have been considered sheep driven to the slaughter, to be killed, exterminated, beaten, and shamed. Yet, in all this, we have not forgotten Your Name. Do not forget us, Lord, God of Israel. Turn away from Your anger, and regret the evil destined for Your people.[21]

COMMENT: The setting in Psalm 44, one of the most powerful psalms in the Bible, is the defeat of the people in battle. The psalm begins with the call to battle, recounts the defeat experienced by the people, expresses their theological outrage, and then turns to God in a protest prayer, of which the verses cited are but a part. The emotions and theology of this psalm are so powerful that its recitation in the second temple was repressed by the authorities. The second quotation is a medieval liturgical resurrection of the suppressed protest motif. To understand the full effect of Psalm 44 and its liturgical tradition, study it and then pray it out loud, in the rage in which it is written, placing yourself in a concentration camp just before liberation, or as a witness to the continued suffering of a shoah survivor.

Among the protesters of injustice against God, Job is probably the best-known.[22] The entire dramatic tension of the book is based on the fact that Job never denies God's existence or God's power and justice. Rather, he asserts all three forcefully and consistently and, at the same time, maintains his own innocence, thereby calling God to God's "higher," "truer," "more complete" justice. The Book of Job is not about mercy or caring; it is about justice and it is a theology of protest, a work of personal confrontation with God.[23]

There are also biblical figures who challenge God by intercession. Jeremiah, in spite of the fact that God had forbidden him to pray for the people, interceded for them.[24] Ezekiel defined the false prophet as one who did not stand in the breach to challenge God and intercede for the people.[25] Muffs describes the dynamics here very clearly: "By mirroring back to God His underlying love at the hour of His anger, the prophet paradoxically restores the divine balance of emotion . . . One of the functions of the prophet is to cool divine wrath. Thus, the prophet helps God retain the delicate balance between love and justice."[26]

Rabbinic tradition picked up both motifs: protest to God rooted in justice and appeal to God's own "higher" standard of mercy.

> • What did the Holy One, blessed be He, do? He wrapped Himself in His *talit* [prayershawl] as a leader of prayer who passes before the stand and said to Moses, "Pray thus before Me and say, 'Lord, Lord, God, Who loves compassionately and cherishes, Who is patient and overflows with lovingkindness and truth, Who stores up lovingkindness for the thousands of generations, Who forgives purposeful, rebellious, and inadvertent sins—He cleanses'" (Ex. 34:6–7).[27]

COMMENT: The context here is Moses' appearance before God on Mt. Sinai, immediately after the sin of the golden calf. The people are in great danger and Moses must act. This midrash, which specifies what Moses did and prayed, is based on a close reading of the words which immediately precede this prayer. The Hebrew grammar of the original biblical text is ambiguous, leaving open the issue of whether God or Moses is the subject of the sentence: "God came down in a cloud and H/he stood with H/him there, and H/he called in the Name of the Lord. The Lord passed before him and H/he called out . . ." (Ex. 34:5–6). The rabbis read this to say that Moses did not know what to do, so God Godself came down, showed Moses how to prepare himself, and taught him what to say.[28] In yet another very bold midrashic move, note that to make this text a prayer for mercy, the midrash and, following it, the liturgy, must read the verse in a very "ungrammatical" way, reversing the negative in the phrase in the biblical text, "He shall not cleanse."

> • "Now, leave Me be and I will be angry with them. I will destroy them and will make you a great nation" (Ex. 32:10)—Rabbi Abbahu said: "If it were not written in Scripture, it would be impossible to say it. This teaches us that Moses grabbed the Holy One, blessed be He, as a person grabs his friend, by the garment, and said to Him, 'Master of the universe, I shall not let go of You until You forgive and pardon them.'"[29]

COMMENT: This is a variant on the previous midrash, but a much bolder version. The context is the same, the confrontation between God and Moses after the incident of the golden calf, except that here, Moses grabs God and won't let go! The fact that God must say "Leave Me be" allows the midrash to teach that Moses had grabbed God.

> • "Moses implored the presence of God" (Ex. 32:11)—Rabbi Elazar said, "This teaches that Moses stood in prayer before the Holy One, blessed be He, until he healed Him."[30]

COMMENT: Again the context of the confrontation after the golden calf, but with an even bolder thought: that Moses does not just pray and pacify God; he actually heals God! What daring to claim that humanity, through prayer, can not only accomplish the end of mercy for itself but, in that very accomplishment, also heals God Godself!

> • "Moses implored the presence of God" (Ex. 32:11)—Rabbi Berekhia said in the name of Rabbi Ḥelbo who said in the name of Rabbi Yitzḥak: He [Moses] annulled the vow of his Creator. How? At the time that Israel sinned with the golden calf, Moses stood forth to pacify God so that He might forgive them. God said, "Moses, I have already sworn, 'He who offers sacrifice to [another] God shall be destroyed' (Ex. 22:19) and, once an oath has left My mouth, I cannot take it back." Moses said, "Master of the universe, have you not given me power to annul vows as it says . . . ?" Immediately he [Moses] wrapped himself in his *talit* [prayershawl] and sat like a sage and the Holy One, blessed be He, stood before him to ask annulment of His vow. . . . He [God] said to him, "I regret the evil which I have said I will do to My people." Then, Moses said to Him, "It is undone for you. It is undone for you. There is no vow here. There is no oath here."[31]

COMMENT: Again, the context is the meeting between God and Moses after the sin of the golden calf, but this is, in some ways, the boldest of the protest texts presented here. In this text, Moses not only has a position morally superior to that of God (!), he also occupies the role of rabbinic judge for God! In that capacity, Moses sits and God stands (!), and Moses actually dissolves an oath taken by God, using the usual rabbinic formula for the dissolving of vows! The rabbinic understanding of the mutual responsibility of humans and God for justice and mercy within covenant approaches its limits with this astonishingly audacious midrash.

> • The Kotzker rebbe said, "Send us our Messiah, for we have no more strength to suffer. Show me a sign, O God. Otherwise I rebel against You. If You do not keep Your covenant, then neither will I keep the promise, and it is all over: we are through with being Your Chosen People, your unique treasure."[32]

COMMENT: In a much later echo of Moses' boldness, a pre-shoah hasidic rebbe takes a very tough protest stance with God.

As in the material on protest against human authority, the sources on protest against divine authority include midrashim in which God explicitly acknowledges the superior ethical and moral claim of the protestor. This is most astounding: that the Judge of the universe should admit moral failure openly, and then have a change of mind and heart which is more caring and more just than the original position!!

> • The Holy One, blessed be He, told Moses to fight with Sihon and Og as it says, "Engage war with him" (Dt. 2:24). But he did not do thus. Rather, "And I sent messengers from the eastern desert to Sihon, the king of Heshbon, with words of peace" (Dt. 2:26). The Holy One, blessed be He, said to him, "I told you to make war on him, and you opened peace negotiations with him?! By your life, I shall fulfill the decree you have issued—every war which they [the Jewish people] shall wage, they must open with an offer of peace as it says, 'When you draw near to a city to fight with it, you shall offer it peace'" (Dt. 20:10).[33]

COMMENT: The issue here is a contradiction between two verses. In one, God commands an immediate attack on the enemies and, in the other, Moses is reported to have offered them peace terms before the attack. God recognizes the moral superiority of Moses' claim and, then, ordains that all military action should be preceded by an effort to negotiate peace—an issue which is always relevant. Given God's severe negative reaction to Moses' divergence from God's command when he smote the rock, Moses' reaction here is all the more remarkable.[34]

> • In three matters Moses acted on his own and God assented to them. He added one day [to the preparations for Mt. Sinai], he separated himself from his wife [permanently], and he broke the tablets. . . . How did Moses learn this [that it was permissible to break the tablets]? He reasoned, "Just as the Passover sacrifice, which is only one of the 613 commandments, cannot be partaken of by an alien as it says . . . , a fortiori the Torah, which contains all of the 613 commandments, cannot be partaken of by those who have consciously adopted idolatry." How do we know that God assented [to his breaking the tablets]? Scripture says, "the tablets which you broke"— Resh Lakish interpreted, "May your strength be straight [that is, your actions are proper] because you broke them."[35]

COMMENT: There are three instances here in which Moses exceeds God's prescriptions. (1) In Exodus 19:10, God enjoins two days of preparation for the theophany on Mt. Sinai but Exodus 19:15 indicates that Moses ordered three days of preparation. (2) Exodus 19:15 provides that, as part of the preparation for receiving the Torah, men and women must be separated. The rabbis claim that Moses remained permanently separated from his wife, reasoning that he would be in continuous reception of the divine word. (3) God did not tell Moses to break the tablets upon which the first Ten Commandments were written. The rabbis, believing that he did not act on impulse, claim that he had ample reason to do so, on the analogy of the paschal sacrifice. For, as the paschal sacrifice cannot be eaten by an idolater, so the Torah should not be given to a people that has just worshiped a golden calf. Moses, therefore, was justified in breaking the tablets. Furthermore, in each of these three cases, Moses is not only justified but God also accepts the moral position of Moses. The proof for the third case is based on a pun. The verse reads: *'asher shibbarta* ("which you broke"); Resh Lakish reads: *yishar [koḥakha she-] shibbarta* ("may [your strength] be straight [because] you broke"). This is not an accepted "proof" in Western logic but, in midrashic thinking, it is common. Given that, the point is impressive: that Moses modified God's instructions three times and each time God agreed, even assenting to the justice of the shattering of God's own Ten Commandments.

> • Rabbi Yoḥanan said, "How do we know that God admitted that he [Moses] was right? It says, 'I have forgiven according to your arguments'" (Nu. 14:20). . . . [Concerning the phrase] "however, by My life" (Nu. 14:21) Rava said that Rabbi Yitzhak said, "This teaches that the Holy One, blessed be He, said to Moses, 'Moses, you have resurrected Me with your words.'"[36]

COMMENT: According to the first authority, the text of the Torah itself shows that God acceded to Moses' protest. According to the second authority, a close reading of one phrase "by My life" does that. Another unbelievably audacious midrashic idea: that human beings, by exercising moral judgment and by interceding on behalf of others, actually resurrect God![37]

This tradition of protest against God eventually developed the *din Torah,* a trial of God, in which rabbis take on the role of prosecutor, defense attorney, and judge. Such trials of God were even known to have taken place in the concentration camps of nazi Europe.[38] On the basis of this strong interpretation of *brit* (covenant), I have proposed the following post-shoah liturgy for Yom Kippur:

> Our Father, our King, we have sinned before You.
> Our Father, our King, You have sinned before us.
> Our Father, our King, we have no King other than You.
> Our Father, our King, You have no special people other than we. . . .

Our Father, our King, forgive and forbear punishment for all our
purposeful sins.
Our Father, our King, ask forgiveness and forbearance for all Your
purposeful sins.
Our Father, our King, wipe away and remove all our rebellious
and inadvertent sins from before Your eyes.
Our Father, our King, ask erasure and removal of all Your rebellious
and inadvertent sins from before our eyes.
Our Father, our King, efface in Your great mercy all record of our guilt.
Our Father, our King, cause us to do complete repentance before You.
Our Father, our King, do complete repentance before us. . . .
Our Father, our King, write us into the book of forgiveness
and forbearance.
Our Father, our King, write Yourself into our book of forgiveness
and forbearance.[39]

Counter-text[40]

When the German SS troops guarding the concentration camp at Gunskirchen heard the Americans were coming, they suddenly got busy burying the bodies of their victims—or rather, having them buried by inmates—and gave the prisoners who were still alive what they considered
an extremely liberal food ration: one lump of sugar per person and one loaf
of bread for every seven persons. Then, two days or a day and a half before we arrived, the SS left. All this I learned from talking to inmates of
the camp, many of whom spoke English. Driving up to the camp in our
jeep, Corporal DeSpain and I [Captain J. D. Pletcher], first knew we were
approaching the camp by the hundreds of starving, half crazed inmates lin-
ing the roads, begging for food and cigarettes. Many of them had been able
to get only a few hundred yards from the gate before they keeled over and
died. As weak as they were, the chance to be free, the opportunity to escape
was so great they couldn't resist, though it meant staggering only a few
yards before death came.
    Then came the next indication of the camp's nearness—the smell.
There was something about the smell of Gunskirchen I shall never forget. . . . Of all the horrors of the place, the smell, perhaps was the most
startling of all. It was a smell made up of all kinds of odors—human ex-
creta, foul bodily odors, smoldering trash fires, German tobacco. . . . The
ground was pulpy throughout the camp, churned to a consistency of warm
putty by the milling of thousands of feet, mud mixed with feces and
urine. . . .

As we entered the camp, the living skeletons still able to walk crowded around us and, though we wanted to drive farther into the place, the milling, pressing crowd wouldn't let us. It is not an exaggeration to say that almost every inmate was insane with hunger. Just the sight of an American brought cheers, groans, and shrieks. People crowded around to touch an American, to touch the jeep, to kiss our arms—perhaps just to make sure that it was true. The people who couldn't walk crawled out toward our jeep. Those who couldn't even crawl propped themselves up on an elbow, and somehow, through all their pain and suffering, revealed through their eyes the gratitude, the joy they felt at the arrival of the Americans.

12

Teachings of Resistance and Goodness

There is a strong overlap between teachings, norms, principles, and value-concepts.[1] It is hard to know whether a verse or phrase is a teaching, a norm, a principle, a law, or a value-concept. Except insofar as a violation of such a phrase is enforceable in law, the ambiguity of the status of such teaching is not significant; rather, it is the moral thrust that is important. In what follows, therefore, law, ethics, and moral teaching are treated as one.

Hokheah Tokhiah
(You Shall Surely Reprove Your Acquaintance)

The biblical sources are very clear that every person, especially a prophet, has the responsibility to reprove other individuals and society at large:

> • Do not hate your fellow in your heart. You shall surely reprove (Heb., *hokheah tokhiah*) your acquaintance, and do not bear sin on his or her account. Do not take revenge or bear a grudge against your people, but love your other as yourself; I am the Lord (Lev. 19:17–18).
> • The word of the Lord came to me saying: Human being, speak to the members of your people and say to them: "When I bring the sword upon a land, the populace shall take one of their own and set that person as a lookout for them. And, when he or she sees the sword coming upon the land, she or he shall blow the shofar to warn the people. If the hearer hears the sound of the shofar and does not take precautions and the sword comes and takes that person, then that person's blood is on his or her own head. That person has heard the sound of the shofar and did not take precautions; her or his blood is upon him or her; for if one takes precautions, one can save one's life. However, as to the lookout who sees the sword coming and does not blow the shofar so that the people are not warned; if the sword then comes and takes the life of one of them, [even though] he or she [the killed person] is taken because of her or his own sin, I will require that person's blood of the lookout's hand." Now I have set you, human being,

as a watchman for the house of Israel and, when you hear a word from Me, you shall warn them from Me (Ezek. 33:1–6).[2]

COMMENT: The quotation from the Torah includes the Hebrew *'ahikha* (fellow), *'amitekha* (acquaintance) and *rei'ekha* (other) which mean a person who is kin, that is, someone who is Jewish. I do not think that the original sources envisioned these principles as applying to the alien even if he or she is a neighbor. Nonetheless, I have translated all ambiguously to include that possibility because, given the multicultural setting of contemporary Jewish moral thinking, this seems more appropriate. The quotation from the prophet intends to hold the watchman responsible for the death of those he or she is supposed to warn, even though their deaths are justified, because the watchman has not in fact warned, reproved, the people.

This value-concept, norm, and principle of reproof, known by the Hebrew phrase *hokheah tokhiah,* became central in rabbinic moral thinking where it is an obligation on everyone but especially upon the leaders of the community.

- Rabbi Hanina said, "Jerusalem was destroyed only because they did not reprove one another . . . they cast their faces down to the ground and did not reprove one another."[3]
- Rabbi Yose ben Halafta said, "All love that does not include reproof in it is not love." Resh Lakish said, "All peace that does not include reproof in it is not peace."[4]

COMMENT: The allegation that Jerusalem was destroyed because of lack of civil moral courage is very serious, and probably true given the history of fanaticism in the Holy City. (The phrase "cast their faces . . ." has the sense of "buried their heads in the sand.") The realization that neither love nor peace can claim their respective titles if each is not also morally critical is also very true.

- The standard of justice (*middat ha-din*) said before the Holy One, blessed be He, "Master of the universe, what is the difference between these and those?" He said, "These are the completely righteous and those are the completely wicked." It said before Him, "Master of the universe, [the former are not completely righteous because] they could have remonstrated and they did not!" He said, "It is revealed and known to Me that, had they protested, the [people] would not have listened." It said before Him, "Master of the universe, it is clearly known by You, but was it clearly known by them?!"[5]

COMMENT: This midrash is based upon Ezekiel 9:4–11 where the righteous and the wicked are marked on their foreheads, the former with ink and the latter with blood. Justice is arguing that the completely righteous cannot possibly have been completely so, for they could have remonstrated with the wicked of their time. God's answer is weak and the exchange ends with justice "winning" the argument, that is, that no matter how righteous one has been, one could always have done more, especially in remonstrating with those who are on the wrong path.[6]

> • Once a man complained that he was being publicly rebuked by Rabbi Hiya and Rabbi Yose: "You are in a conspiracy against me. Surely you are one of the followers of Rabbi Shimon bar Yohai who have no fear of anyone." They replied, "The Torah teaches us to do so, as it says, 'Wisdom cries aloud in the streets, in the markets she raises her voice' (Prov. 1:21). If we feared to speak words of Torah before you, we should be ashamed before God."[7]

COMMENT: A very good example of appeal to a higher authority to justify reprimanding someone.

Even when administering reproof is difficult, it is obligatory. Thus, the rabbis taught that there are moments when toughness is required:

> • Hate evil. Love good. Establish justice in the gate (Amos 5:15).
> • You who love the Lord hate evil (Ps. 97:10).
> • Rabbi Shimon ben Lakish said, "Whoever becomes merciful where toughness[8] is necessary will, in the end, be cruel where mercy is necessary. . . ." The rabbis taught, "Whoever becomes merciful where toughness is necessary, in the end the standard of justice will strike him. . . ."[9]
> • All this requires toughness—to pursue the wicked and to pressure them in order to return them to the good. One must be tough in the law and not have mercy upon one's relatives, friends, and the poor; rather, one must apply the law [fully].[10]

Lo Tisna' (Do Not Hate Your Fellow in Your Heart)

There is a deep danger in the principle of *hokheah tokhiah* (You shall surely reprove your acquaintance)—that it could be taken to extremes. The rabbis were well aware of this and they created a tension between serious moral criticism and full respect for the other in three ways. First, the rabbis developed the counter value-concept, norm, principle, and teaching known as *lo tisna'* (Do not hate your fellow in your heart) which, to be sure, has biblical roots:

• Do not hate (Heb., *lo tisna'*) your fellow in your heart (Lev. 19:17).

This biblical principle was expanded upon by the rabbis.

• "Do not hate your fellow in your heart" (Heb., *lo tisna'*) (Lev. 19:17)—
Is it possible that one is not allowed to hit, slap, or embarrass him or her
[in order to reprove her or him]? Scripture teaches, "in your heart"—
Scripture speaks of hate in the heart [which is forbidden, not physical re-
proof]. From whence does one know that, if one sees a friend doing something wrong, one is obligated to reprove him or her? It says, "You shall
reprove" (end of same verse). And, if one has reproved her or him and he
or she has not accepted it, from whence does one know that one must reprove yet again? It says, "surely." Does anything go? Even if his face
changes? [No,] it says, "and do not bear sin on his or her account."[11]
• Rabbi Elazar ben Matya said, "If there is something between another
and you, say it to him or her and do not be a sinner on her or his account,
as it says, 'Do not hate your fellow in your heart . . . do not bear sin on his
or her account'" (Lev. 19:17).[12]

COMMENT: The points here are that one may not hate in one's heart, but one
may act aggressively to reprove someone. Furthermore, one must repeat the
reproof if it is not accepted. However, one may not reprove someone in a way
that is itself sinful. Kimelman summarizes the two main types of exegesis of
"and do not bear sin on his or her account": "The first trend maintains that the
verse says that while you should reprove, beware that you do not sin in the process of protest by shaming or doing violence to the person. . . . The second
main trend of interpretation . . . take[s] it as 'lest' arguing that if you do not reprove you will bear his sin."[13] I rather favor the second: that, if one has a genuine grudge against someone else and does not discuss it with that person, one
will come to hate that person in one's heart and, hence, one will come to sin.
It is better, therefore, to reprove and remonstrate with one's acquaintance.

Second, the rabbis also taught that there were moral, as well as practical,
limits to the teaching, principle, norm, and value-concept of *hokheah tokhiah*
(reproof):

• Why did Jeroboam merit sovereignty? Because he protested against
Solomon. And why was he punished? Because he protested against him
publicly. . . . He said thus to him, "Your father, David, made breaches in
the wall so that Israel might make pilgrimage on the festivals but you have
now closed them in order to exact tolls for the benefit of [your wife] Pharoah's daughter."[14]

COMMENT: Jeroboam, son of Nevat, was chosen by God through Aḥiya, the prophet, to split the kingdom of Solomon. He formed the ten northern tribes into the kingdom of Israel and left the rest to Reḥoboam, the son of Solomon, as the kingdom of Judah (I Kings 11–12). This split, which had already existed in David's time but had been unified by him and Solomon, remained to the end of the northern and southern kingdoms. The question of the midrash is, What possible merit could Jeroboam have had that his kingdom endured, especially in view of the fact that it is he who set up a new center for the sacrificial cult and put false gods into the temple in Samaria? And, then, if his merit was so great, why did he fall into such sin and punishment? The answer is that he misused the principle of reproof.

- Do not reprove a fool lest he or she hate you [make you his enemy]. Reprove a wise person and she or he will love you (Prov. 9:8).
- "Your acquaintance" (Lev. 19:17)—the person who is with you in mitsvot, you shall reprove but you do not reprove a wicked person who is your enemy.[15]
- Hate heretics, those who incite to idolatry, those who lead astray, and those who inform as David said, "Do I not hate those whom You hate, Lord, with complete hatred, and fight against those who rise up against You?" (Ps. 139:21) . . . "You shall love your other as yourself; I am the Lord" (Lev. 19:18)—I am the One Who created the other. If he or she works along with you, you must love her or him but, if not, you shall not love him or her.[16]

COMMENT: The rabbis teach, here, that there are the practical limits to reproof: some people just won't listen, or can't hear. In such cases, one should not reprove, and certainly not hate in one's heart. The interpretation of these passages, and others, is based upon the pun in Hebrew, *sone' / sin'a / sin'ut* which means both "hate / hatred" and "enemy / enmity." The midrash in the second source returns to the original verse on reproof in Lev. 19:17–18, refining the definition of "acqaintance" is a realistic way through a play on words in the Hebrew: *'amitekha / 'imkha [be-mitsvot]*. The third source repeats the lesson using the dialectic tension between hatred and reproof of the other.

Finally, the rabbis taught that confrontational reproving of the other was not always the best way.

- Rabbi Ḥiya bar Abba said that Rabbi Simai said, "Three people were consulted [by Pharoah when he wanted to oppress the Jews (Ex. 1:10)]: Balaam, Job, and Jethro. Balaam gave advice, and he was killed. Job kept silent, and he was punished with suffering. Jethro fled, and had the merit of having his children serve in the court of the temple.[17]

COMMENT: Balaam is the non-Jewish prophet whom Balak, king of Moab, hires to curse the Jewish people (Nu. 22–24). According to rabbinic tradition, he was killed for agreeing to this perfidy. Job is also a non-Jewish authority; he is a consultant to Pharoah at the time of the exodus. His silence when consulted is the sin for which he is punished in the book bearing his name. Jethro is the father-in-law of Moses, another non-Jew. When consulted, he flees Egypt so as not to have to give advice. He is rewarded with the honor of having his descendants serve in the temple. There are two points here: (1) silence, like that of Job, is not sufficient as a form of protest and (2) sometimes fleeing is the only effective form of protest. This last piece of advice was repeated by Maimonides, never a man to mince words, to Jews who were being oppressed: "But if one can save one's life and flee the evil king [a government which is persecuting Jews] and one does not do so, one is like a dog who lies in its vomit, one is considered a conscious idol-worshiper, and one will be driven from the world-to-come and go down to the lowest level of hell."[18]

- At the hour that Jacob called Esau "my lord," the Holy One, blessed be He, said to him, "You humbled yourself and called Esau 'my lord' eight times. By your life, I will make eight kings from his sons before your sons [have a king], as it says, 'These are the kings which ruled in the land of Edom before a king ruled over the Israelites'" (Gen. 36:31).[19]

COMMENT: Eight times in Genesis Jacob refers to Esau deferentially as "my lord" (Gen. 32:5, 6, 19 and 33:8, 13, 14 twice, 15). The lesson here is that flattery, rather than courageous confrontation, has its place, as indeed was the case in Jacob's confrontation with Esau.

As Kimelman notes, remonstrating requires strategy and planning, often demanding patience, a soft tongue, self-suffering, and careful self-examination.[20] It can even require praying for one's enemies.[21]

Further, it is also true that disobedience and protest is not always the right response: Abraham does not protest when God asks for the sacrifice of Isaac (Gen. 22) and this is considered the act of faith *par excellence*. Yet, according to rabbinic tradition, Saul tried to argue against God concerning the annihilation of Amalek and was punished for it (I Sam. 15:26–29).[22]

In spite of all these nuances, sometimes rabbinic ethics come very close to the edge in the name of law and norm:

- You shall burn out the evil from your midst. . . .
- One who does not wish to make a sukka, or tsitsit for his [or her] talit, or a mezuza for her or his doorpost—one beats him or her until he or she dies.[23]

COMMENT: The first source is biblical and it provides the justification for the death penalty for the following acts: for a false prophet (Dt. 13:6), for idol worship (17:7), for a rebellious judge (17:12), for a murderer (19:13), for a lying witness (19:19), for a rebellious child (21:21), for a woman who is not a virgin when she marries (22:21), for both adulterers (22:22), for the rapist of an engaged woman (22:27), and for a kidnapper (24:7). The second source is rabbinic and is very strong; I do not believe this came to be the law though it remained a valid teaching and principle.

• Is it permissible [for an individual Jew] to hate him or her [another individual Jew], for is it not written, "Do not hate your fellow in your heart" (Lev. 19:17)? In a case where there are witnesses that the other has committed a sin [it is permissible to hate]. If that is so, then everyone [not just an individual] is permitted to hate that person?! How, then, would the case [of individual hatred] be different? In that the individual saw the other commit a sexually forbidden act. Rabbi Naḥman said, "It is a commandment to hate such a person [personally] as it says, 'The fear of God [requires] hating evil'" (Prov. 8:13).[24]

COMMENT: This source justifies personal hate in one's heart for another, if one has personally witnessed another committing a sexually forbidden act—a powerful verse for survivors of incest and other forms of sexual abuse.

The law on reproof and hating is summarized by Maimonides:

• When a person wrongs another, the one should not bear enmity toward him or her and keep quiet as Absalom did with Amnon . . . (II Sam. 13:22). Rather, it is a commandment to make it known to the other and to say, "Why did you do thus and so to me? Why did you wrong me in such and such a matter?" As it says, "You shall surely reprove your acquaintance . . ." (Lev. 19:17). One who sees a friend who has sinned and gone in the wrong way, it is a commandment to return that person to the good and to let him or her know that she or he is sinning against himself or herself with these wicked deeds, as it says, "You shall surely reprove your acquaintance" (Lev. 19:17).[25]
• How can a Jew have a Jewish enemy since it says, "Do not hate your fellow in your heart" (Lev. 19:17)? The sages said that this is the case of one whom one has observed doing a sin, whom one has warned, and who has not desisted. It is a commandment to hate such a person until he or she repents and desists from her or his wickedness.[26]

Yetser Tov (Good Impulse) and Yetser ha-Ra' (Evil Impulse)

Deep in rabbinic psychology, there is the idea that humanity was created with a *yetser tov* (good impulse) and a *yetser ha-ra'* (evil impulse).[27]

- "And God formed (Heb., *va-yiitser*) the human being from the dust of the earth" (Gen. 2:7)—with two impulses, a good impulse and the evil impulse.[28]

COMMENT: The original biblical Hebrew text spells the word for "formed" with two letters *yod,* implying some sort of double creation. The midrash develops this very elaborately; only the interpretation relevant to *yetser tov* and *yetser ha-ra'* is cited here.

- The Holy One, blessed be He, said to Israel: "My children, I have created the *yetser ha-ra'* and I have created the Torah as a cure [for it]. If you occupy yourselves with Torah, you will not be delivered into its hands as it says, 'Surely, if you do good, there is uplift' (Gen. 4:7). But if you do not occupy yourselves with Torah, you will be delivered into its hands as it says, 'But if you do not do good, sin crouches at the opening' (ibid.). Not only that, but all its dealings will be against you as it says, 'its desire shall be for you' (ibid.). But if you will it, you will rule over it as it says, 'and you shall rule over it' (end of verse)." The rabbis taught: "The *yetser ha-ra'* is so tough that even its Creator called it 'evil' as it says, 'for the *yetser* of the heart of humanity is evil (*ra'*) from its youth'" (Gen. 8:21).[29]

COMMENT: This is a phrase-by-phrase interpretation of God's words to Cain just before he kills Abel; that is, this midrash represents God's warning to humanity just before evil takes over: "Surely, if you do good, there is uplift. But if you do not do good, sin crouches at the opening. Its desire shall be for you, and you shall rule over it" (Gen. 4:7). To this is appended an interpretation of God's rumination on the innate sinfulness of humanity right after the flood (Gen. 8:21). The point is that, on the one hand, God is optimistic and teaches that humankind is sinful but can master sinfulness while, on the other hand, God is pessimistic and notes that sinfulness is naturally, if not existentially, innate to humanness. Interestingly, God's optimism is expressed before the first murder while God's pessimism is expressed after God's failed attempt to "correct" the human evil which prompted the flood.

- Antoninus asked Rabbi, "When does the *yetser ha-ra'* gain control of a person—at the time of its creation or at the time it exits [the womb]?" He replied, "At the time of its creation [in the womb]." Antoninus said, "If that is so, it would disdain its mother's womb and come out [right away]. Rather, [the answer is] from the time it exits [the womb]." Rabbi replied, "I learned this from Antoninus and there is a verse which supports him as it says, 'sin lies at the opening'" (Gen. 4:7).[30]

COMMENT: The question, here, is whether sin, in rabbinic thought, is an existential condition or only a potentiality of real human existence. Rabbi [Judah, the Prince] first argues that it is existential while Antoninus, the pagan emperor, argues that it is only a potentiality of real human existence. In the end, Rabbi Judah accepts the view of the pagan emperor that the *yetser ha-ra'* is not "genetic" or existential but only that it is a real part of human existence. He concludes, therefore, that *yetser ha-ra'* asserts its influence only at birth. This may be a midrash intended to counter the doctrine of original sin as it was emerging in Christian midrash and theology.

- It was said in the name of Rabbi Yoḥanan ben Nuri, "One who tears one's clothes in a moment of anger, or one who breaks useful objects in anger, or one who throws away money in anger should be seen as one who worships idols." For such is the work of the *yetser ha-ra'*—Today it says, "Do this" and tomorrow it says, "Do that" and eventually it says, "Worship idols," and one goes and worships them.[31]
- Rabbi Shmuel bar Naḥmani said that Rabbi Yoḥanan said, "The *yetser ha-ra'* incites a person in this world and testifies against him or her in the world-to-come as it says. . . ."[32]
- Rabbi Yosi ha-Galili said, "The righteous are judged by the *yetser tov*. . . . The wicked are judged by the *yetser ha-ra'* . . . and the intermediate people are judged by both. . . ."[33]
- Rabbi Judah interpreted: "In the end of days, the Holy One, blessed be He, will bring the *yetser ha-ra'* and slaughter it before the eyes of the righteous and the wicked. The righteous will have seen it as a gigantic mountain and the wicked will have seen it as a single hair. . . ."[34]

COMMENT: The danger represented by the *yetser ha-ra'* is clearly shown in these passages. Its action is incremental and leads to increasing evil.[35] The yearly divine judgment is based upon its influence in human affairs, as is the ultimate divine judgment after death. Indeed, the *yetser ha-ra'* can only be fully banished in the messianic mode of existence though, even then, the wicked will not have appreciated its enormous danger.

- Rabbi Yoḥanan said, "A man has a small organ. If he starves it, it will be satisfied as it says. . . ."[36]
- Rabbi Shimon ben Lakish said, "A person's *yetser [ha-ra']* does battle with one and seeks to kill one every day, as it says. . . . Were it not that the Holy One, blessed be He, helps, one would not be able to stand up to it as it says. . . ." Rabbi Yishmael taught, "If you meet that despicable one, drag him to the synagogue. . . ."[37]
- Rabbi Levi bar Ḥama said that Rabbi Shimon ben Lakish said, "One

should always arouse one's *yetser tov* against one's *yetser ha-ra'* as it says, 'Arouse, and do not sin' (Ps. 4:5). If one vanquishes it [this way], fine; if not, one should occupy oneself with Torah as it says, 'say in your heart' (ibid.). If one vanquishes it [this way], fine; if not, one should recall the day of death in its presence as it says, 'and be silent, selah' (end of verse)." [38]

COMMENT: The rabbis connected the evil impulse very closely with the sexual drive which can often be the source of sinfulness. Because of this, rabbinic Judaism devised ways to deal with it. One must have sexual discipline, for excess in sexuality is incremental. One must also pray (God will help) and study (take it to the house of study). One can also call up one's *yetser tov* (good impulse) and recall one's ultimate mortality, that is, the ultimate meaning and context of all life. The last source is a midrash on Psalm 4:5, "Arouse, and do not sin. Say in your hearts on your beds. And be silent. Selah."

That goodness was a part of creation is stated in the first chapter of Genesis. The early sages, thus, felt no impulse to justify the *yetser tov* in any special way. The status of the *yetser ha-ra'*, however, was another matter. On the one hand, it was clearly present in creation and, hence, could not be entirely evil. Yet, on the other hand, it was the source of sinfulness. Rabbinic thought, therefore, decided that the *yetser ha-ra'* is, indeed, evil but it is not only evil; it is also a part of creation, that is, of human nature and, therefore, it must be good for something.

• "Behold it was very good" (Gen. 1:31)—Rav Naḥman bar Shmuel said in the name of Rav Shmuel bar Naḥman, "It says, 'good'—this is the *yetser tov,* but it also says, 'very [good]'—this is the *yetser ha-ra'*. Is then the *yetser ha-ra'* 'very [good]'? [Yes, for] were it not for the *yetser ha-ra'*, a man would not build a house, marry a woman, have children, and engage in business as it says. . . ." [39]

COMMENT: This midrash on Genesis 1:31 proposes an answer to two questions: What is the "it" in the verse; that is, what is the antecedent to the implied pronoun? And, what is the meaning of "very"; that is, what kind of goodness would be "very" good? The answer given here is that the *yetser ha-ra'*, which in rabbinic psychology is the source of sinfulness, contains a germ of goodness in it, for it is the sexual and ego drives that move humanity to achieve. The inclination to do evil, then, is part of the goodness of creation. (There is an alternate midrash that suggests that death is the kind of goodness that is "very" good and, hence, included in creation in Genesis 1:31.)

In a still later development of rabbinic thinking on goodness and evil, the rabbis taught that goodness and evil have their roots in God Godself. [40]

• Why is it called *yetser tov?* Because of the verse, "God is good (*tov*) to all" (Ps. 145:9). The blessed Name, may He be blessed, is the essence of truth. The soul is a piece of the divine on high and the *yetser tov* is the guardian of the soul. Therefore, it is called *tov* because of the True Good (*ha-tov ha-'amiti*), may He be blessed.[41]

• *Yetser tov* and *yetser ra'*—*yetser tov* is on the right [Ḥesed] and *yetser ra'* is on the left [Gevura]. The left which is on high seizes the female [Malk-hut] to be united with it as one body as it says, "His left is under my head and his right embraces me" (Song 8:3). Two messengers are sent to a person to be in union with him or her, one on the right and one on the left. They testify for and against a person. In everything that one does, they are there. They are called *yetser tov* and *yetser ra'*. When one comes to submit and to occupy oneself with the words of Torah, the *yetser tov* immediately is joined to him or her. . . .[42]

COMMENT: In the first of these two passages from medieval rabbinic theology, goodness and God are identical. Or, to put it differently, goodness is good because God is absolute goodness. The second passage is even more bold. The midrash on Song of Songs 8:3 suggests not only that *yetser tov* is one of the dimensions of God but that *yetser ra'* is also one of the dimensions of the divine (one of the *sefirot* of the *Zohar*). *Yetser ra'* in zoharic thought is that dimension of God's being that establishes and enforces limits, that judges, and that can, indeed, seize control of God's providential action.[43]

A century of pessimistic social scientists, Marx and Freud most prominently among them, has maintained that humanity has a basic impulse to exploit and to do evil. The Jewish sources affirm this in asserting the existence of the *yetser ha-ra'* though with certain reservations. The tradition is very careful to assert that the *yetser ha-ra'* is not completely evil but is, under certain conditions, socially positive. Furthermore, the sources make the clear claim that the evil impulse in humanity can always be mastered, particularly by mitsvot, study, and prayer. By contrast with other social scientists, Batson has maintained that humanity has an irreducible altruistic motivation.[44] This view, too, is echoed by the Jewish sources which affirm the existence of a *yetser tov* which impels us to do good. Indeed, the medieval theosophic tradition goes so far as to assert both as part of the divine.

The prophet Jeremiah wrote, "The heart is the most devious of all things. It is human. Who can know it?" (Jer. 17:9). In the complicated workings of human motivation, who is to say when disobedience and protest are a function of *yetser tov* and when they are a function of *yetser ha-ra'*? It is certainly possible that *yetser tov* would motivate a person to obedience and conformity, or to disobedience and protest. It is also possible that *yetser ha-ra'* would motivate a person to both prosocial and antisocial acts. The teaching of the *yetser ha-tov* and of the *yetser ha-ra'*—and of the interaction between the two in God, in creation, and in human motivation—is one of the most profound of the rabbinic teachings on the theme of good and evil.

Kiddush ha-Shem (Martyrdom) [45]

The general rule about the relationship between Jews and the secular (non-Jewish) authority is *dina de-malkhuta dina,* the law of the land is the law. This means that, in all matters where the state claims civil jurisdiction, Jews abide by state law. Notwithstanding this, Jews occasionally broke into open armed rebellion in late antiquity and, until modern times, maintained a complete court system for their own civil administration. (Rabbinic courts still exist though the scope of their action is more limited.) There were, however, limits to *dina de-malkhuta dina* and a whole literature has sprung up on this topic, particularly on the relationship between Israeli law and Jewish law.[46]

The main exception to *dina de-malkhuta dina* is the series of cases where what is demanded of the Jew is so forbidden that martyrdom is to be preferred to obedience. The law on this subject is very complex and has evolved over time. Maimonides summarizes it authoritatively: [47]

- All the house of Israel is commanded [to observe] the sanctification of this great Name as it says, "I shall be sanctified in the midst of the children of Israel" (Lev. 22:32). And they have been warned not to profane it as it says, "You shall not profane My holy Name" (beginning of same verse). How [does one observe this commandment]? If a non-Jew comes and forces a Jew, under threat of death, to transgress any one of the commandments in the Torah, let that person transgress and not be killed as it says concerning the commandments, "which a person should do so that he or she may live through them" (Lev. 18:5)—that one should live through them and not die through them.[48] And if one dies [that is, chooses death] and does not transgress, one puts one's life in jeopardy [that is, one can be prosecuted on capital grounds].
- Under what conditions [is the above ruling about transgressing and not being martyred valid]? [If one is asked to transgress] commandments other than worshiping other gods, incest and adultery, and committing murder. However, [concerning] these three, if one is told, "Transgress one of them or be killed," one must be killed and not transgress (Hebrew, *yei-hareig ve-'al ya'avor*) [that is, one must choose martyrdom]. Under what [further] conditions [is the above ruling about transgressing and not being martyred valid]? [If one is asked to transgress] for the personal benefit of the non-Jew as, for instance, if one is forced to build him a house on Shabbat, or to cook for him [on Shabbat], or if he forced a woman to have

intercourse with him, etc. However, if the non-Jew intended solely to make the Jew violate the commandments then, if the Jew was alone and ten other Jews were not present, one should transgress and not be killed. But, if one were forced to violate the commandments in the presence of ten other Jews, then one should be killed and not transgress, even if the non-Jew intended to force one to violate only one of the commandments.

• All these rules [concerning conditions under which one must choose to transgress and not to be martyred] apply only when there is no organized persecution. However, in time of organized persecution[49]—when a wicked king like Nebuchadnezzar and his cohort rule and they promulgate a decree to abolish the religion of Israel or one of the mitsvot thereof—one must be killed and not transgress even for any other commandment [than the three for which martyrdom is obligatory], whether one is in the presence of ten Jews or only in the presence of the non-Jew.

• Whoever must transgress and not be killed—if that person [chooses to] be killed, he or she puts her or his life in jeopardy [that is, one can be prosecuted on capital grounds]. And, whoever must be killed and not transgress—if that person [chooses to] be killed and does not transgress, she or he has sanctified the Name of God. . . . Whoever must be killed and not transgress—if that person [chooses to] transgress and not be killed, he or she has profaned the Name of God. . . . Even though such a person has transgressed, because he or she acted under duress, one does not [punish him or her in a court of law].[50]

The rules for resistance unto martyrdom, then, are quite direct. One must choose martyrdom:[51] (1) if one must transgress one of the three "cardinal" sins: worshiping other gods, incest or adultery, or murder; (2) if one must transgress even a minor sin publicly, that is, in the presence of ten Jews; and (3) if, at a time of organized religious persecution, one must transgress even a minor sin in private. Thus, according to most authorities, one may not recite the Islamic creed; one is not allowed to hand over a hostage, even if the hostage is named by the enemy unless the hostage is already guilty of a capital crime;[52] and one must endure short-term torture no matter how intense, though one may choose death if torture lasts for more than a year.

The term *kiddush ha-Shem* (the sanctification of God's Name), together with *hillul ha-Shem* (the profanation of God's Name) and the legal principle *yeihareig ve-'al ya'avor* (let that person be killed and not transgress the law), thus, became the value-concepts which define martyrdom in rabbinic tradition.

The stories of martyrdom, as well as the laws, norms, and value-concepts, have, sadly, become an all too familiar part of the Jewish religious and secular tradition: Hannah and her seven sons (II Macc. 7:2), the Ten Martyrs (one form of which is incorporated in the Yom Kippur and Tish'a b'Av liturgies), the elegies for the communities of Europe (also part of the Tish'a b'Av liturgy), the story of Massada (invoked liturgically in secular Israeli circles), the *Memorbücher* for the communities lost in nazi Europe, and the stories of spiritual and physical heroism by those lost in the shoah.[53]

Resistance had its price in Jewish history and tradition.

Counter-text[54]

For the thousands of prisoners in Gunskirchen, there was one twenty-hole latrine. The rule of the SS men was to shoot on sight anyone seen relieving himself in any place but the latrine. Many of the persons in the camp had diarrhea. There were always long lines at the latrine and it was often impossible for many to reach it in time because of the hours spent waiting. Naturally, many were shot for they could not wait in line. Their bodies were still lying there in their own filth. The stench was unbelievable.

Corporal DeSpain and I both remarked later about the appearance of the inmates—that they all seemed to look alike. When men are reduced to skeletons, as these men were, they all resembled one another—the only difference being in their height and the color of their hair. . . .

The hunger in evidence is hard to imagine. We found huge animal bones in camp—the bones of a horse or cow the prisoners had found and smuggled into camp. Usually these prizes were eaten raw, the flesh torn from the bones and swallowed in great gulps.

Rarely did a prisoner have the strength to curb his hunger long enough to cook what food he got. Outside the gate of the camp was the carcass of a horse that had been killed by shellfire. There was a great, gaping wound in his belly. As we passed it, one of the inmates was down on his knees, eating off the carcass. It had been dead several days. The next day when we came back, the whole side had been sliced away. Though our troops got food to them as soon as possible, many could not wait. Of course, we quickly gave away all the rations and cigarettes we had. It was strange to see them eat the cigarettes instead of smoking them. Not one cigarette did I see smoked. They were all swallowed in a hurry.

13

Four Case Studies

'Ein Shaliaḥ le-Dvar 'Avera (Military Disobedience)

One of the issues in the realm of obedience is the issue of defying military orders. Keijzer outlines the three options very clearly:[1] (1) *Respondeat superior*[2] according to which the individual soldier has no culpability if following orders because the superior officer is responsible. This option derives from Roman law—Justinian put it well: "Whoever acted upon orders of his father or master is considered not to have acted willfully"[3]—and is incorporated in pre-1946 German law and the 1882 French Code of Military Justice. In this option, one accused of obeying illegal orders would be acquitted. (2) "Full responsibility" according to which the individual soldier is always responsible for his actions—the International Military Tribunal at Nuremberg put it well: "The true test . . . is not the existence of the order, but whether moral choice was in fact possible."[4] In this option, one accused of obeying illegal orders would accept this principle and argue "yes, but . . ." and claim duress or a mistake of law or fact. This option derives from Christian (and Jewish) morality of individual responsibility and is the current law in England and France. An accused would be held liable and convicted but clemency would be expected as part of the sentencing process.

(3) "Limited responsibility" according to which the individual soldier must obey, even when in doubt, and hence cannot be held liable for following orders unless they are "manifestly unlawful." The criteria for "manifestly unlawful" are said to be "objective," that is, if a man of ordinary sense and understanding would have known the order to be illegal or, if the perpetrator can be shown to have known that it was illegal, the order is considered "manifestly unlawful." In this option, one accused of obeying illegal orders is held responsible. This option derives from canon law—Pudendorf put it well: "[G]ood men are conscious that they must give an account of their actions before the divine tribunal, and that every Kingdom is subject to a still greater Kingdom, and should promise obedience only on condition that they are willing to obey the commands of sovereigns, provided these are not manifestly opposed to the law of nature and of God."[5] This is the current law in the United States, Germany, and Israel.

The position in Israeli law is clearly discussed in a symposium held in 1990 with the participation of law professors and the chief appellate judge of the military court system on the West Bank.[6] Section 24, A, 2 of the Israel Penal Code provides that a person bears no responsibility if he or she was following the order of a legitimate authority unless the order is "clearly not according to the law."[7] Sections 122–124 of the Military Judicial Law provide that a person must obey orders which he or she is given and provide penalties for disobedience. Section 125, however, provides that a person must obey all orders unless it is "surely and openly not legal."[8] Israeli soldiers were convicted under these military rules in the Kafr Kassem case (1957–58), the judge ruling that an order is manifestly illegal "if there is a black flag flying over the order" which would indicate an "illegality that pierces the eye and arouses the heart." This became known as "the black flag test" and other convictions have been achieved under it, the criterion being "the reasonable soldier."

Judge Shoham of the Military Appeals Court summed up the situation very clearly. He pointed out that a soldier may be ordered to exceed the speed limit, or to steal ammunition from an adjacent unit, or to drive under unsafe conditions (all of which are illegal) but he or she is expected to obey— unless the order is "surely and openly not legal." That is, Israeli military law "sets the rule that soldiers have to execute legal orders, but also illegal orders. However, when it is a matter of a particular class of illegal orders defined as orders of the 'black flag,' then it is forbidden to fulfill them. And if one does so, it is clear that that person is to stand trial and, if he or she refuses to fulfill them, the person does not have to stand trial because of the refusal to fulfill orders."[9] Judge Shoham also affirmed the "reasonable person" test as objective and indicated that that standard varies according to rank and responsibility.

The position of halakha on the subject of military disobedience is very complex and has been studied in detail twice.[10] It revolves around a long and complicated story in the Bible: Yoav ben Tseruya was David's loyal general while Avner ben Ner was loyal to Saul. After the death of Saul and Jonathan, the conflict between David and Ishboshet, the remaining son of Saul, continued. At one point, Yoav met Avner and their troops engaged in a battle, in the course of which Yoav's brother, Asa'el, was killed by Avner although Avner had warned him to desist from pursuing him (II Sam. 2). The civil war continued. Avner sued for peace and David agreed. But, when Yoav found out, he sent messengers after Avner, brought him back, and killed him (II Sam. 3:27). David, who wanted peace, was much annoyed but the deed was done.

Later, Abasalom, David's son, rebelled against him and seized the throne. David, not wishing to fight his son, withdrew. Eventually, David fought back and Abasalom was killed accidentally while fleeing; David's general in this battle, Amasa ben Yeter, however, was not killed (II Sam. 15–20). The latter was asked by David to gather his troops and return, but he was late in doing so. Yoav suspected that Amasa had joined another rebellion and, when he met Amasa, Yoav killed him (II Sam. 20:10) and took his troops into David's army.

On his deathbed, King David commanded his son, Solomon, as follows: "Now you know what Yoav ben Tseruya did to the two army commanders of Israel, Avner ben Ner and Amasa ben Yeter, killing them and spilling the blood of war in peacetime[11]. . . . Do according to your wisdom and do not let him go in peace to his grave" (I Kings 2:5–6). Solomon had his own reasons for not trusting Yoav because he had joined the cause of the pretender, Adoniya. So, when Adoniya was killed, Solomon ordered Yoav killed too saying: ". . . remove from me and from the house of my father the innocent blood which Yoav spilled in vain. God will return his blood upon his head, for he slew two men more righteous and better than he, killing them with the sword, though my father David did not know: Avner ben Ner a commander in Israel and Amasa ben Yeter a commander in Judah . . ." (I Kings 2:28–35).

The rabbis interpreted this bloody sequence of events twice, the first time in the context of justified disobedience. The assumption behind this text is that King Solomon cannot arbitrarily execute Yoav. There must have been a trial. The following text reconstructs the trial of Yoav:

> • Solomon brought Yoav and gave him a trial and asked, "Why did you kill Avner?" Yoav replied, "I was avenging the blood of my brother, Asa'el." Solomon said, "But Asa'el was pursuing Avner [and Avner was therefore justified in killing him]." Yoav replied, "Avner could have merely wounded him." Solomon said, "He couldn't." Yoav replied, "If he could pierce him through the fifth rib, could he not have merely wounded him?"

COMMENT: Yoav has argued that Avner could have wounded Asa'el but chose to kill him instead and, hence, he (Yoav) cannot be held guilty of killing Avner as an avenger of his brother's blood.

> • Solomon continued, "Go on, Yoav ("You are innocent on this count" [Rashi, ad loc]). Why did you kill Amasa?" Yoav replied, "Amasa was rebelling against the monarchy, as it says . . . [that he was ordered to gather his troops and return by a certain time and did not do so]." Solomon said, "Amasa was only being very precise in his study and judgment. When he found his troops, they were studying Torah and he said to himself, 'It is written, "Any man who rebels against you and will not obey you in all that you command shall be put to death" (Josh. 1:18). Can this mean that even [if the king commands one to contravene the Torah and interrupt one's] study [one must obey]? No, for it also says [at the end of the same verse], 'just be strong and of good courage' [that is, you must resist the command of the king to assemble the army if that command violates the Torah prescription to study].'"

COMMENT: Solomon has argued that Amasa was exercising proper disobedience and was not rebelling against the king and, therefore, Yoav's killing him was unjustified and his (Solomon's) death sentence for Yoav is correct. The Talmud now speaks in its own voice.

> However, [since it is possible that Yoav did not agree with Amasa's exegesis,[12] Solomon was still justified in executing Yoav] because Yoav himself was one who rebelled against the king as it says, "and Yoav joined the forces of Adoniya" (II Kings 2:28).[13]

This classic passage establishes two important points of Jewish law: (1) There is a duty to rebel, even against the king, when superior orders violate a Torah law—this is the case of Amasa who decides not to disobey God's command to study in order to fulfill the kings' command to produce his troops on time. And (2), anyone who disobeys a royal order in favor of God's command is not liable for such disobedience.

The law is summarized by Maimonides as follows:

> • One who fails to follow the orders of the king because one is engaged in the fulfillment of biblical commandments, even if the religious duty is a minor one, may not be punished. If the words of the Master and the words of the servant are in conflict, the words of the Master take precedence (Heb., *divrei ha-rav ve-divrei ha-'eved, divrei ha-rav kodmin*).[14] Moreover, it is obvious that if the king orders someone to violate a commandment, he need not be obeyed.[15]
> • If one's parent orders one to transgress a positive or a negative commandment set forth in the Bible or even a commandment which is of rabbinic origin, the child must disregard the order for it is said, "You shall, every person, fear his or her mother and her or his father, and you shall keep My Sabbaths" (Lev. 19:3); that is, all of you are bound to honor Me.[16]

The second interpretation of the Avner-Amasa-Yoav story by the rabbis centers not on the issue of justified disobedience but on the question of protest in a military hierarchy.

> • "God will return his blood upon his head, for he [Yoav] slew two men more righteous and better than he . . . Avner ben Ner, a commander in Israel, and Amasa ben Yeter, a commander in Judah" (I Kings 2:32) . . . "more righteous"—in that they received their command by mouth [from Saul to kill the priests in Nob] yet defied it, while his [Yoav's command to arrange for the killing of Uriah so David could have Bathsheba (II Sam. 11:14–15)] came by letter and he obeyed it.[17]

COMMENT: In this last passage, Avner and Amasa are contrasted with Yoav, the former receive (according to the first source) their illegal order from the king directly yet they defy it while the latter receives his illegal order (to arrange for the killing of Uriah) indirectly, in a letter, yet he does not defy that order. Avner and Amasa are, thus, morally superior to Yoav because they refuse an illegal order.

> • "The king [Saul] said to the messengers who were in attendance upon him, 'Go and kill the priests of the Lord [in Nob], for their hand was with David and they knew that he was fleeing and did not tell me.' But the servants of the king did not want to stretch out their hands to kill the priests of the Lord" (I Sam. 22:17). Who were they? Rabbi Shmuel bar Rabbi Yitsḥak said, "They were Avner and Amasa." They replied to Saul, "Do we owe you anything beyond this belt and mantle [insignia of office]? Here, take them back!" [18]
> • Rav Judah said in Rav's name: Why was Avner punished [that is, if Avner was suing for peace, what had he done wrong such that he came to a brutal end? (II Sam. 3:27)]? Because he should have protested to Saul against the execution of the priests of Nob (I Sam. 22:18) but did not. R. Isaac, however, said: He did indeed do so but was not heeded. [19]

COMMENT: These last two passages, taking different readings of Avner and the order to kill the priests of Nob, suggest a major point in Jewish ethics: that, even in a situation of a military hierarchy, merely refusing to carry out an illegal order is not enough; one must protest it, one must actively oppose it.

Another set of classical texts in Jewish law on the subject of superior orders deals with the issue of agency. The general rule is *sheluḥo shel adam kemoto* ("a person's agent is as oneself") [20] which means that anything an agent does at the principal's behest binds the principal. But, what if the principal orders the agent to commit an illegal act?

> • When someone appoints an agent saying, "Go forth and slay that man," the agent is culpable and the principal is innocent. Shammai the Elder, however, said in the name of Ḥaggai the prophet, "The principal is culpable, as it is written, 'And him have you slain with the sword of the children of Ammon.'" [21]

COMMENT: The biblical quotation refers to Nathan's confrontation with David who had ordered Yoav to have Uriah killed in the battle with the Ammonites so David could have Bathsheba. Yoav did do this but Nathan accuses David, the principal, of the killing and does not lay the full blame at the door of Yoav, the agent. Hence, Shammai's opinion, though no such tradition has survived in the writings of the prophet, Ḥaggai.

Using the quotation cited above, Jewish law establishes the principle, *'ein shaliah le-dvar 'avera* ("There is no agency for illegal acts").[22] The commentators go on to account for the difference of opinion in the source as follows: "[A]ll are agreed that a principal who appoints an agent to commit a crime may not bear prime responsibility but is certainly guilty in the eyes of Heaven. The disagreement is merely how great is his guilt in the eyes of Heaven. The first [anonymous] opinion is that the guilt in the eyes of Heaven is of secondary quality, that is, of an accomplice and not a perpetrator. Shammai disagrees, contending that the principal is regarded as a murderer in the first degree, albeit in the eyes of Heaven."[23]

The law is summarized by Maimonides:

• One who hires an assassin to kill his or her fellow, or who sends her or his slaves to kill someone, or who binds and exposes someone to a lion or the like and a wild beast did kill that person, and similarly one who kills oneself—all these are shedders of blood and are guilty of murder; they deserve death by Heaven but may not be executed by the [earthly] courts.[24]

There are, however, several exceptions to the rule, *'ein shaliah le-dvar 'avera* ("There is no agency for illegal acts"); e.g., if the act is one of a series of acts, if it involves misappropriation of a pledge or fencing stolen goods, or if the agent is a minor.[25] One interesting exception is the case of a debtor who points to a third person's property and instructs an ignorant agent to use it to pay his debts. The commentators are divided on who is responsible if the agent acts on such instructions. Some hold that the principal (the debtor) is liable while others claim the agent is responsible, the latter claiming that "[a]n agent acting unwittingly is still acting freely; hence, the principal [here, the debtor] cannot be held liable for the acts of such an agent . . . the principal [however] is in no way absolved of moral responsibility . . . guilt in the eyes of Heaven."[26]

Turning to the case of military disobedience in light of the principle *'ein shaliah le-dvar 'avera* ("There is no agency for illegal acts") and its exceptions, Kirschenbaum concludes that the position of Jewish law is as follows:

The faceless apparatus of bureaucracy, turning the wheels of government, local or national, civil or military, cannot blot out the humanity of the single, individual man *qua* man and cannot transform him into an automaton, an amoral cog. . . . Although, as a result of its insistence upon personal responsibility, Jewish law tends to withhold punishment from accessories before the fact, . . . in criminal and sinful acts of a complex nature . . . it does impute equal responsibility to the principal or to the enticers who aid, abet or initiate the crime committed. . . . Nevertheless, the duty of obedience is not absolute. A soldier need not, nay may not, obey an order to commit a crime. If a soldier, following orders, does commit a crime—if he was aware of the criminal nature of the act, *he and his superior* must bear full responsibility for it;—if he was aware of the criminal nature of the act but was equally cognizant of the rule of law which exempts him from obeying, nay forbids him to obey, his superior . . . *he [the soldier] alone* must bear sole responsibility for the act . . . his commander is no more than an accessory before the fact whose punishment is left to Heaven;—if he was unaware of the criminal nature of the act that he is being commanded to perform, *his commander [alone]* must bear full responsibility for it.[27]

The position of the halakha would seem, then, to be closest to the position of "manifest unlawfulness" with the understanding that the "manifest" quality in halakha is a function of knowledge of halakha, not of civil or natural law. It would also seem that the halakha is more subtle in clearly assigning responsibility to the superior.

Lo Tihye Aḥarei Rabbim Lera'ot (Judicial Dissent)

A judicial system must be able to protect reasonable difference of opinion among members of the judiciary and also to guarantee discipline within the system such that the rulings of the highest instance are enforceable and cannot be defied. To accomplish the latter, the Torah provides for the appointment of courts and charges them with doing justice and also establishes an appeal system with sanctions against anyone who defies the final decision.

> • You shall set courts and police in all your gates . . . and they shall judge the people with just judgment. Do not bend judgment; do not favor anyone; do not take a bribe, for the bribe blinds the eyes of the wise and distorts the words of the righteous. Pursue only justice. . . . When some judicial matter is not clear . . . you shall come to the priest, Levites, and judges who shall be in those days; you shall ask and they will tell you the law. You shall act according to that which they tell you . . . to the Torah which they teach you and the law which they decide for you; you shall not deviate from that which they tell you, neither right nor left. And anyone who shall purposely act so as not to obey the . . . judge, that person shall die . . . and all the people will hear and will see and will not purposely do wrong (Dt. 16 : 18–20; 17 : 8–13).[28]

There are two issues here. The first is judicial discipline.

> • "Neither right nor left" (Dt. 17 : 11)—even if they show you before your eyes that left is right and right is left, obey them.[29]

• Its meaning is: Even if you think in your heart that they are in error and it seems as clear to you as knowledge between your right and your left, do as they command and do not say, "How can I . . . condemn this innocent man?" Rather, say, "So has the Commander of mitsvot commanded me to do all the commands which [they] teach me for, on their understanding, has He given me the Torah, even if they err" . . . The need for this mitsva is very great, for the Torah was given in writing and it is known that, in new matters, interpretations are not always the same and that argument would spring up and the Torah would become many Torot. So Scripture set the law for us that we must obey the highest court . . . even if it seems in your eyes that they confuse right and left . . . for the spirit of God [30] is upon those who serve in His sanctuary and He will not desert His righteous ones. He will always save them from error and stumbling. . . . [31]

COMMENT: These two passages, one early and one medieval, develop the meaning of the biblical verse and establish the general principle of, and rationale for, judicial discipline.

• Do not be after the majority to do evil; do not respond to a dispute by tending toward the majority to cause [others] to tend [that way] (Ex. 23:2).

COMMENT: The Hebrew of this biblical passage is very difficult: *lo tihye aharei rabbim lera'ot; ve-lo ta'ane 'al riv lintot aharei rabbim lehatot.* It, too, seems to be establishing the principle of judicial discipline.

• "Do not be after the majority to do evil"—this means that you may not be after them to do evil, but you may do so to do good. How is this? If twelve vote to acquit and eleven vote to convict, the accused is [obviously] acquitted and if thirteen vote to convict and ten vote to acquit, the accused is [obviously] convicted. However, if eleven vote to acquit and twelve vote to convict, I might think that, since there are twelve to convict [that is, there is a majority of one to convict], the accused should be convicted. [To counter this] the Torah teaches, "do not respond to a dispute by tending toward the majority." [By this] the Torah means to teach: As you convict for capital punishment only on the basis of two witnesses, so you shall convict for capital punishment only on the basis of two votes. [32]

COMMENT: The problem, here, is: how much of a majority of voting judges does one need to convict in a capital case? One might think that a simple majority of one would suffice to acquit or to convict. Following the peculiar syntax of this biblical verse and the precedent governing witnesses in capital cases, the rabbis rule that a simple majority of one can acquit, but a majority of two is needed to convict in such cases. They, thus, read the verse: "Do not be after a majority [of one] to convict."

> • "Do not be after the majority to do evil"—From this they teach that one does not decide a vote on the basis of one judge . . . "tending toward the majority to cause [others] to tend [that way]"—There is a majority after which one does tend, and what is it? When the number voting for conviction is two greater than the number voting for acquittal. And from the fact that it says "do not be after the majority to do evil," I understand that there are times when one must be with them. From this, they learn that, in capital crimes, one follows a majority of one judge to acquit and two judges to convict.[33]

COMMENT: A later restatement of the same rule.

The procedural rules on judicial discipline, then, are: (1) A rabbinic judge who feels his colleagues have erred may rule his own way but he must go to a series of appeals courts, each of which is obligated to hear out the dissenter. However, after the final appeal, the dissenter may not rule, or act himself according to his own opinion and, if he does, he is considered "a rebellious judge," a crime punishable by death.[34] (2) In noncapital crimes, one follows a majority of one to acquit or convict ("tending toward the majority [of one] to cause others to tend [that way]"). But, in capital crimes, one follows a majority of one to acquit ("tending toward the majority [of one] to cause others to tend [that way]") and a majority of two to convict ("do not be after the majority [of one] to do evil").

The second issue is the right of judicial dissent; indeed, the obligation to judicial dissent. The rabbis use the same verse from Exodus to establish these principles.

> • Do not be after the majority to do evil; do not respond to a dispute by tending toward the majority to cause [others] to tend [that way] (Ex. 23:2).
> • "Do not respond to a dispute by tending toward the majority to cause [others] to tend [that way]"—You may not say during the deliberations, "It is enough for the servant to be like the master"[35] [that is, to vote with the majority]. Say what is on your mind.[36]
> • Is it possible that, if they tell you that right is left and left is right, you must obey them (Dt. 17:11)?! [To counter this] the Torah teaches "to go right or left"[37] [that is, only] when they tell you that right is right and left is left.[38]

COMMENT: This is the opposite of the interpretation cited above on the subject of judicial discipline. This basic issue of "'You shall not deviate from that which they tell you, neither right nor left'—even if they say that right is left and left is right" is, then, resolved two ways. Abrabanel argues that "right is left" is true only in times of emergency when everyone agrees the court can suspend parts of Torah law. In such a case, "right is left" is really "right is right"; hence, conforming is quite rational.[39] Hoffman argues that the issue is one of precedence for the plain meaning of Scripture or for the tradition. Those who argue for full obedience invoke the precedence of Scripture and those who argue for reasoned obedience invoke the precedence of tradition (and reason).

- "Do not be after the majority to do evil"—There are many interpretations of the sages of Israel on this verse but the language of Scripture does not sit properly on its wheels with them. . . . I say, in order to set Scripture properly on its wheels, according to its simple meaning, that this is its interpretation: "Do not be after the majority to do evil"—If you see the wicked tending judgment, do not say, 'Since they are many, I will follow them.'
  "Do not respond to a dispute by tending toward the majority to cause [others] to tend [that way]"—If the accused in that case questions you about the judgment, do not respond to the dispute with something that tends after that majority, causing judgment to tend from its truth. Rather, say the judgment as it is and let the punishment rest with the majority.[40]

The right—indeed, the obligation—of judicial dissent, then, is guaranteed by strong interpretational support for not going along with the majority when a judge thinks that majority is wrong, even in a capital case.

The need for judicial discipline and the need to protect judicial dissent are clearly in conflict. The commentators strove to reconcile these two traditions and needs.

- If the [highest] court ruled to uproot a principle of the Torah—saying, there is no law concerning menstruating women in the Torah or, there is no law of Shabbat in the Torah, or there is no law concerning idolatry in the Torah—they [judges who defy the highest court] are innocent [of the law of the rebellious judge].[41]
- If the judge was an extraordinary scholar on the court and disagreed, studied, and taught others according to that judge's opinions, but did not rule [for himself or others] to act [according to those opinions], that judge is not liable [under the law of the rebellious judge]. For it says, "And anyone who shall purposely act so as not to obey the . . . judge"—not that one speaks purposely, but that one rules for others to act, or that one acts [oneself]—[only such a judge shall be prosecuted].[42]
- There is, however, a condition to this [the discipline of the court system] which one who looks at the beginning of [*Talmud*] Horayot carefully will

understand. To wit, that, if there were a fully qualified sage at the time of the Sanhedrin and if the Great Court had ruled to permit something and that sage thought they had erred in their ruling, that sage does not have to obey the words of the [other] sages and is not allowed to permit to oneself that which is forbidden. Rather, such a person should practice the strict law for oneself and *a fortiori* if one was one of the judges on the Great Court. Further, such a sage must come before them and make his [or her] arguments, and they must enter into discussion with that person and, if they all agreed that this opinion was invalid and they broke down all the arguments, such a sage should repent and act according to their ruling after they have removed them [the arguments], but they must reach an agreement about this opinion.[43]

The guarantees for judicial dissent, then, include: that a judge should speak his or her mind even if that judge is in a minority; that a judge can teach and expound her or his minority opinions even though the judge may not rule according to them; and that a judge can practice the stricter law, but not the more lenient law, privately, even if it is a minority position.

Lo Ta'amod (The Obligation to Rescue)

One of the issues in the realm of altruism is the issue of rescue, sometimes known as the problem of the Good Samaritan (Luke 10:30–7).[44] Halakha starts neither from a particular illustrative incident like the Good Samaritan nor from an assumption of altruism on the part of human beings. Rather, halakha formulates the issue as an obligation, as mitsva (a commandment from God), and then proceeds to discuss the conditions under which the duty to rescue is obligatory as well as those under which such a duty is optional or *middat ḥasidut* (the standard of the pious) for sensitive rabbinic Jews.[45]

There are three key sources for the obligation to rescue.

• You shall not stand by the blood of your other;[46] I am the Lord (Lev. 19:16).

COMMENT: This verse from the Torah is the origin of the obligation to rescue and it bears several schools of interpretation. One of them takes "stand" in the sense of "rise up against," hence, "to scheme against." In this meaning, the verse forbids one to "scheme against the life of one's fellow, whether by cunning or violence, by speech or deed."[47] Another school of interpretation takes "stand" in the sense of "stand idly by." In this meaning, the verse forbids one to be a passive bystander when another is attacked.

- Whence do we know that if a person sees one's fellow drowning in a river, mauled by beasts, or attacked by robbers, one is obligated to save the other? From the verse, "You shall not stand by the blood of your other" (Lev. 19: 16). Whence do we know [that one must save one's neighbor from] the loss of his or her own self? From the verse, "You shall surely return it [the person's self, life] to him or her" (Dt. 22:2).[48]

COMMENT: The obligation to rescue is, according to this source, derived from two biblical verses, the law in Leviticus forbidding one to be a bystander and the law in Deuteronomy enjoining return of lost objects, including the possible loss of life. Jewish law, however, recognizes these laws, together with others, as unenforceable: "Jewish law views failure as nonfeasance, a formal offence of inaction . . . where action is a duty required by the law."[49]

A third source for the obligation to rescue derives from the value-concept and legal principle of *pikuah nefesh* ("saving a life").[50] In general, Jewish law provides that *pikuah nefesh* ("saving a life") takes precedence over all other Jewish law. Three examples of this prioritization:

- Rabbi Matthia ben Heresh said, "If one has pain in one's throat, one may pour medicine into one's mouth on the Sabbath because there is a possibility of danger to human life, and *every danger to human life suspends [the laws of] the Sabbath.*"[51]

COMMENT: The preparation and administration of medicines involve the violation of the Shabbat restrictions on human activity; however, in the case of even possible danger to a life, one must violate Shabbat law.

- One must remove debris to save a life on the Sabbath; and the more energetic one is, the more praiseworthy is one; and one need not obtain permission from the rabbinical court. The energetic one is praiseworthy, the [authority who would be consulted] is insulted, and the inquirer is a murderer.[52]

COMMENT: Removing debris is, under normal circumstances, forbidden on Shabbat; however, if a life is at stake, one is obligated to remove debris to save someone. Indeed, one sins if one takes the time to consult an authority on this subject.

- When such things [which are violations of Shabbat] must be done [to save the life of a person who is ill], they should not be left to non-Jews, minors, slaves, or women lest these should come to regard Shabbat observance as a trivial matter. [Rather,] they should be done by important and scholarly Jews.[53]

COMMENT: Violating the Shabbat to save a life is not a violation; therefore, such acts must be done by community leaders to model correct behavior explicitly. The converse is also true. The two classic cases of the foolish saint (Hebrew, *ḥasid shote*) are: he who sees a woman drowning and refuses to save her for reasons of man-woman modesty and he who sees a child drowning and delays saving the child so that he can remove his tefillin.[54]

Pikuaḥ nefesh ("saving a life"), then, is really a form of *lo ta'amod* ("rescue") and it applies in all cases, even those where there is only possible danger to a life and even when prolonging life, not saving it, is at stake.[55] It applies with particular rigor to doctors and other health care personnel, who can even endanger a human life in order to save it.[56] A person with a contagious disease is obligated to disclose (a relevant stance in the AIDS disclosure debate).[57] A victim must be rescued even if he or she refuses rescue and protests against being saved.[58] One who is pursuing another with the intent to kill, may in turn be killed if that is the only way to stop the pursuer; but, if the pursuer can be kept from killing by anything short of death, one must do so.[59]

The basic rule, then, is that *lo ta'amod* (the obligation to rescue) is present at all times in its properly qualified senses. The obligation to rescue established in these verses and their interpretation, however, raises a series of questions concerning the limits of rescue. Is one obligated to attempt rescue even at the loss of one's life? What if it is only likely, or only possible, that one might lose one's life? Are there limits to what one must do to save another person? What, if any, are the financial liabilities of the rescuer—to the victim, to others whom he or she may hurt, and to property she or he may damage in the act of rescue? Does the rescuer have a way to recover any expenses he or she may incur in the course of rescue, and from whom? (One problem need not detain us: The Jewish sources do not distinguish between natural dangers [a river or beasts] and human-generated dangers [robbers]).[60]

The issue of risk will be considered first.

- If two are traveling on a journey and one has a pitcher of water—if both drink, they will die but, if only one drinks, that person can reach civilization [that is, will be saved]. The son of Patura taught: "It is better that both should drink and die rather than that one should behold his companion's death." But Rabbi Akiva came and taught, "[It is written, 'You shall fear the Lord, your God] so that your fellow live with you' (Lev. 25:36)—your life takes precedence over the other's life."[61]
- A person exiled [to a city of refuge for accidental homicide (Nu. 35:9– 34)] may never leave the city of refuge, not even to perform a scriptural commandment . . . or even to save a life with his or her evidence, or to save someone from invading troops, or from a river in flood, or from a fire, or from a fallen ruin. Indeed, not even if all Israel needs her or his help . . .

[For] if one does leave, one surrenders oneself to death [at the hands of the blood redeemer (Nu. 35:26–27)].[62]

COMMENT: The law in the case of sure personal danger to the rescuer is clear. A rescuer is not obligated to rescue if it is certain that he or she will be killed, nor does any moral blame attach to such a decision.[63] Further, the status of someone who volunteers to give up his or her life under conditions of sure danger is subject to dispute: Maimonides considers such an act sinful while the Tosafot consider it meritorious.[64]

- However, if the *possibility* of death to the would-be rescuer is close to *certainty,* he need not sacrifice his own life to save his fellow. Nay, if the possibility is more-or-less half favorable and half unfavorable ("fifty-fifty"), he is not obligated to sacrifice his life; for 'what makes you think that your blood is redder; perhaps his blood is redder.'[65] Where, however, the possibility is not half-and-half [and] it rather tends toward safety and he will not be [seriously] endangered, if he does not strive to rescue, he has indeed violated, *Thou shall not stand idly by the blood of thy neighbor* (Lev. 19:17).[66]
- How can one imagine that a person would allow his eye to be blinded or his hand or foot be cut off so that his fellow not die? I, therefore, see no justification for his [Recanati's] decision [that it is obligatory to sacrifice a nonvital limb to save another's life]. It is an act of saintliness (*middat ha-sidut*),[67] [that is, above and beyond the halakhic requirement], and happy is the man who can live up to it. If, however, there is a possible risk of life, then [one who agrees to the amputation] is a foolish saint (*hasid shoteh*),[68] for the *possible* danger to oneself takes precedence over the *certain* danger to one's fellow.[69]

COMMENT: In the case of only likely, or possible, danger of life to the rescuer, the sources are mixed. Radbaz, cited in the preceding quotations, rules that "possibility" and "likelihood" are a matter of intelligent percentages, including those involved in the loss of a limb. If the percentages are reasonable, there is still no obligation because of the danger that remains. It is, rather, an act of extraordinary caring to run a reasonable risk. He also rules that anyone who acts against intelligent odds is a fool.

The halakha on this issue is summarized well by Kirschenbaum:

This question as to whether the Good Samaritan need put his own life in *possible* danger to save his fellow from *certain* death is the subject of sustained controversy among rabbinic authorities. Summarized briefly, *rabbinic law today declares that there is no such duty,* but qualifies this declaration in a number of ways: it exhorts the citizen, "One must not overly protect oneself. . . ." the volunteer who does endanger his life and limb is extolled as acting above and beyond the call of duty and as performing a caring act (*middat ḥasidut*). . . . the degree of jeopardy which legally exempts the bystander from his duty must be a most substantial one. . . .[70]

A further limit to *lo ta'amod* is found in the provision that a rescuer may not commit idolatry, murder, or incest or adultery to save any victim, including oneself.[71] The law is summarized by Maimonides:

  • But if someone is pursuing another to kill that person, even if the pursuer is a minor, all Israel are commanded to save the pursued person from the pursuer even at the cost of the life of the pursuer.
      How [is this possible] . . . since he or she is still pursuing [and has not yet actually killed that] she or he can be killed? If one can save the pursued person by maiming a limb of the pursuer—for instance, by striking with an arrow or a stone or a sword such that one cuts off a hand or breaks a leg or blinds an eye—one does that. But if one cannot intend to save the pursued unless one kills the pursuer, one kills him or her even though she or he has not yet killed. . . .[72]
  • Anyone who is capable of saving another and does not do so transgresses [the commandment], "You shall not stand idly by the blood of your other" (Lev. 19:17). Similarly, if one sees one's fellow drowning in the sea, or under attack by robbers, or a wild animal about to set upon him or her, and one is capable of saving her or him by oneself, or by hiring others to save that person, and one does not do so; or if one heard that non-Jews or informers were planning evil against someone or setting a trap for someone, and one does not advise one's fellow and tell him or her; or if one knew of a non-Jew or an exploiter who was about to set upon one's fellow, and one is able to pacify [the persecutor] on behalf of the friend and to remove that intention, and one does not pacify [the persecutor]; and all such similar situations—whoever so acts transgresses [the commandment], "You shall not stand idly by the blood of your other" (Lev. 19:17).[73]

Another limit to *lo ta'amod,* the issue of priorities—that is, whom is one obligated to rescue and whom is one not obligated to rescue—is also clearly discussed. One is not obligated to rescue non-Jews, recidivist robbers, murderers, those who incite others to idolatry, and defiant heretics on the general grounds that these people are under a death sentence already or, at the minimum, are not considered "one's other" (Lev. 19:17).[74] Men take precedence over women on the general ground that they have the greater responsibility in the observance of mitsvot,[75] and city populations seem to take precedence over suburban populations.[76]

The provisions concerning financial obligations and liabilities of a rescuer are very interesting. First, *lo ta 'amod* is understood to teach that a rescuer must use his or her own money to rescue and must generally come to the aid of persons in distress even if they are not in danger. Kirschenbaum summarizes the issue clearly:

> Thus, the later rabbis in the Talmud itself raise the question of the apparent superfluity of the two verses teaching the same duty to rescue ["You shall not stand by the blood of your other; I am the Lord" (Lev. 19:16) and "You shall surely return it [the person's self, life] to him or her" (Dt. 22:2)]. They come to the conclusion that the verse *Thou shalt not stand idly by,* broadens the duty from the person to the purse, that is, it obligates the bystander to go to extraordinary lengths to save the victim—even to the extent of actually hiring help. . . . Early medieval scholars . . . *Thou shalt restore it to him* . . . includes the duty to come to the assistance of one who is in distress but not in any peril, e.g., one who is lost in a forest but would eventually be able to find his way out. . . .[77]

Second, in spite of halakha's enormous respect for property and property rights, a rescuer is immune from all tort damages he or she may inflict in the course of rescue:[78]

- One who was pursuing a pursuer to save [a victim from murder] and who damaged property either of the pursuer, or the victim, or anyone else, is free [from all liability]. But is he or she not liable according to the law? [No] because, if you do not rule this way, no one would ever save one's fellow from a pursuer.[79]
- Even if one is in mortal danger and must steal from one's fellow in order to save his or her own life, one may do so [but] only on condition that one intends to make subsequent restitution.[80]
- If a ship threatens to break up because of the weight of its load and one of those on board lightens the load by throwing some of the objects overboard, that person is exempt [from compensating the owner] because the load carried is regarded as pursuing the passengers to kill them. Such a person fulfills an important religious duty in throwing some of the load overboard and saving the passengers.[81]
- One who sees one's fellow wandering in the vineyards is permitted to cut one's way through when going up [to the person] and to cut one's way through when coming down, ruining thereby the place upon which one is treading, until one brings the other into town or onto the road. And just as

it is meritorious to do so on behalf of one's fellow, so it is meritorious to do so on behalf of oneself.[82]

Third, a rescuer, while not entitled to any compensation for fulfilling a commandment, is entitled to compensation for costs entailed in rescue.[83] This includes full compensation for loss of livelihood due to rescue.[84] Furthermore, a rescuer is entitled to reimbursement for any direct expenses incurred: "[I]n order to save the victim, the rescuer has the right to sue the rescued party in order to recover the money expended. This holds true even if the victim protests, wishes not to be rescued, and later refuses to compensate the rescuer."[85] This recovery of costs is, however, limited in several ways: the victim's subsequent fortune is not liable, the victim's heirs are not liable, and the victim is not liable at all unless the operation is successful.[86] Finally, halakha protects the rescuer from liability: "The cost of damages and disabilities incurred by the rescuer in the course of the rescue operation, however, could *not* be recovered by the rescuer. The Jewish law of tort obligates the tortfeasor, and the tortfeasor only, for damages incurred; no one else—not even the one as interested as the rescued party himself—is so obligated."[87]

Noting that, in American law contrary to halakha, others, including the rescued party, can sue the Good Samaritan, Kirschenbaum concludes: "Is legislation then necessary? Would not the adoption of the provisions of Jewish law—guaranteeing the Good Samaritan compensation for his losses, exemption from all other duties that devolve upon him at the time, and immunity from tort liability—be sufficient in putting society, as expressing itself in its legal system, on record as creating a legal duty to rescue and as holding said duty in the highest regard?"[88]

Violence and Nonviolence

There is a strong stream of violence in Jewish tradition, as indeed such a tendency exists in all traditions.[89]

God, Godself, threatens, promises, and does acts of violence: God destroys the whole of civilization in the flood (Gen. 6–7). God commands the annihilation of Amalek (Ex. 17:14–15, Dt. 9:1–5, 25:17–19). God commands the annihilation of the six nations (Dt. 20:16–18). God threatens the annihilation of the Jewish people (Ex. 23:23–24, Lev. 26:14–45, Dt. 9:11–29, 28:15–69).

- It will be that, as God rejoiced over you doing good for you and multiplying you, so the Lord will rejoice over you to destroy you and annihilate you . . . (Dt. 28:63).
- God saw and was enraged, angry at his sons and daughters.
He said, "I will hide My Face from them, and see what will become of them.

For they are a reprobate generation,
children in whom one can have no confidence. . . ."
Indeed, fire flames within Me, burning to the bottom of hell,
consuming the earth and its produce,
setting fire to the foundations of the mountains.
I will multiply evils upon them, I will empty My arrows against them.
The ravages of hunger, lightning, wars, bitter poison, and the teeth
of beasts
will I send against them, together with crawling things. . . .
See, now, that I am indeed He, there is no other God beside Me;
I kill and I give life, I crush and I heal,
there is no escape from My hand. . . .
I will make My arrows drunk from blood, My sword will eat meat,
from the blood of the dead and the captured,
from the heads of the leaders of the enemy. . . .

COMMENT: This comes from the great concluding song of Deuteronomy (chap. 32). In it, God threatens ultimate revenge on His enemies, Jewish and non-Jewish. No translation captures the lapidary power of the Hebrew poetry.

Humans follow God's example in action: Moses struck mortal blows to Midian and Bashan (Nu. 31, Dt. 3:3–7). Joshua tried, even if he did not succeed, in annihilating the six nations (Josh. 6:20–21, 8:20–29, 10:28–43, 11:10–15).[90] The Levite abused and killed his concubine (Judges 19). Samuel ordered the annihilation of Amalek, killing Agag with his own hand when Saul failed to do so (I Sam. 15). David, fighting against the Philistines, wiped out whole cities (I Sam. 27:8–12).

Humans also echoed God's violence in their language, in the graphic violence of their imagery, in the threats that they put into the very mouth of God.

• Now I shall expose her nakedness before the eyes of her lovers; no man can save her from Me (Hos. 2:12).
• And I passed by and saw you rolling in your blood and I said: "In your very bloodiness, live! In your very bloodiness, live!" ". . . I spread My garment over you, I covered your nakedness; and I swore a covenant to you," said the Lord, "and you became Mine. . . ." Thus says the Lord: "Since your lewdness has been poured forth and you have revealed your personal parts in your carryings-on with your lovers . . . Therefore, I shall gather all your lovers to whom you pledged yourself, those whom you loved together with those whom you hated, I shall gather them all against you round about, and I shall expose your private parts to them and they shall see your nakedness. . . . I shall give you over to their power and they shall break your back and shatter your proud points; they shall strip you of your

clothes and take your valuable things, and leave you nude and naked. . . .
Then I shall have satisfied My wrath against you and My jealousy shall pass
from you; I shall be calm, and I will be angry no longer" (Ezek. 16:6–8,
36–42).[91]

Apocalyptic threats of violence are also an aspect of this human counter-
part to God's violence.[92] So is the depiction of hell in rabbinic (and Christian)
literature.[93]

When humans could not exercise violence, they prayed for it:

• Pour out Your wrath on the nations which do not acknowledge You
and on the states which do not call upon Your Name.
For they have eaten up Jacob, and laid waste its sanctuary.

COMMENT: This is from Psalm 89:6–7 with a near parallel in Jeremiah 10:25.
It is included in the *Haggada* as part of the rabbinic liturgy of Passover night.

• Let His people chant it against the nations,
indeed, God will avenge the blood of His servants,
He will return vengeance to His enemies,
cleansing His people and His land (Dt. 32:43).
• I will cleanse the blood I have not yet cleansed,
the Lord resides in Zion (Joel 4:21).
• . . . let the avenging of the spilled blood of Your servants
be known publicly among the nations (Ps. 89:10).
• He will exercise judgment on nations filled with corpses,
He will crush heads all over the land,
He will drink from a stream by the wayside,
then He will raise a head (Ps. 110:6–7).

COMMENT: These verses became part of the weekly Shabbat memorial prayer
for Jewish martyrs. For other biblical prayers for violence, see Psalms 44, 109,
136, etc.
The theme of revenge became so strong that the word, *nekama* ("revenge"),
together with its verb forms, became a value-concept on its own.

• Our Father, our King. Avenge before our eyes
the vengeance of the spilled blood of Your servants.

COMMENT: This is part of the penitential liturgy recited on Yom Kippur and
other fast days. Halakhic responsa written during and after the shoah almost
always end with a call for *nekama,* for God to avenge the blood of the fallen
martyrs of God's people.[94]

To be sure, Judaism also teaches a doctrine of justified violence—either as self-defense or as an educational tool:

- If he comes to kill you, kill him first.[95]
- You shall burn out the evil from your midst. . . .[96]
- Hate evil. Love good. Establish justice in the gate (Amos 5:15).
- You who love the Lord hate evil (Ps. 97:10).
- Rabbi Shimon ben Lakish said, "Whoever becomes merciful where toughness[97] is necessary will, in the end, be cruel where mercy is necessary. . . ." The rabbis taught, "Whoever becomes merciful where toughness is necessary, in the end the standard of justice will strike him. . . ."[98]
- All this requires toughness—to pursue the wicked and to pressure them in order to return them to the good. One must be tough in the law and not have mercy upon one's relatives, friends, and the poor; rather, one must apply the law [fully].[99]

The effort to evolve a doctrine of justified violence led to a valiant attempt to reinterpret texts where the violence seemed wholly gratuitous or downright wrong. In fact, the lion's share of biblical, and especially rabbinic, theology on the subject of violence is devoted to interpreting such passages. In the rabbinic reading, violence is justified and the texts become lessons in conscientious toughness and moral pedagogy.

- It will be that, as God rejoiced over you doing good for you and multiplying you, so the Lord will rejoice over you to destroy you and annihilate you . . . (Dt. 28:63).

COMMENT: This passage, also cited above, is so violent in God's desire to wreak destruction on the people that the rabbis, reading the verb in the independent clause in its causative form, interpret: "He does not rejoice—[because God does not rejoice in the fall of the wicked]—but He causes [or allows] others to rejoice over you[r destruction]."[100]

- Rabbi Yoḥanan said in the name of Rabbi Shimon ben Yehotsadak: "It is better that one letter of the Torah be uprooted and the Name of Heaven be sanctified in public. For [non-Jewish] passers-by were saying, 'Who are these men? They are [after all] the sons of a king! What have they done?!' [To this, some Jews answered], 'They had stretched out their hands against poor converts [to take their food—Rashi].' They [the non-Jewish passers-by then] said, 'There is no nation as worthy to cling to as this. If this is how they treat even sons of kings [who have exploited others], how much more so are they [just] with everyone! And, if this is how they treat poor converts, how much more so are they [respectful] of full Jews!'" Immediately, 150,000 people joined the Jewish people.[101]

COMMENT: In II Samuel 21:1–14, David gives up the sons of Saul, except Mefiboshet son of Jonathan, to the Gibeonites to be impaled publicly. This act of violence as recorded in Scripture seemed terribly wrong. It seemed gratuitous violence and it violates the rule about not letting corpses remain unburied, as indeed the continuation of the biblical story reveals. The rabbis interpret that this was done with cause: the sons of Saul had exploited poor converts. This interpretation also had the virtue of showing non-Jews how firmly criminals, even members of the royal family, are dealt with, as well as how respectfully converts are treated. The violence is, thus, justified.

The task of reinterpreting gratuitous violence also generated a mighty effort in the area of theodicy—the justification of God—in the wake of the destruction of the temples and later Jewish persecution. It took the form of the doctrine of *u-mipnei ḥat'einu* ("because of our sins") which is present already in the Bible and became a major part of rabbinic thinking and liturgy.[102]

> • From the mouth of the Ultimate One do not come evils and good. . . . Let us examine our ways and probe them, and return to the Lord. . . . We sinned and rebelled, and You did not forgive (Lam. 3:38–42).[103]
> • One finds that, by the very limb by which Israel sinned, they were punished and will be comforted. They sinned with the head as it says . . . they were punished in the head as it says . . . and they will be comforted in the head as it says . . . ear . . . eye . . . nose . . . mouth . . . tongue . . . heart . . . hand . . . foot . . . fire. . . .[104]

Just as there is a strong stream of violence in the biblical and rabbinic sources, attenuated and justified in some cases, so there is also a strong tradition of nonviolence in the Bible and the rabbinic sources.[105]

> • Do not say, "As the other has done to me, so shall I do to him or her; I will repay the person according to her or his actions" (Prov. 24:29).
> • Do not envy a person of violence and do not choose any of his or her ways (Prov. 3:31).
> • One who gives back evil for good, evil will not leave her or his house (Prov. 17:13).
> • It is good for a man[106] to bear a yoke in his youth. He should sit alone and be silent, accepting what has been put upon him. He should put his mouth into the dust, perhaps there will be hope. He should turn his cheek to him who strikes him. He should be surfeited with shame (Lam. 3:27–30).
> • Despised, rejected of men, a man of sorrows, and acquainted with grief

... he does not open his mouth, like a lamb led to slaughter, like a sheep dumb before those who shear it ... he suffers their iniquities ... he bears the sin of the many (Is. 53).

COMMENT: In the hands of the rabbis these, and similar biblical verses, became the cornerstone of the doctrine of nonviolence which, as Kimelman has shown, flourished in Jewish Palestine between 250 and 400 C.E.[107] The last lines cited above, set so beautifully to music in Handel's "Messiah" and understood by Christians to refer to Jesus, are interpreted in Jewish tradition to refer to the Jewish people who suffer in nonviolence within a violent non-Jewish world.

The first step in nonviolence is not imitating the ways of the wicked.

• Rabbi Shimon ben Abba said: "'One who gives back evil for good, evil will not leave her or his house' (Prov. 17 : 13)—Not only in the case of one who returns evil for good, but even in the case of one who returns evil for evil, 'evil will not depart from her or his house.'"[108]

COMMENT: This exegesis of Proverbs shows that evil comes upon those who act evilly, even if it seems justified by evil previously done to them.

• "May the Lord bless you and keep you ... and grant you peace" (Nu. 6 : 22). This bears on what is written in Scripture "Do not envy a person of violence and do not choose any of his or her ways" (Prov. 3 : 31). The "person of violence" is Esau ... Edom ... you must not do according to their deeds.[109]

COMMENT: This exegesis of the concluding line of the great priestly blessing shows that peace cannot derive from the way of violence practiced by Esau and Edom which, in the context of the midrash, is understood to be Rome, though the moral lesson is surely not limited to late antiquity.

The second step in nonviolence is learning passivity.

• A person should always strive to be rather of the persecuted than the persecutors, as there is none among the birds more persecuted than doves and pigeons, and yet Scripture made them [alone among the birds] eligible for the altar (Lev. 1 : 14).[110]

COMMENT: There are a fair number of animals that can be used as sacrifices but the only birds which one can use as a sacrifice are the dove and the pigeon. This passage reflects on that peculiar choice and uses it as the basis for a moral lesson of passivity as a virtue in nonviolence.

• The rabbis taught: "They are insulted but do not insult, they hear themselves reviled but do not retort, they act out of love, and they rejoice in their suffering—of these Scripture says, 'Those who love Him are as the sun when it rises with power'" (Ju. 5:31).[111]

COMMENT: In this passage, one of the standard messianic verses is used to advocate nonviolent passivity.

• "You will not let your pious (caring) one (*hasidkha*) see the pit" (Ps. 16: 10)—The Holy One, blessed be He, is called *hasid* as it says, "'For I am *hasid*' says the Lord" (Jer. 3:12) and David called himself *hasid* as it says, "Watch over my soul, for I am *hasid*" (Ps. 86:2). Rabbi Huna said in the name of Rabbi Alexandri, "Anyone who hears oneself cursed and remains silent is *hasid*. David heard himself cursed and was silent (II Sam. 16: 5–13). It is correct, therefore, that he is called *hasid*."[112]

COMMENT: Shim'i ben Gera' cursed King David as he fled Jerusalem during the rebellion of Absalom. David refused to let his officers attack and kill Shim'i for cursing him. This is taken by the rabbis of Jewish Palestine of the third and fourth centuries as a virtuous nonviolent act, which they then associate with the value-concept *hasidut* (caring/nonviolence).

The third step in nonviolence is being proactively loving. This behavior seems to us, today, to be very "Christian," yet it was clearly part of good rabbinic practice in third- and fourth-century Jewish Palestine and, from there, became part—albeit, not a major part—of the nonviolent stream of Jewish teaching.

• "If your enemy is hungry, give him or her bread to eat; if she or he is thirsty, give her or him water to drink. For you heap coals of fire on their heads and the Lord will reward you" (Prov. 25:21–22). Do not read "reward (*yeshalem*)" but "He will cause your enemy to be at peace (*yeshalmeno*) with you."[113]

COMMENT: This text, based on a punning reading of the Hebrew in Proverbs, teaches how to bring peace even with an enemy. It is followed by two similar teaching texts.

• Who is a hero of heroes? One who controls one's urge . . . Others say, one who makes of one's enemy a friend.[114]
• . . . for by seeing that one is trying to please the other, the other's heart will change and he or she will repress her or his hate.[115]

When all else fails, one should pray for one's enemies. This is the fourth step in nonviolence, though one could argue that it is also the first step.

- There were once some highwaymen in the neighborhood of Rabbi Meir who caused him a great deal of trouble. Rabbi Meir accordingly prayed that they should die. His wife, Beruria, said to him, "How do you act so? It is written, 'Let sins (*hata'im*) cease' (Ps. 104:35). Is it written 'Let sinners (*hot'im*) cease'? [No.] Further, look at the end of the verse, 'the wicked will be no more'—since the sins will cease, there will be no more wicked persons. Rather, pray for them that they repent and there will be no more wicked people." Rabbi Meir did pray for them and they did repent.[116]

COMMENT: Psalm 104:35 actually uses a professional noun form for sinners (*hatta'im*) and not the noun for sins (*hata'im*). The authors of this narrative about Rabbi Meir knew that but chose to pun on the text and use it to teach an important moral lesson: It is wickedness, not the wicked, that is repulsive to humanity and God.

- One should avoid victory over the enemy, rather one should feel sorry that God's will is not being done. Hence, even for one's enemy one should pray—that he or she worship God. . . . Only by praying for one's enemy does one fulfill the commandment, "Love your other as yourself" (Lev. 19:18).[117]

COMMENT: With this, rabbinic teaching comes a full circle. Beginning with the realization that one need not love one's other more than oneself, rabbinic teaching arrives at the recognition that only by loving one's other more than oneself does one really love oneself. The *Sefer Ahavat Ḥesed* puts it differently: "It is a mitsva to love the wicked."[118]

Surveying the literature on violence and nonviolence, it is very clear that some violence was recognized as justified or legitimate—in action, in threat, and in prayer. It is also clear, however, that alongside the normative tradition which sanctions violence, there exists a standard of caring which decries violence and encourages nonviolence—in action and in prayer.

*   *   *   *   *

Four issues within the realm of obedience and altruism have been examined: the need to compel obedience and yet to cultivate and protect disobedience in a military hierarchy; the requirement to enforce judicial discipline and yet to encourage and protect judicial dissent; the obligation to rescue and its personal and financial limits; and the tension between gratuitous and legitimate violence and nonviolence. In the course of this study, the Jewish sources have shown themselves abundant and thoughtful. They are certainly rich enough to serve as the basis for education in the arts and skills of resistant and caring prosocial living.

Counter-text [119]

No citizen of Dachau is without a deep sense that something was wrong, terribly wrong, on the outskirts of their town.

The majority of them take the position described above ["We were lied to in every respect." "It was all very horrible, but what could we do?"]. That they are honest in this attitude for the most part allows of no doubt whatever.

Those who didn't give a tinker's damn [sic] what happened to the poor souls whom they saw pass through their streets for years—so long as business was good and the SS Hauptsturmführer paid his handsome rent— were really few. Today they are the ones who plead "Ja—wir wussten überhaupt nichts was passiert [sic] da draussen!" ("But we really didn't know what was going on out there!"). "Da draussen"—as if it were on another planet! They are liars, and guilty as sin—everyone.

The very few who dared show some opposition ran great risk and should be honored as the courageous men and women they are. . . .

If one is to attempt the tremendous task and accept the terrific responsibility of judging a whole town, assessing it en masse as to the collective guilt or innocence of all its inhabitants for this most hideous of crimes, one would do well to remember the fearsome shadow that hangs over everyone in a state in which crime has been incorporated and called the government.

14

Hierarchy, Authority, and Autonomy in Teaching Judaism

Applying the Lessons

When the rabbis would have before them two juxtaposed texts which, however, seemed to have nothing to do with one another, they would ask, "What does . . . have to do with . . . ?" That is our position now: In part 1, we reviewed and analyzed the social-psychological and historical evidence on obedience and altruism and worked out a field theory for why ordinary people do good and do evil. We saw that hierarchy and role, teaching and praxis, and early childhood disciplinary patterns were crucial in both cases. In part 2, we moved from the descriptive-analytic to the prescriptive-normative and reviewed the affections, value-concepts, and teachings of the prosocial life. We saw that morality, justice, caring, empowerment, protest, compassion, critical consciousness, and many other clearly identifiable and communicable values were crucial in creating a more prosocial world. We also examined several very strong recommendations, including specific practical suggestions, for encouraging prosocial attitudes and behaviors. Finally, in part 3, we studied the Jewish sources in the area of the prosocial life, including Jewish prosocial value-concepts, Jewish stories and teachings of resistance, and Jewish texts pertaining to military obedience, judicial dissent, the obligation to rescue, and nonviolence. Now we must ask, what does the one have to do with the other? What do the insights gained from social psychology, history, and moral education in the area of prosocial behavior have to do with the Jewish texts and teachings on prosocial issues?

To answer the question, we must bear in mind what we learned in the general discussion of the move from descriptive-analytic to prescriptive-normative discourse; namely, that the social-scientific evidence is clear that religious education and affiliation is not a crucial factor in the formation of the prosocial life.[1] Thus, the Princeton experiment showed that study of prosocial texts did not increase one's actual performance of altruistic actions.[2] Similarly, the Oliners' study showed that active identification with a religious community did not, in itself, increase participation in prosocial (rescue) work.[3] In yet another study,[4] Batson and Ventis showed that, given three people from very different but actively religious backgrounds, it was not the religious setting but the context of social roles, norms, and reference groups that provided the best predictors of religious identity (31–48). Also, asking about people's attitudes and then checking their actual behaviors, Batson and Ventis concluded that seeing oneself as prosocially motivated and actually performing prosocial actions were not the same: "The more religious may *see* themselves as more helpful and caring; they may even be seen this way by others. But when it came to action, there is no evidence that they are" (289, italics original).

In chapter 8, I proposed "Four Very Strong Recommendations for Encouraging Prosocial Attitudes and Behaviors." There is nothing specifically Jewish about these recommendations. There shouldn't be. Goodness is not a "Jewish" trait; nor is it the monopoly of Christianity, Islam, or any other religion or ideology. Prosocial activity is not "Jewish"; nor is it the sole concern of any one religion or ideology.[5] Quite the contrary is true. Goodness and prosocial activity are quintessentially human traits and concerns; they are common to all humankind. That is how it is, and how it should be. Judaism, as shown above, has its own very rich sources on the subject of goodness and prosocial action. It also has its own highly developed traditions on authority, obedience, and even on violence. To teach goodness in the best way in a Jewish context, I suggest implementing the Four Very Strong Recommendations, together with their specific suggestions, using Jewish value-concepts, Jewish stories, and Jewish verses, phrases, and principles. In each case, this must be done together with the general recommendations and suggestions already made. This might be accomplished as follows:[6]

FIRST, ADMIT FAILURE. Judaism teaches the value-concept of *teshuva* (repentance).[7] Teshuva presupposes that everyone is human and, in that state, makes errors, serious errors. However, Judaism teaches one can recover from sin by recognizing one's sins, by remorse, by desisting from further sin, by restitution where that is possible, and by confession. Admitting failure in our efforts at moral education and taking steps to correct that failure is not only a good recommendation, it is, from a Jewish point of view, the ineluctable first step toward reconstructing the prosocial life.

SECOND, GIVE FORMAL INSTRUCTION. Judaism teaches the value-concept of *Torah* (teaching) and its corollary *talmud Torah* (the study and teaching of Torah). Jewish civilization can hardly be envisioned without the value and praxis of formal education. This second very strong recommendation includes five specific suggestions as follows:

(1) Teach prosocial value-concepts. The list of Jewish value-concepts includes (but is not limited to) the following: *tikkun 'olam* (repair / restoring of the world); *tsedaka* (charity, righteousness); *tsedek* (justice); *pikuaḥ nefesh* (saving a life); *middat ḥasidut* (caring / standard of the pious / nonviolence);

gemilut ḥasadim (doing of good deeds); and *yetser ha-ra'* (the impulse to do evil) together with *yetser tov* (the impulse to do good).[8] These must be taught together with the general value-concepts of: inclusiveness, extensivity, caring, bonding, humanness, etc. and the complements: oppression, inhumanity, exclusiveness, etc.

(2) Use the language of justice and caring. Some of the relevant Jewish verses, phrases, and principles are: *latse't yedei shamayim* (fulfillment of duty in the sight of heaven); *lifne 'iver lo titen mikhshol* (do not put a stumbling block before the blind); *lifnim mishurat hadin* (within the line of the law); *lo ta'amod 'al dam rei 'ekha* (you shall not stand idly by the blood of your other); *lo tisna'* (you shall not hate your fellow in your heart, but you should hate his or her ways); *'ein shaliaḥ le-davar 'avera* (there is no agency for illegal acts); *dina de-malkhuta dina* (the law of the land is the law, with exceptions); *patur mi-dinei 'adam ve-ḥayav be-dinei shamayim* (exempt from human law but liable under divine law); and *ve-'asita ha-tov veha-yashar be-'einei Hashem* (do what is right and good in the eyes of God).[9] These must be taught together with the general terms: compassion, affection, respect, intimacy, etc. and the complements: pain, sorrow, grief, suffering, terror, etc.

(3) Identify and actively teach prosocial texts and traditions. The chapters preceding this one have cited much material from the biblical as well as the rabbinic sources, including the stories of Shifa and Pu'a, the officers of Saul, and the tradition of martyrdom. There is much more. These sources must be taught together with the general sources on the American and French Revolutions, the period of slavery, the civil rights movement, and the antiwar protest.

(4) Teach the nature of social processes. Some of the value-concepts and phrases here are: *'akhzariyut* (toughness); *rodef* (pursuer); *nekama* (vengeance); *talmud Torah* (Torah study); and *aharei rabbim lehatot* (do not respond to a dispute by tending toward the majority to cause [others] to tend [that way]).[10] This must be taught together with the technical terms of social process: authority, obedience, resistance, norms, rules, values, normocentrism, identification, socialization, modeling, peer support, etc., as well as in conjunction with the books and films on the subject of obedience and altruism.

(5) Teach critical thinking. The very essence of *talmud Torah* (the study of the tradition), which the rabbis valued above all other activities, encouraged the critical reading of narrative and legal texts. Every question is permitted, even though there may not always be adequate answers at hand.

> • These are the things which bear fruits in this world but whose main reward is reserved for the world-to-come . . . but *talmud Torah* (Torah study) is the greatest of all.[11]

Critical thinking must also be taught together with the skills which teach one how to identify a lie, how to determine what is propaganda, whose power is at stake, and who is manipulating whom in communication, as well as how to disagree intelligently.

THIRD, TEACH PROSOCIAL SKILLS. Judaism never envisioned study as cut off from action. On the contrary, one of the justifications of study is that it leads to action, for it is action that counts. It is for our acts that we are judged. Prosocial skills are paths of action and, hence, crucial to Jewish moral education. This third very strong recommendation includes seven specific suggestions as follows:

(1) **Perspective-taking and empathy**—*middat ḥasidut* (standard of caring / of the pious / of nonviolence), *kevod ha-beriyot* (dignity of the creatures), and *ve-'ahavata le-rei'akha kamokha* (you shall love your other as yourself);[12] together with such questions as: "What do you think he or she feels?" "What does she or he feel, even if she or he cannot express it?" "What is the difference between sympathy and empathy? between pity and compassion?"

(2) **Identifying and coding one's own feelings**—*yetser ha-ra'* (the impulse to do evil), *yetser tov* (the impulse to do good), and *tom lev* (purity of heart);[13] together with such questions as: "What did I feel when I saw . . . ?" "Can I recall moments of deep anger, of great joy, of profound immodesty, of power, of powerlessness?" "How did I handle those moments?"

(3) **Identifying authorities, hierarchies, norms, roles, and social processes**—*talmud Torah* (Torah study) and *aharei rabbim lehatot* (do not respond to a dispute by tending toward the majority to cause [others] to tend [that way]);[14] together with such questions as: "What is the social hierarchy here? Who is subordinate to whom?" "Upon what is the legitimacy of the authority in this situation based? Do I assent to it?" "What would I have to do to challenge the authority? to reverse the hierarchy?" "Am I being a reasonable authority? Am I leaving my subordinates free to disagree and challenge my authority?"

(4) **Externalizing repressed prosocial impulses**—*gemilut ḥasadim* (doing of good deeds) and *yetser tov* (the impulse to do good);[15] together with such questions as: "What could I do today that would be really kind?" "Have I done an act of spontaneous goodness today?" "Whom do I know who is really caring? Why do I consider him or her to be good?"

(5) **Conflict management skills**—*shalom* (peace) and *mipnei darkhei shalom* (for the sake of peace);[16] together with such terms as: superordinate goals, win-win, the stakes for each of the parties involved, mediation, stakeholder, etc.

(6) **Networking**—*tsibbur* (community), *kelal Yisrael* (the whole community of Israel), and *brit* (covenant); together with such questions as: "How can I broaden support for what I believe in?" "Who are my natural allies?" "How do I also involve bystanders, and even opponents?" "How do I bring the authorities to appreciate the cause I espouse?"

(7) **Protesting**—*tsedek* (justice), *raḥamim* (mercy), and *din Torah* (the trial of God); together with the skills of coalition-building, social organization, negotiation, reconciliation, mediation, and nonviolent protest.[17]

FOURTH, PAY ATTENTION TO CONTEXT AND PROCESS. *Kavvana* (intentionality) is a key concept in Judaism. Every act, ritual as well as legal, depends in large part on one's kavvana, one's intention and attentiveness. Without it, life is rote and routine. With kavvana, life is lived in the presence of God. With kavvana, life is lived in the light of God's Torah, of God's will for us. Kavvana gives spiritual meaning to what we do.[18] This fourth very strong recommendation includes five specific suggestions as follows:

(1) **Establish a means by which authority can be challenged.** (a) Favor epistemic authority;[19] that is, favor authority which is based on learning and not on charisma, tradition, or blind obedience. This should be true not only in intellectual matters such as the interpretation of individual texts but also in matters of moral judgment because, often, correct moral judgment is exercised by people who do not occupy a place of authority in the social hierarchy. The value-concept involved here is *talmud Torah* (Torah study):[20]

- Rabbi Ḥanina said, "I learned many things from my teachers, and more from my colleagues but, from my students, I learned the most."[21]

(b) Teach that challenging authority is a *mitsva,* a commandment from God, a religious duty, a calling. The phrases involved here are: *'aḥarei rabbim lehatot* (do not respond to a dispute by tending toward the majority to cause [others] to tend [that way]) in its sense of judicial protest, *hokheaḥ tokhiaḥ* (you shall surely reprove, remonstrate with, your acquaintance), and *divrei ha-rav ve-divrei ha-'eved, divrei ha-rav kodmin* (If the words of the Master and the words of the servant are in conflict, the words of the Master take precedence).[22] This must be implemented together with the general suggestions of: an ombudsperson, a whistle-blowing mechanism, a care team, etc.

(2) **Act. Do. Implement prosocial action.** The Jewish list of specific projects includes: honoring one's father and mother, *gemilut ḥasadim,* attending synagogue prayers morning and evening, hospitality, visiting the sick, dowering the bride, accompanying a corpse to the grave, studying the liturgy, bringing peace among one's fellows, and *talmud Torah;*[23] clothing the naked, releasing the captives, and caring for the stranger, the orphan, and the widow.[24]

- *Tsedaka* (charity, righteousness) is equal to all the other mitsvot.[25]

This must be implemented together with the general suggestions of: maintaining personal contact with the disadvantaged (positive salience with the oppressed), a feedback mechanism to help participants digest their experiences, etc.

(3) Model prosocial attitudes and behaviors. The Jewish value-concepts and phrases involved here are: *hasid* (caring person), *tsaddik* (righteous person), *talmid hakham* (student-sage), and *mehanekh* (educator, spiritual guide).[26] This must be implemented together with the general suggestions of: moving prosocial action out of the formal educational setting into the community, using prosocial commitment as a criterion for hiring and promotion, developing a way to honor prosocial heroes and heroines, etc.

(4) Develop syllabi and curricula in prosocial action. I have presented some texts, particularly the four case studies in prosocial teaching[27] and the stories of protest, altruism, and resistance.[28] There are, however, an endless number of texts and anthologies.[29] Various Jewish organizations have also developed syllabi and curricula—for children, teenagers, and adults—over the years. One of these is summarized in the appendix. A source index is also given. These must be implemented together with the general suggestions of: using theory-praxis learning methods, hiring a person whose special task is to develop and integrate prosocial attitudes and actions across the whole curriculum, etc.

(5) Be intentional about what you are doing. Here, again, Jewish tradition has much to say. We are called by God to refrain from evil and to do good. This means that the doing of good is not a function of some utilitarian principle but transcends psychology and society. Prosocial attitudes and behaviors are a *mitsva,* a commandment, a calling. Rooting prosocial action in God creates an alternate authority for which those who wish to do good and may be hesitating and for those who are torn between conflicting authorities.[30] The following value-concepts should be invoked: *brit* (covenant), *mitsva* (commandedness), *tselem* (image / *imitatio Dei*), and the text from Ezekiel on being a watchman.[31]

For Jews, the study of Jewish sources to help develop moral qualities is crucial. However, other religions, and even secular ideologies, have their own rich traditions on these issues, and studying those sources is important for those who identify with those traditions. I encourage colleagues everywhere to search their traditions for prosocial (and antisocial) texts, and to study and teach those texts. Prosocial action, however, is not dependent only on the teachings of a given tradition but on how that tradition is embodied in the lives of its adherents. In this sense, too, the factors which facilitate good and evil cross traditions. Again, I encourage colleagues everywhere to search the actions of their communities for prosocial (and antisocial) patterns, and to study and teach those patterns. For the purpose of educating people toward a prosocial orientation, any tradition can serve as a base of study, as long as it is combined with the insights from the social sciences on the nature of the factors that facilitate good and evil.[32] I encourage others to make this effort and welcome dialogue on the subject.[33]

Counter-text

COMMENT: The Book of Lamentations closes with two verses: Lamentations 5 : 21–22. The first of these verses is a prayer invoking God's help in our *teshuva,* in our return to God and to a better / older time. The second verse returns to the bitterness of the destruction of the temple and the Davidic kingdom which is the setting of this work. The Book of Lamentations as written, thus, ends on bitterness after hope. When Lamentations is read liturgically in the synagogue, however, the rabbis ordained that the penultimate verse about hope be the ending. The liturgical ending, therefore, is hope, followed by despair, followed by hope. And still, the echo of despair remains. It is with this tension between good and evil, in its very banality, resolved only in its sabbatical-messianic rendering, that this book ends.

השיבנו ה אליך ונשובה, חדש ימינו כקדם.

כי אם מאס מאסתנו, קצפת עלינו עד מאד.

השיבנו ה אליך ונשובה, חדש ימינו כקדם.

כי אם מאס מאסתנו, קצפת עלינו עד מאד.

השיבנו ה אליך ונשובה, חדש ימינו כקדם.

כי אם מאס מאסתנו, קצפת עלינו עד מאד.

השיבנו ה אליך ונשובה, חדש ימינו כקדם.

כי אם מאס מאסתנו, קצפת עלינו עד מאד.

השיבנו ה אליך ונשובה, חדש ימינו כקדם.

כי אם מאס מאסתנו, קצפת עלינו עד מאד.

השיבנו ה אליך ונשובה, חדש ימינו כקדם.

כי אם מאס מאסתנו, קצפת עלינו עד מאד.

השיבנו ה אליך ונשובה, חדש ימינו כקדם.

. . .

Return us, O Lord, to You; and we shall return.
   Indeed, You have certainly reviled us; You have been exceptionally
      wrathful with us.
Return us, O Lord, to You; and we shall return.
   Indeed, You have certainly reviled us; You have been exceptionally
      wrathful with us.
Return us, O Lord, to You; and we shall return.
   Indeed, You have certainly reviled us; You have been exceptionally
      wrathful with us.
Return us, O Lord, to You; and we shall return.
   Indeed, You have certainly reviled us; You have been exceptionally
      wrathful with us.
Return us, O Lord, to You; and we shall return.

Indeed, You have certainly reviled us; You have been exceptionally
   wrathful with us.
Return us, O Lord, to You; and we shall return.
   Indeed, You have certainly reviled us; You have been exceptionally
   wrathful with us.
Return us, O Lord, to You; and we shall return.
   . . .

Aftermatter

Just as the features of human beings are not alike, so also their views are not alike. . . . Moses, at the moment of his death, asked the Holy One, blessed be He, "Master of the universe, the opinion of each person is manifest and known to you and one view is not like another. On my departing this life, I ask you to appoint for them a leader who will bear patiently with each one of them according to the view they hold."

—*Bamidbar Rabba* 21:2, *Tanḥuma,* Pinḥas 10

One who sees a very large crowd of people makes the benediction, "Blessed be He Who discerns secret things, for their features are dissimilar and their views unalike."

—*Tosefta,* Berakhot 6:5; *Talmud,* Berakhot 58a

APPENDIX A

The New Ethical Code of the IDF*

The Spirit of the IDF is an expression of the identity, values and norms of the IDF. It underlies every action performed in the IDF by each and every serviceman and servicewoman. (Hereafter the term *servicemen* will be construed as applying to both servicemen and servicewomen.)

The Spirit of the IDF comprises eleven core IDF values. It defines and presents the essence of each of them, and includes basic principles which express these values.

The Spirit of the IDF draws its values and basic principles from three traditions:

- The tradition of the Jewish People throughout its history.
- The tradition of the State of Israel, its democratic principles, laws and institutions.
- The tradition of the IDF and its military heritage as the Israel Defense Forces.

The Spirit of the IDF is the ethical code by which all IDF enlisted personnel, officers, units and corps act. It is the norm to guide them in forming their patterns of behavior. They are expected to educate and critically evaluate themselves and others in accordance with these values and principles.

The complex nature of military activity in general, and combat in particular, may generate tensions with the values and basic principles of The Spirit of the IDF, and may raise problems of judgment about the proper balance needed between theory and practice.

The obligation to fulfill the mission and ensure military victory will be the compass guiding any effort to balance these values and basic principles of The Spirit of the IDF. The striving for proper balance according to this compass will

---

*Taken from the website of the Israel Defense Forces <http://www.idf.il/English/docs. htm>. The Hebrew original alone is authoritative. As in the Hebrew, the values following "Perseverance in Mission" have been arranged in alphabetical order. The order, therefore, differs from that of the original.

make it possible to preserve the IDF as a body of high quality, imbued with values, and which fulfills its duties and missions appropriately.

Perseverance in Mission

The IDF serviceman will fight and conduct himself with courage in the face of all dangers and obstacles; he will persevere in his mission courageously, resolutely and thoughtfully even to the point of endangering his own life.

The perseverance of IDF servicemen in their mission is their capability and readiness to fight courageously in the face of danger and in most challenging situations; to strive unremittingly to achieve the military goal effectively, with full regard for the particular circumstances, notwithstanding any difficulty, stress or adversity or even mortal danger. They will do so with proper judgment and with due regard for risks.

Comradeship

The IDF serviceman will always go to the aid of his comrades when they need his help or depend on him, despite any danger or difficulty, even to the point of risking his life.

The fellowship of IDF servicemen is their bond as comrades in arms. It is their unwavering commitment to each other, their readiness to extend appropriate assistance, to go to the aid of a comrade, and even risk their lives on his behalf. In all their actions they will uphold and strengthen the solidarity of their unit in full cooperation with other units, and in support of the overall goals of the IDF.

Discipline

The IDF serviceman will execute completely and successfully all that is required of him according to the letter and spirit of his orders and within the framework of the law.

The discipline of IDF servicemen is their readiness to act to the full extent of their abilities, to carry out what is demanded of them completely, according to their understanding of the letter of the orders they have received, and successfully, according to the spirit of their orders. It is their readiness to obey orders amidst a constant striving to execute them with understanding and dedication. They will take care to issue only legal orders, and disavow manifestly illegal orders.

Human Life

The IDF serviceman will, above all, preserve human life, in the recognition of its supreme value and will place himself or others at risk solely to the extent required to carry out his mission.

The sanctity of life in the eyes of the IDF servicemen will find expression in all of their actions, in deliberate and meticulous planning, in safe and intelligent training and in proper execution of their mission. In evaluating the risk to self and others, they will use the appropriate standards and will exercise constant care to limit injury to life to the extent required to accomplish the mission.

Loyalty

The IDF serviceman will act with complete dedication in the defense of the State of Israel and its citizens, according to IDF orders, within the framework of the laws of the State and democratic principles.

The loyalty of IDF servicemen is their dedication, in all actions, to their homeland, the State of Israel, its citizens and armed forces, and their constant readiness to fight and devote all their power, even at the risk of their own lives, in the defense of the sovereign State of Israel and the lives and the safety of its inhabitants, according to the values and orders of the IDF, while following the laws and the democratic principles of the State.

Personal Example

The IDF serviceman will comport himself as is required of him and will, himself, act as he demands of others, thoughtfully and dedicatedly, aware of his ability and responsibility to serve as a role model to those around him.

The personal example of the IDF servicemen is their acting as is demanded of them and as they themselves demand of others, their clear and convincing readiness to serve as an example to those around them, in their actions and comportment, to create, uphold and foster mutual identification and joint responsibility in properly carrying out their tasks and accomplishing their missions in all areas of military activity.

Professionalism

The IDF serviceman will aspire to be familiar with and understand the body of knowledge pertaining to his military position and will master every skill necessary for carrying out his duties.

The professionalism of IDF servicemen is their ability to correctly perform their military duties through striving to constantly excel in and improve their unit's and their individual achievements. They will do so by broadening their knowledge, and increasing proficiency, based upon the lessons of experience and study of the heritage and by expanding and deepening their understanding of the body of military knowledge.

Purity of Arms

The IDF serviceman will use force of arms only for the purpose of subduing the enemy to the necessary extent and will limit his use of force so as to prevent unnecessary harm to human life and limb, dignity and property.

The IDF servicemen's purity of arms is their self-control in use of armed force. They will use their arms only for the purpose of achieving their mission, without inflicting unnecessary injury to human life or limb; dignity or property, of both soldiers and civilians, with special consideration for the defenseless, whether in wartime, or during routine security operations, or in the absence of combat, or times of peace.

Representativeness

The IDF serviceman will constantly see himself as a representative and an emissary of the IDF. As such he will act solely on the basis of the authority he has been given and orders he has been issued.

The representativeness of IDF servicemen is their consciousness, expressed in all their actions, that the armed force placed in their hands and the power to use it are given to them only as members of the IDF and its authorized representatives, duly executing their orders in accordance with the laws of the State of Israel and is subject to its Government.

Responsibility

The IDF serviceman will see himself as an active participant in the defense of his country and its citizens. He will carry out his duties decisively, resolutely and with vigor, within the limits of his authority.

The responsibility of IDF servicemen is their active partnership and their readiness to use their utmost abilities in the defense of the State, its sovereignty, and the lives and safety of its citizens, within the framework of authority granted them by the IDF. They will carry out their duties fully, diligently, and with determination, commitment and initiative, in clear awareness that they are answerable for any consequences.

Trustworthiness

The IDF serviceman will strive in all his actions to fulfill his duties correctly and at the highest professional level, from exacting and thorough preparation through to true, honest, complete and precise reporting.

The trustworthiness of IDF servicemen is their reliability in fully carrying out their charge, using their military skills, with the sincere belief and conviction that they are acting professionally. They are ready at all times to present things as they are, in planning, executing and reporting truthfully, completely, courageously and honestly.

Basic Principles

Values

The IDF serviceman will, in all his actions and conduct, express the basic values of the IDF:

Perseverance in the mission, comradeship, discipline, respect for human life, loyalty, personal example, professionalism, purity of arms, representativeness, responsibility, and trustworthiness, as defined above and as appropriate to the specific circumstances.

The IDF serviceman, when acting in the framework of his military role, will be ever cognizant that he bears responsibility not only for the outcomes of his acts and omissions, but also for the patterns of behavior which they help to create, whether by order or personal example, by direct or indirect influence, whether intentionally or unintentionally.

On Military Service

The IDF serviceman will view himself, in each of his actions, as bearing full responsibility for the lives and safety of the servicemen and all others who are dependent on his actions or decisions.

The IDF serviceman will be ready to place his own life at risk when confronting the enemy or to save human life to the extent required, but he will preserve his own life and that of others in all other military situations.

The IDF serviceman will take into account, in every practical context, not only the proper concern for human life, but also the influence his actions may have on the physical well-being and spiritual integrity and dignity of others.

The IDF serviceman will endeavor fully to exercise his capabilities as called upon in accordance with the priorities assigned by the IDF to combat, command, combat support and combat service support roles.

The IDF serviceman, in all his actions, will take care to uphold the honor of the State, its institutions, monuments and symbols, including the honor of the IDF and its symbols.

The IDF serviceman will show special respect for the fallen of the IDF. The serviceman will behave with deference in ceremonies, at memorial sites, and at memorial and honor ceremonies, and will treat bereaved families with proper respect.

The IDF serviceman will maintain the tradition of the IDF by showing honor and respect for IDF wounded and disabled.

The IDF serviceman will maintain the tradition of the IDF, will study the IDF's military heritage and will promote esprit de corps.

The IDF serviceman will carry out his military activities without obtruding his personal views in matters beyond his sphere of responsibility, authority and professional expertise. He will take special care not to inject his personal opinions on issues subject to public controversy of a political, social or ideological nature.

The IDF serviceman will make use of his military authority or status, whether command or professional, solely for the benefit of the IDF. He will never use his military authority or status improperly to advance a personal objective, or to go beyond the limits of his authority and responsibility, in letter or spirit, within or without the IDF.

The IDF serviceman will hold himself responsible for the outcomes of his orders. He will support those who have acted in accordance with those orders or as is proper, and will view himself as responsible for the patterns of behavior which he imposed.

The IDF serviceman will support his unit and its commanders in every way necessary to fulfill the unit's mission of building, promoting and employing military force. The serviceman will obey his commanders in accordance with the law and maintain respect for his commanders, peers and subordinates.

The IDF servicemen will never conspire to conceal any offense or mishap, and will not entertain any proposal to be party to such a conspiracy. When confronted with an offense or mishap, the serviceman will act as is reasonable and proper to correct the aberration.

The IDF serviceman who participates in a discussion or dispute dealing with an activity in which the IDF is involved, whether before, during or after its implementation, will express his views in accordance with his professional knowledge and conviction, with honesty, candor and courage.

The IDF serviceman will use the authority at his disposal towards others only as is fair, self-controlled, reasonable and professional. He will show due respect for the person and the privacy of those with whom he interacts.

The IDF serviceman will view his appearance in an IDF uniform as an expression of his loyalty to the values and basic principles of the IDF.

When Confronting the Enemy

The IDF serviceman will use the force at his disposal, in all actions in the face of the enemy, manifesting perseverance in his mission, courage and judgment, always ready to carry out his duties despite danger to his life.

The IDF serviceman will be ready to do whatever is required, and even to endanger his own life, to come to the aid of his comrades or to recover wounded comrades from the battlefield.

The IDF serviceman will act, when confronting the enemy, according to the letter and spirit of the laws of war. He will adhere strictly to the principle of purity of arms and to the ethics of combat.

The IDF serviceman will treat enemy troops and civilians in areas controlled by the IDF in accordance with the letter and spirit of the laws of war and will not exceed the limits of his authority.

The IDF serviceman will act fairly with self-control, reasonably, and professionally, in carrying out the responsibilities of his position, in all his contacts with civilians in areas controlled by the IDF, whether in the course of battle or afterward. He will show respect towards the beliefs, values, sacred and historical sites of all civilians and military personnel as they deem proper and to the extent possible, in keeping with the values and basic principles of the IDF and in accordance with military needs and the given circumstances.

The IDF serviceman will fight and exert himself to the utmost, even placing his life at risk so as not to surrender to the enemy but to overcome him. He will not surrender as long as he has a chance of carrying out his mission. Even in the absence of such a possibility, he will not surrender as long as he has contact with his commander or the ability to extricate himself from his compromised position.

The IDF serviceman who, despite all efforts, has been taken prisoner will act according to IDF orders; responsibly, reasonably and honorably.

Relations with Civilian Bodies

The IDF serviceman will give preference to promoting the IDF's goals, as is required of him, in accordance with regulations, orders, values and basic principles, over the advancement of the goals of any civilian body, in any instance of conflict of interests between the IDF's goals and those of that body.

The IDF serviceman, in all official contact with civilian bodies, will act professionally and without compromising the IDF's values, basic principles or honor.

The IDF serviceman may be involved in the activities of a commercial or civilian body only in accordance with the letter and spirit of existing orders and procedures, and within the limits of his position.

The IDF serviceman will refrain from receiving personal benefits as a result of his position, rank, status or actions. He will not request, nor will he agree to accept any favors from any agent, inside or outside the IDF, directly or indirectly, for himself or others, except in accordance with due orders and procedures.

The IDF serviceman will ensure that every public appearance, especially in the mass media, has prior approval, expresses outright and unreserved loyalty to the value and basic principles of the IDF, reflects the IDF's policies and decisions, and contributes to the public's confidence in the IDF.

The IDF serviceman will ensure that his behavior even in private circumstances cannot be interpreted as compromising the IDF's values or basic principles, does not detract from the public's confidence in the IDF, and will not contribute to the creation of patterns and behavior that could harm the implementation of the IDF's values and basic principles.

Reserve Duty and Retirement

The IDF serviceman, during his reserve duty, will act according to the same values and basic principles of the IDF as those that apply to servicemen in regular service.

The discharged serviceman may make private use of special or sensitive information which he gained or which came to his attention during his service only after he has received the proper authorization to make commercial media or other such use of such knowledge outside of the IDF framework.

The discharged serviceman may make use of his military status, including his reserve or retired rank, or may grant permission to others to do so, only in civilian contexts that do not compromise the IDF's values and basic principles, or its honor and the trust which it enjoys in the public mind.

APPENDIX B

The Ten Commandments of the Solomon Schechter Day School Community*

אִם אֵין תּוֹרָה אֵין דֶּרֶךְ אֶרֶץ
אִם אֵין דֶּרֶךְ אֶרֶץ אֵין תּוֹרָה (פרקי אבות ג:כא)

(*im ayn Torah ayn derekh eretz, im ayn derekh eretz ayn Torah*)
Without *Torah* there is no *Derekh Eretz*
Without *Derekh Eretz* there is no *Torah*. (Pirkei Avot 3:21).

At Solomon Schechter Day School, we work together to treat each other
with DEREKH ERETZ.
RESPECT FOR GOD, TORAH, AND MITZVOT
GUIDE ALL OUR ACTIONS.
We expect all members of the Schechter community, both adults and students,
to honor the following TEN COMMANDMENTS:

1. RESPECT EACH OTHER AND ACCEPT INDIVIDUAL DIFFERENCES.
   אֵי־זֶהוּ מְכֻבָּד? הַמְכַבֵּד אֶת הַבְּרִיּוֹת. (פרקי אבות ד:א)
   (*ayzehu m'khubad? ham'khabed et ha-briot*)
   Who deserves respect? Someone who respects others. (Pirkei Avot 4:1)
2. BEHAVE HONESTLY.
   מִדְּבַר שֶׁקֶר תִּרְחָק. (שמות כג:ז)
   (*midvar sheker tirhak*)
   Stay away from dishonesty. (Exodus 23:7)

---

*Prepared by The Derekh Eretz subcommittee of the Educational Policy Committee of the Solomon Schechter Day School of Greater Boston 1994–95 Board of Trustees.

3. SHOW THOUGHTFULNESS, CONSIDERATION AND
   APPRECIATION.

   הֱוֵי מְקַבֵּל אֶת־כָּל־הָאָדָם בְּסֵבֶר פָּנִים יָפוֹת. (פרקי אבות א :טו)

   (*hevay m'kabayl et kol ha-adam b'sayver panim yafot*)

   Greet every person cheerfully. (Pirkei Avot 1:15)

4. LISTEN RESPECTFULLY TO OTHERS.

   אֵיזֶהוּ חָכָם? הַלּוֹמֵד מִכָּל אָדָם. (פרקי אבות ד :א)

   (*ayzehu hakham? ha-lomed me-kol adam*)

   Who is wise? Someone who learns from every person. (Pirkei Avot 4:1)

5. TAKE RESPONSIBILITY FOR THE SAFETY OF YOURSELF
   AND OTHERS.

   כָּל־יִשְׂרָאֵל עֲרֵבִים זֶה לָזֶה. (שבועות לט)

   (*kol Yisrael aravim zeh lazeh*)

   All Jews are responsible for each other. (Talmud, Shavuot 39a)

6. USE RESPECTFUL LANGUAGE.

   מָוֶת וְחַיִּים בְּיַד־לָשׁוֹן (משלי יח :כא)

   (*mavet v'hayyim b'yad lashon*)

   Death and life can depend upon the tongue. (Proverbs 18:21)

7. RESOLVE DIFFERENCES IN AN APPROPRIATE WAY.

   בַּקֵּשׁ שָׁלוֹם וְרָדְפֵהוּ. (תהילים, לד :טו)

   (*bakesh shalom v'radfayhu*)

   Seek peace and pursue it. (Psalms 34:15)

8. MAKE AMENDS IF YOU HURT OTHERS.

   צָרִיךְ לִשְׁאַל מִמֶּנּוּ שֶׁיִּמְחַל לוֹ. (תשובה ב :ט)

   (*tsarikh l'ratzoto v'lish'ol mimenu sheyimbal lo*)

   The wrongdoer must make peace with the injured person and ask that
   person's pardon. (Mishne Torah, Repentance 2:9)

9. RESPECT EACH OTHER'S AND SCHOOL PROPERTY.

   יְהִי מָמוֹן חֲבֵרָךְ חָבִיב עָלֶיךָ כְּשֶׁלָּךְ. (פרקי אבות ב :יז)

   (*yehi mamon havayrakh haviv alekha k'shelakh*)

   The property of others should be as precious to you as your own. (Pirkei
   Avot 2:17)

10. SHARE IN EACH OTHER'S JOYS AND SUPPORT EACH OTHER
    IN TIMES OF NEED.

    וְאָהַבְתָּ לְרֵעֲךָ כָּמוֹךָ.

    (*v'ahavta l'ray'akha kamokha*)

    You shall love your fellow person as yourself. (Leviticus 19:18)

YOU ARE AN IMPORTANT PART OF OUR COMMUNITY!!!
YOU DO MAKE A DIFFERENCE!!!

אַל תִּפְרוֹשׁ מִן הַצִּבּוּר. (פרקי אבות ב :ה)

(*al tifrosh min ha-tzibur*)

Do not keep yourself apart from the community. (Pirkei Avot 2:5)

APPENDIX C

198 Methods of Nonviolent Action*

Practitioners of nonviolent struggle have an entire arsenal of "nonviolent weapons" at their disposal. Listed below are 198 of them, classified into three broad categories: nonviolent protest and persuasion, noncooperation (social, economic, and political), and nonviolent intervention. A description and historical examples of each can be found in volume two of *The Politics of Nonviolent Action,* by Gene Sharp.

THE METHODS OF NONVIOLENT
PROTEST AND PERSUASION
Formal Statements
1. Public Speeches
2. Letters of opposition or support
3. Declarations by organizations and institutions
4. Signed public statements
5. Declarations of indictment and intention
6. Group or mass petitions
**Communications with
a Wider Audience**
7. Slogans, caricatures, and symbols
8. Banners, posters, and displayed communications
9. Leaflets, pamphlets, and books
10. Newspapers and journals
11. Records, radio, and television
12. Skywriting and earthwriting
Group Representations
13. Deputations
14. Mock awards

15. Group lobbying
16. Picketing
17. Mock elections
Symbolic Public Acts
18. Displays of flags and symbolic colors
19. Wearing of symbols
20. Prayer and worship
21. Delivering symbolic objects
22. Protest disrobings
23. Destruction of own property
24. Symbolic lights
25. Displays of portraits
26. Paint as protest
27. New signs and names
28. Symbolic sounds
29. Symbolic reclamations
30. Rude gestures
Pressures on Individuals
31. "Haunting" officials
32. Taunting officials
33. Fraternization
34. Vigils

*Reprinted from G. Sharp, *The Politics of Nonviolent Action* (Boston, Porter Sargent; 1973). Distributed by The Albert Einstein Institution, 50 Church St., Cambridge, MA 02138, USA.

Drama and Music
35. Humorous skits and pranks
36. Performances of plays and music
37. Singing
Processions
38. Marches
39. Parades
40. Religious processions
41. Pilgrimages
42. Motorcades
Honoring the Dead
43. Political mourning
44. Mock funerals
45. Demonstrative funerals
46. Homage at burial places
Public Assemblies
47. Assemblies of protest or support
48. Protest meetings
49. Camouflaged meetings of protest
50. Teach-ins
Withdrawal and Renunciation
51. Walk-outs
52. Silence
53. Renouncing honors
54. Turning one's back

THE METHODS OF SOCIAL
NONCOOPERATION
Ostracism of Persons
55. Social boycott
56. Selective social boycott
57. Lysistratic nonaction
58. Excommunication
59. Interdict
**Noncooperation with Social Events,
Customs, and Institutions**
60. Suspension of social and sports
activities
61. Boycott of social affairs
62. Student strike
63. Social disobedience
64. Withdrawal from social institutions
Withdrawal from the Social System
65. Stay-at-home

66. Total personal noncooperation
67. "Flight" of workers
68. Sanctuary
69. Collective disappearance
70. Protest emigration (*hijrat*)

THE METHODS OF ECONOMIC
NONCOOPERATION: *ECONOMIC
BOYCOTTS*
Actions by Consumers
71. Consumers' boycott
72. Nonconsumption of boycotted
goods
73. Policy of austerity
74. Rent withholding
75. Refusal to rent
76. National consumers' boycott
77. International consumers' boycott
Action by Workers and Producers
78. Workmen's boycott
79. Producers' boycott
Action by Middlemen
80. Suppliers' and handlers' boycott
Action by Owners and Management
81. Traders' boycott
82. Refusal to let or sell property
83. Lockout
84. Refusal of industrial assistance
85. Merchants' "general strike"
**Action by Holders of Financial
Resources**
86. Withdrawal of bank deposits
87. Refusal to pay fees, dues, and
assessments
88. Refusal to pay debts or interest
89. Severance of funds and credit
90. Revenue refusal
91. Refusal of a government's money
Action by Governments
92. Domestic embargo
93. Blacklisting of traders
94. International sellers' embargo
95. International buyers' embargo
96. International trade embargo

THE METHODS OF ECONOMIC
NONCOOPERATION: *THE STRIKE*

Symbolic Strikes
97. Protest strike
98. Quickie walkout (lightning strike)

Agricultural Strikes
99. Peasant strike
100. Farm Workers' strike

Strikes by Special Groups
101. Refusal of impressed labor
102. Prisoners' strike
103. Craft strike
104. Professional strike

Ordinary Industrial Strikes
105. Establishment strike
106. Industry strike
107. Sympathetic strike

Restricted Strikes
108. Detailed strike
109. Bumper strike
110. Slowdown strike
111. Working-to-rule strike
112. Reporting "sick" (sick-in)
113. Strike by resignation
114. Limited strike
115. Selective strike

Multi-Industry Strikes
116. Generalized strike
117. General strike

Combination of Strikes and Economic Closures
118. Hartal
119. Economic shutdown

THE METHODS
OF POLITICAL
NONCOOPERATION

Rejection of Authority
120. Withholding or withdrawal of allegiance
121. Refusal of public support
122. Literature and speeches advocating resistance

Citizens' Noncooperation with Government
123. Boycott of legislative bodies
124. Boycott of elections
125. Boycott of government employment and positions
126. Boycott of government depts., agencies, and other bodies
127. Withdrawal from government educational institutions
128. Boycott of government-supported organizations
129. Refusal of assistance to enforcement agents
130. Removal of own signs and placemarks
131. Refusal to accept appointed officials
132. Refusal to dissolve existing institutions

Citizens' Alternatives to Obedience
133. Reluctant and slow compliance
134. Nonobedience in absence of direct supervision
135. Popular nonobedience
136. Disguised disobedience
137. Refusal of an assemblage or meeting to disperse
138. Sitdown
139. Noncooperation with conscription and deportation
140. Hiding, escape, and false identities
141. Civil disobedience of "illegitimate" laws

Action by Government Personnel
142. Selective refusal of assistance by government aides
143. Blocking of lines of command and information
144. Stalling and obstruction
145. General administrative noncooperation
146. Judicial noncooperation

147. Deliberate inefficiency and selective noncooperation by enforcement agents
148. Mutiny

Domestic Governmental Action

149. Quasi-legal evasions and delays
150. Noncooperation by constituent governmental units

International Governmental Action

151. Changes in diplomatic and other representations
152. Delay and cancellation of diplomatic events
153. Withholding of diplomatic recognition
154. Severance of diplomatic relations
155. Withdrawal from international organizations
156. Refusal of membership in international bodies
157. Expulsion from international organizations

THE METHODS OF NONVIOLENT INTERVENTION

Psychological Intervention

158. Self-exposure to the elements
159. The fast
    a) Fast of moral pressure
    b) Hunger strike
    c) Satyagraphic fast
160. Reverse trial
161. Nonviolent harassment

Physical Intervention

162. Sit-in
163. Stand-in
164. Ride-in
165. Wade-in
166. Mill-in
167. Pray-in
168. Nonviolent raids

169. Nonviolent air raids
170. Nonviolent invasion
171. Nonviolent interjection
172. Nonviolent obstruction
173. Nonviolent occupation

Social Intervention

174. Establishing new social patterns
175. Overloading of facilities
176. Stall-in
177. Speak-in
178. Guerrilla theater
179. Alternative social institutions
180. Alternative communication system

Economic Intervention

181. Reverse strike
182. Stay-in strike
183. Nonviolent land seizure
184. Defiance of blockades
185. Politically motivated counterfeiting
186. Preclusive purchasing
187. Seizure of assets
188. Dumping
189. Selective patronage
190. Alternative markets
191. Alternative transportation systems
192. Alternative economic institutions

Political Intervention

193. Overloading of administrative systems
194. Disclosing identities of secret agents
195. Seeking imprisonment
196. Civil disobedience of "neutral" laws
197. Work-on without collaboration
198. Dual sovereignty and parallel government

APPENDIX D

Six Steps for Nonviolent Social Change*

The Six Steps for Nonviolent Social Change are based on Dr. King's nonviolent campaigns and teachings which emphasize love in action. Dr. King's philosophy of nonviolence, as reviewed in the Six Principles of Nonviolence, guide these steps for social and interpersonal change.

1. Information Gathering: To understand and articulate an issue, problem or injustice facing a person, community, or institution you must do research. You must investigate and gather all vital information from all sides of the argument or issue so as to increase your understanding of the problem. You must become an expert on your opponent's position. Some of the many sources from which you can gather information are: past and present newspaper and magazine articles, radio and television (including the archives of radio and television stations). Many organizations often have expertise in some aspect of the issue; these organizations should be asked to help. The public library, personal discussions and interviews, the more than 4,000 electronic data bases can also be used.

2. Education: It is essential to inform others, including your opposition, about your issue. This minimizes misunderstandings and gains you support and sympathy. You can write articles for newspapers and magazines. You can appear on radio and television talk programs. You can hold seminars, workshops and build coalitions on the issue. You can conduct mass rallies. You can write statements for pastors, priests and rabbis to include in their sermons.

---

*Derived from "Letter from Birmingham Jail," in *Why We Can't Wait* (New York, Penguin Books: 1963). Copyright 1990 by The Martin Luther King, Jr. Center for Nonviolent Social Change, Inc. This material cannot be reproduced without written permission from the Martin Luther King, Jr. estate and The Martin Luther King, Jr. Center for Nonviolent Social Change, Inc., Atlanta, Georgia.

3. Personal Commitment: Daily check and affirm your faith in the philosophy and methods of nonviolence. Eliminate hidden motives and prepare yourself to accept suffering, if necessary, in your work for justice.

4. Negotiations: Using grace, humor and intelligence, confront the other party with a list of injustices and a plan for addressing and resolving these injustices. Look for what is positive in every action and statement the opposition makes. Do not seek to humiliate the opponent but call forth the good in the opponent. Look for ways in which the opponent can also win.

5. Direct Action: These are actions taken to morally force the opponent to work with you in resolving the injustices. Direct action imposes a "creative tension" into the conflict. There are over 250 different direct action tactics, including: boycotts, marches, rallies, rent strikes, work slowdowns, letter-writing and petition campaigns, bank-ins, property occupancy, financial withdrawal, and political denial through the ballot. Direct action is most effective when it illustrates the injustice it seeks to correct.

6. Reconciliation: Nonviolence seeks friendship and understanding with the opponent. Nonviolence does not seek to defeat the opponent. Nonviolence is directed against evil systems, forces, oppressive policies, evil and unjust acts, not against persons. Reconciliation includes the opponent being able to "save face." Through reasoned compromise, both sides resolve the injustice with a plan of action. Each act of reconciliation is one step closer to the "Beloved Community." Not only are individuals empowered, but so is the entire community. With that come new struggles for justice and a new beginning.

Appendix E

Six Principles of Nonviolence*

Principle One: Nonviolence is a way of life for courageous people.
It is active nonviolent resistance to evil.
It is aggressive spiritually, mentally and emotionally.
It is always persuading the opponent of the righteousness of your cause.
It is only passive in its non-aggression towards its enemy.

Principle Two: Nonviolence seeks to win friendship and understanding.
The end result of nonviolence is redemption and reconciliation.
The purpose of nonviolence is the creation of the Beloved Community.

Principle Three: Nonviolence seeks to defeat injustice not people.
Nonviolence recognizes that evil doers are also victims and are not evil
    people.
The nonviolent resister seeks to defeat evil not people.

**Principle Four: Nonviolence holds that suffering can educate
and transform.**
Nonviolence accepts suffering without retaliation.
Nonviolence accepts violence if necessary, but will never inflict it.
Nonviolence willingly accepts the consequences of its acts.
Unearned suffering is redemptive and has tremendous educational and
    transforming possibilities.
Suffering has the power to convert the enemy when reason fails.

Principle Five: Nonviolence chooses love instead of hate.
Nonviolence resists violence of the spirit as well as the body.
Nonviolent love is spontaneous, unmotivated, unselfish and creative.

---

*Derived from "Pilgrimage to Nonviolence" in Dr. King's *Stride Toward Freedom* (Harper & Row: 1958). Copyright 1990 by The Martin Luther King, Jr. Center for Nonviolent Social Change, Inc. This material cannot be reproduced without written permission from the Martin Luther King, Jr. estate and The Martin Luther King, Jr. Center for Nonviolent Social Change, Inc., Atlanta, Georgia.

Nonviolent love gives willingly, knowing that the return might be hostility.

Nonviolent love is active, not passive.

Nonviolent love is un-ending in its ability to forgive in order to restore community.

Nonviolent love does not sink to the level of the hater.

Love for the enemy is how we demonstrate love for ourselves.

Love restores community and resists injustice.

Nonviolence recognizes the fact that all life is interrelated.

Principle Six: Nonviolence believes that the universe is on the side of justice.

The nonviolent resister has deep faith that justice will eventually win.

Nonviolence believes that God is a God of justice.

APPENDIX F

List of Prosocial Sources on the Web

The World Wide Web, known to many as the Internet, is an endless source of material on all subjects. The way to begin is to get on the web and to use one of the search engines. Enter the words "altruism" or "prosocial." Depending upon how advanced a search engine you use, you will have very many references. They will be very diverse; you must choose and look until you find what you want. This is time-consuming, but there is no other way. Another tip: All learning, a teacher once told me, is in the "cfs."; that is, in the beginning indicator in the footnotes. We learn by following footnotes. The web expands our "footnotes" enormously, but learning is still in the surfing.

To help reduce the confusion of a general search, I list the following websites with a brief characterization. All references begin: <http://>. Most sites have email capacity embedded in their pages so that you can communicate directly with each of these organizations and, of course, each site has its own links to other sites. This list represents my personal selection; the reader / surfer must do his or her own search.

www.giraffe.org/giraffe
Site of the Giraffe Project. Probably the best site for prosocial resources on the net. The Project, designed to give publicity to people "who stick out their necks" to do good, is described together with examples. The K–12 curriculum for prosocial education is also displayed alongside television programming and publications. They also have great links to individual "Giraffes" and other organizations dealing with the dangers of tobacco, environmental hazards, performers who go to hospitals, prevention of sexual abuse and abduction, racism, the arts, disabilities, and hunger. The links page (/links.html) also includes a section for children!

www.bev.net/education/schools/bms/bfalato/hrights.htm
Site of Facing History and Ourselves, an organization, with a regular journal, that draws up school units on human rights and social justice based on material from the shoah. They are sometimes attacked for "using" the shoah but, in the spirit of this book, I recommend their efforts.

www.splcenter.org/teachingtolerance.html

Site of *Teaching Tolerance,* a magazine devoted to fighting antisemitism, homophobia, race hatred, and religious bigotry. It is published by the Southern Poverty Law Center, a nonprofit organization founded by Morris Dees, which maintains a Klanwatch and pursues hatemongerers in court. *Teaching Tolerance* has resources including poster, video and text kits, etc. especially for K–8. It also administers a one year fellowship program to enable people to join their staff for a year, as well as grants up to $2000 for K–8 instruction.

www.humboldt.edu/~spol

Site of the Altruistic Personality Project run by Sam and Pearl Oliner. The project is described, publications listed, plans displayed, and links are being set up.

www.impactonline.org

Site of an organization that cultivates and aids volunteering on line, including a matching service for volunteers and those in need—a real database of volunteers.

www.indiana.edu/~eric_rec/ieo/bibs/characte.html

A good bibliography in character education.

www.concentric.net/~Wskills

The site of Wise Skills, a character education program for K–8.

www.familynetwork.org/wecare

Site of the Family Support Network which is devoted to encouraging mutual helping.

www.kumo.swcp.com/service

Site of the Human Services Alliance which gives training in mediation, care for the terminally ill and the developmentally disabled, etc.

www.giraffe.org/giraffe/ziv.htm

Site of the Ziv Tsedakah Project which combines the Giraffe philosophy with Jewish charity. This site needs to be developed.

www.6seconds.org

Site of the Six Seconds group. The concept of "emotional intelligence"—a kind of know yourself discipline, if I understand correctly—is discussed, seminars listed, and training materials made available.

www.nicsl.coled.umn.edu

Site of the National Service-Learning Clearinghouse. The method of learning through doing service is discussed, the partners are listed, as are publications including bibliographies, and dozens of organizations scattered throughout the US.

nch.ari.net

Site of the National Coalition for the Homeless. It lists the myths about homelessness, NCH projects and publications, and has further links on this issue.

www.whocares.org

Site for a publication called "Who Cares" which also publishes a tool kit in prosocial activity. This site needs to be developed.

www.habitat.org
Site of Habitat for Humanity which builds houses for the poor all over the world.

www.americanpromise.com
Site of a project to teach democracy in the schools and includes stories and teachers' guides.

www.globalethics.com
Site of an organization seeking to find and implement global common goals. It includes a corporate service entitled "Ethical Fitness," educational programs including ones on character building and decision making, and public policy initiatives.

www.voa.org
Site of Volunteers of America, one of the oldest human service organizations in the US with roots in Christian mission. They service the elderly, poor, disabled, victims of substance abuse, and ex-offenders.

www.korrnet.org
Site of East Tennessee branch of the National Coalition Building Institute. The national office has no website at this time. The goals of the organization—prejudice reduction, multiculturalism, antidiscrimination, etc.—are explained and local workshops listed.

www.nccj.com
Site of the National Council for Community and Justice, formerly the National Council of Christians and Jews. They have expanded into many areas of social justice and intergroup understanding.

www.internships.com
A commercial site that produces books on internships and temporary employment in various places in the United States.

www.bsr.org
Site of Business for Social Responsibility, an organization for businesses concerned with demonstrating respect for ethical values, people, communities, and the environment through socially responsible business policies and practices. They hold very good conferences with business leaders who speak on their work. It is expensive to join, though not for a corporation.

www.cnt.org
Home of the Center for Neighborhood Technology. They develop self-sufficient neighborhood economies, teaching appropriate technologies to help create a sustainable environment on the local level. Rooted in Chicago, it has a housing abandonment warning system for Chicago's neighborhoods and an initiative to re-craft the relationship between metropolitan areas and the federal government.

APPENDIX G

The Problem of Evil*

A Social-Psychological Approach
(revised 11/97)

Religion 330
TT 2:30–3:45
Callaway S 102

Spring, 1997
Writ. req.

Instructor:
Professor David R. Blumenthal (7-7545; 634-3833)
Adam Halberg, asst. (2-8374)

Content:

This course, dubbed "Advanced Evil" by the students, deals with the existence of both evil and good. These phenomena can be approached textually, philosophically, and literarily. However, the question remains: how do people actually reach moral judgements. The evidence from the social sciences and contemporary history is accumulating on this question and this course will attempt to confront that evidence.

First, we will examine the nature of social conformity (obedience). Then, we will turn to the phenomenon of moral resistance (disobedience) with emphasis on altruistic studies. Then, we will study a field theory to answer the question, what inclines people to do evil and good. Having examined the social scientific and historical evidence, we will engage in pro-social action on campus in groups to accomplish something good as well as to help us test our theory. Finally, we will ask, what have we learned from the social sciences and history that can help us better teach and act as good people.

---

*A course given at Emory University, Atlanta. Updates and other material available at <http://www.emory.edu/UDR/BLUMENTHAL>

Texts:
- S. Milgram, *Obedience*
- A. Miller, *For Your Own Good*
- S. Oliner, *The Altruistic Personality*
- P. Oliner, *Toward a Caring Society*
- H. Arendt, *Eichmann in Jerusalem*
- C. Browning, *Ordinary Men*
- H. Kelman and V. Hamilton, *Crimes of Obedience*

Reserve:
- W. Peters, *A Class Divided Then and Now* ("Eye of the Storm")
- P. Zimbardo in Z. Rubin, *Doing Unto Others* (the Stanford experiments)
- R. Tomsho, *The American Sanctuary Movement*
- Darley and Batson, "From Jerusalem to Jericho" (copied reading)
- E. Staub, "Helping Distressed Persons" (copied reading)
- D. Kittering, "Those Who Said 'No'" (copied reading)

Particulars:
Students will be expected to participate *very* actively in the class.
There will be some films outside of class; they are obligatory.
There will be one short exam and a final exam / paper.
This course is co-sponsored by the Emory Center for Ethics.

Syllabus

I. *Introduction*—1/16

The Descriptive-Analytic Enterprise

II. *Obedience and the Propagation of Social Evil*
   A. The obedience studies: evidence from social psychology
       Obedience—film (45 min.) and book—1/21
       The Stanford Prison Experiment—slide presentation
       (50 minutes) and article—1/23
       The Eye of the Storm—film (20 minutes) and book—1/28
   B. The banality of evil: evidence from history
       the holocaust—H. Arendt, *Eichmann**—1/30
       ch. 8, Epilogue, Postscript, [14,15]**

---

*See guide questions.
**Chapters or pages listed between square brackets are highly recommended.

the holocaust—Browning [Kittering]**—2/4
   The Wannsee Conference, optional film (87 min.), outside
      class—2/3***
Vietnam: the My Lai massacre—Kelman and Hamilton*—
   2/6, 11
   ch. 1–5, 6–8, 11, 13
   Remembering My Lai, required film (58 min.), outside
      class—2/9***

C. The psychopathology of obedience—2/13, 18
   A. Miller, *For Your Own Good,** 3–102, 142–97
D. Open session—2/20
   The Wave, optional film (46 min.), outside class—2/19***
E. Short exam—2/25

III. *Resistance and the Propagation of Social Good*

A. The altruistic studies: evidence from social psychology
   Milgram and Zimbardo revisited: When did some resist?
      Reread your notes; Kelman and Hamilton, ch. 13
      Kittering—2/27
   the Princeton and Staub experiments
      Darley and Batson + Staub—3/4
B. The class projects—3/6—guest facilitator
   (see handout)

[3/11, 13—no classes, spring break]

C. The banality of goodness: evidence from history
   the holocaust—3/18, 20
      S. and P. Oliner, *The Altruistic Personality,** ch. 1–2,
         5–8, 9–10
   the holocaust—class discussion—3/25
      Weapons of the Spirit, required film (90 min.), outside
        class—3/24***
   the sanctuary movement—3/27
      The New Underground Railroad—film (39 min.) and book
D. Business and Education: evidence from the real world—4/1
   Oliner, *Toward a Caring Society,* ch. 4,5,7,10

---

*See guide questions.
**Chapters or pages listed between square brackets are highly recommended.
***Outside films are in Candler Library 425 at 8:00 p.m.

IV. *A Field Theory*
Professor Blumenthal's field theory—4/3

The Prescriptive-Normative Enterprise

V. *Class Projects*
   A. Group Reports—4/8,10
   B. Generalizations from the Reports—4/15
   C. Professor Blumenthal's "Seven Steps to Prosocial Action"
      (handout)—4/17

[4/22—no class, Passover]

VI. *Conclusions*—4/24
Final papers due—Thursday, May 1st, 5:00 p.m.,
   Department of Religion Office

APPENDIX H

Social Action Rabbinics Curriculum
*NA'ASEH VE-NISHMA'**
(A Curriculum for Middle School Students)

Students in Middle School have entered a complex stage of adolescence in which they begin to make their own choices and develop the skills they will require as they become young adults. The Epstein School has designed a varied and challenging program which respects students' growth toward independence. At the same time it offers the direction, guidance and support of a school program designed to teach the complex area of mitzvah through action.

Overview of Present Program

Jewish survival in a time of assimilation depends on Jewish identity fostered by both learning and doing. The Epstein School seventh and eighth grade rabbinics curriculum, *Na'aseh ve-Nishma'*, ("We will do and we will understand," Ex. 24:7) aims to teach mitzvah as a value and a practice to create a real membership in the community and a sense of responsibility to its well-being.

This study program uses social action experiences, textual study, and student reflective writing to expand the traditional approach to our precious classical texts by allowing children a personal context for the fulfillment of mitzvah.

In this unique and innovative social action-based program, every seventh and eighth grader has the opportunity to do concentrated community service

---

*This curriculum was originally developed by The Epstein School, a Solomon Schechter School, of Atlanta, GA, in 1992. It was subsequently revised in 1996. The material presented here represents a précis of the original proposal and the revised curriculum. Copies of the full curriculum are available from: The Epstein School, 335 Colewood Way NW, Atlanta, GA 30328 (404-843-0111). My thanks to the director, Cheryl Finkel, for her support of my work and for her permission to reprint this here. For additional curricular material, see S. Frost, et al., *A Curriculum for the Jewish Day School* (New York, United Synagogue of America, Commission on Jewish Education, Solomon Schechter Day School Association: n.d.).

and then study the traditional rabbinic texts to learn what Jewish tradition teaches.

This school year will focus on three action-based community mitzvah projects. Every student will spend twelve weeks doing and then learning about each of these mitzvot.

Objectives

Na'aseh ve-Nishma' is what the Jews answered when given the Torah at Mt. Sinai. This response, to do, and through doing, to learn, is the principle on which this social action rabbinics curriculum is developed. The philosophy of the program is, further, consistent with the School's ethical and educational beliefs:

- kindness to our fellow human beings and responsibility to the community, and
- an integrated understanding of self and an integrated world view gained through interwoven Judaic and general studies curricula.

Curriculum objectives include:

- learning Mishna and Talmud texts regarding the mitzvot of gemilut hasadim and tzedakah
- developing leadership skills in a required program of community service
- studying Jewish ethical values in a meaningful integrated way.

Implementation Process

The three action-based community service mitzvah projects this year include serving the elderly, the hungry, and others with special needs. Students spend approximately three and one-half hours each Friday engaging in related activities.

Specific tasks involved in experiencing these mitzvah projects include:

- *Vehadarta p'nei zaken* (cherishing the elderly). To fulfill this mitzvah students work at the Louis Kahn Group Home and the Atlanta Jewish Community Center's Weinstein Center visiting the residents, offering friendship, and celebrating holidays with them. Students also help residents make physical preparations for Shabbat.
- *Ma'achil re'ayvim* (feeding the hungry). To fulfill this mitzvah students provide direct services stacking cans and distributing donated food at the Atlanta Food Bank, prepare meals to be served at the Zaban and Shearith Israel shelters for the Atlanta homeless, and deliver challot and flowers to elderly

homebound on Erev Shabbat. Students are also responsible for coordinating a school-wide food drive for Operation Isaiah at Yom Kippur, and for other food drives at Sukkot, Thanksgiving, and Purim.

• *Meshaneh ha-beriyot* (assisting those with special needs). To fulfill this mitzvah, students work with a group of severely disabled children at the Woodland Elementary School under the direction of the classroom special education teacher. They read and tell stories to these children, help them with schoolwork, and establish friendships.

Resources

Each of these practical experiences is followed by text study led by community rabbis. These texts include selections from various classical sources, as follow (n.b. Talmud refers to the Babylonian Talmud unless otherwise noted)

- *Vehadarta p'nei zaken* (cherishing the elderly)
  Talmud: Avot, Shabbat, Niddah, Bava Mezi'a, Sukkah
  Tanḥuma: Meketz, Ḥayei Sarah
  Midrash Shir Hashirim Rabbah
- *Ma'achil re'ayvim* (feeding the hungry)
  Talmud: Pesaḥim, Bava Metzi'a, Shabbat, Bava Batra, Betzah, Eruvin, Avot
  Avot D'Rabbi Nathan
  Jerusalem Talmud: Brachot
- *Meshaneh ha-beriyot* (assisting those with special needs)
  Talmud: Nedarim, Shabbat

Scholars for this phase of learning this academic year are congregational rabbis who have agreed to teach the appropriate texts to our students. They include Rabbi Shalom Lewis, Congregation Etz Chaim; Rabbi Donald Tam, Congregation Beth Tikvah; Rabbi Stephen Weiss, Congregation Ahavath Achim; and Rabbi Mark Zimmerman, Congregation Beth Shalom.

Faculty members implementing this program include Barbara Rosenblit, Nancy Seifert-Gorod, Miriam Rosenbaum, and Marc Medwed.

Evaluation

Formal evaluation requirements include:
- Periodic exams measuring comprehension of text and concepts.
- Three research papers, each focusing on a different topic related to the mitzvah being studied.
- A year-long journal of ethical awareness and development. This journal

is a way for students to record their new experiences (as stewards of the community) and to reflect on their meaning.

In addition, informal methods of evaluation are used. This experience is designed to build life-long skills, enabling each student to develop a sense of self-worth, of involvement, of accomplishment and of being a person committed to performing mitzvot. Internalizing the commitment to give of oneself by serving the community promises benefits long after the course evaluation— well into decades to come.

As a result of teaching Jewish values through community service, the *Na'aseh ve-Nishma'* social action-based mitzvah program is already impacting the students. Rabbi Stephen Weiss stated in his letter to the editor of the *Atlanta Jewish Times* on November 11, 1991, "More than just a school requirement, these students were there out of love for these, their new friends. When it comes to *hiddur p'nei zakken*—bringing light, warmth and dignity to the elderly—these students are a model we should all follow."

Introduction to the Revised Curriculum**

The unifying principle of this curriculum is that action precedes understanding. This means that the performance of mitzvot is critical to understanding the mitzvah, leading ultimately to self-awareness. This principle assumes that these acts, whether performed willingly or not, initially yield simple sensitivity to the less fortunate; secondarily, a sense of self-importance and self-worth and, ultimately, a sense of obligation.

This principle of learning is not confined to a certain age or stage. We, however, are most concerned with the middle school child, ages 11–14. This is a unique time of growth. Developmentally, middle school is a time when children need to feel in control at the very time that they are under everyone else's control. This is the time to stake out and declare who you are uniquely, but this drive toward independence manifests itself through an insistence on being just like everyone else. These contradictions and conflicts expose themselves at home, at school, and everywhere in between. Alongside this emotional minefield develops a maturing body that has become increasingly unfamiliar and unpredictable. These physical and emotional realities are the essential challenges facing the school, the home, and the synagogue.

Yet concurrently grows a child willing to act, to do, to experience, to matter. Staking out who you are means figuring out how you count. Experimenting

---

**This revised curriculum catalogues and expands a vibrant course created and implemented at The Epstein School in Atlanta, Georgia. The curriculum pieces for *Hiddur Mitzvah* and *Mishaneh Ha-Beriyot* were written by Barbara Ellison Rosenblit, with guidance and inspiration from Rabbi Stephen Weiss and Rabbi Shalom Lewis.

with various persona means trying on roles. Consequently, we have structured *Na'aseh ve-Nishma'* to capitalize on these strengths of middle school development rather than bemoan its difficulties.

First of all, this course is purposely scheduled for the final two hours on Friday afternoons. There are several reasons for this particular strategy. Tying the time to lunch extends the time that can be used for mitzvah-doing during that part of the course cycle.

Based on a 12-week cycle, three weeks are set aside for the introduction of the area being studied, including its social urgency, emotional components, sensitivity training, perhaps its historical background. In this part of the cycle, outside speakers, films, field trips, and sensitivity exercises are generally used, depending on the nature of the mitzvah and the availability of speakers, programs in the community, etc. The next six weeks are spent "in the field," actually performing the mitzvah. The last three weeks are spent studying related Rabbinic texts with a rabbi.

This program emphasizes the **doing** of mitzvah. Rabbis, our community experts, teach relevant Biblical and Talmudic texts so that we can employ less scholarly but vitally energetic role models for the initial parts of the cycle. This division of labor and fit of the teacher to the task is an important element in the success of this curriculum; the instructor's willingness to model the **joy** of mitzvah-doing complements our goals of action and study. We compromise neither the opportunity to employ less scholarly but highly-involved community people nor the scholarly and teacherly among our rabbinic community.

Though we attempt to evaluate this program through diaries and term projects, its true yield is far longer range, conceivably affecting one's entire life, coloring forever the eyes through which we view both God's gifts and our own power to make this world better.

The *Na'aseh ve-Nishma'* program faces the developmental, emotional, structural and educational challenges and reinterprets them as assets. In this program, each child confronts and takes control of his or her contribution. One's worth is equated with one's struggle and success in performing mitzvot rather than the memorization of often-distant texts.

The critical course requirements for each mitzvah studied varies and is outlined in the individual descriptions below, but one unvarying component of each term's work is the keeping of a diary. These diaries, viewed by the students as summaries of their activities and feelings after each class, are for us the year-long record of a child's ethical development. We have been pleased with the blend of action and insight that we see in these journals. In Judaic portfolio assessments, an opportunity to display the year's accomplishments before an evaluation committee in the spring, *Na'aseh ve-Nishma'* journals are one of the ten required components. Students verify at that time that this course mattered.

Mitzvah 1: Hiddur Mitzvah (Beautifying a Mitzvah)

Lesson 1: Who are the homeless?
Lesson 2: Enhancing the Shelter
Lessons 3–8: Creating Elements to Enhance the Shelter
Lesson 9: Is More Better? (texts on *lifnim mi-shurat ha-din*)
Lesson 10: Can Commandments Contradict One Another? (various texts)
Lesson 11: How Much is Too Much? (texts on *hiddur mitzvah*)
Lesson 12: Exhibition of the Projects
Final requirements include: diary, research project of 5–8 pages, creation and exposition of an original piece of Judaica

Mitzvah 2: Meshaneh ha-Beriyot (Assisting Those with Special Needs)

Lesson 1: What is the Problem?
Lesson 2: Using My Left Foot to Move Forward
Lesson 3: What If It Were Me?
Lessons 4–9: *Na'aseh* (Doing: site work at the Woodland Hills School)
Lesson 10: The Message of the Blessings (texts from the liturgy)
Lesson 11: What the Torah Teaches Us (Torah texts on the blind, deaf, lame, etc.)
Lesson 12: What the Talmud Teaches Us (talmudic texts)
Final requirements include: research paper of 5 pages, write a story or midrash

APPENDIX I

Holocaust and Human Behavior*

An Overview

The first two chapters in the Resource Book use literature to introduce the key concepts developed in Facing History. Those ideas are then applied to real individuals and real events in history. The opening chapters engage students in thinking about behavior and introduce them to the principles of decision-making. They also help students build a vocabulary of morality. In Chapter 1, for example, students explore the connections between individuals and the society in which they live. And they discover why Martha Minow argues that "when we identify one thing as like the others, we are not merely classifying the world; we are investing particular classifications with consequences and positioning ourselves in relation to those meanings. When we identify one thing as unlike the others, we are dividing the world; we use our language to exclude, to distinguish—to discriminate."

Chapter 1 also begins an exploration of many of the central questions developed in the program:

How is our identity formed?
How do our attitudes and beliefs influence our thinking? How does our thinking affect our actions?
How can we keep our individuality and still be a part of a group?
How does our tendency to see us as unique but them as members affect our behavior as well as our attitudes?

Chapter 2 then outlines the ways various nations, including the United States, have defined their identity. And it helps students understand the significance of those definitions. After all, those who define a nation's identity determine who is a part of its "universe of obligation." Early in the chapter, the focus is on the United States and the way three sets of ideas shaped those definitions

---

*Drawn from the Introduction to *Holocaust and Human Behavior,* a publication of "Facing History and Ourselves," 16 Hurd Rd., Brookline, MA 02146-6919, USA.

in the nineteenth and early twentieth centuries: *democracy, race,* and *nationalism.* All three concepts have had tremendous appeal to people all over the world. And all three, when carried to an extreme, have been abused. False ideas about "race" have on occasion turned nationalism into ethnocentrism and chauvinism. At the same time, some democrats have confused equality with conformity. Others have viewed differences as proof that "they" are less human than "we" are.

The next few chapters focus primarily on the decisions that resulted in the Holocaust and relate those decisions to issues important to students' lives today—particularly to issues of racism, antisemitism, violence, conformity, and power. Chapter 3, which marks the beginning of the case study, examines the choices people in Europe and the United States made after World War I. The chapter highlights German efforts to build a lasting democracy after the humiliation of defeat and explores the values, myths, and fears that threatened those efforts. Chapters 4 through 8 examine *how* the Nazis turned Germany into a totalitarian state by turning neighbor against neighbor in order to break the moral backbone of a citizenry and *why* the German people allowed them to do so. Students also consider the way individuals and nations defined their "universe of obligation" in the 1930s and 1940s and the consequences of those definitions. It is in these chapters that students begin to wonder, "What might I have done?" And it is in these chapters that students see connections to their own world and come to understand why Cynthia Ozick warns that "when a whole population takes on the status of bystander, the victims are without allies; the criminals, unchecked, are strengthened; and only then do we need to speak of heroes. When a field is filled from end to end with sheep, a stag stands out. When a continent is filled from end to end with the compliant, we learn what heroism is."

As they read these chapters, some teachers and students emphasize the acts of courage that rekindle hope in humanity. But, to study only heroes and speak solely of human dignity is to distort and distract from the painful reality of this history. Thinking about the victims and perpetrators of mass murder requires a new "vocabulary of annihilation." The "choiceless choices" of this history of human behavior in extremity do not reflect options between right and wrong but between one form of abnormal response and another.

In the last three chapters, students move from thought to judgment, and then to action. As students think about judgment in moral and legal terms, they consider such questions as:

What is the difference between crimes against humanity and killings sanctioned by war?
What is the purpose of a trial? Is it to punish evil-doing or set a precedent for the future?

Are individuals responsible for their crimes if they have obeyed the laws of their nation? Or are there higher laws?

How does one determine punishment? Is everyone equally guilty? Or do some bear more responsibility than others? Can an entire nation be guilty?

Chapters 10 and 11 consider issues related to prevention by returning to themes developed in the first two chapters in the book. Chapter 10 explores how we remember the past and considers the ways those memories shape the present. It also focuses on the ways individuals and nations avoid, revise, deny, or rewrite their history. In the words of journalist Judith Miller, "Knowing and remembering the evil in history and in each of us might not prevent a recurrence of genocide. But ignorance of history or the suppression of memory removes the surest defense we have, however inadequate, against such gigantic cruelty and indifference to it." What then fosters memory? For Miller, it is anything that makes the past more real and encourages empathy and caring. As part of this chapter, students examine the way we memorialize the past through monuments, museums, and schooling.

Chapter 11 further develops the idea of prevention by considering what it takes to be a good citizen. The chapter is organized around the idea that "people become brave by doing brave acts. People become compassionate by doing compassionate acts. People become good citizens by engaging in acts of good citizenship." Many of the individuals highlighted in Chapter 11 help us understand what it takes to keep democracy alive. The chapter also promotes participation through acts of community service.

Notes

Chapter 1

1. On not capitalizing "nazi," see pp. 12–13.

2. G. Blackburn, *Education in the Third Reich* (Albany, NY, SUNY Press: 1985), esp. chap. 3.

3. P. Sichrovsky, *Born Guilty: Children of Nazi Families,* transl. J. Steinberg (New York, Basic Books: 1988). Most of the behaviors of my Jewish nazi appear in the testimonies of the children of nazis contained in this book.

4. Blackburn, 22–23, 67–73, 106, 127, 178.

5. H. Arendt, *The Origins of Totalitarianism* (New York, Harcourt Brace Jovanovich: 1951) and idem, *Eichmann in Jerusalem: A Report on the Banality of Evil* (New York, Viking Press: 1963).

6. Sichrovsky, 127–8.

7. A. Miller, *For Your Own Good* (New York, Farrar, Straus, Giroux: 1983) is the classic text on abuse in nazi culture. See 84–89.

8. On not capitalizing "führer," see pp. 12–13.

9. E. Staub, *The Roots of Evil: The Origins of Genocide and Other Group Violence* (Cambridge, Cambridge University Press: 1989) 50.

10. See pp. 35–36, chap. 3.

11. On various and multiple "universes of discourse" as an analytic tool, see D. Blumenthal, *Facing the Abusing God: A Theology of Protest* (Louisville, KY, Westminster / John Knox: 1993) chap. 4.

12. On not capitalizing "third reich," see pp. 12–13.

13. *Weapons of the Spirit,* a film about Le Chambon sur Lignon, by Pierre Sauvage.

14. C. ten Boom, *The Hiding Place* (Old Tappan, NJ, Spire Books: 1971) 99.

15. H. C. Kelman and V. L. Hamilton, *Crimes of Obedience* (New Haven, Yale University Press: 1989) 8.

16. See the story of Marion Pritchard told in *The Courage to Care,* ed. C. Rittner and S. Myers (New York, New York University Press: 1986) 28–33 and in *Rescuers: Portraits of Moral Courage,* ed. G. Block and M. Drucker (New York, Holmes and Meier: 1992) 33–41.

17. See Note 18 on my use of "shoah."

18. On the "use" of the shoah, see D. Blumenthal, "The Holocaust and Hiroshima: Icons of Our Century," available on my website <http://www.emory.edu/UDR/ BLUMENTHAL> and "From Anger to Inquiry," *From the Unthinkable to the Unavoid-*

able, ed. C. Rittner and J. Roth (Westport, CT, Greenwood Press: 1997) 149–55, also available on my website.

19. Westminster / John Knox: 1993. See also my "Theodicy: Dissonance in Theory and Praxis," *Concilium* 1 (1998) 138–54.

20. S. Katz, "The 'Unique' Intentionality of the Holocaust," in *Post-Holocaust Dialogues,* ed. S. Katz (New York, New York University Press: 1985) 287–317. Idem, *The Holocaust in Historical Context* (New York, Oxford University Press: 1994).

21. Ibid.

22. For a preliminary attempt, see E. Staub, *The Roots of Evil: The Origins of Genocide and Other Group Violence* (Cambridge, Cambridge University Press: 1989) and idem, "Psychological and Cultural Origins of Extreme Destructiveness and Extreme Altruism," *Handbook of Moral Behavior and Development,* ed. W. Kurtines and J. Gewirtz (Hillsdale, NJ, Lawrence Erlbaum: 1991) 425–46.

23. One should also include other historical data fields such as Vietnam, African-American slavery, etc.

24. As Elie Wiesel has noted, while not all the victims were Jewish, all the perpetrators and bystanders were Christian.

25. Susan Shapiro, "Hearing the Testimony of Radical Negation," *Concilium,* 1985; idem, "Failing Speech: Post-Holocaust Writing and the Discourse of Postmodernism," *Semeia* 40:1987; and idem, review of Fackenheim, *Religious Studies Review* 13:3 (July 1987) 204–13; L. Langer, *Holocaust Testimonies: The Ruins of Memory* (New Haven, Yale University Press: 1991) xi. A similar, though ritual, step was taken after the destruction of the second temple: ceremonies were introduced to commemorate that terrible moment in Jewish history, the most well-known is the breaking of a glass at Jewish wedding ceremonies.

26. For a fuller statement, see Blumenthal, *Facing the Abusing God,* at the Index, "autobiographical moments." See also, "From *Wissenschaft* to Theology: A Mid-Life Re-Calling," available on my website.

27. See, for example, L. Davidowicz, *History and the Historians* (Cambridge, MA, Harvard University Press: 1981); D. Blumenthal, "Scholarly Approaches to the Holocaust," *Emory Studies on the Holocaust,* ed. D. Blumenthal (Atlanta, GA, Emory University: 1985) 1:14–35.

28. For a fuller statement of this, see *Facing the Abusing God,* xxii.

29. For a fuller statement of this, see *Facing the Abusing God,* xxii, 40–41, 64; *God at the Center* (San Francisco, Harper and Row: 1988; reprinted Northvale, NJ, Jason Aronson: 1994) xxx; and "What American Jews Believe," *Commentary* (Aug. 1996) 23–24.

30. For a feminist reading of Psalm 51, the psalm recited by David right after this incident, see B. Ellison Rosenblit, "David, Bat Sheva, and the Fifty-First Psalm," *Cross Currents* (Fall 1995) 326–40.

Chapter 2

1. Cited from her autobiography in R. Abzug, *Inside the Vicious Heart* (Oxford, Oxford University Press: 1985) 58.

2. On my preference for "shoah," see p. 13. On "holocaust," see Z. Garber and B. Zuckerman, "Why Do We Call the Holocaust 'The Holocaust'? An Inquiry into the Psychology of Labels," *Modern Judaism* 9 (1989) 197–212, etc., cited in A. Rosenfeld, *The Americanization of the Holocaust,* D. W. Beilin Lecture (Ann Arbor, University of Michigan: 1995) 7. On this and other terms used to label the holocaust, see I. Wollaston, *A War Against Memory* (London, Society for Promoting Christian Knowledge: 1996) 1–5, citing especially U. Tal, "On the Study of Holocaust and Genocide: Excursus on Hermeneutical Aspects of the Term *Sho'ah,*" *Yad Vashem Studies* (Jerusalem: 1979) 7–52, as well as Garber and Zuckerman.

3. T. W. Adorno et al., *The Authoritarian Personality,* abridged edition (New York, W. W. Norton and Co.: 1950, 1982).

4. G. Allport, *The Nature of Prejudice* (Reading, MA, Addison-Wesley: 1954).

5. S. E. Asch, "Effects of Group Presssure Upon the Modification and Distortion of Judgements," *Groups, Leadership, and Men,* ed. H. Guetzkow (Pittsburgh, Carnegie Press: 1951).

6. P. G. Zimbardo et al., "The Psychology of Imprisonment: Privation, Power, and Pathology," *Doing unto Others,* ed. Z. Rubin (Englewood Cliffs, NJ, Prentice-Hall: 1974); available in slide presentation and, later, in a film, *Quiet Rage;* see *New York Times Magazine,* April 8, 1973.

7. S. Milgram, *Obedience to Authority: An Experimental View* (New York, Harper and Row: 1974); also available as a film. See also the film: *In the Eye of the Storm* and later in *A Class Divided;* the latter appeared as a book by W. Peters, *A Class Divided Then and Now* (New Haven, Yale University Press: 1987).

8. H. Arendt, *The Origins of Totalitarianism* (New York, Harcourt Brace Jovanovich: 1951) and idem, *Eichmann in Jerusalem: A Report on the Banality of Evil* (New York, Viking Press: 1963).

9. T. Des Pres, *The Survivor: An Anatomy of Life in the Death Camps* (Oxford, Oxford University Press: 1976); reviewed by me in *Journal of Jewish Studies* (1979) 41:330–2.

10. H. Fein, *Accounting for Genocide* (New York, Free Press: 1979).

11. L. Davidowicz, *The War Against the Jews: 1933–1945* (New York, Holt, Rinehart, and Winston: 1975).

12. M. Mayer, *They Thought They Were Free: The Germans 1933–1945* (Chicago, University of Chicago Press: 1955, 1966).

13. B. Bettelheim, *Surviving and Other Essays* (New York, Vintage Books: 1952, 1972).

14. E. A. Cohen, *Human Behavior in the Concentration Camps* (New York, W. W. Norton and Co.: 1953).

15. E. Fromm, *Escape from Freedom* (New York, Avon Books: 1965).

16. G. W. Blackburn, *Education in the Third Reich* (Albany, NY, SUNY Press: 1985).

17. G. Cocks, *Psychotherapy in the Third Reich: The Göring Institute* (New York, Oxford University Press: 1985).

18. C. Koonz, *Mothers in the Fatherland* (New York, St. Martin's Press: 1987).

19. I. Müller, *Hitler's Justice: The Courts of the Third Reich,* transl. D. L.

Schneider (Cambridge, MA, Harvard University Press: 1991); reviewed by me in *Modern Judaism* (1993) 13:95–106.

20. R. J. Lifton, *The Nazi Doctors: Medical Killing and the Psychology of Genocide* (New York, Basic Books: 1986) and R. Proctor, *Racial Hygiene: Medicine under the Nazis* (Cambridge, MA, Harvard University Press: 1988); see also "The Value of the Human Being: Medicine in Germany 1918–1945," an exhibition sponsored by Ärztekammer Berlin in Zusammenarbeit mit der Bundesärztekammer, published as a catalogue edited by C. Pross and G. Aly, *Der Wert des Menschen: Medizin in Deutschland 1918–1945* (Berlin, Hentrich: 1989).

21. R. Ericksen, *Theologians under Hitler* (New Haven, Yale University Press: 1985) and M. Weinreich, *Hitler's Professors* (New York, Yiddish Scientific Institute [YIVO]: 1946).

22. B. Bellon, *Mercedes in Peace and War* (New York, Columbia University Press: 1990) and J. Borkin, *The Crime and Punishment of I. G. Farben* (New York, Free Press: 1978).

23. E. Klee et al., *"The Good Old Days,"* transl. D. Burnstone (New York, Free Press: 1988, 1991).

24. C. Browning, *Ordinary Men: Reserve Police Battalion 101 and the Final Solution in Poland* (New York, HarperCollins: 1992).

25. P. Sichrovsky, *Born Guilty: Children of Nazi Families,* transl. J. Steinberg (New York, Basic Books: 1988) and D. Bar-On, *Legacy of Silence* (Cambridge, MA, Harvard University Press: 1989).

26. J. Dimsdale, *Survivors, Victims, and Perpetrators: Essays on the Nazi Holocaust* (New York, Hemisphere Publishing Co.: 1980).

27. F. Katz, *Ordinary People and Extraordinary Evil* (Albany, NY, SUNY Press: 1993).

28. E. Staub, *The Roots of Evil: The Origins of Genocide and Other Group Violence* (Cambridge, Cambridge University Press: 1989) and idem, "Psychological and Cultural Origins of Extreme Destructiveness and Extreme Altruism," *Handbook of Moral Behavior and Development,* ed. W. Kurtines and J. Gewirtz (Hillsdale, NJ, Lawrence Erlbaum Associates: 1991) 425–46.

29. A. Miller, *For Your Own Good,* transl. H. and H. Hannum (New York, Farrar, Straus, Giroux: 1983).

30. I. Charny, *How Can We Commit the Unthinkable?* (Boulder, CO, Westview Press: 1982). See also Staub, parts I and III, and especially S. Katz, "The 'Unique' Intentionality of the Holocaust," in *Post-Holocaust Dialogues,* ed. S. Katz (New York, New York University Press: 1985) 287–317; now in book form, *The Holocaust in Historical Context* (New York, Oxford University Press: 1994).

31. H. C. Kelman and V. L. Hamilton, *Crimes of Obedience* (New Haven, Yale University Press: 1989).

32. C. Zahn-Waxler et al., *Altruism and Aggression: Biological and Social Origins* (Cambridge, Cambridge University Press: 1986).

33. D. Olweus et al., *Development of Antisocial and Prosocial Behavior* (New York, Academic Press: 1986).

34. E. Staub, *The Roots of Evil,* is really a study in obedience based in social psychology and shoah studies. His last section on the creation of caring societies, while

very useful and rooted in his work in altruistic studies, is only a rudimentary adden-
dum to the main work of the book. See also, idem, "Extreme."

35. N. Eisenberg et al., *Social and Moral Values* (Hillsdale, NJ, Lawrence Erlbaum Associates: 1989).

36. J. A. Piliavin and H. W. Charng, "Altruism: A Review of Recent Theory and
Research," *American Review of Sociology* 16 (1990) 27–65.

37. P. Oliner et al., *Embracing the Other: Philosophical, Psychological, and Historical Perspectives* (New York, New York University Press: 1992); reviewed by me in
Pastoral Psychology 46:2 (1997) 131–34.

38. P. and S. Oliner, *Toward a Caring Society: Ideas into Action* (Westport, CT,
Praeger: 1995).

39. S. and P. Oliner, *The Altruistic Personality: Rescuers of Jews in Nazi Europe*
(New York, Free Press: 1988); reviewed by me in *Critical Review of Books in Religion*
3 (1990) 409–11.

40. E. Fogelman, *Conscience and Courage: Rescuers of Jews during the Holocaust* (New York, Anchor Books: 1994); reviewed by me in *Journal of Psychology and
Theology* 23 (1995) 62–63.

41. N. Tec, *When Light Pierced the Darkness* (Oxford, Oxford University Press:
1986); *In the Lion's Den: The Life of Oswald Rufeisen* (Oxford, Oxford University Press:
1990); and *Defiance: The Bielski Partisans* (Oxford, Oxford University Press: 1993).

42. G. Block and M. Drucker, *Rescuers: Portraits of Moral Courage in the Holocaust* (New York, Holmes and Meier: 1992).

43. The best known is S. Spielberg's *Schindler's List* (1993, 1994) but it is not the
best. There is also a documentary called *Schindler* by Jon Blair (London, Thames
Television: 1983, 1995) and the book (T. Keneally, *Schindler's List* [New York, Simon
and Schuster: 1982]). Cf. also L. Rappoport and G. Kren, "Amoral Rescuers: The Ambiguities of Altruism," *Creativity Research Journal* 6 (1993) 129–36, for an analysis
of Schindler and other such rescuers. Pierre Sauvage's film dealing with Le Chambon
sur Lignon, *Weapons of the Spirit,* and several dealing with the Denmark story are also
very moving. See Fogelman's bibliography which also lists films.

44. T. Des Pres, *The Survivor: An Anatomy of Life in the Death Camps* (Oxford,
Oxford University Press: 1976) chap. 5, esp. 136–40.

45. Film, *The New Underground Railroad* and book, R. Tomsho, *The American
Sanctuary Movement* (Austin, TX, Texas Monthly Press: 1987). See also G. Wiltfang
and D. McAdam, "The Costs and Risks of Social Activism: A Study of Sanctuary
Movement Activism," *Social Forces* 69:4 (June 1991) 987–1010.

46. T. Wyatt and R. Gal, *Legitimacy and Commitment in the Military* (New York,
Greenwood Press: 1990). The work of Gal on the Israeli military, including the issues
of conscientious resistance, is very good. See also R. Linn, *Not Shooting and Not Cry-
ing* (Westport, CT, Greenwood Press: 1989) and idem, *Conscience at War: The Israeli
Soldier as a Moral Critic* (New York, SUNY Press: 1996); reviewed by me in *Jewish
Spectator* (Summer 1998) 52–53.

47. L. M. Thomas, *Vessels of Evil: American Slavery and the Holocaust* (Philadelphia, Temple University Press: 1993); reviewed by me in *Jewish Spectator* (1996)
60–62.

48. Film of the same name; I. Guest, *Behind the Disappearances: Argentina's*

Dirty War against Human Rights and the United Nations (Philadelphia, University of Pennsylvania Press: 1990).

49. W. Beardslee, "Commitment and Endurance: Common Themes in the Life Histories of Civil Rights Workers Who Stayed," *American Journal of Orthopsychiatry* 53 (Jan. 1983) 34–42.

50. *Washington and Lee Law Review* 48 (Winter 1991), whole issue devoted to the topic; T. Terrell, "Violence, Human Rights, and the Rule of Law," *Emory Law Journal* 32 (1983) 383–404.

51. Oliner, *Toward;* see also, *Embracing,* 369–89; and *The Altruistic Personality,* end.

52. Staub, *The Roots of Evil,* 264–83; *Embracing,* 390–42.

53. H. C. Kelman and V. L. Hamilton, *Crimes of Obedience,* 307–38.

54. A. Kohn, *Punished by Rewards: The Trouble with Gold Stars, Incentive Plans, A's, Praise, and Other Bribes* (New York, Houghton Mifflin: 1993) and D. Heath, *Schools of Hope* (San Francisco, Jossey-Bass: 1994). See also Batson, 217–19; Piliavin and Charng, 58; Fogelman, 317–22; and Colby and Damon, end.

55. G. Sharp, *The Politics of Nonviolent Action,* 3 vols. (Boston, P. Sargent Publishers: 1973) and R. Holmes, *Nonviolence in Theory and Practice* (Belmont, CA, Hadsworth Publishing: 1990).

56. The Giraffe Project is devoted to identifying and acknowledging publicly people who do altruistic deeds (who stick their necks out; hence, the name of the project). The Giraffe Project is located at Box 759, Langley, WA 98260 and, in addition to publicity packets for "Giraffes," the project has teaching kits and runs seminars all over the world.

57. See "The Holocaust and Hiroshima: Icons of Our Century," available on my website <http://www.emory.edu/UDR/BLUMENTHAL>.

58. Hillel's dictum, "That which is hateful to you do not do unto others" (*Talmud,* Shabbat 31a), is the minimalist formation of this definition.

59. "By evil, I mean *actions* that have consequences. We cannot judge evil by conscious intentions, because psychological distortions tend to hide even from the perpetrators themselves their true intentions. . . . Frequently, their intention is to create a 'better world,' but in the course of doing so they disregard the welfare and destroy the lives of human beings. Perpetrators of evil often intend to make people suffer but see their actions as necessary or serving a higher good. . . ." (Staub, *The Roots of Evil,* 25).

60. Cf. C. D. Batson, *The Altruism Question: Towards a Social-Psychological Answer* (Hillsdale, NJ, Lawrence Erlbaum Associates: 1991) 67–73 on the contrast of Aristotelian and Galilean scientific methods.

61. E.g., S. and P. Oliner, *The Altruistic Personality;* A. Colby and W. Damon, *Some Do Care: Contemporary Lives of Moral Commitment* (New York, Free Press: 1992). See also the parallel studies of perpetrators and their children.

62. The term is drawn from Krebs et al. in Oliner, *Embracing,* 149.

63. This is most forcefully stated by C. D. Batson, *The Altruism Question,* 66: "We cannot assume that the helper knows his or her own ultimate goal." It is certainly true of perpetrators, too, that they distort history to protect themselves.

64. The work of Staub, Hoffman, Midlarsky, Rushton, Krebs, as well as Milgram, Zimbardo, and others in developmental and social psychology falls into this category.

It is they who criticize the strictly laboratory method as "ecologically invalid" (Oliner, *Embracing,* 255).

65. See Batson, 63–74, for his vigorous defense of his scientific "Galilean" methodology and his attack on the "exemplar" (or "paragon") method as one which focuses on behavior, not on motivation.

66. An additional methodology involves studying animal behavior and drawing conclusions from that data for aggression and altruistic studies. I have not followed this data as closely as I have followed the data of the other methodologies.

67. Montada cites a source listing forty-four different kinds of altruistic actions (Oliner, *Embracing,* 226).

68. Zahn-Waxler, 138, emphasis added; repeated in Eisenberg, 50, where "rule orientation" is listed as the other primary moral value orientation.

69. Zahn-Waxler, 136, emphasis added.

70. Eisenberg, 46–8, emphasis added.

71. Smolenska in Oliner, *Embracing,* 217–19, emphasis original. While Smolenska evolved this theory for prosocial behavior only, the typologies seem to me to hold true for antisocial behavior as well.

72. Oliner, *The Altruistic Personality,* 188.

73. This argument, based on very precisely-calibrated laboratory experimentation, is Batson's (*The Altruism Question*).

74. One could arrive at the same structure by defining two types of altruisic motivations, egocentric and allocentric, but that seems linguistically cumbersome. I shall follow the definitions and typology set here.

75. E. Staub, *The Roots of Evil,* the final two chapters; idem, "Extreme"; and Kelman and Hamilton, 307–38.

76. On the primacy of the altruistic motive, see Batson. On the coexistence of the impulse to do good and the impulse to do evil in each person, see the discussion of the rabbinic terms *yetser ha-ra'* and *yetser ha-tov,* pp. 188–93.

77. For these three terms see pp. 115–19, 123–24, 149, 160, and 182.

78. Even conscience, which is usually understood as individual and personal, is embedded in personal development and has its place in the hierarchy of authorities among which all humans live. In this sense, it, too, is "institutionalized."

79. This midrash appears as part of my multivocal commentary to Psalm 44 in *Facing the Abusing God: A Theology of Protest* (Louisville, KY, Westminster / John Knox: 1993) 99–100. On reading rabbinic texts, see pp. 147–48.

Chapter 3

1. S. Milgram, *Obedience to Authority: An Experimental View* (New York, Harper and Row: 1974); also available as a film.

2. Film, *In the Eye of the Storm* and later in a film, *A Class Divided;* the latter appeared as a book by W. Peters, *A Class Divided Then and Now* (New Haven, Yale University Press: 1987).

3. This is clear from *A Class Divided.* My students tell me that Mrs. Elliot appeared on the Oprah Winfrey show with great success.

4. H. C. Kelman and V. L. Hamilton, *Crimes of Obedience* (New Haven, Yale University Press: 1989).

5. See pp. 45–55.

6. H. Arendt, *Eichmann in Jerusalem: A Report on the Banality of Evil* (New York, Viking Press: 1963).

7. This is confirmed by the analysis of the Rorschach data for the Nuremberg accused. No psychopathology was found (G. Borofsky and D. Brand, "Personality Organization and Psychological Functioning of the Nuremberg War Criminals: The Rorschach Data," in J. Dimsdale, *Survivors, Victims, and Perpetrators: Essays on the Nazi Holocaust* [New York, Hemisphere Publishing Co.: 1980] 359–403).

8. On this term, see p. 5.

9. E. Klee et al., *"The Good Old Days,"* transl. D. Burnstone (New York, Free Press: 1988, 1991).

10. C. Browning, *Ordinary Men: Reserve Police Battalion 101 and the Final Solution in Poland* (New York, HarperCollins: 1992). The issue of "putative duress" seems to be very complicated. Browning (171) implies that there was none at all, at least not for his subjects since they were specifically given the opportunity not to participate by their commanding officer in Jósefow. The first quotation from Klee indicates that there was a distinct subjective, though not objective, putative duress; the second sets the issue in the context of willing obedience.

11. Browning, *Ordinary Men*. See also, idem, "Ordinary Germans or Ordinary Men," *Address and Response at the Inauguration of the Dorot Chair of Modern Jewish and Holocaust Studies,* ed. D. Blumenthal (Atlanta, GA, Emory University: 1994) 7–14.

12. "Ordinary Germans or Ordinary Men," 11; see also page 9 where he calls these men "grass roots" killers.

13. It is now well-known that there is not one single case of a person put to death for refusing to kill Jews. See Browning, 170; Klee, 75–86, with 80 and 82 for Himmler's verbal and written orders on the subject; and D. Kitterman, "Those Who Said, 'No!': Germans Who Refused to Execute Civilians during World War II," *German Studies Review* 9:2 (May 1988) 241–54. See Browning, 103, that those who resisted were yelled at but not disciplined.

14. M. Mayer, *They Thought They Were Free: The Germans 1933–1945* (Chicago, University of Chicago Press: 1955, 1966).

15. I. Müller, *Hitler's Justice: The Courts of the Third Reich,* transl. D. L. Schneider (Cambridge, MA, Harvard University Press: 1991); reviewed by me in *Modern Judaism* (1993) 13:95–106.

16. J. M. Darley and C. D. Batson, "From Jerusalem to Jericho: A Study of Situational and Dispositional Variables in Helping Behavior," *Journal of Personality and Social Psychology* 27:1 (1973) 100–8.

17. E. Staub, "Helping a Distressed Person," L. Berkowitz, *Advances in Experimental Social Psychology* (New York, Academic Press: 1974) 7: 293–341.

18. L. Eron and L. Huesmann, "The Role of Television in the Development of Prosocial and Antisocial Behavior," D. Olweus et al., *Development of Antisocial and Prosocial Behavior* (New York, Academic Press: 1986) 285–314.

19. Called by authors "observational learning" (309).

20. L. Baron, "The Dutchness of Dutch Rescuers: The National Dimension of Altruism," P. Oliner et al., *Embracing the Other: Philosophical, Psychological, and Historical Perspectives* (New York, New York University Press: 1992) 306–27; reviewed by me in *Pastoral Psychology* 46:2 (1997) 131–34.

21. In the film, *Weapons of the Spirit*. One of the most moving moments in the film occurs when the visiting nazi finishes his speech and shouts "Heil Hitler." He is greeted by silence and, in that silence, one person shouts, "Long live Jesus Christ."

22. E. Fogelman, *Conscience and Courage: Rescuers of Jews during the Holocaust* (New York, Anchor Books: 1994); reviewed by me in *Journal of Psychology and Theology* 23 (1995), 62–63.

23. E. Kurek-Lesik, "The Role of Polish Nuns in the Rescue of Jews, 1939–1945," Oliner, *Embracing*, 328–34.

24. See pp. 134, 136, 224.

25. The Milgram experiments probably could not be conducted today because of stricter rules on experimentation with human subjects but, if one were to redo these experiments, one would need to redesign this part to test more fully the role of peer support in defying authority. More importantly, the Stanford Prison experiment (P. G. Zimbardo et al., see below) would have to be completely redesigned to test for resistance to add, for example: a resisting confederate among the guards, the prisoners, and the parents; or, a series of humanizing moments such as joint meals between prisoners and guards, a built-in reminder of the experimental framework, etc.

26. Staub, "Helping," 316–21.

27. Interestingly, prohibition did not seem to inhibit helping. Further, subjects alone also helped at very high levels because, consistent with Latané and Darley's work, subjects alone feel more responsibility.

28. S. and P. Oliner, *The Altruistic Personality: Rescuers of Jews in Nazi Europe* (New York, Free Press: 1988).

29. See also C. D. Batson, *The Altruism Question: Toward a Social-Psychological Answer* (Hillsdale, NJ, Lawrence Erlbaum Associates: 1991) 160, that low-empathy persons need feedback on their helping activities.

30. P. G. Zimbardo et al., "The Psychology of Imprisonment: Privation, Power, and Pathology," *Doing Unto Others*, ed. Z. Rubin (Englewood Cliffs, NJ, Prentice-Hall: 1974); available in slide presentation and, later, in a film, *Quiet Rage;* see also *New York Times Magazine*, April 8, 1973.

31. Kelman and Hamilton remark that students do homework because it is required, not because it is good for them; i.e., because of role, not reason (95). Using the rule-, role-, value-oriented model, we should probably conclude that rule-oriented students do homework because it is their duty to do work assigned; that role-oriented students do homework because that is their place in the hierarchy called the university; and that value-oriented students do homework because they accept the worldview that values knowledge. It is my observation, however, that most students are motivated by quizzes, not the search for knowledge; i.e., that most students are motivated by role and not value.

32. I admit to a certain countertransferential anomie and anger at the collapse of the assigned roles, as well as to the fear of a possible vigorous attack by the students. The following class I almost put the chairs back into rows to reestablish the authority hierarchy and role patterns. A suggestion that bean bags to be thrown at one another be distributed next year was rejected by me on the grounds that that would probably need the permission of the university committee on human experimentation; this proved a sobering thought to a not-so-humorous suggestion.

33. M. Weinreich, *Hitler's Professors* (New York, Yiddish Scientific Institute [YIVO]: 1946).

34. J. Sabini and M. Silver, "Destroying the Innocent with a Clear Conscience," in Dimsdale, 329–58.

35. P. Sichrovsky, *Born Guilty: Children of Nazi Families,* transl. J. Steinberg (New York, Basic Books: 1988).

36. J. Steiner, "The SS Yesterday and Today: A Sociopsychological View," in Dimsdale, 405–56.

37. This role identification with nazism was not limited to the SS or even to Germans. Mayer reports the following: "I was sitting in a cinema with a Jewish friend and her daughter of thirteen, while a Nazi parade went across the screen, and the girl caught her mother's arm and whispered, 'Oh, Mother, Mother, if I weren't a Jew, I think I'd be a Nazi!'" (51).

38. E. Staub, *The Roots of Evil: The Origins of Genocide and Other Group Violence* (Cambridge, Cambridge University Press: 1989).

39. To this, one should add, based on Staub's own evidence: a strong leader.

40. *The Altruistic Personality,* chap. 8, one of the more remarkable chapters in the book.

41. Empathically oriented persons account for 37% of the sample and principled persons account for 11%.

42. Even someone with low empathy scores will act courageously if motivated normocentrically (208).

43. Page references in this paragraph are to *Embracing.*

44. This figure seems high. It seems to me that many more Jews would have been saved if 62% of the women's religious communities had been engaged in helping and hiding them.

45. In Olweus et al., 310.

46. *Conscience and Courage,* especially chap. 5.

47. Cf. also Fogelman, 225, on the development of the rescuer self among child rescuers; 148, on the development of a rescuer self among children of rescuers; and 273, for the rescuer self developed by a whole town.

48. In N. Eisenberg et al., *Social and Moral Values* (Hillsdale, NJ, Lawrence Erlbaum Associates: 1989).

49. A. Colby and W. Damon, *Some Do Care: Contemporary Lives of Moral Commitment* (New York, Free Press: 1992).

50. W. R. Beardslee, "Commitment and Endurance," *American Journal of Orthopsychiatry* 53:1 (January 1983) 34–42.

51. On reading rabbinic texts, see pp. 147–48.

52. Commentary of the Vilna Gaon to Proverbs 6:4 cited in M. Elon, *Jewish Law,* 4 vols. (Philadelphia, Jewish Publication Society: 1994) 1:180.

53. *Talmud,* Sanhedrin 7a. See also *Mishna,* Avot 3:14.

54. *Talmud,* Ketubot 33a; Bava Kama 83b.

55. Z. W. Falk, *Legal Values and Judaism: Toward a Philosophy of Halakha* (Hebrew) (Jerusalem, Hebrew University: 1980) 41.

56. Maimonides, *Code of Law,* Hilkhot Avadim 9:8.

57. Specifically on *middat ḥasidut,* see pp. 157, 161, 179, 206–10.

58. *Talmud,* Bava Metsiʻa 30b, discussed in Berman (see pp. 162–64) 91–95.

59. On the value-concept of caring, see p. 120; esp. 162–64 on "within the line of the law."

Chapter 4

1. E. Staub, *The Roots of Evil: The Origins of Genocide and Other Group Violence* (Cambridge, Cambridge University Press: 1989) 50, emphasis original, context supplied in square brackets.

2. See M. Weinreich, *Hitler's Professors* (New York, Yiddish Scientific Institute [YIVO]: 1946) chap. 5; I. Müller, *Hitler's Justice: The Courts of the Third Reich,* transl. D. L. Schneider (Cambridge, MA, Harvard University Press: 1991); reviewed by me in *Modern Judaism* 13 (1993) 95–106, chap. 12; and R. Proctor, *Racial Hygiene: Medicine Under the Nazis* (Cambridge, MA, Harvard University Press: 1988). See also "The Value of the Human Being: Medicine in Germany 1918–1945," an exhibition sponsored by Ärztekammer Berlin in Zusammenarbeit mit der Bundesärztekammer, published as a catalogue edited by C. Pross and G. Aly, *Der Wert des Menschen: Medizin in Deutschland 1918–1945* (Berlin, Hentrich: 1989). The title and content of the exhibit nicely catch the cultural continuity of racial thinking.

3. See G. W. Blackburn, *Education in the Third Reich* (Albany, NY, SUNY Press: 1985) chaps. 6–7.

4. C. Browning, *Ordinary Men: Reserve Police Battalion 101 and the Final Solution in Poland* (New York, HarperCollins: 1992) 179–84.

5. Müller, chap. 12.

6. Claudia Koonz, *Mothers in the Fatherland* (New York, St. Martin's Press: 1987) 105, 149, 399.

7. Müller, chaps. 13–14.

8. Blackburn, 119, 181.

9. Weinreich, 172–77; Müller, 108; and S. Katz, "The 'Unique' Intentionality of the Holocaust," in *Post-Holocaust Dialogues,* ed. S. Katz (New York, New York University Press: 1985) 287–317 on the aryanization of some Gypsies.

10. Blackburn, chaps. 5–6; Müller, 77–79. Almost all books have a list; this is a composite.

11. M. Mayer, *They Thought They Were Free: The Germans 1933–1945* (Chicago, University of Chicago Press: 1955, 1966) 105.

12. Staub, 130.

13. P. Sichrovsky, *Born Guilty* (New York, Basic Books: 1988) 30. The Reichsparteitaggelände, the open space in Nuremberg where the great nazi party rallies were held and where Riefenstahl's famous film, *Triumph of the Will,* was photographed still exists. It, and the stadium on which the podium at which Hitler stood, is open to the public. (I admit to visiting there and standing at that podium with a mixture of awe and

justice because I wore there a watch left to me as an inheritance from a great uncle who was a survivor.) The videotape which introduces the Reichsparteitaggelände contains interviews with men who had been there. One of them says, quite honestly, that it was an honor, a privilege, to have been there at that time; it was the high point of his life. The videotape also juxtaposes the healthy male camaraderie of the nazi days with the degenerate rock concerts which are now held in the same arena; this too easily evokes a nostalgia for what Mayer calls "the good old days" of order and healthy values.

14. Note Steiner's telling phrase, "from existential angst to esprit de corps" (J. Steiner, "The SS Yesterday and Today: A Sociopsychological View," in J. Dimsdale, *Survivors, Victims, and Perpetrators: Essays on the Nazi Holocaust* [New York, Hemisphere Publishing Co.: 1980] 418).

15. Blackburn, 116. See also Staub, 113–15.

16. See Weinreich, chaps. 31–33, for the debate on extermination of the Poles, especially 183 for Hitler's intention.

17. Weinreich, 177, quoting: "so long as the individual does not possess traces of alien races (Jewish, Negroid, Asiatic, etc.); as to alien races, refolking is to be denied by principle."

18. Claudia Koonz has convincingly argued that nazi ideology linked race and gender (3). "Hitler overtly demanded what other nationalist politicians only hinted at: 'Aryan' victory over the Jew and male triumph over the emancipated woman. Hitler, who vacillated on nearly every other crucial political issue, never relented on two biological axioms: Separate the sexes and eliminate the Jews" (53). Even in the gas chambers, Jews were separated by sex (405–6). Aryan women were excluded but there was never an intent to exterminate them.

19. L. Davidowicz, *The War Against the Jews: 1933–1945* (New York, Holt, Rinehart, and Winston: 1975); S. Katz, "Intentionality." See also D. Goldhagen, *Hitler's Willing Executioners* (New York, A. Knopf: 1996).

20. In view of the special place of antisemitism in nazi thinking and taking into consideration the results of that praxis, I think the term "antisemitism," itself a recent term, is too mild, too academic, too civilized. I prefer "Jew-hatred"; it is truer to the facts and, hence, stronger. I shall use it from now on to designate the hatred of Jews and Judaism which is rooted deep in the psyche and which takes on social, political, religious, and racial forms of thought and practice.

21. On the continuing nature of the link between racial thinking, Jew-hatred, and history, see Deborah Lipstadt, *Denying the Holocaust: The Growing Assault on Truth and Memory* (New York, Free Press: 1993).

22. See S. Katz, "Intentionality."

23. During a recent visit to the beaches of Normandy, I realized that *Aktion Reinhard,* the code name for the extermination of the Jews of Poland, had been closed down in November 1943, six months before the landings. D-day had come too late (see D. Blumenthal, "Can Jews Celebrate D-Day?" *Atlanta Jewish Times,* June 3, 1994).

24. The Jewish nightmare, which is worse than the shoah, is contemplating what would have happened if Hitler had not invaded Russia and had withdrawn from parts of France. Would England, Russia, and the United States have entered the war? If not, Hitler would have had all the time necessary to exterminate systematically **all** the Jews of nazi-occupied Europe and to have concealed that from history, as Himmler had promised (see the novel by Robert Harris, *Fatherland* [New York, Random House: 1992] for such a scenario).

25. A. Miller, *For Your Own Good,* transl. H. and H. Hannum (New York, Farrar, Straus, Giroux: 1983).

26. Sichrovsky, 169, quoting Hitler but without footnote; Blackburn, 69.

27. See Staub, 109, for the Lutheran roots for this attitude.

28. Müller's chapter 26 deals with the double-standard definition of criminality while chapter 29 deals with the trials of the jurists (war crimes trial #3); both are excellent. I didn't believe there could be so many forms of denial and defense.

29. Dimsdale, 344, 353–54.

30. F. Katz, *Ordinary People and Extraordinary Evil* (Albany, NY, SUNY Press: 1993) 83–4, original italics (this text is followed by examples). This is an otherwise disappointing book though the title and topic are crucial.

31. Brutalization of children is also an extreme form of authoritarian teaching; this is dealt with pp. 84–96.

32. Mayer, 258.

33. On the connection of this to Nietzsche, see Blackburn, 16–17, and Staub, 112.

34. The movie, *A Few Good Men,* is a good example of rationalization by higher authorities because it is the ideologies of anticommunism and group solidarity that form the basis of the whole plot. The moral confusion in the conception of the movie is evident when one asks: Who are the "good" men? And, who gets tried for manslaughter?

35. E. Midlarsky, "Helping in Late Life," P. Oliner et al., *Embracing the Other: Philosophical, Psychological, and Historical Perspectives* (New York, New York University Press: 1992) 253–75; reviewed by me in *Pastoral Psychology* 46:2 (1997) 131–34.

36. J. A. Piliavin and H. W. Charng, "Altruism: A Review of Recent Theory and Research," *American Review of Sociology* 16 (1990) 27–65.

37. E. Staub, "A Conception of the Determinants and Development of Altruism and Aggression: Motives, the Self, and the Environment," C. Zahn-Waxler et al., *Altruism and Aggression: Biological and Social Origins* (Cambridge, Cambridge University Press: 1986) 135–88, especially 145.

38. A. Colby and W. Damon, *Some Do Care: Contemporary Lives of Moral Commitment* (New York, Free Press: 1992) especially chaps. 4 and 10.

39. S. and P. Oliner, *The Altruistic Personality: Rescuers of Jews in Nazi Europe* (New York, Free Press: 1988); reviewed by me in *Critical Review of Books in Religion* 3 (1990) 409–11.

40. E. Fogelman, *Conscience and Courage: Rescuers of Jews during the Holocaust* (New York, Anchor Books: 1994); reviewed by me in *Journal of Psychology and Theology* 23 (1995) 62–63.

41. Intellectual and moral abilities, while separable in some areas, are deeply intertwined in others, especially in the exercise of intelligent moral judgment. I, therefore, link them as one affection.

42. See, for instance, D. Krebs and F. Van Hesteren, "The Development of Altruistic Personality," in Oliner et al., *Embracing,* chap. 6, for a summary of the main schools of thought and their own proposal for six "invariant" stages in the development of the altruistic personality.

43. The feminist movement has done a great deal to point out the biases of these hierarchies. To this I add that designating the ultimate of these steps as "love" or "reconciliation" is a bias of the Christian culture, even in its secularized form, in which we work and live.

44. "Altruism: A Review," 32.

45. *Embracing,* 219–20.

46. For a very similar quotation from a different rescuer, see Oliner, *The Altruistic Personality,* 217.

47. *The Altruistic Personality,* especially chap. 10.

48. *Embracing,* 369–89.

49. "Commitment and Endurance: Common Themes in the Life Histories of Civil Rights Workers Who Stayed," *American Journal of Orthopsychiatry* 53:1 (Jan. 1983) 34–42.

50. The teaching of extensivity is itself rooted in the teaching of universal humanness of the secular human rights tradition or in the teaching of the divine image in which humanity is created of the biblical tradition.

51. On the distinction between altruism and prosocial attitudes and actions, see p. 25.

52. M. L. Hoffman, "Empathy and Prosocial Activism," N. Eisenberg et al., *Social and Moral Values* (Hillsdale, NJ, Lawrence Erlbaum Associates: 1989) 65–85. For a list of Hoffman's writings, see also the bibliography in Batson.

53. C. D. Batson, *The Altruism Question: Toward a Social-Psychological Answer* (Hillsdale, NJ, Lawrence Erlbaum Associates: 1991) and the earlier essay, "Personal Values, Moral Principles, and the Three-Path Model of Prosocial Motivation," in Eisenberg, 213–28.

54. Hoffman's position, together with that of Krebs, Rosenhan, Karylowski, and others is nicely summarized by Batson, 43–58.

55. The Oliners return to empathy as a core affection facilitating prosocial action in their prescriptive book, *Toward a Caring Society: Ideas into Action* (Westport, CT, Praeger: 1995) chap. 3.

56. The teaching of empathy is itself rooted in the teaching of love of one's neighbor, especially of the poor and disadvantaged, of the biblical tradition and, for Christians, in the teaching of agape (see pp. 130–31).

57. C. Gilligan, *In a Different Voice* (Cambridge, MA, Harvard University Press: 1982) 164ff.

58. L. Montada, "Predicting Prosocial Commitment in Different Social Contexts," *Embracing,* 226–52.

59. The term "ideology" is used in its descriptive sense, with Staub (above), and not in its often pejorative, evaluative sense.

60. Citations are from *The Roots of Evil.*

61. This is, significantly, reflected in the post-war situation, for no decision by any nazi court has ever been declared null and void by a German court or legislature (287), not even the decisions of the explicitly political People's Court (292).

62. G. Cocks, *Psychotherapy in the Third Reich: The Göring Institute* (New York, Oxford University Press: 1985).

63. "For the Nazi hierarchy, anti-Semitism was to be pursued as an expression of the Führer's will, and thus as active Nazi policy at home and abroad. For Göring, as for most of the German psychotherapists, such racism, while building on a widely-held prejudice, was probably more or less an occasionally necessary means of expression to a professional end" (115).

64. I find myself offended by Cocks's last sentence, a theme echoed at the beginning of his book: "It is not the intent of this book to attempt to justify or condemn the morals and ethics of psychotherapists in the Third Reich, or to assess the degree of their historical responsibility for the advent and actions of the Nazis. Rather, it means to demonstrate and explain the psychotherapists' success within, and often against, the medical establishment in Germany between 1933 and 1945, and to record the sometimes perilous course they navigated between the chaotic features of Nazi party and state" (5). This apologetic rhetoric pervades Cocks's book and, while it is praiseworthy to set forth the slimy facts, a little more prophetic passion seems to me to be called for.

65. P. G. Zimbardo et al., "The Psychology of Imprisonment: Privation, Power, and Pathology," *Doing unto Others,* ed. Z. Rubin (Englewood Cliffs, NJ, Prentice-Hall: 1974); available in slide presentation and, later, in a film, *Quiet Rage;* see *New York Times Magazine,* April 8, 1973.

66. S. Milgram, *Obedience to Authority: An Experimental View* (New York, Harper and Row: 1974); also available as a film.

67. This is true about criminals who are not caught or who receive minimal punishment; they logically conclude that they can, at least, repeat their crime and / or that they can move incrementally to the next level of crime.

68. For the last, see Koonz, 215–17, 244–46, 279–83. For the others, see the various works cited here passim.

69. For the best presentation of this, see, for example, R. Hilberg, *The Destruction of European Jews* (Chicago, Quadrangle Press: 1961).

70. See C. Browning, *Fateful Months: Essays in the Emergence of the Final Solution* (New York, Holmes and Meier: 1991) esp. 3–27.

71. See Dawidowicz, 147–48, in the footnote, for four speeches prophesying the destruction of world Jewry.

72. S. Spielberg, *Schindler's List* (film), 1993, 1994.

73. H. Arendt, *Eichmann in Jerusalem: A Report on the Banality of Evil* (New York, Viking Press: 1963).

74. See Müller, 148–49, that bills were sent to the families charging them for the execution of criminals.

75. Kelman and Hamilton, 18; Davidowicz, 203–5; Dimsdale, 427; Koonz, 412.

76. *Altruistic,* 132–35.

77. See also Staub, 156.

78. See Fogelman, chap. 15, for a very sensitive account of the difficulties faced by rescuers after the war, ranging from threats on their lives, to neglect and poverty, to barriers to self-acceptance.

79. In Zahn-Wexler, 154–56.

80. On reading rabbinic texts, see pp. 147–48.

81. *Vayikra Rabba* 27:5, cited in R. Kimelman, "Non-Violence in the Talmud," *Judaism* 17 (1968) 331, with parallels.

82. See Kimelman, "Non-Violence," 316, and pp. 165–66, 212–19.

83. Magen Avraham and Mishna Berura to *Shulḥan Arukh,* Orah Ḥayyim 703, cited in N. Rakover, *Modern Applications of Jewish Law,* 2 vols. (Jerusalem, Jewish Legal Heritage Society: 1992) 543–44. The phrase *she-yekabel teshuva* probably means to "do penance," not "repentance," and I have so translated.

Chapter 5

1. A. Miller, *For Your Own Good,* transl. H. and H. Hannum (New York, Farrar, Straus, Giroux: 1983).

2. E. Bass and L. Davis, *The Courage to Heal* (New York, HarperCollins: 1988, 1994); E. Bass, *I Never Told Anyone: Writings by Women Survivors of Child Sexual Abuse* (New York, HarperCollins: 1983); D. Blumenthal, *Facing the Abusing God: A Theology of Protest* (Louisville, KY, Westminster / John Knox: 1993) at bibliography; J. C. Brown and C. R. Bohn, *Christianity, Patriarchy, and Abuse* (Cleveland, OH, Pilgrim Press: 1989); M. Fortune, *Sexual Violence: The Unmentionable Sin: An Ethical and Pastoral Perspective* (Cleveland, OH, Pilgrim Press: 1983); B. Hooks, *Sisters of the Yam: Black Women in Recovery* (Boston, South End Press: 1993); J. Leehan, *Defiant Hope* (Louisville, KY, Westminster / John Knox: 1993); J. Leehan, *Pastoral Care for Survivors of Family Abuse* (Louisville, KY, Westminster / John Knox: 1989); P. Rutter, *Sex in the Forbidden Zone: . . . Therapists, Doctors, Clergy, Teachers, etc.* (New York, Fawcett Crest: 1989); Evelyn C. White, *Chain, Chain, Change* (Seattle, WA, The Seal Press: 1985).

3. F. Bolton, *Males at Risk: The Other Side of Child Sexual Abuse* (Newbury Park, CA, Sage Publications: 1989); E. Gil, *Treatment of Adult Survivors of Child Abuse* (Walnut Creek, CA, Launch Press: 1988); K. Steele, "The Healing Pool," *Voices,* 24:3 (1988) 74–8; idem, "Sitting with the Shattered Soul," *Pilgrimage: Journal of Personal Exploration and Psychotherapy* 15:6 (1989) 19–25.

4. Fortune, 164, reports recent statistics which indicate that 38% of all females and 10% of all males will have been sexually molested by age eighteen. Furthermore, she reports, fully half of child abuse takes place within families and, hence, also constitutes incest. The taboo on admitting this and on speaking of it publicly is very strong—when was the last time the reader heard a sermon on incest?—but is slowly breaking down.

5. Much of adult behavior seems completely unreasonable to the child. This is the point of *Alice in Wonderland,* a play that should be seen by adults from the point of view of the child.

6. "For parents' motives are the same today as they were then: in beating their children, they are struggling to regain the power they once lost to their own parents. . . . Although parents *always* mistreat their children for psychological reasons; that is, because of their own needs, there is a basic assumption in our society that this treatment is good for children" (Miller, 16, emphasis original). "One mother got into bed with her seven-year-old son whenever she felt lonely or unhappy, and many parents, often in competition with each other, urgently sought out the affections of their children . . ." (Miller, 89).

7. "Beatings, which are only one form of mistreatment, are *always* degrading, because the child not only is unable to defend himself or herself but is also supposed to show gratitude and respect to the parents in return" (Miller, 17, emphasis original).

8. "It is hard to go wrong if one bends a sapling in the direction in which it should grow, something that cannot be done in the case of an old oak" (cited in Miller, 37).

9. See for example, Bolton, 19–30, for the "abuse of sexuality" model which is broader, and more useful, than the "sexual abuse" model and Fortune, 10 and elsewhere, on "coercive," "assaultive," and "consensual" sexuality.

10. See Fortune, 17, 113–20 and 164 with the notes, for the argument on Freud's inability to acknowledge incest and child abuse and, hence, his movement into female hysteria and male instinctuality. See also Miller, 60.

11. J. C. Brown and C. R. Bohn, *Christianity, Patriarchy, and Abuse* (Cleveland, OH, Pilgrim Press: 1989).

12. Sometimes called "doubling." Staub strenuously objects to splitting and doubling: "People function best when they can integrate their goals by living and acting in ways that combine the fulfillment of important motives. . . . While splitting realms can develop into doubling, people tend toward integration. As they evolve, most perpetrators develop unitary selves by changes in their motives, their world views, and beliefs, and by achieving highly differentiated orientations to different groups of people" (145–7). He is undoubtedly correct that people tend to integrate and not split, but splitting does occur and it is a very powerful adjustment tool and developing "different orientations to different groups of people" may be a rationalized part of that.

13. Quoted in Fortune, 163. In sexual abuse situations, it is not uncommon to see pictures of a girl at a window looking in on the same girl in bed being abused by an older male.

14. The cartoon, "Calvin and Hobbes," is a good example of splitting, though one could debate whether Calvin is in need of intensive treatment or just a child with a very, very active imagination. I think the popularity of "Calvin and Hobbes" comes from the fact that readers identify with the little boy who splits into a space hero who battles monsters (real world authority figures) and who splits his stuffed tiger into a protective friend. (Is there a man who would not admit to such fantasies and to such an imaginary friend at some time in his life, and not necessarily only in childhood?)

15. When this process is conscious, I think the term "suppression" is probably better because it distinguishes the unconscious from the conscious types of memory control.

16. This widely used term was developed by Lifton (R. J. Lifton, *The Nazi Doctors: Medical Killing and the Psychology of Genocide* [New York, Basic Books: 1986]) and it is noted by Browning, 161.

17. "As a reaction against the underlying hostility, there is often a rigid glorification and idealization of the parents" (T. W. Adorno et al., *The Authoritarian Personality,* abridged edition [New York, W. W. Norton and Co.: 1950, 1982] 258).

18. E. A. Cohen, *Human Behavior in the Concentration Camps* (New York, W. W. Norton and Co.: 1953) 177–78, 200, and 188–93 for the resulting self-hatred.

19. Miller points out that Eichmann, who had no regrets about exterminating Jews, was embarrassed when he had to be told to stand up during sentencing; he should have known better (67).

20. P. Sichrovsky, *Born Guilty: Children of Nazi Families,* transl. J. Steinberg (New York, Basic Books: 1988) interviewed children of prominent nazis. He cites, again and again, the screaming rages and emotional coldness of those homes (89–104).

21. In the psychobiographical section on Hitler (142–97), Miller gives evidence that Hitler's father was abusive and also that Hitler had a personality that was split and seriously repressed, that he idealized and identified with his father, and that he projected his idealized father into the image of the führer while he projected the part of his childhood that needed to be repressed and extinguished onto the Jews (156ff., 176–80).

22. This would be especially true in the camps, using Katz's concept of a "culture of cruelty" (F. Katz, *Ordinary People and Extraordinary Evil* [Albany, NY, SUNY Press: 1993] 78, 83–90, 135).

23. To be sure, not all abused children become abusers. Bolton's report of a 30% intergenerational transmission rate (85) seems to me to be low. This rate would, however, be especially high in authoritarian cultures: ". . . those who are intimidated will be intimidating, those who are humiliated will impose humiliation" (Miller, 232); and ". . . if permitted to do so by outside authority, the same person [the authoritarian personality] may be induced very easily to uncontrolled release of his instinctual tendencies, especially those of destructiveness. Under certain conditions he will even join forces with the delinquent, a fusion found in Nazism" (Adorno, 258).

24. *The Authoritarian Personality,* cited above.

25. E. Fromm, *Escape from Freedom* (New York, Avon Books: 1969).

26. E. Staub, *The Roots of Evil: The Origins of Genocide and Other Group Violence* (Cambridge, Cambridge University Press: 1989) 129, quoting G. M. Kren and L. Rappoport, *The Holocaust and the Crisis of Human Behavior* (New York, Holmes and Meier Publishers: 1980) 51.

27. M. Mayer, *They Thought They Were Free: The Germans 1933–1945* (Chicago, University of Chicago Press: 1955, 1966).

28. I think Mayer is wrong is indicating that this constellation of character is unique to Germans and could not occur elsewhere (242). It seems to me that there is a unique conjunction of economic, cultural, and psychological factors at work in nazi Germany; however, the authoritarian personality and the culture which sustains it is not unique to any Western society.

29. The desperation of psychological totalitarianism is also seen in the tale of Horst Wessel and in the new religion developed by nazism, complete with its triumphalist messianism, rituals, holidays, martyrs, sacred books, priesthood, and even its ethics. See G. W. Blackburn, *Education in the Third Reich* (Albany, NY, SUNY Press: 1985) chap. 4.

30. *The Altruistic Personality* (New York, Free Press: 1988); reviewed by me in *Critical Review of Books in Religion* 3 (1990) 409–11, 182–83.

31. All first-year psychology students are familiar with the experiments in which rats who are subjected to erratic and excessive electric shocks are driven "insane."

32. *Ordinary People and Extraordinary Evil,* cited above. See also p. 63.

33. E. Fogelman, *Conscience and Courage: Rescuers of Jews during the Holocaust* (New York, Anchor Books: 1994); reviewed by me in *Journal of Psychology and Theology* 23 (1995) 62–63, 255–57.

34. Hoffman and others, cited in *The Altruistic Personality,* 178–79.

35. E. Staub, "A Conception of the Determinants and Development of Altruism and Aggression: Motives, the Self, and the Environment," in C. Zahn-Waxler et al., *Altruism and Aggression: Biological and Social Origins* (Cambridge, Cambridge University Press: 1986) 150–2 (emphasis original), citing many sources. Cf. also J. A. Piliavin and H. W. Charng, "Altruism: A Review of Recent Theory and Research," *American Review of Sociology* 16 (1990) 41.

36. For more on the role of discipline, see pp. 8, 61–62.

37. *The Altruistic Personality* (1988), cited above; *Embracing the Other: Philosophical, Psychological, and Historical Perspectives* (New York, New York University Press: 1992); reviewed by me in *Pastoral Psychology* 46:2 (1997) 131–34; and *Toward a Caring Society: Ideas into Action* (Westport, CT, Praeger: 1995).

38. See p. 25.

39. *The Altruistic Personality,* chap. 10, is devoted to this composite portrait and the contrasting "constricted" personality of the bystander and perpetrator.

40. See more on this in chap. 8.

41. Piliavin and Charng, 41–42. Cf. also Staub in Zahn-Waxler, 153, citing many sources.

42. M. Hoffman, "Empathy and Prosocial Activism," N. Eisenberg et al., *Social and Moral Values* (Hillsdale, NJ, Lawrence Erlbaum Associates: 1989) 80.

43. On reading rabbinic texts, see pp. 147–48.

44. *Talmud,* Menaḥot 99a-b. See also Shabbat 87a.

45. Maimonides, *Code of Law,* Hilkhot De'ot 6:1.

46. Maimonides, *Code of Law,* Hilkhot De'ot 6:3. The text refers only to fellow Jews. In the spirit of our times, I have rendered it more universally. On this, see p. 183.

47. Maimonides, *Code of Law,* Hilkhot Talmud Torah 4:4 with egalitarian language added.

48. Maimonides, *Code of Law,* Hilkhot Rotseaḥ 5:5–6.

Chapter 6

1. See A. J. Heschel, *God in Search of Man* (New York, Farrar, Straus, Giroux: 1955) and David R. Blumenthal, *Facing the Abusing God: A Theology of Protest* (Westminster / John Knox: 1993) chaps. 1–5.

2. Genesis 6: 6–7. See p. 13, on the use of gendered language in quotations and liturgy.

3. Jeremiah 31:19.

4. *Eikha Rabba,* Petihta, 24.

5. *Pirkei Rabbenu ha-Kadosh (Otsar ha-Midrashim)* 3:15. For a stunning zoharic reinterpretation of this motif, see *Zohar* 3:74b.

6. Isaiah 6:10

7. Isaiah 1:2–3.

8. *Eikha Rabba,* Petihta, 24.

9. This is not true of all parent-child relationships and certainly not true of all aspects of any given parent-child relationship. But the principle holds true: parents hope, expect, and do, and children try and then go their own way, which is sometimes the wrong way.

10. Unlike the problem of theodicy, which is God's problem. I wrote *Facing the Abusing God: A Theology of Protest,* taken together with my "Theodicy: Dissonance in

Theory and Praxis," *Concilium* 1 (1998) 138–54 to answer the question of theodicy (as best I could) and I have written this book to answer the question of sin and repentance.

11. "Atonement" is the state of being absolved from sin. "Penance" is an act undertaken to atone mechanically for sin. Doing the act (or acts) of penance brings atonement; the act itself is efficacious. "Penance" is not at all the same as "repentance" which is the process of turning one's actions, one's thoughts, and one's intentions away from sin. For a fuller statement on this theme, see my "Repentance and Forgiveness," *Cross Currents* (Spring 1998) 75–81 and my review of S. Wiesenthal, *The Sunflower, Jewish Social Studies* 40 (1978) 330–32.

12. Hosea 14:2.

13. Isaiah 44:22. On *teshuva* as applied to God, see Numbers 10:36, and Psalms 6:5 and 90:13, with *Pesikta Rabbati* 44:11.

14. Jeremiah 3:22 and 17. This is a triple pun on *teshuva* which I have tried to catch in English.

15. *Devarim Rabba* 2:24.

16. *Tanna de-Bei Elihayu Zuta* 24:1.

17. Maimonides, *Code,* Hilkhot Teshuva 2:2.

18. Maimonides, *Code,* Hilkhot Teshuva 2:1.

19. These include: continuously crying out to God even with tears, significant charity, putting great distance between one and the locus of sin, identifying oneself as a person no longer capable of that sin, changing one's general patterns of behavior for the good, and even going into exile (Maimonides, *Code,* Hilkhot Teshuva 2:4).

20. Maimonides, *Code,* Hilkhot Teshuva 1:1.

21. Maimonides, *Code,* Hilkhot Teshuva 3:5.

22. They can be found in any traditional Yom Kippur prayerbook in the *Amida* (Silent Devotion).

23. When I was younger, I would recite these liturgical lists and wonder why I was confessing most of those sins. Now that I am older, I find more and more of them apply to me. On the "intentional" use of liturgy, see pp. 138, 225, on *kavvana*.

24. The *'Al Ḥet'* is a double acrostic. Adding these lines in their proper alphabetic places destroys the double quality of the acrostic; the rupture itself is intentional. So is the use of modern Hebrew which jangles the ear of one accustomed to rabbinic Hebrew. The number of lines, twelve, is also intentional, though I intend no symbolism with the initial letters in Hebrew which I have chosen. It should also be noted that some of the lines already in the confession are very much in the spirit of what I have added; e.g., unknowingly, in secret and in public, by exploiting another, with fantasy, with violence, by acceding to the evil impulse, by stubbornness, with needless hatred, and with a stunned heart. My thanks to my friend and colleague, Naftali Stern of Bar Ilan University, for help with the Hebrew phrasing.

25. See pp. 168–75, 174–80.

26. W. Brueggemann, "A Shape for Old Testament Theology," *Catholic Biblical Quarterly* 47 (1985) 28–46 and 395–415. See also his *Theology of the Old Testament: Testimony: Dispute, Advocacy* (Minneapolis, Fortress Press: 1995).

27. Brueggemann notes that all authority tends to respond to sin by trying to repress the existence of pain: "A theology of contractual coherence must excommunicate all the pained and pain-bearers. . . . Indeed, the presence of pain-bearers is a silent refutation of the legitimated structures, and therefore must be denied legitimacy and visibility. Visible pain-bearers assert that the legitimated structures are not properly functioning" (44).

28. Brueggemann notes that this bipolarity also produces an ongoing tension, which cannot ever be definitively resolved, in Godself, for it is God Who gives and enforces the covenant and Who yet embraces the real pain of the other: "[T]he text permits entry into the disclosure of God's own life, which is troubled, problematic, and unresolved" (44; see also 397–99 and 414).

29. Maimonides, *Code,* Hilkhot Teshuva 10:1–2, 3. The whole last chapter (chap. 10) is devoted to this theme of love and true repentance.

30. Micah 3:7.

31. *Vayyikra Rabba* 10:5, the implication being that Adam, had he done *teshuva,* might have avoided being expelled from Eden.

32. *Talmud,* Shabbat 104a, Yoma 38b, etc.

33. Based on the early morning daily liturgy. Again, my thanks to my friend and colleague, Naftali Stern of Bar Ilan University, for help with the Hebrew phrasing.

34. Poem and comment by John Hines, Gorham, ME.

Chapter 7

1. See David R. Blumenthal, "The Holocaust and Hiroshima: Icons of Our Century," forthcoming; also available on my website <http://www.emory.edu/UDR/BLUMENTHAL>.

2. P. and S. Oliner, "Promoting Extensive Altruistic Bonds: A Conceptual Elaboration of Some Pragmatic Implications," P. Oliner et al., *Embracing the Other: Philosophical, Psychological, and Historical Perspectives* (New York, New York University Press: 1992); reviewed by me in *Pastoral Psychology* 46:2 (1997) 131–34, 369–89, which was later developed into P. and S. Oliner, *Toward a Caring Society: Ideas into Action* (Westport, CT, Praeger: 1995). In the latter, the Oliners outline eight elements in the cultivation of prosocial behavior: bonding, empathizing, education, practicing, diversifying, networking, conflict resolution, and globalism.

3. E. Staub, "A Conception of the Determinants and Development of Altruism and Aggression: Motives, the Self, and the Environment," C. Zahn-Waxler et al., *Altruism and Aggression: Biological and Social Origins* (Cambridge, Cambridge University Press: 1986) 135–88, and E. Staub, *The Roots of Evil: The Origins of Genocide and Other Group Violence* (Cambridge, Cambridge University Press: 1989) 264–83. These were later developed in "The Origins of Caring, Helping, and Nonaggression: Parental Socialization, the Family System, Schools, and Cultural Influence," *Embracing,* 390–412. In the latter, Staub outlines several elements in the cultivation of prosocial behavior: nurturance, reasoned discipline, encouraging prosocial activity, helping children identify their feelings, training parents in positive parenting, and education in school for cooperative learning, critical consciousness, shared humanity, identifying and dealing with stereotyping, and knowledge of the social processes in life.

4. H. C. Kelman and V. L. Hamilton, *Crimes of Obedience* (New Haven, Yale University Press: 1989) 307–38. In these pages, Kelman and Hamilton respond to the typology they constructed of rule- , role- , and value-oriented persons. They propose specific remedies for obedience for each of these types of persons: for rule-oriented persons, empowerment; for role-oriented persons, developing multiple perspectives and roles; and for value-oriented persons, heightened awareness of the situation and agency involved.

5. Don Saliers, *The Soul in Paraphrase: Prayer and the Religious Affections* (New York, Seabury Press: 1980) cited in David R. Blumenthal, *Facing the Abusing God: A Theology of Protest* (Westminster / John Knox: 1993) 59.

6. In what follows, I offer a series of loose definitions. I acknowledge that none is comprehensive and I invite readers to refine what I have set forth and to be in touch with me. The discussion of these matters is itself important.

7. See pp. 32–33, 67–70.

8. See pp. 74–75.

9. On this, see *Facing,* 16–17 and at the index.

10. M. Kadushin, *The Rabbinic Mind* (New York, Jewish Theological Seminary: 1952). See also pp. 67–70, 116, on "intelligent moral judgment."

11. Kadushin argues forcefully, and in my mind correctly, that value-concepts also clearly inform our worship life. See his *Worship and Ethics* (n.p., Northwestern University Press: 1964).

12. In what follows, I offer a series of loose definitions. I acknowledge that none is comprehensive and I invite readers to refine what I have set forth and to be in touch with me. The discussion of these matters is itself important.

13. C. D. Batson, *The Altruism Question: Toward a Social-Psychological Answer* (Hillsdale, NJ, Lawrence Erlbaum Associates: 1991).

14. ". . . the most important point about altruistic motivation is its existence . . ." (208).

15. *Talmud,* Shabbat 31a.

16. On righteous anger, see pp. 74–75, 116.

17. Leviticus 19:18, cited by Jesus in Mark 12:28–31.

18. See the Oliners, *The Altruistic Personality,* at index.

19. On extensivity as well as globalism, see the Oliners, *Embracing,* 370–78, and *The Altruistic Personality,* at index. Extensivity is also a teaching of goodness (see pp. 70–72, 98–99).

20. This differs slightly from the Oliners' usage where extensivity is taken in the human context and, hence, very close to inclusiveness.

21. See the Oliners, *Toward,* chap. 2.

22. See the Oliners, *The Altruistic Personality,* at index.

23. I differ on this from the Oliners who seem to see bonding and attachment as synonymous.

24. See the Oliners, *Toward,* chap. 3, and *The Altruistic Personality,* at index.

25. See pp. 51, 71–74. On the relationship of empathy to sympathy, see below.

26. See Staub, *Embracing,* 405; Kelman and Hamilton, 326; and below.

27. Empowerment is close to personal competence and, as such, is also a teaching of goodness (see pp. 66–67).

28. See *Facing,* 85–110 and 249–99.

29. There are, of course, affections, value-concepts and teachings of the anti-social life. They form a mirror image of those of the prosocial life. They, too, are interlinked with one another and with the processes which facilitate the doing of evil. They, too, inform and embody a way of living. We study them, but we do not advocate them.

30. I am not certain, despite the literature on the subject (see pp. 72–74), of the difference between sympathy and empathy. Hence, I did not expatiate on it but only list it. I invite the reader to reflect on this and be in touch with me.

31. On tacking as a basic metaphor for life, see *Facing,* chap. 5, and "Theodicy," cited above.

32. On reading rabbinic texts, see pp. 147–48.

33. *Devarim Rabba,* 5:15.

34. *Tanḥuma,* Bamidbar, Pinhas 3; *Sifre,* Devarim, 42; *Bamidbar Rabba* 21:4; *Peskita Rabbati* 12:3. On *ḥasidut / ḥesed* as caring, see pp. 160–66, 172–74. Not all the rabbis were happy with this *ḥesed-* type exegesis. See *Pesikta de Rav Kahana,* 3:5, that both will be punished in the end for their evils. There is also the example of the Amonites and the Amalekites for whom *ḥesed* is not in question. On loving and hating one's enemies, see pp. 184–88, 218–19.

Chapter 8

1. On reading rabbinic texts, see pp. 147–48.

2. *Pesikta de-Rav Kahana,* Piska 2, at the end (edition Mandelbaum, 1:33–34) and parallels. All three examples are taken from there and are set off here into paragraphs for ease of comprehension.

3. Last phrase added from parallel sources, e.g., *Bamidbar Rabba* 12:13.

4. See, for example, the series of United Nations Covenants in *The Department of State: Selected Documents, #5: Human Rights* (Bureau of Public Affairs and Office of Media Services, Washington, DC: 1977).

5. Sometimes it is called "ideology," though the use of that word by fascists and communists has made that a politically incorrect term.

6. See *The Humanist Manifesto, I and II;* K. Nielsen, *Ethics Without God;* M. Storer, *Humanist Ethics;* and similar works published by Prometheus Press, Buffalo, NY.

7. J. M. Darley and C. D. Batson, "From Jerusalem to Jericho: A Study of Situational and Dispositional Variables in Helping Behavior," *Journal of Personality and Social Psychology* 27:1 (1973) 100–8. See p. 41, for a fuller and more detailed presentation.

8. S. Milgram, *Obedience to Authority: An Experimental View* (New York, Harper and Row: 1974) 62–63, 170.

9. See selected bibliography, under Staub. None of the experiments and analyses lists religion as a factor in prosocial behavior.

10. A. Colby and W. Damon, *Some Do Care: Contemporary Lives of Moral Commitment* (New York, Free Press: 1992). In this study of exemplars religion, again, is not a determinative factor.

11. C. D. Batson and W. L. Ventis, *The Religious Experience: A Social-Psychological Perspective* (New York, Oxford University Press: 1982).

12. S. and P. Oliner, *The Altruistic Personality* (New York, Free Press: 1988); reviewed by me in *Critical Review of Books in Religion* 3 (1990) 409–11, 155–56,

290–92; P. Oliner et al., *Embracing the Other: Philosophical, Psychological, and Historical Perspectives* (New York, New York University Press: 1992); reviewed by me in *Pastoral Psychology* 46:2 (1997) 131–34; chaps. 11–13; especially chap. 14; E. Fogelman, *Conscience and Courage: Rescuers of Jews during the Holocaust* (New York, Anchor Books: 1994); reviewed by me in *Journal of Psychology and Theology* 23 (1995) 62–63, 169–72.

13. See, for example, M. Gilbert, *The Holocaust* (New York, Holt, Rinehart and Winston: 1992) at the index.

14. C. Browning, *Ordinary Men: Reserve Police Battalion 101 and the Final Solution in Poland* (New York, HarperCollins: 1992) chaps. 2 and 18.

15. See, for example, N. Tec, *Defiance: The Bielski Partisans* (Oxford, Oxford University Press: 1993). Religion has also not been a factor in conscientious objection in the Israeli armed forces or in the various Israeli peace movements (though there is one small religious peace movement). See R. Linn, *Conscience at War: The Israeli Soldier as a Moral Critic* (New York, SUNY Press: 1996); reviewed by me in *Jewish Spectator* (Summer 1998) 52–53.

16. R. Rubenstein, *The Cunning of History* (San Francisco, Harper Colophon: 1975).

17. This, in spite of the avowedly secular and atheistic ideology of these totalitarian-Enlightenment states. The "religious republics" of modern neofundamentalist bent do not augur much better treatment of prosocial issues.

18. A. Sagi, "Models of Authority and the Duty of Obedience in Halakhic Literature," *Association for Jewish Studies Review* 22 (1995) 1–24.

19. There are no women rabbis and judges in classic halakhic tradition.

20. See pp. 202–6.

21. See pp. 152–57, 172–74, with Exodus 24:3,7.

22. P. Rigby and P. O'Grady, "Agape and Altruism: Debates in Theology and Social Psychology," *Journal of the American Academy of Religion* 57 (1990) 719–37.

23. The position of Nygren as summarized by Rigby and O'Grady (720).

24. The position of Outka as summarized by Rigby and O'Grady (720).

25. Rigby and O'Grady, 730–31; this is their own position. Of course, they mean "true meaning **for Christians** . . .".

26. S. Welch, *A Feminist Ethics of Risk* (Minneapolis, Fortress Press: 1990).

27. See P. and S. Oliner, *Toward a Caring Society: Ideas into Action* (Westport, CT, Praeger: 1995).

28. C. Gilligan, to whom we owe the distinction between the ethics of justice and caring, also does not specify how one cultivates prosocial attitudes and behaviors, especially in the areas of resisting legitimate authority.

29. See chaps. 3 and 4.

30. For more on this, see especially the Oliners, *Toward a Caring Society*. I have tried to arrange these recommendations in a sequence. But it is possible that I am completely wrong about the sequence or that there is no sequence at all. In either case, the order can safely be ignored. The important thing is to get started facilitating good, no matter where one starts.

31. See pp. 119–22, 123–24, for a fuller discussion of this.

32. See pp. 222–23.

33. See, for example, Colby and Damon. See also the Oliners, *Toward a Caring Society,* passim.

34. The Giraffe Project (Box 759, Langley, WA 98260) keeps track of these, prepares press releases, and has prepared syllabi for all ages on "sticking out one's neck" for a prosocial cause.

35. Rabbinic Judaism is particularly rich in prosocial value-concepts, texts, and traditions (see part 3). Only a list is presented here: *tselem* (image, imitatio Dei); *brit* (covenant); *talmud Torah* (study of Torah); *mitsva* (commandedness); *tsedek* (justice); *lifnei 'iver* (you shall not put a stumbling block before the blind); *ve- 'asita ha-tov veha-yashar* (you shall do what is right and proper); *patur mi-dinei adam ve-ḥayyav be-dinei shamayim* (exempt in a human court but not in heaven); *tsedaka* (righteousness, charity); *middat ḥasidut* (the standard of the pious / caring / nonviolence); *ḥesed* (loyalty, grace, caring); *gemilut ḥasadim* (doing good deeds); *lifnim mi-shurat ha-din* (beyond the line of the law); *shalom* (peace); *mipne darkhei shalom* (for the sake of social peace); *tikkun 'olam* (repairing / restoring the world); *yetser ha-ra'* and *yetser tov* (the impulse to evil / to good); and *pikuaḥ nefesh* (saving a life). There are many more. Prosocial rabbinic texts and traditions also include: norms for proper court procedure and judicial protest; laws commanding one to reprove one another and to rescue someone in trouble; the uses and limits of military disobedience and nonviolence; and the doctrines of "doing good deeds," "going beyond the demands of the law," "honoring God's creatures," and martyrdom.

36. See the selected bibliography. Consult the web.

37. The centrality of this issue accounts for its appearance as an area of formal instruction and also as a social skill.

38. See, for example: The National Coalition Building Institute, 1835 K Street, Washington, DC 20006.

39. See "198 Methods of Nonviolent Action" prepared by The Albert Einstein Institution (1430 Massachusetts Ave., Cambridge, MA 02138; phone: 617-876-0311) reprinted in the appendixes.

40. See, for example: The Martin Luther King, Jr. Center for Nonviolent Social Change, Atlanta, GA, and the "List of Prosocial Resources" in the appendixes.

41. I have never been part of an academic search, even in a department of religion or school of theology, where this was so. Also, my own curriculum vitae, which is quite long, does not include my prosocial activities and commitments, nor have I been asked to add them.

42. See A. Kohn, *Punished by Rewards: The Trouble with Gold Stars, Incentive Plans, A's, Praise, and Other Bribes* (New York, Houghton Mifflin: 1993).

43. See the appendixes for my syllabus and others.

44. See the appendixes for another set of ten commandments. Readers are invited to write their own ten commandments and send them to me.

45. On reading rabbinic texts, see pp. 147–48.

46. Drawing on *Mishna,* Avot 1:10 as, indeed, the rest of this passage is a dialogue between Avot and popular Greek philosophy.

47. *Talmud,* Tamid 32a.

48. *Talmud,* Berakhot 54a.

49. *Talmud,* Berakhot 60b, with parallels in *Talmud Yerushalmi,* Berakhot 33a and Sanhedrin 8b.

50. On this, see pp. 188–93.

Chapter 9

1. I shall make references to Christianity from time to time but am not qualified to write this section from that perspective.

2. On Amos, see especially S. Spiegel, *Amos and Amaziah* (New York, Jewish Theological Seminary: 1957) for a very elegant presentation which was delivered in the presence of President Harry Truman and Chief Justice Earl Warren of the United States Supreme Court.

3. Daube (D. Daube, *Civil Disobedience in Antiquity* [Edinburgh, Edinburgh University Press: 1972] 61) adds Adam and Eve as resistors of unreasonable authority (Gen. 3).

4. Soloveitchik (J. Soloveitchik, "Kol Dodi Dofek: It is the Voice of My Beloved that Knocketh," transl. L. Kaplan, B. Rosenberg and F. Heuman, *Theological and Halakhic Reflections on the Holocaust* [Hoboken, NJ, Ktav Publishing: 1992] 58–62) holds that Job was guilty in two senses of the word: he did not assume his proper share of the communal burdens and he did not properly empathize with the suffering of others. As evidence, Soloveitchik notes that it is only after Job intercedes for his interlocutors that he is restored (Job 42:8–10).

5. For the historical sources, see the encyclopedias under "Bar Kokhba," "The Ten Martyrs," etc. For spiritual resistance to the nazis, see M. Prager, *Sparks of Glory* (New York, Mesorah Publications: 1974, 1985); P. Schindler, *Hasidic Responses to the Holocaust in Light of Hasidic Thought* (Hoboken, NJ, Ktav Publishing: 1990); and I. Rosenbaum, *Holocaust and Halakha* (New York, Ktav Publishing: 1976).

6. See also Maimonides, *Code,* Hilkhot Melakhim 5:4.

7. On texts of terror against women, see P. Trible, *Texts of Terror* (Philadelphia, Fortress Press: 1984) and against Israel, see Ex. 23:23–24, Lev. 26:14–45, Dt. 9:11–29, and Dt. 28:15–69. My thanks to Rabbi Steve Jacobs for his list of "painful passages" from which part of this is drawn.

8. H. Cohn, *Human Rights in Jewish Law* (New York, Ktav Publishing: 1984) 32–34.

9. On *mamzer,* see the encyclopedias. For hate which is zeal, see *Talmud,* Pesahim 113b with Arakhin 16b which echo Amos 5:15 and Ps. 97:10.

10. See chap. 8.

11. Ex. 23:2 and Dt. 17:11.

12. The church did not do much better. It sponsored the inquisition which, among other tasks, burned Jews, witches, and other heretics, and its record during the shoah leaves much to be desired. This is not the issue here.

13. See R. Linn, *Conscience at War: The Israeli Soldier as a Moral Critic* (New York, SUNY Press: 1996)—reviewed by me in *Jewish Spectator* (Summer 1998) 52–53—that there are no religious selective conscientious objectors.

14. On the philosophical and ethical studies, see for example, M. Kellner, *Contemporary Jewish Ethics* (New York, Sanhedrin Press: 1978).

15. The best study, to my mind, is D. Boyarin, *Intertextuality and the Reading of Midrash* (Bloomington, IN, Indiana University Press: 1990)—reviewed by me in *CCAR Journal* (Fall 1995) 81–83.

16. See p. 13.

17. For a fuller statement of this, see *Facing the Abusing God: A Theology of Protest* (Louisville, KY, Westminster / John Knox: 1993) xxii, 40–41, 64; *God at the Center* (San Francisco, Harper and Row: 1988; reprinted Northvale, NJ, Jason Aronson: 1994) xxxiv–xxxv; and "What American Jews Believe: A Symposium," *Commentary* (August 1996) 23–24.

18. A. Gross, "Mr. Gross' Story: A Survivor's Account," *Emory Studies on the Holocaust: An Interfaith Inquiry,* ed. S. Hanover and D. Blumenthal (Atlanta, GA, Emory University: 1988) 2: 11–12. This excerpt portrays life in the early days of the ghetto.

Chapter 10

1. On the subject of Jewish law and morality, see H. Cohn, *Human Rights in Jewish Law* (New York, Ktav Publishing: 1984); M. Elon, *Jewish Law* 4 vols. (Philadelphia, Jewish Publication Society: 1994); Z. W. Falk, *Law and Religion* (Jerusalem, Mesharim Publications: 1981); Z. W. Falk, *Legal Values and Judaism: Toward a Philosophy of Halakha* (Hebrew) (Jerusalem, Hebrew University: 1980); N. Rakover, *Modern Applications of Jewish Law* 2 vols. (Jerusalem, Jewish Legal Heritage Society: 1992); and in general, N. Rakover, *The Multiple-Language Bibliography in Jewish Law* (Jerusalem, Library of Jewish Law: 1990).

2. The term is derived from M. Kadushin, *The Rabbinic Mind* (New York, Jewish Theological Seminary: 1952). See also his *Worship and Ethics* (n.p., Northwestern University Press: 1964). For a fuller exposition of value-concepts and their relation to affections and teachings, see pp. 117–19.

3. *The Rabbinic Mind,* 4.

4. As Kadushin points out, all value-concepts imply all others. They also overlap one another such that a Venn diagram of overlapping circles is a good representation of the dynamic relationship of value-concepts one to another (*The Rabbinic Mind,* chap. 2). On this, see pp. 117–19. It is, therefore, misleading for me to choose only four. These four, however, seem to me to be more central to halakha than others. Still, the reader needs to know that there are many more value-concepts; also, that other scholars may analyze this differently.

5. Kadushin properly remarks (*The Rabbinic Mind,* chap. 3) that, in any given culture, the value-concepts must be in the language of that culture. Hence, in writing about the value-concepts of altruism (pp. 119–22), I used English terms while, in writing about the value-concepts of halakha, I shall use Hebrew terms. Also, as Kadushin notes (*The Rabbinic Mind,* chap. 1), a value-concept need not be present textually in order to be active as a concept and value that informs a text. Hence, the specific value-concepts that I use will not always be specifically mentioned in the texts I cite; they will, however, in all cases be an informing value and concept behind the text.

6. Genesis 1:26–7; 5:3; 9:6. The word is also used to refer to idolatrous and even phallic images. See Maimonides, *Guide for the Perplexed,* 1:1, for a discussion of this term and its multiple meanings.

7. *Mekhilta,* Shira, 3; *Masekhet Sofrim,* 3:13.

8. *Tosefta,* Yevamot 8:5.

9. The idea behind "prooftexting" is that the source is, in some way, divine and expresses God's truth and will. Hence, one can appeal to such a text as "proof" that something is true or morally desirable.

10. By a slight, but permissible, change in the grammar of Genesis 9:6, another reading is possible: "He who spills the blood of a person in a person, his blood shall be shed." Catholic tradition uses this reading to forbid abortion.

11. *Tosefta,* Yevamot 8:5, with variant of Ben Azzai for R. Elazar.

12. *Talmud,* Shabbat 10a. The Hebrew is a play on words: *kol dayyan she-dan din 'emet la-'amito.*

13. *Talmud,* Sanhedrin 7a. See also *Mishna,* Avot 3:14.

14. On value-concepts always coming in clusters, see pp. 117–19.

15. Z. W. Falk, *Legal Values and Judaism: Toward a Philosophy of Halakha* (Hebrew), (Jerusalem, Hebrew University: 1980) 56–7. Halakha does not specifically recognize the concept of "rights" and much is made of various "duties" or "obligations." However, Cohn notes, "As the recognition of a right implies a duty to implement it, so does the imposition of a duty confer a right to have it performed" (20). Falk agrees that duties imply rights and, hence, covenant implies, even if it does not specify, rights (*Law and Religion,* 230–31). Falk points out that the Torah grants basic "rights" even to slaves and animals (e.g., rest on Shabbat and no cruelty), to the human body (no mutilation or suicide), to property (no theft or wanton destruction), as well as to strangers, the marginalized, the oppressed, and even the enemy (*Law and Religion,* 79–82). The index of the *Israel Yearbook for Human Rights* lists 104 separate human rights (21 [1991] 296–9).

16. Exodus 24:7 in contrast with *Talmud,* Shabbat 88a.

17. Heb., *talmid-ḥacham* applies to everyone, for it designates one who is still a student but also already has some authoritative knowledge—a very good way to designate teacher-students and student-teachers. For "student-sages" as another translation of this term, see pp. 154, 226.

18. *Talmud,* Bava Metsi'a 59b.

19. It is difficult to tell which value-concepts are subsets of others (see pp. 117–19). My intellectual instinct is to take value-concepts that are more closely related and to call those "ancillary value-concepts" while leaving those which are more indirectly related as "related value-concepts." But, it really makes no difference because the system of value-concepts is not a hierarchical system (*The Rabbinic Mind,* chap. 2). I have, therefore, adopted the term "associated value-concept" to cover all value-concepts related to one another. See p. 154, for another example: *kevod ha-beriyot* and *gemilut hasadim* as associated value-concepts.

20. *Talmud,* Temura 14b. See also Maimonides, *Code,* Hilkhot Mamrim 2:4.

21. *Law and Religion,* 32.

22. Falk, *Legal Values,* 36–38; Falk, *Law and Religion,* 29–31.

23. *Talmud,* Eruvin 13b. The text goes on to favor the school of Hillel on various grounds but the principle that plurality of interpretive truth exists is established in this text and its parallel (see Cohn, 122, though his explanation of why this is so does not appear to me to be correct).

24. Heb., *talmid-hacham* applies to everyone, for it designates one who is still a student but also already has some authoritative knowledge—a very good way to designate teacher-students and student-teachers. For "scholar-student" as another translation of this term, see p. 153.

25. *Talmud,* Hagiaga 3b, cited in Cohn, 122.

26. Maharal of Prague (sixteenth century), cited in Cohn, 128. Cohn goes on to point out that, while liberal on the matter of free speech, rabbinic culture is very strict on the matter of books which contain heretical writings (129).

27. Cited in Rakover, *Modern Applications,* 211–12 (italics Rakover's).

28. Saadia Gaon, *The Book of Beliefs and Opinions,* 3:3, called these "traditional [or, revealed] commandments" in distinction from "rational commandments." Maimonides, who philosophically denied this distinction, went to very great lengths to show that all commandments are "rational," but Saadia is closer to the mainstream of the tradition.

29. *Tanhuma,* Hukat 8.

30. *Tanhuma,* Hukat 3.

31. *Sifra,* Kedoshim, 9:12.

32. *Otsar ha-Midrashim,* "Le'olam," 14.

33. *Midrash Tehillim* 146:8.

34. Falk, *Law and Religion,* 25, 33 (italics original).

35. Rashi to Leviticus 19:24, quoting *Sifra,* ad loc. See also M. Kasher, *Torah Sheleyma,* ad loc.

36. Nahmanides, *Commentary to the Torah,* Deuteronomy 6:18 and Leviticus 19:2, cited in Elon, 185.

37. Elon, 248.

38. Maimonides, *Code,* Hilkhot Sanhedrin 21:1–3. There are many, many more such rules.

39. Rakover, *Modern Applications,* 270–71.

40. Occurs sixteen times in the *Talmud,* e.g., Bava Kama 54b. See also Kiddushin 43a; Bava Kama 47b, 98a.

41. *Talmud,* Bava Kama 94b, 118a; Bava Metsi'a 37a-b.

42. With textual variants in *Talmud,* Shabbat 121b, Kiddushin 17b, Bava Kama 94b, Bava Metsi'a 48a, Bava Batra 133b, and in positive form, Shabbat 153a, Megilla 16b.

43. Elon structures his chapter on morality and the law according to such a list of phrases and verses (1:141–89).

44. W. Brueggemann, *Theology of the Old Testament: Testimony, Dispute, Advocacy* (Minneapolis, Fortress Press: 1997).

45. Maimonides, *Guide of the Perplexed,* 3:53. On these two meanings, see also, D. Blumenthal, *Facing the Abusing God: A Theology of Protest* (Louisville, KY, Westminster / John Knox: 1993) 152.

46. *Sifre,* Devarim 49.

47. *Talmud,* Bava Kama 30a. The other cases of *ḥasidim ha-rishonim* (there are twenty-eight in the *Talmud* and midrashim) deal with ascetic practices, prayer techniques, nazirite sacrifices, the making of the fringes for a garment, having sex on Wednesday, and tithing regulations.

48. D. Blumenthal, "Creation: What Difference Does It Make?," B. Burrell and J. McGinn, *God and Creation: An Ecumenical Symposium* (Notre Dame, IN, University of Notre Dame Press: 1990) 154–72.

49. *Talmud,* Shabbat 120a.

50. The talmudic discussion goes on to offer another opinion, that of Rava, that these men are clever, not insofar as they are acting piously, but because they are God-fearing and realize that one may not profit on the Shabbat. By compensating the owner, they remove the possibility that they have profited on the Sabbbath.

51. *Talmud,* Ḥulin 130b. The other occurrences of *middat ḥasidut* (there are twenty-three) deal with repaying pledges which have expired and with impurity rules. It is interesting that all eight occurrences of *middat ḥasidut* in Maimonides's *Code* seem to have no direct parallel in the earlier rabbinic literature and, of the seven occurrences of *ḥasidim ha-rishonim,* only the ecology quotation is taken directly from its rabbinic source. Perhaps, Maimonides's medieval definition of *ḥesed* accounts for this.

52. *Talmud,* Berakhot 19b; Shabbat 81b; Eruvin 41b; etc.

53. *Talmud,* Ketubot 37b, Sanhedrin 45a and 52b, etc.; Kasher, ad loc, 269–74.

54. Elon, 156.

55. Saul Berman, in a fine study of this phrase—S. Berman, *"Lifnim Mishurat Hadin," Journal of Jewish Studies* 26:1–2 (1975) 86–104 and 28:2 (1977) 181–93— cites six cases from the legal literature and four from the nonlegal literature to demonstrate the structure of this usage. In each case, he maintains that there is "the undifferentiated law" (*din*), which is followed by "the differentiated law" (*shurat ha-din*), which in turn is followed by a "return to the undifferentiated law" (*lifnim mi-shurat ha-din*). I, however, favor calling the third stage "the superdifferentiated law" as I shall show in these footnotes.

56. *Talmud,* Bava Kama 99b–100a, discussed in Berman, 87–91. The exegesis appears again in *Talmud,* Bava Metsi'a 30b and in the *Mekhilta de Rabbi Shimon bar Yoḥai,* Masekhta d'Amalek, Yitro, 2 (Berman, 186).

57. The standard for all moneychangers is "the undifferentiated law"; that of experts is "the differentiated law"; and in my opinion, that of those who act within the line of the law is "the superdifferentiated law."

58. *Talmud,* Bava Metsi'a 24b, discussed in Berman, 101–2.

59. The case of the usual lost object is "the undifferentiated law"; that of the exemption to bear costs after one year is "the differentiated law"; and in my opinion, that of the father of Shmuel is "the superdifferentiated law."

60. *Talmud,* Berakhot 7a, discussed in Berman, 184–85.

61. On whether this figure is God or something else, see G. Scholem, *Major Trends in Jewish Mysticism* (New York, Schocken: 1941) 356, n.3, cited in Berman, 184, n. 94. Scholars have not adequately dealt with "nodding of the head" as a mystical (?ecstatic) experience, which it most likely was intended to convey.

62. Berman's analysis here differs from his earlier threefold analysis and, in my opinon, he is wrong. One can indeed utilize his threefold analysis as follows: The *din* (the undifferentiated law) is God's full judgment of the people; it would be very severe. The *shurat ha-din* (the differentiated law) is God's judgment of the people with mercy; it would have many exceptions to the law and it would be too lax. The *lifnim mi-shurat ha-din* (the superdifferentiated law) is God's loving justice, that is, a meting out of that which is properly due. This would be a fair and loving mixture of justice and mercy, and would express great piety in that one trusts oneself and God to do the right and proper thing. The *Zohar*, where the phrase is *lego mi-shurat ha-din*, treats this dimension as a function of *ḥesed*, pure grace (2:170a; 3:199b).

63. Berman 191, 193.

64. The Mordecai and the Baḥ cited in Elon, 157.

65. *Talmud*, Sota 14a.

66. That is, one may do as much as one wishes.

67. *Talmud Yerushalmi*, Pe'a 1:1. A slightly different version appears in the daily liturgy.

68. *Talmud*, Sukka 49b; close parallel *Talmud Yerushalmi*, Pe'a 1:5.

69. Rashi, ad loc.; Maimonides, *Code*, Hilkhot Avel 14:2. See also *Encyclopedia Talmudit*, "Gemilut Ḥasadim," 151, n. 32, 33.

70. *Encyclopedia Talmudit*, "Gemilut Ḥasadim," 151–52. There is an associated value-concept here called *Tikkun Olam* (restoration of the world) which valorizes all activity intended to make the world a better place.

71. *Mishna*, Avot 1:2.

72. R. Kimelman, "Non-Violence in the Talmud," *Judaism* 17 (1968) 333–34. For a discussion of this issue, see pp. 165–66, 212–19.

73. The phrase, *mipnei darkhei shalom*, occurs twenty-six times in rabbinic literature (e.g., *Talmud*, Gittin 59a-b).

74. *The Rabbinic Mind*, chap. 4.

75. A. Gross, "Mr. Gross' Story: A Survivor's Account," *Emory Studies on the Holocaust: An Interfaith Inquiry*, ed. S. Hanover and D. Blumenthal (Atlanta, GA, Emory University: 1988) 2:20–21. This excerpt describes the last march from Auschwitz to Gleiweitz and the last voyage from Gleiwitz to Buchenwald, the trip so searingly portrayed in Elie Wiesel's *Night*. (Alex Gross and Elie Wiesel know each other from the camps and from that trip.)

Chapter 11

1. Cited in D. Daube, *Civil Disobedience in Antiquity* (Edinburgh, Edinburgh University Press: 1972) 12, with a parallel in Tobit 1:17.

2. See S. Spiegel, *Amos and Amaziah* (New York, Jewish Theological Seminary: 1957) for a very elegant presentation of this confrontation which was delivered in the presence of President Harry Truman and Chief Justice Earl Warren of the United States Supreme Court.

3. Cited in M. Konvitz, "Conscience and Civil Disobedience in the Jewish Tradition," *Judaism and Human Rights*, reprinted in M. Kellner, *Contemporary Jewish Ethics* (New York, Sanhedrin Press: 1978) 239. Cited also by Daube who notes that, when questioned by the king, the midwives attempted no bravery; they simply lied saying that the Hebrew women gave birth before midwives arrived (9–10).

4. Konvitz, 239.

5. Daube, 9.

6. *Talmud,* Sota 11b.

7. Daube calls this, "a moment when supralegal action is called for" (63).

8. I Samuel 22:17. For more on this important act of resistance, see pp. 197–200.

9. The rabbis understood that Vashti was to come in her royal crown and nothing else (*Esther Rabba,* Introduction, at end, and 1:9), cited in Daube, 14–16.

10. Josephus, *Antiquities* 18:8, cited by Konvitz in Kellner, 243.

11. *Talmud,* Zevaḥim 101a, twice, cited in Z. W. Falk, *Law and Religion* (Jerusalem, Mesharim Publications: 1981) 105.

12. Cited in Daube, 66–67.

13. See M. Prager, *Sparks of Glory* (New York, Mesorah Publications: 1974, 1985) and E. Berkovits, *With God in Hell* (New York, Sanhedrin Press: 1979) 54–76. Prager tells the stories; Berkovits develops a typology of the "authentic Jew" (that is, the orthodox rabbinic Jew) of the concentration camps and contrasts that with the views of Kogan and Frankl. The stories have become models, told over and over again.

14. See pp. 61–62, 97–101.

15. This popular story has its most literary form in the work of Y. L. Peretz.

16. I do not know where I first heard this story, nor of whom it is told.

17. This story is told of several hasidic rebbes and Torah scholars. I first cited it in *Understanding Jewish Mysticism,* vol. 2 (New York, Ktav Publishing: 1982) 104.

18. Commenting on Adam and Eve (Gen. 3), Daube notes: ". . . the so-called story of the Fall. It ought to be called the story of the Rise. . . . God turns out to be lying. They do not die, and their eyes are opened exactly as the serpent, the Prometheus of the Bible, told them" (61). One would need a protest text to make this line of reasoning stick. For a similar position, see E. Fromm, *On Disobedience and Other Essays* (New York, Seabury Press: 1981).

19. On the justice-oriented challenge to God, see D. Blumenthal, *Facing the Abusing God: A Theology of Protest* (Louisville, KY, Westminster / John Knox: 1993). On the intercessory-oriented challenge, see Y. Muffs, "His Majesty's Loyal Opposition: A Study in Prophetic Intercession," *Conservative Judaism* 33:3 (1980) 25–37.

20. For a full interpretation of this psalm and its theology, see *Facing the Abusing God,* 85–110.

21. Weekly penitential liturgy, western European rite, with echoes from Psalm 44.

22. On the tradition of protest, see A. Laytner, *Arguing With God: A Jewish Tradition* (Northvale, NJ, Jason Aronson: 1990) and *Facing the Abusing God,* 249–64.

23. See also Psalm 109 interpreted in *Facing the Abusing God,* 111–56.

24. Jeremiah 7:12–14, 14:11–12, and 15:1, discussed by Muffs, 29–32.

25. Ezekiel 13:4–5 and 22:30–31, discussed by Muffs, 33–34.

26. Muffs, 35–36.

27. *Tanḥuma Buber,* Bereshit, Vayera' 9. On purposeful, rebellious, and inadvertent sins, see *Facing the Abusing God,* 139–41 with the sources cited there.

28. On this as the original "Lord's Prayer," see *Facing the Abusing God,* 139.

29. *Talmud,* Berakhot 32a.

30. *Talmud,* Berakhot 32a.

31. *Shemot Rabba* 43:4. For the same motif, see *Talmud,* Berakhot 32a in the name of Rava.

32. Cited in Laytner, 189 and then in *Facing the Abusing God,* 252.

33. *Devarim Rabba,* Shoftim, 13, cited in Z. W. Falk, *Legal Values and Judaism: Toward a Philosophy of Halakha* (Hebrew) (Jerusalem, Hebrew University: 1980) 39.

34. Falk 39, n. 50.

35. *Talmud,* Shabbat 87a, Menaḥot 99a-b, cited in Z. W. Falk, *Law and Religion,* 113.

36. *Talmud,* Berakhot 32a.

37. I have had students tell me that these texts can't mean what they say; or, that I have made them up to make my point. I invite the reader to check my sources and not underestimate the moral imagination of the tradition.

38. Laytner, 206, n. 50. See also *Facing the Abusing God,* 253 and E. Wiesel, *The Trial of God* (New York, Schocken Books: 1976, 1989).

39. Taken from the new liturgy in *Facing the Abusing God,* 291–95.

40. *The Seventy-First Came . . . to Gunskirchenlager,* foreword by Maj. Gen. W. Wyman, is one of a series of pamphlets published by units of the American Army which liberated the concentration camps. It is a collection of essays and photographs by the men in those units with no date, place, or publishing body listed. It is simple, direct testimony. When, at Emory University, we began to interview liberators in the late 1970s, the men spontaneously brought us these pamphlets. We photo-reproduced them as we received them. This pamphlet was first printed by us (Witness to the Holocaust Project, Emory University) in 1979 and reprinted in 1983; LC #79–51047 (a). The quotation is taken from pages 4–5.

Chapter 12

1. See pp. 123–24, 132–33.

2. Cited in M. Lamm, "After the War—Another Look at Pacifism and Selective Conscientious Objection," *Judaism,* 1971; reprinted in M. Kellner, *Contemporary Jewish Ethics* (New York, Sanhedrin Press: 1978) 223, and retranslated by me.

3. *Talmud,* Shabbat 119b, cited in R. Kimelman, "The Rabbinic Ethics of Protest," *Judaism* 19 (1970) 42.

4. *Bereshit Rabba,* 54:3, cited in Kimelman, 43.

5. *Talmud,* Shabbat 54b–55a. See M. Greenberg, "Rabbinic Reflections of Defying Legal Orders: Amasa, Abner, and Joab," *Judaism* 19 (1970) 34 for a clear discussion of this passage in its rabbinic context. See also Kimelman, 40, on this text.

6. For another excellent quotation, see p. 15.

7. *Zohar* 3:46a, referring to *Talmud,* Shabbat 33b, cited in Kimelman, 44.

8. Hebrew, *'akhzari,* lit., "cruel" but here it clearly means "tough."

9. *Kohelet Rabba,* 7:24.

10. *Orḥot Tsadikim,* "Sha'ar ha-'Akhzariyut" ("The Gate of Toughness").

11. *Talmud*, Arakhin 16b.

12. *Tanna de-bei Eliyahu Rabba*, 18:40.

13. Kimelman, 53–54.

14. *Talmud*, Sanhedrin 101b, cited in Kimelman, 52.

15. *Tanna de-bei Eliyahu*, 18:40.

16. *Avot de-Rabbi Natan*, 16:5.

17. *Talmud*, Sanhedrin 106a, Sota 11a, mentioned in Kimelman, 40.

18. Maimonides, *Code*, Hilkhot Yesodei ha-Torah, 4:5, end.

19. *Bereshit Rabba* 75:11, cited in Kimelman, 44.

20. Kimelman, 49–51, 57.

21. Kimelman, 51, esp. n. 53. See also pp. 165–66, 212–19.

22. *Talmud*, Yoma 22b, cited in Z. W. Falk, *Legal Values and Judaism: Toward a Philosophy of Halakha* (Hebrew) (Jerusalem, Hebrew University: 1980) 39 and Z. W. Falk, *Law and Religion* (Jerusalem, Mesharim Publications: 1981) 107. Falk's conclusion that "everything depends on the individual" (*Legal Values*, 39) seems not adequate.

23. *Talmud*, Ketubot 86a, Ḥulin 132b. See also Maimonides, *Code*, Hilkhot Ḥametz u-Matsa 5:12, for one who eats ḥamets on erev Pesaḥ.

24. *Talmud*, Pesaḥim 113b.

25. Maimonides, *Code*, Hilkhot De'ot 6:6–7.

26. Maimonides, *Code*, Hillkhot Rotseaḥ 13:14.

27. In talmudic texts, it is "*a* good impulse" and "*the* evil impulse" for reasons not clear to me. Later rabbinic literature spoke of both using either the indeterminate or the determinate article, e.g., *yetser ha-tov* and *yetser ha-ra'* (see below, n. 40).

28. *Bereshit Rabba* 14:4; shortened form in *Talmud*, Berakhot 61a.

29. *Talmud*, Kiddushin 30b. On the use of "with all your heart" (Dt. 6:5) for *yetser tov* and *yetser ha-ra'*, see p. 139.

30. *Talmud*, Sanhedrin 91a.

31. *Talmud*, Shabbat 105b.

32. *Talmud*, Sukka 52b.

33. *Talmud*, Berakhot 61b.

34. *Talmud*, Sukka 52a.

35. On the importance of incremental action, see pp. 31, 77–86, 133, 138.

36. *Talmud*, Sukka 52b. See also the quotation from *Bereshit Rabba* 9:7, p. 191.

37. *Talmud*, Kiddushin 30b; Sukka 52a-b.

38. *Talmud*, Berakhot 5a. In later rabbinic literature, the recommendaton to arouse good against evil is reversed: to use one's *yetser ha-tov*, one must first seize upon one's *yetser ha-ra'* (e.g., *Sha'ar ha-'Otiyot*, 'Ot Tav, Teshuka 13).

39. *Bereshit Rabba* 9:7 (note the tradition is from his father and that he bears his grandfather's name).

40. This explains, I think, why this literature sometimes speaks of both *yetser tov* and *yetser ha-ra'* with the indeterminate article, as here, and sometimes of both with the determinate article, *yetser ha-tov* and *yetser ha-ra'*.

41. *Sha'ar ha-'Otiyot*, 'Ot Yod, "Yetser Tov," 7.

42. *Zohar* 1:49b and 1:144b.

43. For more on this, see D. Blumenthal, *Understanding Jewish Mysticism*

(New York, Ktav Publishing: 1978) part 2; I. Tishby, *The Wisdom of the Zohar*, transl. D. Goldstein, 3 vols. (Oxford, Oxford University Press: 1989).

44. See p. 119, though Batson has only given very sketchy indications of how to capitalize on the existence of this impulse.

45. The term *kiddush ha-Shem* properly refers to any action that sanctifies God's Name in the world. It is used commonly in its most extreme setting to refer to martyrdom; hence, its usage here in that sense.

46. See *Encyclopedia Talmudit*, "Dina de-Malkhuta Dina"; and L. Landman, "Civil Disobedience: The Jewish View," *Tradition* 10 (1969) 5–14 and 123–26.

47. Maimonides, *Code*, Hikhot Yesodei ha-Torah, 5:1–4, divided here into four separate paragraphs. Note that Maimonides words the law positively.

48. *Talmud*, Yoma 85b, Sanhedrin 74a, Avoda Zara 27b and 54a.

49. Hebrew, *bi-she'at ha-gezera*.

50. To this Maimonides adds the obligatory escape clause; see p. 187.

51. *Encyclopedia Talmudit*, "Yeihareig ve-'al Ya'avor," for all of these provisions.

52. There is a terrifying case of a man in the camps who consulted a rabbi about bribing a concentration camp guard to obtain the release of his son from a selection knowing that another would be chosen in his place (I. Rosenbaum, *Holocaust and Halakha* [New York, Ktav Publishing: 1976] 4).

53. On the last, see M. Prager, *Sparks of Glory* (Mesorah Publications: 1974, 1985) and N. Tec, *Defiance: The Bielski Partisans* (Oxford, Oxford University Press: 1993), though the literature is vast and growing all the time.

54. *The Seventy-First Came . . . to Gunskirchenlager*, foreword by Maj. Gen. W. Wyman, is one of a series of pamphlets published by units of the American Army which liberated the concentration camps. It is a collection of essays and photographs by the men in those units with no date, place, or publishing body listed. It is simple, direct testimony. When, at Emory University, we began to interview liberators in the late 1970s, the men spontaneously brought us these pamphlets. We photo-reproduced them as we received them. This pamphlet was first printed by us (Witness to the Holocaust Project, Emory University) in 1979 and reprinted in 1983; LC #79–51047 (a). The quotation is taken from pages 9–11.

Chapter 13

1. N. Keijzer, "A Plea for the Defence of Superior Orders," *Israel Yearbook of Human Rights* 8 (1978) 78–103.

2. Lit., let the superior respond / be responsible. This is also known as "Befehl ist Befehl" (an order is an order) and "obéissance passive" (passive obedience).

3. Cited in Keijzer, 80.

4. Cited in Keijzer, 85. The French text for this passage is interestingly different: "Il réside dans la liberté morale, dans la faculté de choisir, chez l'auteur de l'acte reproché."

5. Cited in Keijzer, 95–96.

6. "The Defence of Justification because of Obedience to Illegal Orders: Summary of the Symposium" (Hebrew), *Mishpatim* (1991) 591–621.

7. Hebrew, *be-'alil she-lo ka-din*.

8. Hebrew, *barur ve-galui sheha-pekuda she-nitna hi lo-ḥukit.*

9. "Symposium," 602.

10. M. Greenberg, "Rabbinic Reflections of Defying Legal Orders: Amasa, Abner, and Yoav," *Judaism* 19 (1970) 30–37 and A. Kirschenbaum, "A Cog in the Wheel: The Defence of 'Obedience to Superior Orders' in Jewish Law," *Israel Yearbook of Human Rights* 4 (1974) 168–93. See also: *Encyclopedia Talmudit,* "Ein Shaliaḥ le-Dvar Avera"; Y. Silman, "The Military Order in Light of the Halakha" (Hebrew), *Arakhim be-Mivḥan Milḥama: Musar u-Milḥama bi-R'i ha-Yahadut* (Jerusalem, A. Mizrahi: 1983) 183–89; A. Steinsaltz, "Obedience and Disobedience to Orders" (Hebrew), *ibid.,* 190–95; and Zekharya ben Shelomo, *Hilkhot Tsava* 2 vols. (Shaalavim: 5746 and n.d.). On conscientious objection in the Israeli army, see R. Linn, *Conscience at War: The Israeli Soldier as a Moral Critic* (New York, SUNY Press: 1996); reviewed by me in *Jewish Spectator* (Summer 1998) 52–53. Y. Shachar, "The Elgazi Trials: S.C.O. in Israel," *Israeli Yearbook on Human Rights* 12 (1982) 214–58.

11. That is, in the middle of peace negotiations.

12. Tosafot, ad loc.

13. *Talmud,* Sanhedrin 49a.

14. This phrase became a norm.

15. Maimonides, *Code,* Hilkhot Melakhim 3:9, cited in Kirschenbaum, "Cog," 181.

16. Maimonides, *Code,* Hilkhot Mamrim 6:12, itself based on earlier sources, cited in Kirschenbaum, "Cog," 181, n. 48.

17. *Talmud,* Sanhedrin 49a, cited in Greenberg, 34.

18. *Talmud Yerushalmi,* Sanhedrin 52b, cited in Greenberg, 33, as Sanhedrin 29a.

19. *Talmud,* Sanhedrin 20a, cited in Kirschenbaum, "Cog," 182.

20. Kirschenbaum, "Cog," discusses this issue very clearly.

21. *Talmud,* Kiddushin 43a.

22. *Talmud,* Kiddushin 42b, etc. See also *Encyclopedia Talmudit,* "Ein Shaliaḥ le-Dvar Avera."

23. Kirschenbaum, 172–73.

24. Maimonides, *Code,* Hilkhot Rotseaḥ 2:2, cited in Kirschenbaum, 173. Kirschenbaum cites an interesting difference of opinion among the ancients: ". . . in contrast to Aristotle's teaching that a slave who murders under orders of his master is only an instrument and does not act unjustly (*Nichomachean Ethics* 5.9.11) . . . an interesting parallel may be found in Seneca, *De Beneficiis* 3:20: 'Nor are we able to command all things from slaves, nor are they compelled to obey us in all things; they will not carry out orders that are hostile to the State and they will not lend their hands to any crime'" (173, n. 15).

25. Kirschenbaum, 178.

26. Kirschenbaum, 186–87.

27. Kirschenbaum, 192–93, italics added. The tradition of commentation and argumentation is very complex here, too complex for this book, though the interested reader can begin with the articles cited and follow the sources. Jewish law does not talk explicitly about the standard of "the reasonable man." But there is a general "refusal of the Jewish criminal code to accept the rule *Ignorantia iuris non excusat*" (Kirschenbaum, 184).

28. See also pp. 157–62, 172–75, *tsedek.* The Deuteronomy 16:19 passage has a near parallel in Exodus 23:8.

29. *Sifre,* Shoftim, 154:11.

30. Hebrew, *ruah Hashem.*

31. Naḥmanides, *Commentary to the Torah,* ad loc. Similar language in *Sefer ha-Ḥinukh* (496): ". . . it is better for us to endure one error and have everything under their good authority and not have each do according to his own opinion, for with that there would be the destruction of the religion, division in the heart of the people, and a loss for the whole nation."

32. *Mekhilta,* ad loc. See also, *Tosefta,* Sanhedrin 3:4.

33. Rashi, ad loc, drawing on *Talmud,* Sanhedrin 2a: "Your tending after the law for evil is not like your tending after the law for good. Tending for the good is the case of [acquitting with] a one-judge majority and tending for evil is the case of [convicting with] a two-judge majority."

34. Hebrew, *zaken mamre'.* Deuteronomy 17:12 with *Talmud,* Horayot 2a-4b and Maimonides, *Code,* Hilkhot Mamrim 1–4 in general and specifically, 1:4. Cf. also *Encyclopedia Talmudit,* "Zaken Mamre'," that the dissenter must be properly qualified, that only certain categories of law can be appealed, that the highest instance must be without blemish, etc., for the dissenter to be actually condemned to death.

35. Manuscript variant: "for me to be like my master."

36. *Tosefta,* Sanhedrin 3:4. See also, *Encyclopedia Talmudit,* "Lo Ta'ane al Riv Lintot."

37. The commentators notice that there is no such verse in Deuteronomy 17:11. D. Z. Hoffman speculates that the Yerushalmi may be reading as follows: *ve-'asita al pi ha-davar asher yagidu lekha* ("You shall act according to that which they tell you") / . . . *asher yagidu lekh* ("You shall . . . they tell you 'Go'") (*Melamed Leho'il* [New York, Frankel: 1953] 128).

38. *Talmud Yerushalmi,* Horayot 2b.

39. Cited in M. Elon, *Jewish Law,* 4 vols. (Philadelphia, Jewish Publication Society: 1994) 254.

40. Rashi, ad loc, citing *Talmud,* Sanhedrin 7b on the punishment for causing a judgment to tend in the wrong direction.

41. *Mishna,* Horayot 1:3.

42. Maimonides, *Code,* Hilkhot Mamrim 3:6; see also *Mishna,* Horayot 1:4. There were, and are, no women judges in rabbinic tradition; I have, however, tried to preserve the egalitarian language in these paragraphs.

43. Naḥmanides, *Commentary to Sefer ha-Mitsvot of Maimonides,* First Root. In general, see M. Berger, "The Halakhic Basis for Civil Disobedience in a Democratic State," *The Orthodox Forum Series* (Northvale, NJ, Jason Aronson: in press).

44. After the killing of Kitty Genovese in March 1964, which lasted forty minutes and was witnessed by almost forty neighbors, the legal world devoted substantial effort to the problem of the Good Samaritan. A. Kirschenbaum wrote about the issue from the point of view of Jewish law in two exhaustive articles: "The 'Good Samaritan' and Jewish Law," *Diné Israel* 7 (1976) 7–85 and, in abridged form, "The Bystander's Duty to Rescue in Jewish Law," *Journal of Religious Ethics* (1980) 204–26.

45. On these value-concepts, see pp. 155–57, 160–66, 172–74.

46. As noted on p. 183, the Hebrew, *rei'ekha* means "fellow Jew"; however, given the contemporary context, I use it in a more inclusive sense.

47. "Good Samaritan," 11. One may not, for example, testify falsely against someone in a capital case.

48. *Talmud,* Sanhedrin 73a with parallels, cited in "Good Samaritan," 12–13.

49. "Bystander's Duty," 207; "Good Samaritan," 15–18.

50. *Pikuaḥ nefesh* ("saving a life") is very close to *lo ta'amod* ("rescue") and the two are often treated together.

51. *Mishna,* Yoma 8:6 italics added, cited in "Bystander's Duty," 213.

52. *Talmud,* Yoma 84b, and *Talmud Yerushalmi,* to Yoma 8:5, both cited in "Bystander's Duty," 213.

53. Maimonides, *Code,* Hilkhot Shabbat 2:3, cited in "Good Samaritan," 63.

54. *Talmud,* Sota 21b and *Talmud Yerushalmi,* Sota 16a.

55. "Bystander's Duty," 213, summarizing the sources.

56. *Encyclopedia Talmudit,* "Hatsalat Nefashot."

57. *Encyclopedia Talmudit,* "Hatsalat Nefashot," citing the *Sefer Ḥasidim,* 773.

58. "Good Samaritan," 20 and with note 48 that this is used as the basis of saving a patient against his or her expressed will.

59. *Mishna,* Sanhedrin 8:7 with *Talmud,* Sanhedrin 57a–b.

60. "Good Samaritan," 81, drawing on talmudic sources. Quoting A. Barth, Kirschenbaum notes "that the original Good Samaritan extolled by Saint Luke was fortunate in not arriving on the scene until after the thieves had set upon the traveler, robbed him and beaten him half to death. The Samaritan cared for him and showed him great kindness, but he did not put himself in any peril by doing so" ("Bystander's Duty," 221, n. 13).

61. *Talmud,* Bava Metsi'a 62a, cited in "Good Samaritan," 24; "Bystander's Duty," 210.

62. Maimonides, *Code,* Hilkhot Rotseah 7:8, cited in "Good Samaritan," 50.

63. "Good Samaritan," 28; see also 41, citing the Me'iri, "if the rescuer can do so without endangering himself"; "Bystander's Duty," 210.

64. "Good Samaritan," 28, n. 86; "Bystander's Duty," 221, n.12.

65. Citing *Talmud,* Sanhedrin 74a, Yoma 82b.

66. Radbaz (d. 1573), translated by Kirschenbaum, "Good Samaritan," 46 (grammar and italics Kirschenbaum's).

67. Or, "standard of caring." On this, see pp. 155–57, 160–66, 172–74.

68. On this, see p. 208.

69. Radbaz, translated by Kirschenbaum, "Good Samaritan," 55–56 (grammar and italics Kirschenbaum's).

70. "Bystander's Duty," 211. Of course, if there is no life-threatening danger but only physical harm or other inconvenience, even humiliation, the rescuer is obligated to act ("Bystander's Duty," 213 with notes).

71. See pp. 193–95, on the grounds that, since the other is equally innocent, "the other's blood is not redder than one's own."

72. Maimonides, *Code,* Hilkhot Rotseah 1:6–7.

73. Maimonides, *Code,* Hilkhot Rotseah 1:14.

74. *Encyclopedia Talmudit,* "Hatsalat Nefashot"; Maimonides, *Code,* Hilkhot Rotseah 4:10–11.

75. *Encyclopedia Talmudit,* "Hatsalat Nefashot."

76. "Good Samaritan," 32–36. For other lists of precedence, see Maimonides, *Code,* Hilkhot Matenot Aniyim 8:10, 17–18 and Hilkhot Gezela va-'Aveda 12:1–2.

77. "Good Samaritan," 13–14, citing *Talmud,* Sanhedrin 73a, together with Rabbenu Peretz of Corbeil.

78. See "Good Samaritan," 65–74 and "Bystander's Duty," 214–16 for a discussion of tort liability for the rescuer.

79. *Talmud,* Sanhedrin 74a. See the summary of the law in Maimonides, *Code,* Hilkhot Hovel u-Mazik 8:14, cited in "Good Samaritan," 70 and "Bystander's Duty," 215 where it is cited incorrectly as 8:4.

80. *Shulhan Arukh,* Hoshen Mishpat 359:4, cited in "Good Samaritan," 68 and "Bystander's Duty," 215.

81. Maimonides, *Code,* Hilkhot Hovel u-Mazik 8:15, cited in "Good Samaritan," 71.

82. *Talmud,* Bava Kama 81b, cited in "Good Samaritan," 71 and "Bystander's Duty," 316.

83. "Good Samaritan," 19–23 and "Bystander's Duty," 207–9.

84. "Good Samaritan," 21 and "Bystander's Duty," 208.

85. "Good Samaritan," 20 with the sources; "Bystander's Duty," 208.

86. "Good Samaritan," 22–23 and "Bystander's Duty," 209.

87. "Good Samaritan," 22 and "Bystander's Duty," 208, italics Kirschenbaum's.

88. "Bystander's Duty," 219.

89. Christians sometimes claim that the violence of the Bible is the violence of the "Old" Testament which is then contrasted with the love of the "New" Testament. This is just not true. The "New" Testament contains many violent passages directed against those who do not accept Jesus and the mission of the church. Furthermore, Christianity as a world religion practiced, over the centuries, a great deal of violence against Jews, heretics, and fellow Christians. The violence practiced by Christianity against women has been particularly vicious and subtle. The literature on Christian violence is extensive. One might begin with G. F. Ellwood, *Batter My Heart* (Wallingford, PA, Pendle Hill Pamphlets: 1988) and the works of the Christian feminists. Islam has fared no better. Nor has Hinduism. It is part of human nature that our cultures, including religious cultures, are just plain violent.

I think that there are no value-concepts, properly speaking, for nonviolence and violence. Violence which is vengeance is *nekama* (see p. 214) and nonviolence is *middat hasidut* in a very technical sense (see p. 218). Gratuitous violence may be *hamas* (based on Gen. 6:11, 13; Gen. 49:5; Ps. 18:49; etc.). This needs further study.

90. See Maimonides, *Code,* Hilkhot Melakhim, chap. 5, on "commanded wars" and "permitted wars."

91. See also Jeremiah 13:25–26 and Isaiah 3:16–17. These passages are discussed in D. Blumenthal, *Facing the Abusing God: A Theology of Protest* (Louisville, KY, Westminster / John Knox: 1993), 240–6.

92. Ezekiel 38–39 from which the rabbinic "wars / days of Gog and Magog" come (*Talmud,* Berakhot 7b–10a passim, Shabbat 118a, Sanhedrin 94a–97b passim, and often in the midrashim). Christian apocalyptic eschatology is not far from these rabbinic sources.

93. See S. Lieberman, *Texts and Studies* (New York, Ktav Publishing: 1974) 29–56, 235–72.

94. See for example, I. Rosenbaum, *Holocaust and Halakha* (New York, Ktav Publishing: 1976) 34.

95. *Talmud,* Berakhot 58a. See pp. 210–12, on the law of the pursuer. Note that in November 1995, Prime Minister Rabin of Israel was assassinated by a young man, who had received religious training, on the grounds that Rabin was a "pursuer" of Jews by encouraging the peace process at the expense of Jewish lives lost in the ensuing terror actions.

96. That is, there is a death penalty. Deuteronomy 13:6 for a false prophet, 17:7 for idol worship, 17:12 for a rebellious judge, 19:13 for a murderer, 19:19 for a lying witness, 21:21 for a rebellious child, 22:21 for a nonvirgin who marries, 22:22 for both adulterers, 22:27 for the rapist of an engaged woman, and 24:7 for a kidnapper.

97. Hebrew, *'akhzari,* lit., "cruel" but here it clearly means "tough."

98. *Kohelet Rabba,* 7:24.

99. *Orhot Tsadikim,* "Sha'ar ha-'Akhzariyut" ("The Gate of Toughness").

100. *Talmud,* Megilla 10b.

101. *Talmud,* Yevamot 89a.

102. See the Musaf (Additional) Service for holidays, the middle section of which starts with the words "Because of our sins . . . ," as well as the confessional liturgies. The phrase became a value-concept.

103. See also Lamentations 1:8, 18, 22; 4:6; 5:21.

104. *Eikha Rabba,* 1:57.

105. This has been carefully examined by R. Kimelman, "Non-Violence in the Talmud," *Judaism* 17 (1968) 316–34.

106. Hebrew, *gever,* clearly meaning a male.

107. Kimelman, "Non-Violence," 316, ascribes this to a lessening of religious persecution and an increase in political persecution. He does not, however, argue that case.

108. *Bereshit Rabba* 38:3, cited in Kimelman, "Non-Violence," 316, with parallels.

109. *Bamidbar Rabba* 11:1, cited in Kimelman, "Non-Violence," 329, with parallels.

110. *Talmud,* Bava Kama 93a, cited in Kimelman, "Non-Violence," 330, with parallels.

111. *Talmud,* Shabbat 88b, cited in Kimelman, "Non-Violence," 331 (incorrectly, as 88a), with parallels.

112. *Midrash Tehilim,* 16:11, cited in Kimelman, "Non-Violence," 331, with parallels.

113. *Midrash Mishlei,* ad loc, cited in Kimelman, "Non-Violence," 327, with parallels.

114. *Avot de Rabbi Nathan* 23:1, cited in Kimelman, "Non-Violence," 320, with parallels.

115. *Tosefta,* Bava Metsi'a 2 : 26, cited in Kimelman, "Non-Violence," 317, with parallels.

116. *Talmud,* Berakhot 10a, cited in Kimelman, "Non-Violence," 320, with parallels.

117. *Orḥot Tsadikim,* "The Gate of Joy," chap. 9, cited in Kimelman, "The Rabbinic Ethics of Protest," 51, with full footnote to praying for one's enemies, including the quotation from *Sefer Ahavat Ḥesed.*

118. See Kimelman, "Non-Violence," 333, that this was so for third to fifth century Jewish Palestine. For other sources on loving one's enemies, see M. Amiel, *Ethics and Legality in Jewish Law* (Jerusalem, Rabbi Amiel Library: 1992) 37–43.

119. *Dachau,* foreword by Col. W. Quinn, is another in the series of pamphlets published by the American Army right after the liberation of the camps. It is a collection of essays and photographs without date, place, and publisher. The Witness to the Holocaust Project at Emory University photo-reproduced this pamphlet in 1979; LC #79–51047 (b). The quotation is taken from pages 25–26.

Chapter 14

1. See pp. 128–32, 146. This is true about the antisocial life too.

2. See p. 41, that study of the story of the Good Samaritan did not affect the willingness of students for the ministry to aid a distressed person.

3. See pp. 129, 287, n. 12.

4. C. D. Batson and W. L. Ventis, *The Religious Experience: A Social-Psychological Perspective* (New York, Oxford University Press: 1982).

5. Nor was the social-psychological data generated by the studies drawn from any one religion, ideology, or ethnic group.

6. There are, to be sure, only a few direct parallels in these two sources. The art of interdisciplinary writing is finding insights from one area and cross-reading them with another—in this case, insights from social psychology and history and cross-reading them with sources from the Jewish tradition. This is, in my mind, theology in its highest form. My intertexting reflects my own particular views. Others will see different ways of applying the Jewish sources to these social-psychological insights. I am glad of that and welcome correspondence on this subject.

7. On this, see pp. 108–14 and D. Blumenthal, "Repentance and Forgiveness," *Cross Currents* (Spring 1998) 75–81.

8. See pp. 157–60, 164–66, 174–75, 188–93, 206–10, 212–19.

9. See pp. 155, 160, 162–64, 206–12, 184–88.

10. See pp. 153, 164, 184, 202–6, 214–15, 216–21.

11. *Talmud Yerushalmi,* Pe'ah 1 : 1, with variation in the daily liturgy.

12. See pp. 209–10.

13. See pp. 133, 139, 188–93.

14. See pp. 153, 164, 202–6.

15. See pp. 164–66, 188–93.

16. See pp. 165–66, 212–19.

17. See pp. 157–62, 172, 179.

18. On the matter of *kavvana,* see M. **Kadushin,** *Worship and Ethics* (n.p., Northwestern University Press: 1964) 185–98; D. **Blumen**thal, *God at the Center* (San Francisco, Harper and Row: 1988; reprinted Northvale, NJ, Jason Aronson: 1995) 186–90; and the various encyclopedias.

19. On this, see p. 130.

20. See pp. 153, 164.

21. *Talmud,* Taanit 7a, Makkot 10a.

22. See pp. 155–57, 202–6, 182–84, 199.

23. Daily liturgy based on *Talmud Yerushalmi,* Pe'a 1 : 1. For other versions, see *Talmud,* Shabbat 127a and Kiddushin 39b.

24. Selected from the daily liturgy.

25. *Talmud,* Bava Batra 9a.

26. See pp. 153–54. On *talmid ḥakham,* see also Maimonides, *Code,* Hilkhot Talmud Torah, chaps. 4–6. The term *mehanekh* (educator) is used in contemporary Israeli education to refer to the person who is responsible for the formation of the student into a whole person and it is contrasted with the *moreh / morah* (teacher) who is responsible for the academic progress of the student, though often they are one and the same person. In the orthodox world, the function of *meḥanekh* is fulfilled by a rabbi who is called a *mashpi'a* (influencer); this is parallel to "spiritual father" in Christian tradition.

27. See chapter 13.

28. See chaps. 11 and 12.

29. A few suggestions: Maimonides, *Code,* Hilkhot Matenot 'Aniyim (the laws on charity); as an anthology, C. G. **Monte**fiore and H. Loewe, *A Rabbinic Anthology* (New York, Schocken Books: 1974); and, as a good beginning point, *Encyclopedia Judaica* and *The Jewish Encyclopedia.*

30. On the importance of this, see pp. 133–38.

31. See pp. 150–51, 152–57, 159–64, 172–74, 183.

32. For Christian tradition, see D. **Gushee,** *The Righteous Gentiles of the Holocaust: A Christian Interpretation* (Minneapolis, Fortress Press: 1994). To be sure, in comparative study, one may argue that, on a given topic, one tradition seems more reasonable, or closer to the good, than another. That is a matter of study, and weighing cultures and convictions.

33. At Department of Religion, Emory University, Atlanta, GA 30322, or by e-mail at <reldrb@emory.edu>. More information on my work is also available on my website: <http://www.emory.edu/UDR/BLUMENTHAL>.

Selected Bibliography*

"The Defence of Justification Because of Obedience to Illegal Orders: Summary of the Symposium" (Hebrew), *Mishpatim,* 1991, 591–621.

"The Value of the Human Being: Medicine in Germany 1918–1945," an exhibition sponsored by Ärztekammer Berlin in Zusammenarbeit mit der Bundesärztekammer, published as a catalogue edited by C. Pross and G. Aly, *Der Wert des Menschen: Medizin in Deutschland 1918–1945,* Berlin, Hentrich: 1989.

"198 Methods of Nonviolent Action," prepared by The Albert Einstein Institution, 1430 Massachusetts Ave., Cambridge, MA 02138; phone: 617-876-0311.

Adorno, T. W. et al., *The Authoritarian Personality,* abridged edition, New York, W. W. Norton and Co.: 1950, 1982.

Allport, G. *The Nature of Prejudice,* Reading, MA, Addison-Wesley: 1954.

Amiel, M. *Ethics and Legality in Jewish Law,* Jerusalem, Rabbi Amiel Library: 1992.

Arendt, H. *Eichmann in Jerusalem: A Report on the Banality of Evil,* New York, Viking Press: 1963.

Arendt, H. *The Origins of Totalitarianism,* New York, Harcourt Brace Jovanovich: 1951.

Asch, S. E. "Effects of Group Pressure Upon the Modification and Distortion of Judgments," *Groups, Leadership, and Men,* ed. H. Guetzkow, Pittsburgh, Carnegie Press: 1951.

Bar-On, D. *Legacy of Silence,* Cambridge, MA, Harvard University Press: 1989.

Batson, C. D. *The Altruism Question: Towards a Social-Psychological Answer,* Hillsdale, NJ, Lawrence Erlbaum Associates: 1991.

Batson, C. D. and W. L. Ventis, *The Religious Experience: A Social-Psychological Perspective,* Oxford, Oxford University Press: 1982.

Beardslee, W. R. "Commitment and Endurance: Common Themes in the Life Histories of Civil Rights Workers Who Stayed," *American Journal of Orthopsychiatry,* 53, 1983, 34–42.

Bellon, B. *Mercedes in Peace and War,* New York, Columbia University Press: 1990.

Ben Shelomo, Z. *Hilkhot Tsava,* 2 vols., Shaalavim: 5746 and n.d.

Berger, M. "The Halakhic Basis for Civil Disobedience in a Democratic State," *The Orthodox Forum Series,* Northvale, NJ, Jason Aronson: in press.

---

*See also Appendix F, "Prosocial Sources on the Web," 249–51.

Berkovits, E. *With God in Hell,* New York, Sanhedrin Press: 1979.

Berman, S. *"Lifnim Mishurat Hadin," Journal of Jewish Studies,* 26:1–2, 1975, 86–104 and 28:2, 1977, 181–93.

Bettelheim, B. *Surviving and Other Essays,* New York, Vintage Books: 1952, 1972.

Blackburn, G. W. *Education in the Third Reich,* Albany, NY, SUNY Press: 1985.

Blair, J. "Schindler" (a documentary film), London, Thames Television, 1983, 1995.

Block, G. and M. Drucker, *Rescuers: Portraits of Moral Courage in the Holocaust,* New York, Holmes and Meier: 1992.

Blumenthal, D. "Can Jews Celebrate D-Day?" *Atlanta Jewish Times,* June 3, 1994.

Blumenthal, D. "Memory and Meaning in the Shadow of the Holocaust," *Emory Studies on the Holocaust,* ed. D. Blumenthal, Atlanta, Emory University: 1985, 2: 115–22.

Blumenthal, D. "Scholarly Approaches to the Holocaust," *Emory Studies on the Holocaust,* ed. D. Blumenthal, Atlanta, Emory University: 1985, 1:14–35.

Blumenthal, D. *Facing the Abusing God: A Theology of Protest,* Louisville, KY, Westminster / John Knox: 1993.

Blumenthal, D. *God at the Center,* San Francisco, Harper and Row: 1988; reprinted Northvale, NJ, Jason Aronson: 1994.

Blumenthal, D. review of S. Wiesenthal, *The Sunflower, Jewish Social Studies,* 40, 1978, 330–32.

Blumenthal, D. "From Anger to Inquiry" ed. C. Rittner and J. Roth, *From the Unthinkable to the Unavoidable,* Westport, CT, Greenwood Press: 1997, 149–55.

Blumenthal, D. "From *Wissenshaft* to Theology: A Mid-Life Re-Calling," forthcoming.

Blumenthal, D. "What American Jews Believe: A Symposium," *Commentary,* August 1996, 23–24.

Blumenthal, D. "Theodicy: Dissonance in Theory and Praxis," *Concilium,* 1, 1998, 138–54.

Blumenthal, D. "Repentance and Forgiveness," *Cross Currents,* Spring 1998, 75–81.

Bolton, F. G. *Males at Risk: The Other Side of Child Sexual Abuse,* Newbury Park, CA, Sage Publications, 1989.

Borkin, J. *The Crime and Punishment of I. G. Farben,* New York, Free Press: 1978.

Borofsky, G. and D. Brand, "Personality Organization and Psychological Functioning of the Nuremberg War Criminals: The Rorschach Data," J. Dimsdale, *Survivors, Victims, and Perpetrators: Essays on the Nazi Holocaust,* New York, Hemisphere Publishing Co.: 1980, 359–403.

Boyarin, D. *Intertextuality and the Reading of Midrash,* Bloomington, IN, Indiana University Press: 1990; reviewed by Blumenthal in *CCAR Journal,* Fall 1995, 81–3.

Brown, J. C. and C. R. Bohn, *Christianity, Patriarchy, and Abuse,* Cleveland, OH, Pilgrim Press: 1989.

Browning, C. *Fateful Months: Essays in the Emergence of the Final Solution,* New York, Holmes and Meier: 1991.

Browning, C. "Ordinary Germans or Ordinary Men," *Address and Response at the Inauguration of the Dorot Chair of Modern Jewish and Holocaust Studies,* ed. D. Blumenthal, Atlanta, Emory University: 1994, 7–14.

Browning, C. *Ordinary Men: Reserve Police Battalion 101 and the Final Solution in Poland,* New York, HarperCollins: 1992.

Brueggemann, W. "A Shape for Old Testament Theology," *Catholic Biblical Quarterly,* 47, 1985, 28–46 and 395–415.

Brueggemann, W. *The Theology of the Old Testament: Testimony, Dispute, Advocacy* (Minneapolis, Fortress Press: 1992).

Charny, I. *How Can We Commit the Unthinkable,* Boulder, CO, Westview Press: 1982.

Cocks, G. *Psychotherapy in the Third Reich: The Göring Institute,* New York, Oxford University Press: 1985.

Cohen, E. A. *Human Behavior in the Concentration Camps,* New York, W. W. Norton and Co.: 1953.

Cohn, H. *Human Rights in Jewish Law,* New York, Ktav Publishing: 1984.

Colby, A. and W. Damon, *Some Do Care: Contemporary Lives of Moral Commitment,* New York, Free Press: 1992.

Dachau, foreword by Col. W. Quinn, n.d., n.p. Photo-reproduced by "Witness to the Holocaust Project," Emory University: 1979; LC #79-51047 (b).

Darley, J. M. and C. D. Batson, "From Jerusalem to Jericho: A Study of Situational and Dispositional Variables in Helping Behavior," *Journal of Personality and Social Psychology,* 27:1, 1973, 100–8.

Davidowicz, L. *The War Against the Jews: 1933–1945,* New York, Holt, Rinehart, and Winston: 1975.

Des Pres, T. *The Survivor: An Anatomy of Life in the Death Camps,* Oxford, Oxford University Press: 1976; reviewed by Blumenthal in *Journal of Jewish Studies,* 1979, 41:330–32.

Dimsdale, J. *Survivors, Victims, and Perpetrators: Essays on the Nazi Holocaust,* New York, Hemisphere Publishing Co.: 1980.

Eisenberg, N. et al. *Social and Moral Values,* Hillsdale, NJ, Lawrence Erlbaum Associates: 1989.

Ellwood, G. F. *Batter My Heart,* Wallingford, PA, Pendle Hill Pamphlets: 1988.

Elon, M. *Jewish Law,* 4 vols., Philadelphia, Jewish Publication Society: 1994.

Emory Studies on the Holocaust: An Interfaith Inquiry, vol. 1, ed. D. Blumenthal, 1985; vol. 2, ed. S. Hanover and D. Blumenthal, 1988, Atlanta, Emory University.

Encyclopedia Talmudit, Talmudic Encyclopedia Institute, Jerusalem, multivolume.

Ericksen, R. *Theologians under Hitler,* New Haven, Yale University Press: 1985.

Falk, Z. W. *Law and Religion,* Jerusalem, Mesharim Publications: 1981.

Falk, Z. W. *Legal Values and Judaism: Toward a Philosophy of Halakha* (Hebrew), Jerusalem, Hebrew University: 1980.

Fein, H. *Accounting for Genocide,* New York, Free Press: 1979.

Fogelman, E. *Conscience and Courage: Rescuers of Jews during the Holocaust,* New York, Anchor Books: 1994; reviewed by Blumenthal in *Journal of Psychology and Theology,* 23, 1995, 62–63.

Fortune, M. *Sexual Violence: The Unmentionable Sin: An Ethical and Pastoral Perspective,* Cleveland, OH, Pilgrim Press: 1983.

Fromm, E. *Escape from Freedom,* New York, Avon Books: 1969.

Gilligan, C. *In a Different Voice,* Cambridge, MA, Harvard University Press: 1982.

Giraffe Project, Box 759, Langley, WA 98260.

Goldhagen, D. *Hitler's Willing Executioners: Ordinary Germans and the Holocaust,* New York, A. Knopf: 1996.

Greenberg, M. "Rabbinic Reflections of Defying Legal Orders: Amasa, Abner, and Joab," *Judaism,* 19, 1970, 30–37.

Guest, I. *Behind the Disappearances: Argentina's Dirty War against Human Rights and the United Nations,* Philadelphia, University of Pennsylvania Press: 1990; also available as film.

Gushee, D. *The Righteous Gentiles of the Holocaust: A Christian Interpretation,* Minneapolis, Fortress Press: 1994.

Heath, D. *Schools of Hope,* San Francisco, Jossey-Bass: 1994.

Heschel, A. J. *God in Search of Man,* New York, Farrar, Straus, Giroux: 1955.

Hoffman, M. L. "Empathy and Prosocial Activism," N. Eisenberg et al., *Social and Moral Values,* Hillsdale, NJ, Lawrence Erlbaum Associates: 1989, 65–85.

Hoffmann, D. Z. *Melamed le-Ho'il,* New York, Frankel: 1953.

Holmes, R. *Nonviolence in Theory and Practice,* Belmont, CA, Hadsworth Publishing: 1990.

In the Eye of the Storm and later in *A Class Divided;* the latter appeared as a book by W. Peters, *A Class Divided Then and Now,* New Haven, Yale University Press: 1987.

Israel Yearbook for Human Rights.

Kadushin, M. *The Rabbinic Mind,* New York, Jewish Theological Seminary: 1952.

Kadushin, M. *Worship and Ethics,* n.p., Northwestern University Press: 1964.

Kasher, M. *Torah Sheleyma,* 43 vols., New York, American Biblical Society: 1949–.

Katz, F. *Ordinary People and Extraordinary Evil,* Albany, NY, SUNY Press: 1993.

Katz, S. "The 'Unique' Intentionality of the Holocaust," in *Post-Holocaust Dialogues,* ed. S. Katz, New York, New York University Press: 1985, 287–317.

Katz, S. *The Holocaust in Historical Context,* New York, Oxford University Press: 1994.

Keijzer, N. "A Plea for the Defence of Superior Orders," *Israel Yearbook of Human Rights,* 8, 1978, 78–103.

Kellner, M. *Contemporary Jewish Ethics,* New York, Sanhedrin Press: 1978.

Kelman, H. C. and V. L. Hamilton, *Crimes of Obedience,* New Haven, Yale University Press: 1989.

Keneally, T. *Schindler's List,* New York, Simon and Schuster: 1982.

Kimelman, R. "Non-Violence in the Talmud," *Judaism,* 17, 1968, 316–34.

Kimelman, R. "The Rabbinic Ethics of Protest," *Judaism,* 19, 1970, 38–58.

Kirschenbaum, A. "A Cog in the Wheel: The Defence of 'Obedience to Superior Orders' in Jewish Law," *Israel Yearbook of Human Rights,* 4, 1974, 168–93.

Kirschenbaum, A. "The Bystander's Duty to Rescue in Jewish Law," *Journal of Religious Ethics,* 1980, 204–26.

Kirschenbaum, A. "The 'Good Samaritan' and Jewish Law," *Diné Israel,* 7, 1976, 7–85.

Kitterman, D. "Those Who Said, 'No!': Germans Who Refused to Execute Civilians during World War II," *German Studies Review,* 9:2 May 1988, 241–54.

Klee, E. et al. *"The Good Old Days,"* transl. D. Burnstone, New York, Free Press: 1988, 1991.

Kohn, A. *Punished by Rewards: The Trouble with Gold Stars, Incentive Plans, A's, Praise, and Other Bribes,* New York, Houghton Mifflin: 1993.

Konvitz, M. "Conscience and Civil Disobedience in the Jewish Tradition," *Judaism and Human Rights,* reprinted in M. Kellner, *Contemporary Jewish Ethics,* New York, Sanhedrin Press: 1978, 239–54.

Koonz, C. *Mothers in the Fatherland,* New York, St. Martin's Press: 1987.

Kren, G. M. and L. Rappoport, *The Holocaust and the Crisis of Human Behavior,* New York, Holmes and Meier Publishers: 1980.

Lamm, M. "After the War—Another Look at Pacifism and Selective Conscientious Objection," *Judaism,* 1971, reprinted in M. Kellner, *Contemporary Jewish Ethics,* New York, Sanhedrin Press: 1978, 221–38.

Landman, L. "Civil Disobedience: The Jewish View," *Tradition,* 10, 1969, 5–14 and 123–26.

Laytner, A. *Arguing with God: A Jewish Tradition,* Northvale, NJ, Jason Aronson: 1990.

Lifton, R. J. *The Nazi Doctors: Medical Killing and the Psychology of Genocide,* New York, Basic Books: 1986.

Linn, R. *Conscience at War: The Israeli Soldier as a Moral Critic,* New York, SUNY Press: 1996; reviewed by Blumenthal in *Jewish Spectator,* Summer 1998, 52–53.

Linn, R. *Not Shooting and Not Crying,* Westport, CT, Greenwood Press: 1989.

Lipstadt, D. *Denying the Holocaust: The Growing Assault on Truth and Memory,* New York, Free Press: 1993.

Maimonides, M. *Code of Jewish Law,* New Haven, Yale University Press.

Mayer, M. *They Thought They Were Free: The Germans 1933–1945,* Chicago, University of Chicago Press: 1955, 1966.

Milgram, S. *Obedience to Authority: An Experimental View,* New York, Harper and Row: 1974; also available as a film.

Miller, A. *For Your Own Good,* transl. H. and H. Hannum, New York, Farrar, Straus, Giroux: 1983.

Montefiore, C. G. and H. Loewe, *A Rabbinic Anthology,* New York, Schocken Books: 1974.

Muffs, Y. "His Majesty's Loyal Opposition: A Study in Prophetic Intercession," *Conservative Judaism,* 33:3, 1980, 25–37.

Müller, I. *Hitler's Justice: The Courts of the Third Reich,* transl. D. L. Schneider, Cambridge, MA, Harvard University Press: 1991; reviewed by Blumenthal in *Modern Judaism,* 1993, 13:95–106.

Oliner, P. and S. *Toward a Caring Society: Ideas into Action,* Westport, CT, Praeger: 1995.

Oliner, P. et al. *Embracing the Other: Philosophical, Psychological, and Historical Perspectives,* New York, New York University Press: 1992; reviewed by Blumenthal in *Pastoral Psychology,* 46:2, 1997, 131–34.

Oliner, S. and P. *The Altruistic Personality: Rescuers of Jews in Nazi Europe,* New York, Free Press: 1988; reviewed by Blumenthal in *Critical Review of Books in Religion,* 3, 1990, 409–11.

Olweus, D. et al. *Development of Antisocial and Prosocial Behavior,* New York, Academic Press: 1986.

Piliavin, J. A. and H. W. Charng, "Altruism: A Review of Recent Theory and Research," *American Review of Sociology,* 16, 1990, 27–65.

Prager, M. *Sparks of Glory,* New York, Mesorah Publications: 1974, 1985.

Proctor, R. *Racial Hygiene: Medicine under the Nazis,* Cambridge, MA, Harvard University Press: 1988.

Rakover, N. *Modern Applications of Jewish Law,* 2 vols., Jerusalem, Jewish Legal Heritage Society: 1992.

Rakover, N. *The Multiple-Language Bibliography in Jewish Law,* Jerusalem, Library of Jewish Law: 1990.

Rappoport, L. and G. Kren, "Amoral Rescuers: The Ambiguities of Altruism," *Creativity Research Journal,* 6, 1993, 129–36.

Rigby, P. and P. O'Grady, "Agape and Altruism: Debates in Theology and Social Psychology," *Journal of the American Academy of Religion,* 57, 1990, 719–37.

Rosenbaum, I. *Holocaust and Halakha,* New York, Ktav Publishing: 1976.

Rosenberg, B. and F. Heuman, *Theological and Halakhic Reflections on the Holocaust,* Hoboken, NJ, Ktav Publishing: 1992.

Rubenstein, R. *The Cunning of History,* San Francisco, Harper Colophon: 1975.

Sabini, J. and M. Silver, "Destroying the Innocent with a Clear Conscience," J. Dimsdale, *Survivors, Victims, and Perpetrators: Essays on the Nazi Holocaust,* New York, Hemisphere Publishing Co.: 1980, 329–58; reprinted in J. Sabini and M. Silver, *Moralities of Everyday Life,* Oxford, Oxford University Press: 1982, 55–87.

Sagi, A. "Models of Authority and the Duty of Obedience in Halakhic Literature," *Association for Jewish Studies Review,* 22:1, 1995, 1–24.

Sauvage, P. *Weapons of the Spirit* (a film about Le Chambon sur Lignon).

Schindler, P. *Hasidic Responses to the Holocaust in Light of Hasidic Thought,* Hoboken, NJ, Ktav Publishing: 1990.

Shachar, Y. "The Elgazi Trials: S.C.O. in Israel," *Israeli Yearbook on Human Rights,* 12, 1982, 214–58.

Sharp, G. *The Politics of Nonviolent Action,* 3 vols., Boston, P. Sargent Publishers: 1973.

Sichrovsky, P. *Born Guilty: Children of Nazi Families,* transl. J. Steinberg, New York, Basic Books: 1988.

Silman, Y. "The Military Order in Light of the Halakha" (Hebrew), *Arakhim be-Mivḥan Milḥama: Musar u-Milḥama bi-R'i ha-Yahadut,* Jerusalem, A. Mizrahi: 1983, 183–89.

Soloveitchik, J. "Kol Dodi Dofek: It Is the Voice of My Beloved that Knocketh," transl. L. Kaplan, in B. Rosenberg and F. Heuman, *Theological and Halakhic Reflections on the Holocaust,* Hoboken, NJ, Ktav Publishing: 1992, 58–62.

Spiegel, S. *Amos and Amaziah,* New York, Jewish Theological Seminary: 1957.

Spielberg, S. *Schindler's List* (film), 1993, 1994. See also under Blair and Keneally.

Staub, E. "A Conception of the Determinants and Development of Altruism and Aggression: Motives, the Self, and the Environment," C. Zahn-Waxler et al., *Altruism and Aggression: Biological and Social Origins,* Cambridge, Cambridge University Press: 1986, 135–88.

Staub, E. "Helping a Distressed Person," L. Berkowitz, *Advances in Experimental Social Psychology,* New York, Academic Press: 1974, 7: 293–341.

Staub, E. "Psychological and Cultural Origins of Extreme Destructiveness and Extreme Altruism," *Handbook of Moral Behavior and Development,* ed. W. Kurtines and J. Gewirtz, Hillsdale, NJ, Lawrence Erlbaum Associates: 1991, 425–46.

Staub, E. *The Roots of Evil: The Origins of Genocide and Other Group Violence,* Cambridge, Cambridge University Press: 1989.

Steele, K. "Sitting with the Shattered Soul," *Pilgrimage: Journal of Personal Exploration and Psychotherapy,* 15:6, 1989, 19–25.

Steele, K. "The Healing Pool," *Voices,* 24:3, 1988, 74–78.

Steiner, J. "The SS Yesterday and Today: A Sociopsychological View," in J. Dimsdale, *Survivors, Victims, and Perpetrators: Essays on the Nazi Holocaust,* New York, Hemisphere Publishing Co.: 1980, 405–56.

Steinsaltz, A. "Obedience and Disobedience to Orders" (Hebrew), *Arakhim be-Mivḥan Milḥama: Musar u-Milḥama bi-R'i ha-Yahadut,* Jerusalem, A. Mizrahi: 1983, 190–95.

Tec, N. *Defiance: The Bielski Partisans,* Oxford, Oxford University Press: 1993.

Tec, N. *In the Lion's Den: The Life of Oswald Rufeisen,* Oxford, Oxford University Press: 1990.

Tec, N. *When Light Pierced the Darkness,* Oxford, Oxford University Press: 1986.

The Seventy-First Came . . . to Gunskirchenlager, foreword by Maj. Gen. W. Wyman, n.d., n.p. Photo-reproduced by "Witness to the Holocaust Project," Emory University: 1979; LC #79-51047 (a).

Thomas, L. M. *Vessels of Evil: American Slavery and the Holocaust,* Philadelphia, Temple University Press: 1993; reviewed by Blumenthal in *Jewish Spectator,* 1996, 60–62.

Tomsho, R. *The American Sanctuary Movement,* Austin, TX, Texas Monthly Press: 1987.

Trible, P. *Texts of Terror,* Philadelphia, Fortress Press: 1984.

Washington and Lee Law Review, 48, Winter 1991.

Weinreich, M. *Hitler's Professors,* New York, Yiddish Scientific Institute (YIVO): 1946.

Welch, S. *A Feminist Ethics of Risk,* Minneapolis, Fortress Press: 1990.

Wiesel, E. *The Trial of God,* New York, Schocken Books: 1976, 1989.

Wiltfang, G. and D. McAdam, "The Costs and Risks of Social Activism: A Study of Sanctuary Movement Activism," *Social Forces,* 69:4 June 1991, 987–1010.

Wyatt, T. and R. Gil, *Legitimacy and Commitment in the Military,* New York, Greenwood Press: 1990.

Zahn-Waxler, C. et al. *Altruism and Aggression: Biological and Social Origins,* Cambridge, Cambridge University Press: 1986.

Zimbardo, P. G. et al. "The Psychology of Imprisonment: Privation, Power, and Pathology," *Doing unto Others,* ed. Z. Rubin, Englewood Cliffs, NJ, Prentice-Hall: 1974; available in slide presentation and, later, in a film, *Quiet Rage; see New York Times Magazine,* April 8, 1973.

Glossary

'aharei rabbim lehatot—do not respond to a dispute by tending toward the majority to cause [others] to tend [that way]

'akhzariyut—toughness

brit—covenant

dina de-malkhuta dina—the law of the land is the law

divrei ha-rav ve-divrei ha-'eved, divrei ha-rav kodmin—If the words of the Master and the words of the servant are in conflict, the words of the Master take precedence.

'ein shaliah le-dvar 'avera—there is no agency for illegal acts

'elu ve-'elu divrei 'elohim hayyim—these and those are the words of the living God

gemilut hasadim—doing of good deeds

halakha—Jewish law; rules of Jewish living

hasidut / hesed—caring

hokheah tokhiah—you shall surely reprove, remonstrate with, your acquaintance

kevod ha-beriyot—dignity of the creatures

kiddush Hashem—sanctification of the Name; martyrdom

latse't yedei shamayim—fulfillment of duty in the sight of heaven

lifne 'iver lo titen mikhshol—do not put a stumbling block before the blind

lifnim mishurat hadin—within the line of the law

lo ta'amod 'al dam rei'ekha—you shall not stand idly by the blood of your other

lo tisna'—you shall not hate your fellow in your heart, but you should hate his or her ways

malkhut shamayim—the kingdom of God

middat hasidut—standard of caring / of the pious / of non-violence

mipnei darkhei shalom—for the sake of peace

mitsva—commandedness

nekama—vengeance

patur mi-dinei adam ve-hayav be-dinei shamayim—exempt from human law but liable by divine law

pikuah nefesh—saving a life

rodef—pursuer

shalom—peace

talmid hakham—student-sage, scholar-student

talmud Torah—Torah study

teshuva—repentance

tikkun 'olam—repair / restoring of the world

tom lev—purity of heart

tsedaka—charity, righteousness

tsedek—justice

tselem—image / *imitatio Dei*

ve-'ahavata le-rei'akha kamokha—you shall love your other as yourself

ve-'asita ha-tov veha-yashar be-'einei Hashem—do what is right and good in the eyes of God

vidui—confession

yeihareig ve-'al ya'avor—be killed and not sin

yetser ha-ra'—the impulse to do evil

yetser tov—the impulse to do good

Subject Index*

---

*These subjects are selected and references are not, usually, given to the Endnotes.

scapegoating   60, 90–92
screaming   1, 84, 89
secularism   112, 127–28
shalom   see "non-violence"
sin   108–14, 284 n 11
socialization   29
splitting   87–88
Stanford experiment   45–46, 78, 273 n 25
supererogation   162–64
survey of literature   chapter 2
survivalism   4, 64–66

talmid ḥakham   153, 154, 226, 292 n 17
talmud Torah   152–54, 164, 222–25
teachings   29, 33, 58–75, 123–24, 132–38, 182–95
teshuva   108–14, 222, 227, 284 n 11
tikkun 'olam   222, 295 n 70
toughness   184, 215, 223
tsedaka   165, 222, 225, 257
tsedek   157–60, 162, 172, 174–75, 183, 222, 225
tselem   150–52, 159–64, 226

value-concepts
   definition   117–19, 149, 160, 182, 303 n 89

military   196–202, 231–38
   prosocial   119–22, 123–24, 132–33
ve-'ahavata le-rei'akha kamokha   120, 162, 182, 186, 219
ve-'asita ha-tov veha-yashar   158, 223
vidui   109–10
violence   42
   see also "aggressive texts" and "non-violence"

whistle-blowing   136
women
   Bat Sheva   266 n 30
   Beruria   219
   Raḥav   168–69
   Ritspa bat Aya   169
   Shifra and Pu'a   170
   Tamar   171
   Vashti   171
   under the nazis   276 n 18
   texts of terror   290 n 7

yeihareig ve-'al ya'avor   193–95
yetser ha-ra' and *yetser tov*   113, 133, 139, 188–93, 222, 224
Yoav   197–200

Source Index*

Classic Sources

Hebrew Scriptures

Genesis
  1:26–27   150
  1:31   191
  2:7   189
  4:7   189
  6:6–7   107, 212
  7:21–23   145
  8:21   189
  9:6–7   150–51
  18   143, 164, 175
  21   164
  25:11   164
  36:31   187
  38   143, 171

Exodus
  1:10   186
  1:15–22   143, 170
  2:1–10   144
  2:12   171
  6:17–18   158
  12:28   158
  15:2   150
  17:14–15   145, 212
  18:13   151
  18:20   162–63
  19:15   179
  20:1   154
  22:19–20   157
  23:1–7   56, 153, 157, 159, 163, 203, 204, 239

  23:23–24   212
  25:8   126
  25:22   126
  30:12–13   126
  32:7–11   103, 176–77
  34:1–7   101, 176

Leviticus
  10:18–20   171–72
  18:5   193
  19:3   199
  19:15   157, 159
  19:16   206–12
  19:17   141, 182–84, 185–86, 188
  19:18   120, 141, 162, 182, 186, 219, 240
  19:24   157
  20:26   156
  22:23   193
  24:22–55   209–10
  25:36   208
  26:14–15   212

Numbers
  14:20–21   179
  19:1   155
  22–24   187
  23:28–34   172
  25:7–8   171
  28:2–3   126
  31   145, 213
  35:9–34   208
  35:26–27   209

---

*It is not possible or desirable to give all references. Hence, these are selected for importance.

Medieval Sources

Contemporary Sources*

*Readers should consult the footnotes carefully for fuller references.